Haywood County Tennessee

County Court Minutes

1826–1830

WPA Records

Heritage Books
2024

HERITAGE BOOKS

AN IMPRINT OF HERITAGE BOOKS, INC.

Books, CDs, and more—Worldwide

For our listing of thousands of titles see our website
at
www.HeritageBooks.com

A Facsimile Reprint
Published 2024 by
HERITAGE BOOKS, INC.
Publishing Division
5810 Ruatan Street
Berwyn Heights, MD 20740

Nashville, Tennessee
The Tennessee Historical Records Survey
December 1940

International Standard Book Number
Paperbound: 978-0-7884-8685-2

TRANSCRIPTIONS OF THE COUNTY ARCHIVES

OF TENNESSEE

NO. 38. HAYWOOD COUNTY (BROWNSVILLE)

COUNTY COURT MINUTES

1826-1830

Prepared by

The Tennessee Historical Records Survey
Division of Professional and Service Projects
Work Projects Administration

Sponsored

by

The Tennessee State Library

Nashville, Tennessee
The Tennessee Historical Records Survey
December 1940

The Historical Records Survey Program

       Sargent B. Child, Director
       Madison Bratton, State Supervisor

Research and Records Section

       Harvey E. Becknell, Director
       Milton W. Blanton, Regional Supervisor
       T. Marshall Jones, State Supervisor

Division of Professional and Service Projects

       Florence Kerr, Assistant Commissioner
       Blanche M. Ralston, Chief Regional Supervisor
       Betty Hunt Luck, State Director

WORK PROJECTS ADMINISTRATION

       Howard O. Hunter, Acting Commissioner
       Malcolm J. Miller, Regional Director
       Harry S. Berry, State Administrator

HAYWOOD COUNTY

COUNTY COURT MINUTE BOOK
1826-1830

(p.1)

State of Tennessee)   January Term 1826
Haywood County Court)

At a court of pleas and quarter sessions begun and holden in and for said county of Haywood at the Court House in the Town of Brownsville on the third Monday in January in the year of our Lord one thousand eight hundred and twenty six being the sixteenth day of said month, Present the worshipfull Laurence McGuire, Nicholas T. Perkins and Jonathan T. Jacocks, Esquires Justices of the peace in and for said county; John G. Carithers Sheriff and Britain H. Sanders Clerk:-

A commission from His Excellency William Carroll, Esqr. governor in and over the State of Tennessee for the time being being produced in open Court wherein Joel Estes, Charles Wortham and James L. Wortham were commissioned Justices of the peace in and for the county of Haywood, who thereupon came into court and took the necessary oaths prescribed by Law and took their seats accordingly:-

Filed

The commissioners Heretofore appointed at a former term of this court to-day of and designate and set apart for Mrs. Lucinda Kirksey widow of Bryant H. Kirksey, dec'd and one years' support as contemplated by act of assembly, returned into Court the following report, To wit, we have given and set apart to the widow aforesaid one hundred pounds of seed cotton, fifteen barrels corn, five choice Hoggs, two bushells salt twenty five pounds sugar and eight pounds of coffee, signed

                          N. T. Perkins)
                          C. White   )   Comms.
Filed   B. Reynolds)

Ordered by Court that Samuel Conyers, Alfred Kenedy, Daniel Cherry, Edward Goode and John Williams be appointed a Jury of view to mark and lay of a road the nearest and best way from the Town of Brownsville in the county of Haywood to Harrisses bluff on the south fork of the Forked deer river and make report thereof to the next Term of this Court and that an order issue accordingly -

Issued 1st Feby. 1826

On motion and petition filed, ordered that David Jeffreys, Green L. Harrelson, Herndon Haralson, Laurence McGuire, William Pace, Joel Pace, Oliver Woods, Malcolm Johnson, Charles White, Joseph Shaw, Bowen Reynolds, Julius Sanders and Richard W. Nixon be appointed a Jury of view to lay of and mark a road the nearest and best way from the Town of Brownsville to the county line on a direction to the Town (p.2) of Bolivar in Hardeman County crossing Hatchie River at the nearest and most convenient point on (p.2 con.) said river and that an order issue accordingly and that the said commissioners or a majority of them make report thereof to the next Term of this Court.

Issued 1st Feby. 1826

On motion and petition filed, Ordered by the Court that William Jackson, William B. Taylor, Joel M. B. Herring, Vardy Halsey, Joseph Blythe, Malcolm Johnson and Joel Pace be appointed a Jury of view to mark and lay of a road the nearest and best way from Madison county line to Fayette County line crossing Hatchie River at a point called Murray's Bluff and make report thereof to the next Term of this Court, and that an order issue accordingly-

Issued 1st Feby. 1826

Order that Herndon Harrelson and Hiram Bradford be and are hereby appointed commissioners to settle with the Circuit and County Court Clerks, Trustee and other officers in conformity to and act of assembly passed at Murphresboro November 26th 1825 and report agreeably thereto.

Issued 1st Feby. 1826

Ordered that an order made at a former Term of this Court to view and mark a road from McGuires' Ferry to Summerville in Fayette county as far as the county line be renewed and that an order issue accordingly.

Issued 1st Feby. 1826

Ordered that Laurence McGuire Esqr. Green L. Harrelson, Julius Sanders, Robert Hammell, Matthew Ray, Isham Olive and ___ Chambers or any five of them be a Jury of view to lay of and mark a road the nearest and best way from the Town of Brownsville as a continuance of the road from said Town to Nixons' Warehouse on Hatchie River crossing the same near said landing on a direction to Fayette county line leading immediately to Summerville and make report thereof to next Court.

Issued 1st Feby. 1826

Thomas Ferguson produced in oppen Court the scalps of three wolves over four months old and proved by his own oath that he killed the same in the bounds of Haywood County, it is therefore ordered by the Court that the Clerk make out a certificate to the Treasurer of West Tennessee as the law directs and that the sheriff destroy the same.

Issued to Col. R. W. Nixon

(p.3) Daniel Cherry produced in open Court the scalps of a wolf over four months old and proved by his own oath that he killed the same in the bounds of Haywood County, it is therefore ordered by the Court that the Clerk make out a certificate to the Treasurer of west Tennessee as the law directs and that the sheriff destroy the same.

Issued

James Dorris produced in open Court the scalp of a wolf over four (p.3 con.) months old and proved by his own oath that he killed the same in the bounds of Haywood County. It is therefore ordered by the Court that the Clerk make out a certificate to the Treasurer of west Tennessee as the sheriff destroy the same.

Issued

A Deed of Bargain and sale from A. D. Murphy to Robert Hughs for one thousand acres of land was this day produced in open Court and proven by the oaths of Herndon Harrelson and Green L. Harrelson subscribing Witnesses thereto and ordered to be certified for registration.

A Deed of Bargain and sale from A. D. Murphy to Robert Hughs for eight Hundred and forty acres of land was this day produced in open Court and proven by the oaths of Herndon Harrelson, and Green L. Harrelson subscribing witnesses thereto and ordered to be certified for registration.

A Deed of Bargain and sale from Blackman Coleman to Frances M. Wood for two hundred and ninety acres of Land was this day produced in open court and duly acknowledged, and ordered to be certified for registration.

A Deed of Bargain and sale from William W. Kavanaugh To Francis M. Wood for two hundred acres of land was this day produced in open Court and proven by the oaths of Blackman, Coleman and Will H. Dyre subscribing witnesses thereto and ordered to be certified for registration.

A Deed of bargain and sale from Joel Dyre to Blackman Coleman for two Hundred acres of Land was this day produced in open Court and proven by the oaths of Henry L. Gray and Will H. Dyre subscribing witnesses, thereto and ordered to be certified for registration.

A Deed of Bargain and sale from Blackman Coleman to Charles Wortham for Three Hundred and fifty acres of Land was this (p.4) day produced in open Court and duly acknowledged and ordered to be certified for registration.

A Deed of bargain and sale from Blackman Coleman to William W. Kavanaugh for four hundred and fifty acres of Land was this day produced in open Court and duly acknowledged and ordered to be certified for registration.

A Bill of sale from John G. Carithers sheriff to Blackman Coleman for a certain negro man named Burton was this day produced in open Court and duly acknowledged by the said John G. Carithers the maker thereof and ordered to be certified for registration.

A Bill of sale from John G. Carithers sheriff to Blackman Coleman for a certain negro woman named Lyn was this day produced in open Court and duly acknowledged by the said John G. Carithers sheriff the maker thereof and ordered to be certified for registration.

A Bill of sale from John G. Carithers sheriff to Blackman Coleman for a certain negro Boy named Claiborne was this day produced in open Court and duly acknowledged by the said John G. Carithers the maker thereof and ordered to be certified for registration.

(4 con.) Ordered by the Court a majority being present that Perkins and Elliot be allowed the sum of seventy two dollars and fifty cents for Books and stationary as pr. account filed, and that the county Trustee pay the same out of any monies not otherwise appropriated which shall be good in the settlements of his accounts.

Issued 1st Feby.

James Malden administrator of Brant H. Kirksey Dec'd. this day returned into Court the account of sales of the property of said dec'd. which was accordingly received by the Court and ordered to be filed and recorded.

On motion and with the assent of Blackman Coleman Coleman, Esqr. It is ordered by the Court that the said Blackman Coleman be appointed special Guardian for Drucilla Dyre, Joel Dyre, Charles Dyre, James Dyre, Cornelia Dyre and Sarah Ann Dyre, Infant and minor heirs of Joel Dyre, dec'd. for the purpose of effecting a division of the Lands belonging and owned by the Joel Dyre at his dec'd. between the said Drucilla Dyre, Joel Dyre, Charles Dyre, James Dyre, Cornelia Dyre, and Sarah Ann Dyre and other Legatees and heirs of the said Joel Dyre, dec'd.

(p.5) Ordered by Court that James Smith Hiram Bradford and Matthew Ray be and are hereby appointed commissioners to settle with the sheriff and county trustee agreeable to act of assembly, who entered into bond with James Mauldin their security in the penal sum of one hundred dollars for the faithfull performance thereof which bond is to filed and recorded agreeable to law.

Ordered that the stock mark of Charles Wortham be recorded as follows, To wit, a crop of the left ear and a swallowfork in the right.

Ordered that the stock mark of James F. Wortham be recorded as follows, To wit, a crop off the right ear and swallow fork in the left.

Ordered that the stock mark of William R. Wortham be recorded as follows, To Wit, a crop of the left ear.

John G. Carithers sheriff and collector for the County of Haywood this day handed in his resignation as such, which is accordingly filed, and it is ordered that an election be made on Tomorrow also for County Trustee whose resignation was also made known and that the clerk advertize the same.

Ordered by the Court that Nicholas T. Perkins, Esqr. be appointed Guardian to Nancy M. J. P. Turner and Simon Turner infant heirs and childred of Simon Turner deceased who entered into bond with David Jeffers and Charles White his securities in the sum of ten thousand Dollars, conditioned as the law directs.

Ordered by the Court that tomorrow until two o'clock be set apart for the transaction of County business.

Ordered that John G. Carithers sheriff and collector be allowed the credit of thirty five dollars 4 cts. with the Treasurer of West Tennessee and also the sum of fifty five dollars 31 cts. to the County Trustee and also the sum of ninety three dollars 68 cents to the public printer, sheriff & clerk on land reported for the year 1824 and not sold for want of bidders. Issued June 1st To sheriff & Printer Issued to B. H. Sanders, Clk.

(p. 5 con.)   Ordered by the Court a majority being present that the Taxes on Taxable property be and remain for the present as they were for the last year 1825.

(p. 6)   The Court then adjourned until to-morrow ten o'clock

Richd. Nixon   Cha.
L. McGuire
Jona. T. Jacocks
Blackman Coleman

Tuesday morning January 17th 1826   The Court met according to adjournment.

This day Stephen Howard constable handed in to the Court his resignation as such which was accordingly received.

Ordered by the Court that Thomas Ferguson, Thomas Thweat, John Sanderlin Alfred Kenedy, Charles Howard, Wm. Johnston, Zachariah Thompson be and are hereby appointed a Jury of view to mark and lay of a road from Harris' bluff to Edward Williams at the place called the Frog Jump, on the south fork of Forked deer river and that an order issue accordingly.

Issued 2nd Feby. 1826

It appearing to the satisfaction of the Court that a six hundred and forty acre Tract of land entered in the name of Ivander McIver in range 5 section Ten Entry four has been twice listed for Taxation in the year 1824 and 1825 and that Blackman Coleman the owner of said Tract of land has paid the Taxes due, for sd. years, on the same, and it also appearing to the satisfaction of the Court that one Tract of land owned by Pleasant Nelson of six hundred and forty acres is also twice listed, and also one other Tract of land containing one hundred acres in the name of Joshua Newman the property of Dan'l Cherry, has been twice listed for the same year, it also appearing that the taxes due on the two last mentioned tracts of land has been paid. It is therefore ordered by the Court that John G. Carruthers Esqr, Collector, be allowed his legal charges on said tracts of land in the settlements, and that the sd. above named Tracts of land severally be striken Tax list.

Issued to Shff.

(p. 7)   Ordered by the Court that Samuel Conyers, Alfred Canady, Daniel Cherry, Edward Good, and John Williams be appointed a jury of view to mark and lay off a road from the Town of Brownsville the nearest and best way to Harris Bluff, and an order issue accordingly.

Issued from Page 1

Agreeable to notice on yesterday, and proclamation thereof being duly made the court proceeded to the Election of sheriff and collector for the county of Haywood for the ensueing two years; Whereupon on counting the Ballots it was found that John G. Carruthers was duly and constitutionally elected, and thereupon entered into the necessary Bonds with approved security according to Law, in the sum of Ten Thousand Dollars for the faithful collecting and paying over the State and County Taxes, and also one

(p. 7 con.) other Bond in the sum of Ten Thousand Dollars for the performance of the duties of his office, and thereupon took the oath to support the Constitution of the United States and the Constitution of the State of Tennessee the oath against Duelling and the oath of office.

Agreeably to notice on yesterday proclamation thereof being duly made the Court proceeded to the election of a Trustee of Haywood for the ensuing two years whereupon on counting the ballots it was found that Col. Richard Nixon was duly and constitutionally elected, and thereupon entered into Bond in the sum of Ten Thousand Dollars with approved security for the faithful performance of the duties of his said office and thereupon took the oath to support the Constitution of the United States, to support the Constitution of the state of Tennessee and the oath of office.

A Deed of Bargain and sale from the Commissioners of the Town of Brownsville to Brittain E. Saunders for Lots number of 51-50-52 & 108 was proven in open Court by Hiram Bradford and John G. Caruthers subscribing witnesses thereto and ordered to be certified for Registration.

Certified

Ordered by the Court that Edward Goode be appointed overseer of the road from Harris' Bluff to the County line leading to Jackson in the place of Alfred Kenedy, and that all the hands within the following boundary be allotted to work on said road (p. 8) to wit, beginning at the mouth of Nelson's Creek west of the Bluff thence north with said Creek to the new road leading from Major Dyre's to Blackman Coleman's, thence East with said road to the east boundary of this County, thence south to the Forked Deer River thence west with said River to the beginning and an order issue accordingly.   Issued 2nd Feby.

Robert Hummell and Benjamin King returned into Court the contract of the commissioners for the clearing out of the north end of Washington Street in the the town of Brownsville wherein it appears that that they are agreeable to a former order, entitled to the sum of Thirty five dollars to be drawn from the trustee out of any monies not otherwise appropriated.

Issued June pd.

The Court then proceeded to the election of a constable on the north side of Forked Deer River whereupon after counting out the votes William R. Wortham was declared duly and constitutionally elected and entered into Bond with Francis M. Wood and Charles Wortham securities.

Ordered by the Court that the following named Justices of the peace are appointed commissioners to take in the list of the taxable property for the present year in Haywood County, that is to say, Charles Wortham _____ in Captain Fudge's company including all on the north side of Forked deer river and Richard Nixon in the town of Brownsville and Lawrence McGuire in Captain McGuire's company, and David Jeffreys in Captain Haralson's company and that the said Gentlemen Justices be and they are hereby appointed to take the census of Haywood County in pursuance of the act of assembly.

Issued 3rd. Feby.

The Commissioners appointed to settle with the sheriff of Haywood

(8 cont.) County for the years 1824 and 1825 report that they have performed the duties assigned them, and find a balance in favor of the shff. of $612.76, which said amount the sheriff has credit on by act of assembly until the 1st day (p.9) of July next, and it is ordered by the Court that the said report be received and filed.

The Commissioners appointed to settle with the Trustee of Haywood County report that they have performed the duties assigned them for the years 1824 and 1825, and that they find a balance due in favor of the County Trustee for said years of eight Dollars ninety nine cents, and it is ordered by the Court that the said report be received and filed.

This day came John G. Carithers Esquire Sheriff of This county and made report to the Court in the words and figures Following To wit;

State of Tennessee   )   January Term 1826
Haywood County Court)

I John G. Carithers sheriff and collector of the public Taxes for the County of Haywood do hereby report to Court the following Tracts of land as having been given in for the Taxes for the year 1825. That the Taxes thereon remain due and unpaid by the respective owners or claimants thereof who have no goods or chattels within my county on which I can destrain for said Taxes To wit.

Owners Names	No. Acres	Dist.	Range	Sec.	No. Entry or Grant	Water Course	
Arthur William	640	10	5	9	1137	F.D.	4.80
Armstrong Martin Reprs.	500	"	6	6	418	B.H.	3.75
Baldridge Francis	640	"	4	8	986	"	4.80
Brown Peter	500	"	"	"	"	"	3.75
Bagler Nathan	800	"	4	7	"	"	6.00
Barrow & Vaulx	410	"	5	11	773	F.D.	3.07½
Buckhannon John	640	"	4	10,11	104	S.F.D.	4.80
Brooks Robert	640	"	6	6	274	"	4.80
Brown John	1000	"	4&5	7	Gr.269	"	7.50
Same	1000	"	5	7.8	Gr.271	"	7.50
Blackfan Jessie	86½	"	6	11	E.961	F.D.	.65
(p.10)							
Braham John	112	"	6	11	962	"	.84
Brown Thomas	1000	"	4&5	8	Gr.272	B.H.	7.50
Same	1000	"	5	8	" 270	"	7.50
Bryan J. H. & J.Freeman	1000	11	1	9-10	E.808	F.D.	7.50
Campbell Arthur	640	11	1	6	" 593	B.H.	4.80
Childress John Reprs.of	935	11	1	6	453	"	7.01¼
Carpenter Benjamin	1250	10	4	11	632 F.Deer part of 1500 acres		9.37½
Craig John	583	"	6	6	379	B.H.	4.37½
Dougherty Thomas	500	"	4	7	77	"	3.75
Dyne Joel	2510	"	5	11	----	F.D.	18.82½
Same	1000	"	6	9	---	"	7.50
Daugherty George	2500	11	2	9&10	408	"	18.75
Dennet Robert	640	"	1	5&6	---	B.H.	4.80

(p.10 con.)

Owners Name	No. Acres	Dist.	Range	Sec.	Entry or Grant	Water Course	
Erwin Alexander	380	10	4	9	525	F.D.	2.85
Golson Benjamin	50	-	5	9	1294	"	.37½
Greer Joseph	1500	-	5	8	Gr.303	B.H.	11.25
Greer J.S.&W.B.Sims	125	-	6	9	-	-	.93¾
Greer Thomas	1685	-	4	8	E.804	" "	12.63¾
Gerard Charles	640	-	3&4	7	433	-	4.80
Huntsman Adam & R. Chester	640	-	6	8	1572	F.D.	4.80
Huling Frederick W.	640	-	4	10	53	F.D.	4.80
Same	274	-	5	10	230	-	2.05½
Same	640	-	4&5	10-11	49		4.80
Same	640	-	6	9	329		4.80
Henderson William	100	-	5	10	626		.75
~~Hoard William~~	~~2100~~	~~/~~	~~4~~	~~9~~	~~506~~	~~B.H.~~	~~$15.75~~
Hays O. B.	210	11	1	6	-	B.H.	1.37½
Hughs Robert	840	10	5&6	7&8	Gr.298	" "	6.30
Henderson Thomas	640	"	4&5	9	E.516	F.D.	4.80
Hill, William B.	181	"	4	7&8	833	B.H.	1.35¾
Same	365	"	4	7&8	91	" "	2.73¾
Hart Anthony	434	11	2	7	230	-	3.25
Jones Henry	45	10	5	8&9	1331	F.D.	.33¾
Joiner David	159	"	4	10	560	-	1.19¼
	30714½						$230.35½

(p. 11)

Johnston Thomas	2100	10	5&6	8	-	B.H.	$15.75
							(2500 acres)
King Thomas	640	-	6	6	425	-	4.80
Lewis William T.	329¼	-	4	11	243	F.D.	2.47½
Leonard Jacob	819½	11	3	6	-	B.H.	6.15
Long Nicholas	480	10	4	9	331	F.D.	3.60
McLemore, J. C. & J. Murray	50	"	6	8	1576	B.H.	.37½
Same	20	"	6	8	1593	-	.15
Same	59	"	6	8	1577	-	.30
Same	20	"	4	6	1503	-	.15
Same	100	"	4	8	1279	-	.75
McIver Evander	640	"	5	10	-	F.D.	4.80
Madin Daniel	470	"	5	11	-	"	3.52½
McDonald John	450	"	4&5	11	195	"	3.37½
McAllister John	1000	"	6	9	527	"	7.50
McIver John	640	-	5	6	665	B.H.	4.80
Same	100	-	4	10	-	F.D.	.75
Same	1000	11	2	10&11	597	"	7.50
Same	1000	"	2	9&10	497	"	7.50
Murray John	10	10	4	6	1504	B.H.	.07½
Moore William	1320	"	4	7	589	"	9.90
Murray John & B. Golson	70	"	6	8	1322	"	.52½
Newton Edward	640	11	2	9&10	572	F.D.	4.80
Overton John	1000	10	5	11	Gr.155	"	7.50
Philpot John W.	500	"	4	8	319	B.H.	3.75
Same	360	"	1	8	-	"	2.70

(p.11 con.) Owners Name	No. Acres	Dist.	Range	Sec.	Entry or Grant	Water Course	
Patrick John	274	10	4	10	931	B.H.	2.05½
Polk Thomas	1434	"	5	6	406	B.H.	10.75
Same	623	"	5	5&6	430	-	4.67¼
Same	500	"	4	7	77	-	3.75
Same	500	"	4	7	-	-	3.75
Person John	2500	11	1	6	266	-	18.75
Phillip Abner	1500	10	6	8	Gr.279	-	11.25
Robertson Elijah	332½	"	6	9	1143	F.D.	2.49½
Same	180½	"	4	7&8	985	B.H.	1.35½
Robertson James	1000	"	6	6&7	428	B.H.	7.50
Rice, John	5000	11	1	8	2205	-	37.50
Smith Richard	640	10	4	6	1133	-	4.80
Same	640	"	4	6	1133(Listed twice		4.80
(p. 12)							
Shelbon David	4000	10	5&6	11&10	-	S.F.D.	22.50
Sullivan Lee	2000	11	1&2	6	275	B.H.	15.00
Stewart David	400	10	4	9	527	F.D.	3.00
Smith Benjamin	250	"	4	11	632	"	1.87½
Sims Walter B.	213½	"	6	9	530	F.D.	1.60¼
Sims W.	60	11	1	6	-	B.H.	.45
Stubblefield Clement	228	10	5	6	364	"	1.71
Steed Jesse	1035	10	4	7&8	Gr.308	B.H.	7.76¼
Smith G. and J. McLemore	440	"	6	8	1594	"	3.30
Turner Henry H.	160	"	4	8	704	"	.20
					(part of 5000)		
Terrell John	640	"	4	8	968		4.80
Tisdale James H.	7606	11	2	11	Gr.412	F.D.	57.04½
Same	5000	"	1	11	414	"	37.50
Same	5592	10&11	1	10	415	"	41.94
Same	3496	10	6	10	410	"	26.22
Same	6934	"	6	11	411	"	52.00½
Todd George	200	"	4	8	320	"	1.50
					(part of 1000)		
Tate Mark A.	640	"	5&6	6	1085	B.H.	4.80
Talifero Benjamin	1000	"	6	6	145	"	7.50
Valch Adrian	500	11	1&2	7&8	278	"	37.50
Walker, James W.	3518¾	10	4	7&8	704	"	26.39½
					(part of 5000)		
Same	1000	"	4	7	1608	"	7.50
Weakly Robert	1875	"	4&5	11	447	F.D.	14.06¼
Windsor John	1000	"	5	7&8	1259	B.H.	7.50
William W. Woodfolk	1456	"	4	10	775	S.F.D.	10.92
Same	172¼	"	4	10	344	"	1.28¼
Wilson George	83	"	5	11	120	"	.62¼
Walker James	5000	"	5	6&7	635	B.H.	37.50
Williams Sam'l. & J. Greer	1000	"	6	6	213	"	7.50
Wheaton Daniel	12	"	5	9	-	F.D.	.09
Wheaton and Tisdale	640	11	1	9	-	-	4.80
No. acres	119,287½					Taxes	$894.63

(p.13) Whereupon it is considered by the Court that Judgment be and the same is hereby entered against the aforesaid Tracts of Land in the name of the state for the amount of the Taxes, costs and charges due severally thereon for the year 1825 and it is ordered by the Court that said several Tracts of land or so much thereof as shall be sufficient of each of them to satisfy the said Taxes costs and charges be sold as the Law directs.-

John G. Carithers esquire Sheriff of Haywood County makes return upon the Venire Facias returnable to this Court that he hath summoned the persons therein named, except James Mauldin, Anderson Turpin & Beverly Scurlock- The following persons named in the Venire Facias returnable to this Court were drawn, elected & sworn as a grand Jury for the present Term to wit.

Hiram Bradford, Foreman)	John F. Turner
Robert Axley)	Samuel Conner
Tobias C. Henderson)	Vincent Harrelson
Robert F. Smith)	Lewis Powers
Nathan Bridgeman)	Benjamin Huckaby
Jedediah Cusick)	Allen H. Howard and Alfred Kennady who having

received their charge retired to consider of the duties assigned them. Reubin Alfin was sworn as a constable to attend the grand Jury.

The Grand Jury returned into Court a bill of Indictment against Willie Dodd for an assault and battery on the body of Hardy L. Blackwell "a true bill" and retired to consider of further business.

The Court then adjourned until to-morrow 9 o'clock.

L. McGuire
Jona. T. Jacocks
Blackman Coleman

(p. 14) Wednesday Jany. 18th 1826

The Court met according to adjournment present the worshipful Blackman Coleman, Laurence McGuire and Jonathan T. Jacocks Justices of the peace in and for said county.

Dawson Bond assee)
   vs   ) Covenant
Britain H. Sanders)

This day came the parties by their attornies and thereupon came a Jury of good and lawful men (To Wit) Hiram Bradford, Robert Axley, Tobias C. Henderson, Nathan Bridgman, Jedediah Cusick, John T. Turner, Samuel Conner, Robert T. Smith, Vincent Harrelson, Lewis Powers, Benja. Huckabee and Alfred Kenedy who being elected, tried and sworn say the truth upon the issue joined, upon their oaths do say that the defendant hath not performed his covenant as in pleading he hath alledged, and they assess the plaintiffs damages by reason thereof to one hundred and fifty dollars, besides costs.

Execution Issued

Therefore it is considered by the Court here that the said plaintiff do recover against the said defendant the Damages aforesaid by the Jury

(p. 14 con.) aforesaid in form aforesaid assessed and his and his costs by him about his suit in this behalf expended, and the said defendant in mercy &c.

Bennet R. Butler
(for the use of Austin A. David Parish)
    vs
Britain H. Sanders

    This day came the said parties by their attornies & thereupon came also a jury of good and lawful men to wit, Hyram Bradford, Alfred Kennady, Samuel Conner, Robert Axley, Benjamin Huckaby, Lewis Powers, Nathan Bridgeman, Robert T. Smith, Jedediah Cusick, Allen H. Howard, Vincent Harrelson, & Tobias C. Henderson, who being elected tried and sworn well and truly to try the matters in dispute between the parties upon their oath aforesaid do say they find for the Defendant. It is therefore considered by the Court here that said Defendant go hence without day & recover against said plaintiff his costs by him about his Defence in this behalf expended &c- (p. 15) The plaintiff being dissatisfied with the judgment rendered against both prayed and obtained an appeal to the Circuit Court of Haywood County, he having given bond and security to prosecute the same.

    It is ordered by the Court that the following persons be summoned to attend as jurors the next Circuit Court for Haywood County to wit, Jonathan T. Jacocks, Laurence McGuire, Joel Estes, Richard Nixon, Nicholas, T. Perkins, David Jeffreys, Charles Wortham, Herndon Harrelson, Matthew Ray, Benjamin Noax, Charles White, Vincent Harrelson, William W. Doutheatt, Joshua Abstain, John Williams, Thomas C. Nixon, Bignal Crook, A. D. Gordon, John Roddy, Benjamin Huckaby, Mason F. Johnson, Richard W. Nixon, John McWhite, Lewis Powers, Eli Jones, and Caleb Warren. And it is further ordered by the Court that Reubin Alfin be summoned to attend said Court as constable, and that a Venire facias issue accordingly.
Issued 3rd Feby.

    It is Ordered by the Court that the following persons be summoned to attend at the next Court of pleas and Quarter sessions for the County of Haywood County then and thereto serve, as grand, or petit Jurors as the case may be, to wit, Henry A. Powell, Charles Howard, Thomas Ferguson, Daniel Cherry, Francis M. Wood, Edward Goode, William Johnson, James Barrington, Alfred Kennady, John Sanderlain, James Dorris, Mark Spence, Nathan Bridgeman, William Waddell, Levi Garner, _____ Marberry, Robert Hammell, Robert Penn, Francis L. Dillard, Samuel Elliott, Benjamin King, Robert T. Smith, Jerediah Cusick, Wyatt F. Tweedy, John Parker and Allen H. Howard. And it is further ordered by the Court that Reubin Alfin be summoned to attend said Court as a constable and that a venire facias issue accordingly.
Issued 3rd Feb. 1826

    A Deed of Bargain and sale from John McIver to Joel Dyre for five thousand acres of Land was this day produced in open Court and proven by the oaths of Joel Dyre and Blackman Coleman subscribing witnesses thereto and ordered to be certified for registration.

    A deed of Bargain and sale from the commissioners of the Town of Brownsville to Hiram Bradford for Lot no. 1 was produced in open Court and duly acknowledged, and ordered to be certified for registration.
Certified

(p. 16)   The commissioners appointed to Let out the building of a temporary Courthouse in the town of Brownsville in Haywood County report to Court that they have performed the duties assigned them, that they let the building of the same to Hiram Bradford for the sum of six hundred Dollars; that it has been completed by said Bradford according to contract and has been received by the said commissioners.

Ordered by the Court that Hiram Bradford be allowed the sum of six hundred Dollars for the building of the temporary Court house in the town of Brownsville, Haywood County as per contract made with the commissioners appointed for that purpose, and that the same be paid by the County trustee of Haywood County out of any monies in his hands not otherwise appropriated and that the receipt of the said Bradford shall be a good voucher in the hands of said Trustee in the settlement of his accounts.
Issued 23rd Jany. 1826

The Grand jury came into Court & there appearing no further businesses for their consideration at the present Term were dismissed & received their certificate.

Richard W. Nixon was this day qualified as a Deputy Sheriff, under John G. Caruthers, Sheriff of Haywood County.

The Court then adjourned until Court in course.
                                    Blackman Coleman
                                    L. McGuire
                                    Jona. T. Jacocks

(p. 17)   State of Tennessee)   March Term 1826
           Haywood County   )

At a court of pleas and quarter sessions Began and held at the Court House in the Town of Brownsville on the second Monday in March In the year of Lord one thousand eight hundred and Twenty six. It being the 13th day of said month Present the worshipful Laurence McGuire, Nicholas T. Perkins and David Jeffers, Esqr.

Ordered by the Court that tomorrow be and is hereby set apart for county Business.

The Court then adjourned until tomorrow 10 o'clock.
                                    Richd. Nixon, Chm.
                                    L. McGuire
                                        Jona. T. Jacocks

Tuesday morning March 14th 1826

The Court met according to adjournment, present Laurence McGuire, Jonathan T. Jacocks, and Richard Nixon, Esqr.

A Deed of Bargain and sale from Lee Sulivan to Robert I. Chester for one thousand acres of Land was this day produced in open Court and the probet thereof being certified by the Clerk of Smith County Court it is ordered to be certified for Registration.
Taken out by H. Harrelson

(Page 17 Con.)   James Farris this day produced in open Court the scalps of Two wolves over four months old and proved by his own oath that he killed the same in the bounds of Haywood County. It is therefore ordered by the Court that the clerk make out a certificate to the Treasurer of west Tennessee as the law directs and that the Sheriff destroy the scalps.
Issued and fees paid 14th March

Thomas Carnahan this day produced in open Court the scalp of one wolf over four months old and proved by his own oath that he killed the same in the bounds of Haywood County it is therefore ordered by the Court that the Clerk make out a certificate to Treasurer of west Tennessee as the law directs and that the sherriff destroy the scalp.
Issued March 28th fees paid

(p.18)Ordered by the court that the original Venire Facias issued from January Term 1826 To April term 1826 and Issued by the clerk the third of February 1826 be renewed.
Issued March 29th

Order by the Court that the original Venire Facias as Issued at January 1826 to March Term 1826 be Renewed and that the sheriff summons the same to attend the next Legal court.
Issued March 29th

This day James Cosby appeared in open Court and took the ____ oath as deputy Clerk in the county Court.

A Deed of bargain and sale from Alexander B. Bradford To James Cosby for lot No. 6 in the town of Brownsville was this day produced in open Court and proven by the oaths of Thomas G. Nixon and Jonathan Nixon subscribing witnesses thereto and ordered to be certified for registration.
Certified June 10th

A Bill of Sale from Henry L. Gray and Mary H. Gray his wife to James Cosby for a certain negro girl named Malvina was this day produced in open Court and proven by the oath of Paton Woodard subscribing witness thereto and ordered to be certified for registration.
Taken out

Ordered that in addition to a former order at July Term 1825 that all the hands south of the public square of the town of Brownsville work on the road Leading from the town of Brownsville to Nixon's Warehouse.
Issued 30th March

Ordered that a former order for a review for a road Leading from Brownsville in a direction to bolivar in Hardaman County to cross Hatchie River at Perkins Sanders and Jeffreys bluff be renewed and order Issue accordingly.
Issued

Ordered by the Court that tomorrow be set apart for the transaction of County business.

(p.19)   John G. Carithers Sheriff and collector of Haywood County this day appeared in open court and proclamation being made whereupon the Court proceeded to elect a sheriff and collector for the county of Haywood, for the

(p. 19 con.) county of Haywood, for the Insuing two years, on counting the balotts it was found that John G. Carithers was duly and constitutionally elected and thereupon entered into the necessary Bonds with approved security according to law In the sum of Ten Thousand dollars for the faithfull collecting and paying over the state and county Taxes and also another bond in the sum of ten thousand dollars for the performance of the duties of his office and thereupon took the oath to support the Constitution of the United States and the constitution of the state of Tennessee the oath against dueling and the oath of office.

The court then proceeded to the election of Constable in Capt.McGuire's company whereupon after counting out the votes Reubin Alfin was declared duly and constitutionally elected and entered into Bond with suficent security and took the nesary oaths of office.

State of Tennessee)
Haywood County Court) March Term 1826

Whereas this Court has been convened and held at the town of Brownsville in the county aforesaid under the belief that the last Legislature of the State of Tennessee had authorised the same particularly from the publications in the Jackson Gazette, but without any official authority, the Court feeling it their duty thus situated to support their charter and do what was Legal and right have directed and do hereby order that all the orders processes and other business and Papers returnable to this term be renewed and continued over untill the second Monday in June next at which term we have reason to believe will be the term Legal by the statue and we further order and direct (for want of such official information) that the sheriff of this County summon the Jurors appointed at last term to attend at next Court accordingly and whereas and whereas for want of such official authority are equally at a loss to appoint our officers of Law except the sheriff and Constable from a presumption that all our acts now in error (if any) will be Legalized by law.

(p. 20)   On petition of Col. John Murray it is ordered by the court that there be allowed a public Ferry at Murry's bluff on Hatchie river where the road Leading from Jackson to Summerville will cross said river and that the rates of Ferrage be equal to that of Lawrence McGuire's ferry on said river. Issued fees pd.

This day came John G. Carithers Esqr. Sherriff of this county and delivered to the court the original tax list as by him reported at January Term 1826 therefore it is ordered by the Court that the same stand good as recorded in the proceedings of said term and renewed at the present term of this court.

Ordered that the court adjourn untill tomorrow ten o'clock.

State   ) A. B.
  vs   )
John M. White)

In this case the defendant came into Court Together with William W. Doughert and Mathew Ray his securities and acknowledged themselves Indebted to the State in the sum of one Hundred Dollars that is to say the said

(p. 20 con.) John M. White in the sum of fifty Dollars and the said Wm. W.
Doughart and Mathew Ray in the sum of twenty five Dollars each to be levied
of there Goods and chattels for the use of the State, void on condition that
the above Bound John M. White shall well and truly make his personal appearance before the next County Court to be holden for the County of Haywood at
the Courthouse in the Town of Brownsville on the second Monday in June next
to answer the State in a charge of assault and Batery & not depart the same
without leave.
Issued

State　　　　　) A. B.
　vs　　　　　　)
Doctor C. Stricklin)

In this case the defendant came into Court Together with William W.
Douthett and Mathew Ray his securities and acknowledged themselves Indebted
to the state in the sum of one hundred dollars that is to say the said
Doctor C. Stricklin in the sum of fifty Dollars and the said Wm. W. Douthett
and Mathew Ray in the sum of twenty five dollars each to be levied of their
goods and chattels for the use of the state, void on condition that the
above bound Doctor C. Stricklin shall well and truly make his personal appearance (p. 21) before the next county court to be holden for the county of
Haywood at the Courthouse in the town of brownsville on the second Monday in
June next to answer the State in a charge of assault and batter and not depart
the same without Leave.

State　　　　　) A. B.
　vs　　　　　　)
Caleb Warren)

In this case the defendant came into court together with Thomas G. Nixon
his security and acknowledged themselves indebted to the state in the sum of
one hundred dollars that is to say the said Caleb warren in the sum of fifty
dollars and the said Nixon in the sum of Fifty dollars to be levied of their
goods and chattels for the use of the state void on condition that the above
bound Caleb Warren shall well and truly make his personal appearance before
the next county court to be holden for the county of Haywood at the Courthouse
in the town of Brownsville on the second Monday in June next to answer the
state in a charge of assault and battery and not depart the same without leave.
Issued

State　　　　　) A. B.
　vs　　　　　　)
Burrell Hunter)

In this case the defendant came into court Together with John M. White
his security and acknowledged themselves indebted to the state in the sum of
one hundred dollars, that is to say the said Burrell Hunter in the sum of
fifty dollars and the said John M. White in the sum of fifty dollars to be
levied on their goods and chattels for the use of the State void on condition
that the above bound Burrell Hunter shall well & truly make his personal
appearance before the next county court to be holden for the County of Haywood at the Courthouse in the town of Brownsville on the second Monday in
June next to answer the state in a charge of assault and battery and not

(p. 21 con.) depart the same without leave.
Issued

State   ) A. B.
 vs   )
Julius Sanders)

  In this case the defendant came into court together with Reubin Alfin
his security and acknowledged themselves indebted to the State in the sum of
one hundred dollars that is to say the said Julius Sanders in the sum of
fifty dollars and the said Reubin Alfin in the sum of fifty dollars to be
levied on their goods and chattels for the use of the State. Void on condition that the above bound Julius Sanders shall well and truly make his
personal apearance before the next county court to be holden for the county
of Haywood at the courthouse in the town of Brownsville on the second Monday
in (p. 22) June next to answer the state in a charge of assault and Battery
and not depart the same without Leave.

State   ) A. B.
 vs   )
James Dorris)

  In this case the defendant came into court together with John G.
Carithers and Rubin Alfin his securities and acknowledged themselves indebted to the state in the sum of one hundred dollars that is to say the said
James Dorris in the sum of fifty and the said John G. Carithers in the sum of
twenty five dollars and the said Rubin Alfin in the sum of twenty five dollars
to be levied on their goods and chattels for the use of the state void on condition that the above bound James Dorris shall well and truly make his personal appearance before the next county court to be holden for the county of
Haywood at the Courthouse in the town of Brownsville on the second Monday in
June next to answer the state in a charge of assault and Battery and not
depart the same without Leave.   Isd.

State   ) A. B.
 vs   )
John Rutherford)

  In this case the defendant came into court together with Burrell Hunter
Julius Sanders, Allen H. Howard, John M. Smith, Green L. Harrilson, Henry
Hunter, Rubin Alfin his securities and acknowledged themselves indebted to the
State in the sum of one hundred dollars that is to say the said John Ruther-
ford in the sum of fifty dollars and the said Burrell Hunter, Julius Sanders,
Allen H. Howard, John M. Smith, Green L. Harrelson, Henry Hunter and Rubin
Alfin each in the sum of eight dollars to be Levied on the goods and chattels
for the use of the state. Void on condition that the above Bound John
Rutherford shall well and truly make his personal appearance before the next
county court to be holden for the county of Haywood at the courthouse in the
town of Brownsville on the second Monday of June next to answer the state in
a charge of assault and Battery and not depart the same without Leave.

(p. 23) This day came John G. Carithers Esqr. sheriff and collector of this
county and made report to the court in the words and figures Following to wit

(p. 23 con.)   State of Tennessee   )
                Haywood County Court) March Term 1826

I John G. Carithers sheriff and collector of the public Taxes for the county of Haywood do hereby report to court the following tracts of Land as having been given in for the taxes for the year 1825 that the taxes thereon remain due and unpaid by the respective owners or claimants thereof who have no goods or chattels within my county on which I can distrain for said Taxes To Wit

Owners Names	No. Acres	Dist.	Range	Sec.	Ent.vs Grant	No.Entry Water or Grant Course
Arthur William	640	10	5	9	Ent	1137
Armstrong Martin R.	500	"	6	6	"	410
Baldridge Frances	640	"	4	8	"	986
Brown Peter	500	-	-	-	-	-
Bayler Nathan	800	"	4	7	"	-
Barrow & Vaulx	410	"	5	11	"	775
Buckhannon John	640	"	4	10&11	"	104
Brooks Robert	640	"	6	6	"	274
Brown John	1000	"	4&5	7	Gt.	269
Same	1000	"	5	7&8	"	271
Blackfan Jessee	86½	"	6	11	Ent.	961
Braham John	112	"	6	11	"	969
Brown Thomas	1000	"	4&5	8	Gt.	272
Same	1000	"	5	8	"	270
Briant J. H. & J. Freeman	1000	11	1	9&10	Ent.	808
Campbell Arthur	640	"	1	6	"	595
Childress John Reps.of	935	"	1	6	"	453
Carpenter Benjamin	1250	10	4	11	Ent.	632
Craig John	583	"	6	6	"	379
Daugherty Thomas	500	"	4	7	""	77
Dyre Joel	2510	"	5	11	-	-
Same	1000	"	6	9	-	-
Daugherty George	2500	11	2	9&10		408
Dannet Robert	640	"	1	5&6	-	-
(p.24) Erwin Alexander	380	10	4	9	Ent.	525
Gholson Benjamin	50	"	5	9	"	1294
Green Joseph	1500	"	5	8	Grt.	303
Greer J.S. & W. Sims	125	"	6	9	"	"
Greer Thomas	1685	"	4	8	Ent.	804
Gerard Charles	640	"	3&4	7	"	435
Huntsman A. & R. Chester	640	"	6	8	"	1572
Huling Frederic W.	640	"	4	10	"	53
Same	274	"	5	10	"	230
Same	640	"	4&5	10&11	"	49
Same	640	"	6	9	"	329
Henderson William	100	"	5	10	"	626
Head William	2100	"	4	9	"	506
Hays O. B.	210	11	1	6	-	-
Hughs Robert	840	10	5&6	7&8	Grt.	298
Henderson Thomas	640	"	4&5	9	Ent.	516
Hill William B.	181	"	4	7&8	"	833
Same	365	"	4	7&8	"	91
Hart Anthony	434	11	2	7	"	230

(p. 24 con.) Owners Names	No. Acres	Dist.	Range	Sec.	Entry or Grant	No.Entry or Grant	Water Course
Jones Henry	45	10	5	8&9	-	1331	
Joiner David	159	"	4	10	"	560	
Johnston Thomas	2100	10	5&6	8	ent.	-	
King Thomas	640	"	6	6	"	425	
Lewis William T.	329¼	"	4	11	"	243	
Leonard Jacob	819¼	11	3	6	"	-	
Long Nicholas	480	10	4	9	"	331	
McLemore J. C.							
& J. Murray	50	"	6	8	"	1576	
Same	20	"	6	8	"	1593	
Same	39	"	6	8	"	1577	
Same	20	"	4	6	"	1503	
Same	100	"	4	8	"	1279	
McIver Evander	640	"	5	10	-	-	
Madin Daniel	470	"	5	11	-	-	
McDonald John	450	"	4&5	11	-	195	
McAllister John	1000	"	6	9		527	
McIver John	640	"	5	6	"	665	
Same	100	"	4	10	-	-	
Same	1000	11	2	10&11		597	
Same	1000	"	2	9&10		497	
(p.25) Murray John	10	10	4	6	Ent.	1504	
More William	1320	"	4	7	"	589	
Murray John &							
B. Gholson	70	"	6	8	"	1322	
Newton Edward	640	11	2	9&10	"	572	
Overton John	1000	10	5	11	Grant	155	
Philpott John W.	500	"	4	8	"	319	
Same	360	"	1	8	-	-	
Patrick John	274	"	4	10	-	931	
Polk Thomas	1434	"	5	6	"	406	
Same	623	"	5	5&6	"	430	
Same	500	"	4	7	"	77	
Same	500	"	4	7	"	-	
Person John	2500	11	1	6	"	266	
Philip Abner	1500	10	6	8	"	279	
Robertson Elijah	332½	"	6	9	"	1143	
Same	180½	"	4	7&8	"	985	
Robertson James	1000	"	6	6&7	"	428	
Rice John	5000	11	1	8	"	2205	
Smith Richard	640	10	4	6	"	1133	
Same	640	"	4	6	"	1133	
Shelton David	3000	"	5&6	10&11	-	-	
Sulivan Lee	2000	11	1&2	6	"	275	
Stewart David	400	10	4	9	"	527	
Smith Benjamin	250	10	4	11	"	632	
Sims Walter B.	213¼	"	6	9	"	530	
Sims W.	60	11	1	6	-	-	
Stubblefield Clement	228	10	5	6	-	364	
Steed Jessee	1035	10	4	7&8	Grt.	308	
Smith G. &							
J. McLemore	440	"	6	8	-	1594	
Turner Henry H.	160	"	4	8	-	704	
Terrill John	640	"	4	8	-	968	
Tisdale James Hrs. of	7606	11	2	11	-	412	

(p.25 con.) Owners Name	No. Acres	Dist.	Range	Sec.	Entry or Grant	No.Ent or Grt.	Water Course
Tisdale James Hrs. of	5000	11	1	11	Grt.	414	
Same	5592	10&11	1	10	"	415	
Same	3496	10	6	10	Part Grt.	410	
Same	6934	10	6	11	"	411	
Todd George	200	"	4	8	Ent.	320	
Tate Mark	640	"	5&6	6	"	1085	
Taliaferro Benjamin	1000	"	6	6	"	145	
(p. 26) Valch Adrian	5000	11	1&2	7&8	Grt.	278	
Walker James W.	3518$\frac{3}{4}$	10	4	7&8	"	704	
Same	1000	10	4	7	"	1608	
Weakley Robert	1875	"	4	5	"	447	
Winsor John	1000	"	5	7&8	"	1259	
Woodfolk William W.	1456	"	4	10	"	775	
Same	172$\frac{1}{2}$	"	4	10	"	344	
Wilson George	83	"	5	11	Ent.	120	
Walker James	5000	"	5	6&7	"	635	
Williams Saml. & J. Greer	1000	"	6	6	"	213	
Wheaton Daniel	12	"	5	9	"	-	
Wheaton & Tisdale	640	11	1	9	-	-	

Whereupon it is considered by the court that Judgment be and the same is hereby entered against the the aforesaid tracts of Land in the name of the state for the amount of the tax cost and charges due severally thereon for the year 1825 and it is ordered by the court that the said several Tracts of Land or so much thereof as shall be of sufficient of each of them to satisfy the said tax cost and charges be sold as the law directs.

Ordered that court adjourn to meet tomorrow morning ten o'clock.

N. T. Perkins J. P.
Jon. T. Jacocks
L. McGuire

Wednesday morning March 15 1826 Court met agreeable to adjournment present the worshipfull Lawrence McGuire Jonathan T. Jacocks and Nicholas T. Perkins.

(p. 27) Ordered by the court that former bonds of the sheriff given at January Term 1826 the same be and remain filed in the clerks office untill the next term of this court also the Bonds given by said sheriff at this term of this court.

A deed of Bargain and sale from the commissioners of the town of Brownsville To John Reed for lots number seventy and eighty was this day produced in Court and duly acknowledge by Lawrence McGuire, Wm. H. Henderson, N. T. Perkins and Thomas G. Nixon Commissioners of said Town and ordered to be certified for registration.
Certified June 10th

A Deed of bargain and sale from the commissioners of the town of Brownsville to Richard W. Nixon for lots numbers 16 and 45 was this day

(p. 27 con.) produced in open Court and duly acknowledged by Lawrence McGuire Wm. H. Henderson, N. T. Perkins and Thomas G. Nixon Commissioners of said town and ordered to be certified for registration.
Certified

A Deed of Bargain and sale from the commissioners of the town of Brownsville To Solomon Reese for lot number 18 was this day produced in open court and duly acknowledged by Lawrence McGuire Wm. H. Henderson N. T. Perkins and Thomas G. Nixon Commissioners of said town and ordered to be certified for Registration.
Certified & fees pd. 26th March

A Deed of Bargain and sale from the commissioners of the town of Brownsville To Matthew Ray for lots number 66 and 68 was this day produced in open court and duly acknowledged by Lawrence McGuire, Wm. H. Henderson, N. T. Perkins and Thomas G. Nixon Commissioners of said town and ordered to be certified for Registration.
certified

Ordered by the court that the clerk of Haywood Cty. Court issue an order of sale against the property of Bennett R. Butler as levied on by an attachment issued by Richard Nixon Justice of the peace of said county issued the 27th day of January 1826 levied on lots no. 41 and 45 in the town of Brownsville on the 27th of January 1826 Returned to clerks office the 15th day of March 1826.
Order Void

(p. 28) A former order at January Term 1826- For the purpose of appointing persons to take the List of Taxable Property and also the Census as the Law directs Be and is hereby renewed.

Ordered by the Court the case between Bennett R. Butler and John Henry be continued until next Court and that the clerk keep the papers filed in his office and that the plaintiff & Defendant be permitted to plead at said Term.

Ordered by the court that the taxes on taxable property be and remain the same as it was last year also that each lot in the town of Brownsville be taxed equal to the State tax.

The court then adjourned untill Court in course
N. T. Perkins J. P.
Jona. T. Jacocks
L. McGuire

(p. 29)   State of Tennessee   )   June Term 1826
Haywood County Court)

At a court of pleas and quarter sessions began and holden in and for said county of Haywood at the Court House in the year of our Lord one thousand eight hundred and twenty six, being the 12th day of said month. Present the worshipfull Richard Nixon Nicholas T. Perkins, Laurence McGuire and others their fellow Justices of the peace. Britain H. Sanders Clerk and John G. Carithers Sheriff.

(p.29 con.)   Edmond Richmond
               William R. Hess
               William H. Loving
               William Stoddart and Samuel S. Copeland esquires, councellors
at law, this day appeared in open Court and severally took the several
oaths prescribed by law, and are admitted to the practice of the law in the
county of Haywood.
twelfth

        Blackman Coleman was this day appointed Special Guardian for Drucella
Dyre, Joel S. Dyre, Charles C. Dyre, James W. Dyre, Cornelia Dyre and
Sarah Ann Dyre.

        Upon the Petition of Daniel Mading and Mariah T. Maden his wife,
formerly Mariah T. Dyre, Sarah J. Dyre setting forth that they, together
with the minor heirs of Joel Dyre deceased, to wit, Drucilla Dyre, Joel S.
Dyre, Charles C. Dyre, James W. Dyre, Cornelia Dyre, and Sarah Ann Dyre are
entitled to certain lands in the County of Haywood, to wit the said Sarah
J. Dyre widow of said Joel Dyre to nine hundred and ten acres on the north
and south waters of the south fork of Forked deer river, the residue of the
surplus of five thousand acres granted by the State of North Carolina to
Benjamin Smith and conveyed by John McIver to said Joel Dyre. The said
Daniel Mading in right of his wife Mariah (p.30) Madden formerly Mariah
T. Dyre, Drusilla Dyre, Joel S. Dyre, Charles C. Dyre, James M. Dyre,
Cornelia Dyre and Sarah Ann Dyre to three hundred acres, part of a tract of
two thousand acres sold & conveyed by John McIver to said Joel Dyre on the
north waters of the south fork of Forked Deer River granted by the state of
North Carolina to Benjamin Smith by Patent no. 405, also two thousand acres
on the north waters of the south fork of Forked deer river adjoining the
above mentioned tract on the north, granted by the State of North Carolina
to Benjamin Smith by Patent No.417 and conveyed to said Joel Dyre now dec'd.
by John McIver also one thousand acres on the south waters of the South
waters of the south fork of Forked deer river, being part of a three thous-
and acre tract granted by the State of North Carolina to Benjamin Smith by
Patent No.406, and conveyed by said John McIver to said Joel Dyre and praying
this Court to appoint commissioners to allot set apart and apportion in
severally to said Petitioners and said minor Heirs their and each of their
respective proportions in said tracts of land, herein before mentioned and
specified- It is therefore ordered by the Court here that William Harris,
Charles Wortham, William H. Henderson, Vincent Harrelson, Charles White,
and Thomas G. Nixon be and are hereby appointed commissioners for that purpose, and hereupon Blackman Coleman, Guardian for the minor heirs of said
Joel Dyre deceased appeared here in open Court (p. 31) and acknowledged
the legal service of notice and waved all exceptions as to all informal-
ities and irregularities as to the time and manner of the service of the
same and says he is content and willing, as special guardian for the said
minor heirs, that the said Petition & all things appertaining thereto
should now at this time be acted on.

        A Bill of sale from Alsey H. Smith to Robert T. Smith for a certain
negro man named dick was this day produced in open Court and acknowledged
and ordered to be certified for Registration.
certified

        A Deed of Bargain and sale from William Polk By his attorney Samuel
Dickens to James W. Walker for twenty seven hundred and forty three $\frac{3}{4}$
Acres of Land was this day produced in open Court and proven by the oaths

(p. 31 con.) of Nicholas T. Perkins and B. H. Sanders and ordered to be certified for Registration.
certified

A Deed of Bargain and sale from F. W. Huling To Simon Turner for six hundred and forty Acres of Land was this day produced in open Court and proven by the oath of Jonathan J. Nixon and Richd. Nixon subscribing witnesses thereby and ordered to be certified for Registration.
certified

Ordered by the Court that William Jackson Vardy Halsell, William Taylor Jacob Watson, Joseph Blythe, Joel Pace & Malcolm Johnson, be appointed a jury of view, or any five of them to view and mark out a road from a point where the road from Jackson on a direction to Somerville crosses the Madison County line crossing Big Hatchie at Murray bluff to the county line at Fayette County in a direction to (p.32) Somerville and make report thereof to the next term of this Court.
Issued June 23

On motion and petition filed, ordered by the Court that John G. Carithers Thomas G. Nixon, Clement F. Walker, Thomas Lamoin and Reubin Alfin be appointed a jury of view to mark out and lay off a road leading from the town of Brownsville through the lands of Simon Turner in a direction to the Key Corner to the County line between the counties of Haywood and Dyer and make report to the next term of this Court.
Issued June 23rd

Ordered by the Court that the Clerk of this Court be authorized and required to receive enumerative lists of the taxable inhabitants of Haywood county at any time previous to making his return of the agregate amount of the free male inhabitants to the security of State &c.

The Court then proceeded to the election of a constable in Capt.Curry's company, Cato Freeman in nomination when upon on counting the votes it appeared that the said Cato Freeman was duly and constitutionally elected a constable in the bounds of Capt. Curry's company of malitia in Haywood county for the two ensuing years.

Ordered by the court that David Jeffreys, James Malden, N. T. Perkins, Edwin Joy Osborne, Bowen Reynolds, Eli Jones, Charles White, Lewis Powers and William Jackson be appointed a jury of view to mark and lay off a road the nearest and best way from the town of Brownsville in a direction to the town of Bolivar in Hardeman County to cross Hatchie river, at a bluff known by the name of Jeffrey's,Sanders and Perkins' bluff and make report to the next term of this Court, the foregoing order is a _____ on order made at a former Term of this Court.
Issued June 23

This day William Alred produced in open court five Justices being present three wolf scalps over four months old, and proved the killing of the same, within the bounds of Haywood County by his own oath having no other evidence to prove the fact. Ordered by the Court that a certificate issue to the Treasurer of West Tennessee.
Issued F -

(p. 33) Ordered by the Court that Herndon Haralson and Hiram Bradford be and they are hereby appointed commissioners to examine the settlements, as

(p. 33 con.) also all proceedings in _____ to the revenue in the offices of the Clerk of the County Court and also of the Circuit Court of Haywood County, for the years 1822-1823-1824 and 1825, and make report thereof accordingly. Issued

On motion and petition filed, Ordered by the Court that Laurence McGuire, William Henderson, Matthew Ray, Blackman Coleman, Robert Penn, Henry Welch, Hiram Bradford Thomas Potter John Rogers John G. Caruthers,
Or any five of them be and they are hereby appointed a jury of view impartially to mark and lay off a road the nearest and best way by a line run with a compass from the town of Brownsville to the Eastern boundary of Haywood County in a direction to the south end of the bridge and causeway across the forked Deer river near the town of Jackson Madison county and that they make report of their proceedings to the next term of this Court.
Issued June 26th

On motion and petition filed it is ordered by the court that Nathaniel D. Lilly be appointed overseer on the McGuire's Road Leading from Jackson to McGuires ferry and that part of the road between Parson Bigges and McGuire's and that the following hands work with him Mr. Ross Smith, Marberry, Bigges Womble, Morris Able and that an order Issue accordingly.

It is ordered by the court that a former order for a Jury of view for a road Leading from Harrisburgh to Burks ferry near the frog Jump, ~~in a direction to the town of Trenton in Gibson County~~, be and is hereby renewed and that James Wortham Junr., Francis Wood Daniel Cherry Broadwaters Matney and Thomas Ferguson be appointed to view said road and that an order issue accordingly.
Issued June 23rd

(p. 34)   State of Tennessee
It is ordered by the court Laurence McGuire Green L. Harrelson Julius Sanders Robt. Hamonds Herndon Harrilson Benjamin Woodard or any five of them be a Jury of view to Lay off and mark a road the nearest and best way from the town of Brownsville as a continuance of the road from said town to Nixons warehouse on Hatchie River crossing the same near said Landing on a direction to Fayette county Line amediately to Summerville in said county and make report to next court.
Issued June 23rd 1826

A Deed of Bargain and sale from Thomas H. Taylor to the commissioners of the town of Brownsville for three acres more or less of ground for a buring ground was this day produced in open Court and proven by the oaths of Richard Nixon and Jonathan J. Nixon and ordered to be certified for Registration.
certified

A Deed of Bargain and sale from Thomas H. Taylor to the Elders of the presbyterian church was this day produced in open Court and proven by the oaths of Herndon Harrilson and Blackman Coleman subscribing witnesses thereto and ordered to be certified for Registration.
certified

A Deed of Bargain and sale from the commissioners of the town of Brownsville to Willie B. Dyer for one town lot no. 8 was this day produced in open Court and duly acknowledged and ordered to be certified for Registration.
certified

(p. 35)   A Deed of Trust from Jacob H. Fort to the commissioners of the town of Brownsville was this day produced in open Court and duly acknowledged and ordered to be certified for Registration.
certified

A Deed of Trust from James Casby to the commissioners of the town of Brownsville was this day produced in open Court and duly acknowledged and ordered to be certified for Registration.
certified

A Deed of Trust from David Sanders & Co. to the commissioners of the town of Brownsville was this day produced in open Court and duly acknowledged and ordered to be certified for Registration.
certified

A Deed of Trust from A. B. Bradford to the Commissioners of the Town of Brownsville was this day produced in open Court and duly actd. and ordered to be certified for registration.
certified

A Deed of Bargain and sale from the commissioners of the Town of Brownsville to James Casby for four lots no. 135-143-147-137 and was duly acknowledged and ordered to be certified for registration.
certified

A Deed of Bargain and sale from Samuel Dickens to Isaac Koonce for five hundred acres of Land was this day produced in open Court and proven by the oaths of David Jeffreys and William H. Henderson subscribing witnesses thereto and ordered to be certified for Registration.
certified fees pd.

Ordered that William Allred who produced in open Court the scalps of Three wolves over the age of four months, and having no other evidence proved the killing of the same by his own oath within the bounds of Haywood County, whereupon the clerk is directed to issue an order to the Treasurer of West Tennessee as the law directs.

(p.36) Ordered by the Court that Benjamin Noakes, Nathan Bridgman Laurence McGuire John R. McGuire Ephraim Paddy Alexander Roddy and James Jackson be appointed a Jury of view to mark and lay off a road the nearest and Best way from McGuires Ferry on Hatchie River to the County Line of Fayette County in a direction to summerville and make report to next Court.
Issued June 23rd 1826

On motion of Alexander B. Bradford Attorney General of the 14th District Britain H. Sanders clerk of the Court of pleas and quarter sessions, of Haywood County produced in open Court his receipts for the amount of monies he was bound to the the Treasurer of West Tennessee and the Trustee of the County of Haywood which one in the word and figures following to wit;
Nashville December 23rd 1825
Received of Brittain H. Sanders, Clerk of the Court of pleas and quarter sessions for Haywood County- One hundred and six dollars sixty two cents being the amount of State tax by him received for the year ending the first day of October eighteen hundred and twenty five, which by law he is bound to account for.   Tho. Crutcher Treasurer
$106.62   of West Tennessee
Rec'd. of Britain H. Sanders clerk of the Court of pleas and quarter

(p. 36 con.) sessions the taxes due on five and for futures and amendments
the sum of six and one fourth cents for the years 1824 and five.
Isd. pd.   Richd. Nixon C Treas.
                                                             Octo. 1825

        Ordered by Court that the following persons, To Wit, Samuel Conyers,
Robert Axley, Daniel Cherry, James F. Wortham, and Francis M. Wood or any
five of them be and are hereby appointed a Jury of view to mark and lay off
(p. 37) a road leading from Harrisburgh to or in a direction to the Town of
Trenton in the County of Gibson and make report thereof to next Court.
Issued June 21

        The Court then adjourned until Tomorrow Ten o'clock after after sitting
aside until Twelve o'clock for Transacting county Business.
Issued June 20th   Jona. T. Jacocks J. P.
                                                           Chas. Wortham J. P.
                                                           Joel Estes J. P.

        Tuesday Morning June 13th 1826

        Court met according to adjournment present Jona. T. Jacocks Charles
Wortham & Joel Estes
Bill of sale from John G. Caruthers Sheriff of Haywood County to Blackman
Coleman for a negro woman named Lyn was produced in open Court & duly
acknowledge by said John G. Carithers and ordered to be certified for registration.
certified

        Bill of sale from John G. Caruthers Sheriff of Haywood County to
Blackman Coleman for a negro man named Burton was produced in open Court &
duly acknowledge by said Jno. G. Caruthers and ordered to be certified for
registration.
certified

        A Bill of Sale from John G. Carithers Sheriff of Haywood County to
Blackman Coleman for a certain negro Boy known by the name of Claiborn, was
this day produced in open Court and Duly acknowledged by said Carithers and
ordered to be certified for registration.
certified

        On motion and petition filed it is ordered by the Court that a Jury of
view be appointed to mark and lay off a road beginning at the Court house
going west with ____ in a direction to intersect the rode leading to Haywood
Bluff and make return to the next term, Jury of view Thos. G. Nixon, Wm. H.
Henderson, Saml. Elliott, Herndon Haralson & Henry Welch.   Issued

(p. 38)   Ordered by the Court that the county Treasurer pay to Jonathan T.
Jacocks the sum of Five dollars for the purchase of a Blank Book for the
office.
Issued

        This day Wyatt F. Tweedy produced one wolf scalp over the age of 4
months and having no other evidence proved the same by his own oath and it is
hereby ordered by the Court that a certificate be issued accordingly.
Issued 26th Decr.

        This day John Johnston produced in open Court two wolfs scalps over the
age of four months and having no other evidence proved the same by his own

(p. 38 con.) oath and it is hereby ordered by the Court that a certificate issue accordingly.
Issued July 18th

Ordered by the Court that the following persons be appointed a Jury of view (viz) J. L. Henderson, Tobias Henderson, Joshua Absten, Thos. White, Stephen Booth, Eli Jones & Vinsent Haralsen exammoning the property of turning the rode leading from Col. Nixons to the Town of Jackson on the north side of Jedediah Cusick's house and make report to the next term.
Issued June 26th

Cater Freeman who was duly and constitutional elected a constable in Capt. Curry company appeared in open Court and took the oath agreeable to law, and entered into bond with Robert Burns Burrell Hunter & Washington Barrington as his security.
Fees Paid $1.00

This day Charles G. Manning appeared in open Court and proved by his own oath (having no other evidence) the killing one wolf over the age of four months and the Court ordered a certificate to issue accordingly.
Fees Paid 25¢

This day appeared in open Court Charles Wortham and Joel Estes and took the oaths of a magistrate agreeable to Law and entered upon the duties of their office.

(p. 39)   Ordered by the Court that the commissioners be authorised to employ hands to clean out the streets and public square in the town of Brownsville, and they are authorised to draw from the treasurer of the County or sufficient sum of money to defray the expence thereof out of any money not otherwise appropriated.
Issued 11th August

Ordered by the Court that Laurence McGuire be appointed to superintend the running the county lines between Haywood & Gibson also Haywood and Tipton in conjunction with commissioners appointed from sd. County.
Issued 26 June

Proclamation being made the Court then proceeded to the election of County Treasurer candidates Richard Nixon, who was duly and constitutionally elected, and taking the oaths as the law directs entered into Bond with Blackman Coleman, Joel Estes & Jonathan T. Jacocks as his securities.

Theophilus Sanders appeared and took the oaths of office as deputy Clerk being appointed by Britain H. Sanders Clerk.

Thomas Ferguson appeared in Court and was released from serving as a Juror to the present term by his own affidavit.

Ordered by the Court that tomorrow, and that at each succeeding Court Wednesday be set apart for States business.

Deed of bargain and sale from William W. Kavanaugh for two Hundred acres Land to Frances M. Wood was this day proven in open Court by the oaths of Blackman Coleman, also the signature of William B. Dyre.
certified

(p. 39 con.)   Deed of bargain and sale from Mathew Ray to A. D. Murphy was this day acknowledged in open Court and certified for registration.
certified

(p. 40)   A Deed of bargain and sale from Blackman Coleman to Charles Wortham for three Hundred & fifty acres was this day acknowledged in open Court and certified for registration.
Is'd. pd.

A Deed bargain and sale from Blackman Coleman To William W. Kavanaugh for four Hundred & fifty acres was this day acknowledged in open Court and certified for registration.
certified

A Deed bargain and sale from A. D. Murphy by his attorney in fact Robt. Hughs to James W. Russell being in the 10th Surveyors Dist. 8 & 9 ___ & 6 the range Lot 3 ___ was this day acknowledged in open Court and certified for registration.
certified

A Deed bargain and sale from Blackman Coleman to Francis M. Wood for Two Hundred and ninety acres land was this day acknowledged in open Court and certified for registration.
certified

A Deed of Trust from Charles White to the Commissioners for the town of Brownsville for two Lots no. 29 & 37 was this day acknowledged and certified for registration.
certified

A Deed of bargain and sale from Jno. McIver to Joel Dyre for five thousand acres land in two tract one for Two thousand the other for three thousand was this day proven in part by the oath of Blackman Coleman, which proven at Jany. term by the oath of Joel H. Dyre ~~and certified for registration~~ and filed for further probate.

A Deed of Bargain and sale from Joel Dyre to Blackman Coleman for 200 acres of Land was this day produced in open Court (having been proven at and illegal Term heretofore) by the subscribing witnesses thereto, is now proven by one of the same the other being Dec'd. which is by the oath of Henry L. Grey who further swears that he saw William H. Dyer the other subscribing witness attest the same in the presence of the said Joel Dyer and he the said witness is now dead and ordered to be certified for registration.

(p. 41)   John C. Carithers Sheriff returned into Court the Venire Facias for the present term with the following endorcement (viz) By virtue of the within Venire Facias to me directed, I have proceeded to summon all the within named persons to serve as a jury except Henry A. Powell, James Barrington & Nathaniel Bridgement and all persons so summoned as inhabitants of said County and the age of twenty one years & are free holders or house holders of said County.

Jno. Carithers Shff.

Whereupon the sheriff proceeded to call at the Court House door the aforesaid persons named in the Venire who answered to these names with the exception of Henry A. Powell, James Barrington and Nathaniel Bridgement.
The Court then proceeded to empannel the grand Jury and thereupon the

(p. 41 con.) following persons good and lawful men of said County were drawn (viz) Daniel Cherry (Foreman) Robert T. Smith, Frances M. Wood, Jedediah Cusick, John Sanderlin, John Parker, William Waddle, Alfred Kenada, James Dorris, Wyatt F. Tweedy, Levi Gardner, John Marbra & Benjamin King who being elected drawn and sworn received there charge and retired together with Reubin Alfin Cble. sworn as an officer to attend them to consider of their presentments.

The Grand jury returned into open Court under the case of the officer sworn to attend them the following bills of indictment, that is to say, a bill of indictment against Robert Neal for an assault & battery on the body of John Potter; a bill of Indictment on Willie Dodd for an assault and battery on the body of Hardy L. Blackwell, a Bill of indictment against against Julius Sanders and John Rutherford for an affray and a bill of Indictment against John M. White, and Dr. C. Stricklin for an affray, which were severally endorsed"by the foreman of the Grand Jury thus: "A true bill, Dan'l. Cherry five men of the Grand jury."
(p.42) The Court adjourned until tomorrow morning 9 o'clock.

Blackman Coleman   J.P.
Joel Estes   J. P.
Chas. Wortham J. P.

Wednesday Morning June 14, 1826 Court met persuant to adjournment. Present Blackman Coleman, Joel Estes & Charles Wortham esqr. Justices.

The State of Tennessee)   Ast. & Battery
      vs   )
Robert Neal   )

This day came as well the State of Tennessee by Alx. B. Bradford, esquire attorney General, as the defendant in his proper person, and thereupon the said Defendant being solemnly charged, saith that he is guilty in manner & form as charged in the Bill of Indictment & puts himself upon the grace and mercy of the Court. It is therefore considered by the Court here that the Defendant make his fine with the State of Tennessee by the payment of seven dollars & fifty cents and the costs in this behalf expended and that he be taken &c.
Issued 18th 1826

The State of Tennessee)
    vs   )
John Rutherford   )

This day came as well the State by Alexander B. Bradford, esquire attorney General, as the Defendant in his proper person, and thereupon the said Defendant in his proper person, and thereupon the said Defendant being solemnly charged saith he is Guilty in manner and form as charged in the Bill of (p. 43) Indictment and puts himself upon the grace and mercy of the Court. It is therefore considered by the Court that the said Defendant make his fine with the State of Tennessee by the payment of Five dollars and the costs in this behalf expended and that he be taken &c.

The State of Tennessee)   Affray
    vs   )
Julius Sanders   )

This day came as well the State of Tennessee by Alexander B. Bradford,

(p. 43 con.) esquire Attorney General; as the said defendant in his proper person, who being solemnly charged saith that he is not guilty in the bill of Indictment, and thereupon came a Jury of good and lawful men, to wit; Thomas F. Dillard, Samuel Elliott, Robert Hammell, Herndon Harelson, Thomas G. Nixon, Henry Welch, James White, Benjamin Huckaby, Bignal Crook, William W. Douthit, Robert Penn and Henry Wooten, who being elected, tried and sworn well and truly to try the issue of traverse upon their oath do say that the defendant is not guilty in manner and form as charged in the bill of Indictment. It is therefore considered by the Court that the defendant go hence without day and upon motion of the Attorney General it is ordered by the Court that the County trustee pay all legal costs in this behalf expended and & c.
Issued June 18th 1826

Blackman Coleman)
    vs   )
Charles Wortham   )

Upon motion of plaintiff by his attorney to amend his Declaration filed in this case and upon argument being heard thereon and by the Court here fully understood, it is ordered by the Court that the motion be sustained.

(p. 44)   Dawson Bond assee)   Covenant
              vs   )
            Britain H. Sanders)

This day came the said Defendant in his proper person and with drawing his plea by him heretofore pleaded, saith he cannot gainsay the said plaintiffs action for one hundred and fifty three dollars damages. It is therefore considered by the Court that the said plaintiff do recover against the said defendant the Damages aforesaid by the said defendant in this behalf assumed and the costs in this behalf expended & the said Defendant in mercy.
Issued June 22nd 1826

The State of Tennessee)
      vs   )
Doctor C. Strickland   )

By the knowledge- Upon motion of the attorney General and by the knowledge and consent of the Court, a nole prosequi is entered, and thereupon Matthew Ray and William W. Douthit, comes here in open Court and assumes upon themselves to pay all costs in this behalf expended and agree that execution may issue against them for the same.

The State of Tennessee)   Assault & Battery
      vs   )
John M. White   )

This day came as well the State of Tennessee by Alexander B. Bradford esqr. Attorney General as the Defendant in his proper person and thereupon the Defendant being solemnly charged saith he is guilty in manner and form as charged in the Bill of Indictment, and puts himself upon the grace and mercy of the Court. It is therefore considered by the Court here that the Defendant make his fine with the (p. 45) State of Tennessee by the payment of Five Dollars and all costs in this behalf expended & that he be taken &c.

(p. 45 con.)   Amos Chambers, James Chambers and Benjamin McDonald who were severally bound in a recognizance to appear at this term to answer a charge of the state of Tennessee, to wit: the said Amos Chambers in the sum of Five hundred dollars and the said James Chambers and Benjamin McDonald in the sum of two hundred and fifty dollars each were this day severally solemnly called to come into Court as they were bound to do came not but made default. It is therefore considered by the Court here that the State of Tennessee recover against the said Amos Chambers the said sum of Five hundred dollars, and also that the State of Tennessee do recover against the said James Chambers and Benjamin McDonald severally the sum of two hundred and fifty dollars and that writs of Scire Facias issue severally against them.

The Grand jury empannelled, charged & sworn to enquire for the body of the County of Haywood at the present Term, returned into Court with the following bills of Indictment. A Bill against Amos Chambers for Petit Larceny "a true bill" - also a Bill against Amos Chambers for trading with a negro "a true Bill" and retired to consider of further business.

Alfred Kennedy this day produced in open Court (there being five Justices of the Peace present) the scalp of a wolf over the age of four months, and he being duly sworn saith that he killed the wolf off of which said scalp was taken in said (p. 46) County of Haywood. It is therefore ordered that the same be certified to the Treasury of West Tennessee.

It is ordered by the Court that Richard Taylor, John Williams, James F. Wortham, Jr., Samuel Conyers and Daniel Cherry be & are hereby appointed to complete the reviewing of a road from Brownsville to Harrisburg & make report to next Court.
Issued July 18th 1828

It is ordered by the Court that Allen Howard be and is hereby allowed the sum of fifty five dollars for work done on the West end of Main Street, also the further sum of thirty-five dollars for work done on the north end of Lafayette Street, to be paid out of any unappropriated money in the hand of the County trustee.
Issued June 19th fees not paid

Jonathan P. Hardwick for the ___ of)   Attachment
Joel W. Hardwick   )
        vs   )
Hudson Morris   )   In Debt

This day came the plaintiff by his attorney and it appearing to the satisfaction of the Court, that the defendant is not an inhabitant of this State; It is ordered by the Court that all proceedings in said Court be Stayed six months, and that publication be made thereof for three successive weeks in the Jackson Gazette in the town of Jackson, Tennessee, the last of which publication shall be at least two months before the December Term, next of this Court, notifying him to the said defendant to appear in this Court on or before the 2nd Monday in December next replevy his property, attached & plead to issue or demur, otherwise Judgement fine will be entered against him.
Sent on to be printed 26th July

(p. 47)   Robert A. Penn)   Debt
                 vs   )
            John M. Smith   )

(p. 47 con.) This day came the plaintiff by his attorney and dismisses his
suit herein: It is therefore considered by the Court that the defendant go
hence without day and recover of the plaintiff his costs by him in this behalf
expended and the ptff. for his false demur be in mercy &c.-

It is ordered by the Court that the following persons be summoned to
attend at the next term of this Court then and there to serve as grand or
petit Jurors as the case maybe (To Wit) Henry Welsh, Thos. G. Nixon,
Benjamin Huckabee, Richard Taylor, James C. Russell, Thos. _____, Phillip
Coonce, Clement T. Walker, Francis Lamoin, Thos. Potter, James Barrington,
Joshua Absten, Tobias C. Henderson, John M. White, Caleb Warren, Eli Farris,
Henry Wooten, John Rogers, John Fudge, James Stalcup, William Hollingsworth,
George W. Jones, Samuel Elliott, Malcomb Johnson, Benjamin Roland, William
W. Douthit, and also that Reubin Alfin & William R. Wortham attend said
Court as Constables & that a venire Facias issue accordingly.
Issued July 18th 1826

The Grand jury returned into Court & there appearing no further business for their consideration at the present Term, were discharged & received
their certificates to wit. James Dorris two days Jedediah Cusick two days,
John Parker two days F. M. Wood two days, //////two days/ Danl. Cherry two
days, A. Kenady, two days. Wyatt Tweedy two days, Levi Gardner two days,
Robt. Smith two days, William Weddle two days, John Marberry, two days,
Benjamin King two days & also the following of the Petit jury received
their certificates to wit, Allen Howard, F. S. Dillard, Mark Spence, Robert
Hamil, Sam'l. Elliott,

(p. 48) Court adjourned until Court in Course

Richd. Nixon Ch-
Blackman Coleman
L. McGuire

State of Tennessee)
Haywood County   ) September Term 1826

At a court of pleas and quarter sessions began and holden in and for
said county of Haywood at the Court house in the Town of Brownsville on the
second Monday in September in the year of our Lord one thousand eight hundred and twenty six being the 11th day of said month, Present the worshipful
Richard Nixon, Charles Wortham, Willie Dodd, James L. Wortham, and others
their fellow Justices of the Peace; John G. Carithers Sheriff and
Britain H. Sanders Clerk-

Ordered by the Court a majority of the acting Justices being present
that Joshua Abstain be appointed overseer of the Road, leading from Brownsville by the way of Col. Richard Nixon to Jackson from the county line to
Mud Creek including the creeks and Jonathan T. Jacocks be overseer of the
road from mud Creek to where General Blackman Coleman now lives and Col.
Richard Nixon overseer from Colemans to Brownsville and that they divide the
hands subject to work thereon in like proportion.
Issued 16th Sept. 1826

Ordered by the Court that a precinct election be held on south side of
Hatchie River at the place where Samuel P. Ashe now lives for the purpose of
electing members to the Legislature, and Congress, as well as all other civil
appointments-
Issued

(p. 48 con.) The Jury of view from where the road leading from the town of
Jackson to this county line in a direction to Summerville in Fayette County
returned their report into Court. Whereupon it is ordered by the Court a
majority being present that William Jackson be appointed overseer of the
same on the north side of Hatchie River, and that Hugh Black, John Black,
John Hill, Jacob Watson, Isaac Taylor, Sullivan and Son and William Kavanaugh
be subject (p.49) to work under him as such, in opening and keeping the
same in repair. Issued 16th Sept.

Ordered by the Court a majority of the acting Justices being present,
that Benjamin Wilks be appointed overseer of the road on the south side of
Hatchie river in a direction from Jackson to Summerville as far as our County
line and that Joseph Wilks, Vardy Halsey, Malcomb Johnston, Joseph Shaw, ___
Brazzeal, Trus Patton, Peter Young and Joel Pace be subject to work under
him as such in opening and keeping the same in repair.
Issued 18th Sept.

A Bill of sale from Hudson Morris to Joseph Lowry for two negroes to
wit; Nat, and Sarah, was this day produced in open Court and duly proven by
the oath of James Baxter a subscribing witness thereto and ordered to be
certified for registration.
certified Delivered Oct. 1826

Ordered by Court a majority of the acting Justices being present that
Lewis Powers be appointed overseer of what is called the McGuire road from
the county line of Madison to where Laurence McGuire now lives, in place of
William Mauldin and the following hands work under him as such (to wit) - all
hands east of said McGuires and south of said road as far as Big Hatchie
river, and that an order issue accordingly with the exception of Bowen
Reynolds and smith.
Issued 18th Sept.

Ordered by Court that an order made at the last Term of this Court be
renewed, which is as follows, to wit; on motion and petition filed ordered
by Court that Laurence McGuire, William Henderson, Matthew Ray, Blackman
Coleman, Robert Penn, Henry Welch, Hiram Bradford, Thomas Potter, John Rogers,
John G. Carithers or any five of them be and they are hereby appointed a
Jury of view impartially to mark and lay of a road the nearest and best way
by a line run with a compass from the town of Brownsville to the eastern
boundary of Haywood County in a direction to the south end of the Bridge and
causeway across the Forked Deer river near the town of Jackson in Madison
County and that they make report of their proceedings to the next term of
this Court.
Issued 18th Sept.

Ordered by the Court a majority of the acting Justices being present,
that Jonathan Jones be appointed overseer of the road leading from the Town
of Brownsville to McGuire's. (p. 50) ferry on Big Hatchie river in place of
Maliche Jackson and work the hands heretofore ordered on said road.

On motion and petition filed it is ordered by the Court a majority of
the acting Justices being present that a Jury of view be appointed to mark
and lay of a road, begining at the south end of Lafayette Street, thence run
in a direction to intersect the road leading to Haywood Bluffs, at some convenient point, and make a report of their proceeding to the next term of this
Court (Jury of Views), To Wit; Thos. G. Nixon, William H. Henderson, Samuel
Elliott, Herndon Harrelson, Henry Welch and Mason F. Johnston. Issued 18th Sept.

(p. 50 con.)   The Jury of view returned their report into Court, whereupon
it is ordered, a majority of the acting Justices being present that Azariah
Thompson be appointed overseer of the road leading from Harrisburgh to the
County line in a direction to Trenton in Gibson County and that all the hands
east of the range line that runs near Charles Wortham's Esqr. (except on-half
of Daniel Cherry hands) work under him as such in opening the same and keeping it in repair.
Issued 18th

Ordered by Court a majority of the acting Justices being present that Frances
Lamoin be and hereby is appointed overseer of a road leading from Brownsville
through the lands of Simon Turner to the District line in a direction to the
Key Corner and that all the hands within two miles north and south of said
road work under him as such.
Issued 14th Sept.

The Jury of view returned their report, whereupon it is ordered by the
Court a majority of acting Justices being present that Julius Sanders be
appointed overseer of the road leading from a point near Nixon's Ware House
as a continuance of the road from Brownsville to the same, as far as the
County line in a direction to Summerville and that all the hands at said
Nixon's Ware house, the hands of Herndon Harralson, Laurence McGuire, Henry
Wooten, Malcomb Johnston, Henning Pace, Robert Hammell, Eli Woodard and all
those persons on the south side of the river living between the fourth and
sixth range lines, to work on and open the same. received-

(p. 51)   Ordered that an order made at the last Term of this court making it
the duty of the commissioners of the town of Brownsville to employ persons to
clean out the public square and streets be and is hereby recinded.

Ordered by the Court a majority of the acting Justices being present that
Hiram Bradford be appointed overseer to call out all the hands in the town of
Brownsville to work and clean off the public square and streets of said town
and the said hands are therefore exempt from working on any road and that an
order issue accordingly.
Issued 22nd Sept.

Ordered by Court a majority of the acting Justices being present that
Laurence McGuire, Nathan Bridgman, John R. McGuire, Ephraim Roddy, Alexander
Roddy, Benjamin Noaks, James Jackson, Samuel P. Ashe, Isaac Edwards, Griffeth
Edwards, John Roddy, and James Fields be appointed a Jury to view mark and lay
off a road, begining at McGuire's Ferry and run through the bottom of Hatche
river in such a direction to the summit of the high lands on the south side so
as to suit a road to branch off from thence to Memphis, and to Summerville and
to continue to mark out that part (or branch) of the road leading from the same
in the best direction to Summerville and make report of their proceedings to the
next term of this Court.   Issued 22 Sept.

Ordered by the Court that Charles White overseer of the road leading
the town of Brownsville in a direction to the town of Jackson as far as the
County line, work the hands of John R. Leigh, Henry Wooten and the hands of Hay,
Eli Farris, Joseph Murphy, Phillip Bruce, _____ Grisum, Lowrence Womble in
addition to those heretofore allotted him and an order issue accordingly.
Issued 22nd Sept.

Ordered by Court a majority of the acting Justices being present that

(p. 51 con.) Griffeth Edwards be appointed overseer of the road as now used from McGuires ferry on Hatche River to the House of Samuel P. Ashe, and to keep the same passable, for which purpose he is authorized to call out and work the hands on the south side of the river and west of Big Muddy Creek, and that an order issue accordingly. Issued 22nd Sept. 1826

(p. 52) Ordered by the Court a majority of the acting Justices being present that James F. Wortham be appointed overseer of the road leading from Harrisburgh to Bucks Ferry as far as the first creek below the Hurricane, and that one-half of the hands of Daniel Cherry and all the hands from the 4th range line to the Hurricane out to the County line north, work under him as such, and an order issue accordingly.
Issued 22nd Sept.

Ordered by the Court a majority of the acting Justices being present that William Johnston Jr. be appointed overseer of the road leading from Harrisburgh to Bucks Ferry, from the first creek below the Hurricane to Thomas Furgerson's and all the hands in the following bounds, To wit, all those being east of a north line from Furgerson's to the County line and west of the Hurricane be subject to work under him as such.
Issued 22 Sept.

Ordered by the Court a majority of the acting Justices being present that Thomas Furguson be appointed overseer of the road from his own house to Buck's Ferry and that all the hands west of a north line from his house to the County line be subject to work under him as such.
Issued 23rd Sept.

Ordered by the Court a majority of the acting Justices being present, that the road leading from the Town of Brownsville in a direction to the Flour Island Bluff be and the same is hereby established a public road as far as the County line.
Is'd.

The Court proceeded to the election of a Constable in Captain Blackwell's company, whereupon after counting the votes Wiatt F. Tweedy was declared duly and constitutionally elected, who thereupon took the necessary oaths prescribed by Law, and entered into bond with Azariah Thompson and Daniel Madden his securities.

The Court proceeded to the election of a constable in Captain Fudge's company, whereupon after counting the votes Azariah Thompson was declared duly and constitutionally elected, who thereupon took the necessary oaths of office prescribed by law and entered into bond to-gether with Wiatt F. Tweedy and William R. Wortham his securities.

(p. 53) A Deed of Bargain and sale from William W. Kavanaugh to Francis M. Wood, for two hundred acres of land was this day produced in open Court, and further proven by the oath of Edward Williams Jr., a subscribing witness thereto, having been heretofore proven in part; and ordered to be certified for registration.

Wilie Dodd produced the scalp of a wolf over the age of four months and proved the killing the same within the bounds of Haywood County by his own oath having no other evidence whereby he could prove the same it is therefore ordered that a certificate issue to the Treasurer of West Tennessee accordingly. Issued

(p. 53 con.)

Alexander D. Gordan produced in open Court the scalp of a wolf over the age of four months, and proved the killing the same within the bounds of Haywood County by his own oath and the oath of John Marberry, it is therefore ordered that a certificate issue to the Treasurer of West Tennessee accordingly. Iss'd.

Ordered by the Court a majority of the acting Justices of the peace being present that Margaret Carter an illegitimate child now of the age of fifteen years be bound as an apprentice unto Willie Dodd, Esquire until she shall arrive at the age of eighteen years to learn the art and mystery of spinster and that the said Dodd at the expiration of said term furnish her, the said Margaret Carter with two good suits of common clothes, one dress suit, together with two pair of shoes, one of leather, and one of Morocco, one cow and calf and one sow and pigg, as freedom dues; and that the said, Dodd enter into bond and security as the law directs.   Bond given

William Harris, Charles White, Vincent Harrelson and Thomas G. Nixon, four of the commissioners appointed at the last term of this Court to divide set apart & allot to Sarah J. Dyer, widow of Joel Dyer, Dec'd. & to the several heirs of the said Joel, dec'd. their respective portions of land mentioned in petition filed at last Court, report to this Court that they have done the same, & herein open Court return a plott of said division. (p. 54) together with a description of the several tracts as set apart, all of which is ordered to be recorded & certified for registration.

Ordered by the Court that tomorrow until eleven o'clock be set apart for County business.

The Court then adjourned until tomorrow 9 o'clock.
Blackman Coleman, J. P.
Richd. Nixon, Cham.
Willis Dodd
J. L. Wortham

Tuesday Morning September the 12th 1826 Court met persuant to adjournment present, Richard Nixon, Blackman Coleman, Wilie Dodd and James L. Wortham and others their fellow Justices of the peace.

On motion and petition filed, it is ordered by Court a majority of the acting Justices of the peace being present that James L. Wortham, William Alread, Joshua Abstain, Washington Barrintine, John Parker, William Waddle and Robert Burns be appointed a Jury of view, to mark and lay off a road* from the town of Jackson to Harrisburg crosses the County line at or near James L. Wortham's the nearest and best way in a direction to Brownsville to intersect the Jackson road and make report of their proceedings to next Court. Issued 23rd Sept.

Ordered by the Court a majority of the acting Justices of the peace being present, that Caleb Warren be appointed overseer of the road leading from Brownsville in a direction to Bolivar as far as where the same crosses the road known by the name of the McGuire road and all the hands within the following bounds, to wit; All the hands east of the road leading from Brownsville to Haywood Bluffs and south of the road passing Richard Nixon's, Esqr. and west of Range 4 and north of McGuire's road, work under him as such in opening the same.   Issued 23rd Sept.

(p. 55)   Ordered by Court a majority of the acting Justices being present that *from where the road leading

(p. 55 con.) James Malden be appointed overseer of the road leading from Brownsville to Bolivar from the McGuire road to Big Hatche River, and that all the hands south of McGuire's road east of Range five and north of the river together with Smith, be subject to work under him as such in opening the same.
Issued 23rd Sept. 1826

Ordered by Court a majority of the acting Justices of the peace being present, that Gideon Pace be appointed overseer of the road from Brownsville in a direction to Bolivar, from Big Hatche River to Hardeman County line, and that all the hands south of said river and east of the 6th range line be subject to work under him as such in opening the same and it is further ordered that the overseer in cutting out the above named road be authorized to vary on either side of the present marked way forty poles if by so doing they can run the same on better ground.
Issued 23 Sept.

Reuben Alfin appeared in Court and took the necessary oaths as Deputy Sheriff under John G. Carithers, Sheriff of this County.

Ordered by the Court a majority of the acting Justices being present that Henry Wooten and the hands of D. Hay be subject to work on the road leading from Brownsville to Haywood Bluffs, and all orders subjecting them to work on other roads be recinded.
Issued.

Henry L. Gray appeared in open Court and took the several oaths prescribed by law, and is admitted to the practice of law in the County of Haywood.

Eli Jones produced in open Court the scalps of a wolf over the age of four months, and proved the killing the same by his own oath within the hands of Haywood County. It is therefore ordered that a certificate issue to the Treasurer of West Tennessee accordingly.
Issued 15th Sept.

A Deed of Bargain and sale from Isaac Koonce to David S. Nunn for two hundred and forty acres of land was this day produced in open Court and proven in part by the oath of Henry A. Powell, a subscribing witness thereto, and ordered to be filed for further probate.

(p.56) A power of Attorney from Joel W. Hardwick to Jonathan J. Hardwick was this day produced in open Court and duly acknowledged, and ordered to be certified for registration.

John G. Carithers Esquire, sheriff of Haywood County makes return upon the Venire Facias returnable to this Court that he has summoned the persons therein named except James Stalcup, all of whom are freeholders or house holders of this county.
The following persons named in the Venire facias returnable to to this Court, was drawn, elected and sworn & charged at a Grand Jury for the present Term, (To. wit);

Joshua Abstain, foreman	Phillip Koonce	Tobias C. Henderson
Henry Welch	Clemment T. Walker	John M. White
Thos. G. Nixon	Francis Lamoin	Caleb Warren
Benjamin Huckabee	Thomas Potter	John B. Fudge
		George W. Jones

(p. 56 con.) who having received their charge retired to consider of the duties assigned them; Wiatt F. Tweedy constable was sworn to attend them.

John Potter   )
      vs   )   Assault and Battery
Robert Neale   )

This day came the parties by their attorneys and thereupon came a Jury of good and lawfull men, to wit; Eli Farris, Thomas Thweeatt, James W. Russell, Henry Wooten, John Rogers, James T. White, Mark Spence, Eli Jones, Joseph T. Harrilson, William Waddle, Willis Holland and Robert Hammell who being elected tried and sworn the truth to speak upon the issue joined upon their oaths do say that the defendant is guilty of the tresspass, assault and battery as the plaintiff in his declaration hath alledged, and do assess the plaintiffs damages by reason thereof to eighty two dollars and fifty cents besides his costs. It is therefore considered by the Court that the plaintiff recover of the defendant the damages aforesaid in form aforesaid by the Jury aforesaid assessed, and also his costs by him about his suit in this behalf expended and the defendant may be taken &c.
Transcript made out

(p. 57)   Robert Neale)
              vs   )   Slander
           John Potter   )

This day came the defendant in his proper person and filed his affidavit for a continuance in this cause, whereupon by order of the Court the same is continued until the next term.

Robert Neale)
      vs   )   Slander
John Potter   )

This day came the defendant in his proper person and filed his affidavit for a continuance of this cause whereupon by order of the Court the same is continued until next term.

John Watson   )
      vs   )   Covenant
Francis Dillard)

This day came the parties by their attornies and thereupon came a jury of good and lawful men, to wit; Eli Farris, Thomas Thweatt, James W. Russell, Henry Wooten, John Rogers, James T. White, Mark Spence, Eli Jones, Joseph Harralson, William Waddle, Willis Holland and Robert Hammel who being elected tried and sworn the truth to speak upon the issue joined upon their oaths do say the find the issue in favor of the plaintiff and do assess the plaintiff damages by reason of the breach of covenant in the plaintiffs declaration mentioned to one hundred and sixty-seven dollars eighty four cents besides his costs. It is therefore considered by the Court that the plaintiff recover of the said defendant the damages aforesaid by the jury aforesaid in form aforesaid assessed, and also his costs by him about his suit in this behalf expended, and the said defendant in mercy. Whereupon the defendant prayed and obtained (p. 58) an appeal to the next Circuit to be holden for this

(p. 58 con.) County and entered into bond together with Hiram Bradford and Henry Welch conditioned as the law directs.
Transcript made out

William Newsom)
    vs   )   Debt
Daniel Cherry)

      This day came the parties by their attorneys and thereupon came a Jury of good and lawful men, to wit; Eli Farris, Thomas Thweeat, James W. Russell, Henry Wooten, John Rogers, James T. White, Mark Spence, Eli Jones, Joseph T. Harrelson, William Waddle, Willis Holland and Robert Hammell who being elected, tried and sworn the truth to speak upon the issues joined upon their oath do say that the Defendant hath not paid the debt of two hundred and thirty-four dollars & seventy-five cents in the declaration mentioned as the plaintiff in replying hath alledged and the jurors aforesaid upon their oath aforesaid do further say that there is no set off, and they assess the plaintiffs damages by reason of the detention of that debt to nine dollars & ninety-two cents, besides costs. It is therefore considered by the Court here that the said plaintiff do recover against the said defendant the debt aforesaid in the declaration mentioned, and the damages aforesaid by the jury in form aforesaid assessed, and his costs in this behalf expended and the said defendant in mercy & c. From which judgement the defendant hath prayed & obtained an appeal to the next Circuit of Haywood County, which is granted, he having given bond & security to prosecute the same. Transcript

(p. 59)   Blackman Coleman   )
                vs   )
      Francis M. Wood & Charles Wortham)

      This day came the said parties by their attornies & thereupon came also a jury of good and lawful men to wit, James Hollingsworth, Mason F. Johnson, Francis L. Dilliard, Nathan Williamson, Julius Sanders, James T. White, Peter Lankford, Joseph King, Allen H. Howard, James W. Russell, Eli Farris & John Potter who being elected, tried and sworn well and truly to try the issue joined between the parties, upon their oath do say that the defendant hath paid all the debt in the plaintiffs declaration mentioned except two hundred and ten dollars part thereof- and the jurors aforesaid upon their oath aforesaid do further say that there was no tender of payment or set off, and they assess the plaintiff's damages by reason of the detention of the residue of that debt to fifteen dollars and fifty cents besides costs. It is therefore considered by the Court here that the said plaintiffs do recover against the said defendants the residue of the debt aforesaid together with the damages aforesaid assessed and his costs in this behalf expended and the defendants in mercy &c. From which judgement the defendants hath prayed and obtained an appeal to the next Circuit Court of Haywood County, in the nature of a writ of error they having given bond & security to prosecute the same. Transcript

(p. 60)   Charles Carson, assee)
             vs   )
    John R. Leigh &   )
    Richard W. Nixon   )
Execution issued

(p. 60con.)This day came the plaintiff by his attorney & saith that he intends
no further to prosecute his said action against the said defendants. And
thereupon the said defendants assume to pay all costs in this behalf expended.
It is therefore considered by the Court here that the said plaintiff do recover against the said defendants his costs by them assumed & the defendants
in mercy etc.
execution issued

   The court then adjourned until tomorrow morning 9 o'clock.
              Richd. Nixon Cham.
              Blackman Coleman J. P.
              J. L. Wortham
              N. T. Perkins
              W. Dodd

   Wednesday morning September 13th 1826 the Court met according to
adjournment, present the worshipful Richard Nixon, Nicholas T. Perkins,
Blackman Coleman and others their fellow justices of the peace-

Robert Neal)
  vs)
Thomas Potter)

   On motion of the defendant by his counsel, leave is granted the said
defendant to take depositions Generally in giving the adverse party twenty
days notice if taken within the state & thirty days if taken without
Commissions issued

Robert Neal)
  vs)
John Potter)

   On motion of the defendant by his attorney, leave is granted the said
defendant to take depositions Generally upon giving the adverse party, twenty
days notice if taken, within the State & thirty days notice if taken without
Commissions Issued

(p. 61) It is ordered by the Court that Richard Nixon, Lawrence McGuire,
Nicholas T. Perkins, David Jeffers, Willie Dodd, Charles Wortham, Joel Estes,
Samuel P. Ashe, Henry W. Turner, Charles White, Vincent Harrelson, Joshua
Abstain, David Cherry, Jonathan T. Jacocks, Hyram Bradford, Henry Welch,
William Waddle, Herndon Harrelson, Henry Wooten, Francis Lamoin, Thomas G.
Nixon, Thomas Potter, James W. Russell, John Rodgers, John Williams, and
Richard Taylor be summoned to attend as grand or Petit jurors at the next
Circuit Court to be holden for this County, and that a venire Facias issue
accordingly and that Wyatt F. Tweedy be also summoned to attend said Court
as constable.
Iss'd 26th Sept. 1826

   It is ordered by the Court that Benjamin Noax, Benj. Rucker, James
Axley, Samuel Conner, Alfred Kennady, James Barrington, William Hollingsworth,
James Dorris, Robert Burns, Levi Gardner, Allen H. Howard, Benjamin Huckaby,
Benjamin King, Alexander D. Gordon, Caleb Warren, Eli Jones, Julius Sanders,
Jedediah Cusick, James Malding, Robert T. Smith, John M. White, Thomas
Rutherford, Matthew Ray, John Potter, John Hardwick and Peter Lankford, be
summoned to attend at the next County Court of this County, then & thence to

(p. 61 con.) serve as grand or Petit jurors as the case may be, and that a venire facias issue accordingly and also that Cato Freeman be summoned to serve said court as constable.

(p. 62)   Frederick Jones)
                vs   )
          Edwin J. Osborne)

This day came the said parties by their attornies and thereupon came also a jury of good & lawful men, to wit, Eli Farris, James Hollingsworth, James W. Russell, John Rogers, Thos. Thweatt, Samuel White, Nathan Williamson, Robert T. Smith, Lee H. Burks, Benjamin Noax, Peter Lankford and James T. White who being elected tried and sworn the truth to speak upon the issue joined upon their oath do say that the defendant hath not paid the debt of one hundred forty five dollars in the declaration mentioned as the plaintiff in declaring hath alledged and they assess the plaintiff's damages by reason of the detention of that debt to eight dollars besides costs.
Execution issued Sept. 26 1826
It is therefore considered by the court here that the said plaintiffs do recover against the said defendant the debt aforesaid in the declaration aforesaid mentioned together with his damage aforesaid by the jury aforesaid in form aforesaid assessed and his costs in this behalf expended, & the said defendant in mercy etc.

Robert F. Smith)
      vs   )
Robert G. Green)

This day came the said parties by their attornies and thereupon came also a jury of good and lawful men, to wit Eli Farris, James Hollingsworth, James W. Russell, John Rogers, Thomas Thweatt, Samuel White, Nathan Williams, Allen H. Howard, Lee H. Burks, Benjamin Noax, Peter Lankford and James T. White who being elected (p. 63) tried and sworn well & truly to try the matters in dispute between the parties upon their oath aforesaid do say they find for the defendant. It is therefore considered by the court here that the said defendant go hence without delay and recover against the said plaintiff his costs by him about his defence in this behalf expended and the said plaintiff in mercy & etc.

The grand Jury returned into Court the following presentments to wit the State of Tennessee to Robert Neal and Lee H. Burks for Gambling. The state vs Lee H. Burks and Levi Richards for gambling. The state vs Thomas J. Smith, Lee H. Burks, Benjamin Noaks and James Dorris for Gambling- The State vs Alexander Stewart and Peter Lankford for gambling. The State vs Robert Lackey and Thomas Chaney for gambling and also a presentment the State vs Levi Richards for retailing spiritous liquors without a licence, and retired to consider of other duties.

The State of Tennessee)
            vs   )
Willie Dodd   )

This day came as well the State of Tennessee by the attorney General as the defendant in his proper person, and the said defendant being solemnly

(p. 63 con.) charged saith that he is guilty in manner and form as charged in the Bill of Indictment and puts himself upon the grace and mercy of the Court. It is therefore considered by the Court that the defendant make his fine with the State of Tennessee by the payment of three dollars and all costs in this behalf expended and that the defendant be taken.
Execution issued

(p. 64)   John Potter)
                 vs   ) On motion for a new trial.
           Robert Neal)

On motion of the defendant by his attorney for a new trial in this cause and upon solemn agreement being had thereon on both sides by Councel learned in the law and by the Court here learned and fully understood it is considered by the court that the motion be overruled. And thereupon the defendant prayed and obtained in appeal to the next Circuit Court of Haywood County he having given bond and security to prosecute the same.

State   )
    vs   ) Presentment
Levi Richards)

This day came as well the State of Tennessee by the attorney general as the defendant, in his proper person and the said defendant being solemnly charged saith that he is guilty in manner and form as charged in the bill of Indictment, and puts himself upon the grace and mercy of the court, It is therefore considered by the court that the defendant make his fine with the state of Tennessee by the payment of one dollar and all costs in this behalf expended and the defendant be taken-
Execution issued

Ordered by the court that the overseer of the road leading from Brownsville to Capt. Estes be authorized to turn said road opposite John Rodgers, a quarter of a mile in such a way as he may think will be to the advantage of said road.

The court then adjourned until nine o'clock tomorrow morning-
                                   Rich'd. Nixon Cham-
                                   B. Coleman J.P.
                                   L. McGuire

(p. 65)   Thursday morning September 14, 1826
The Court met according to adjournment present the worshipful Richard Nixon, Blackman Coleman and Laurance McGuire, esquires.

A deed of Bargain and sale from A. D. Murphy, by his attorney in fact (Robt. Hughs) to John Rogers for two hundred and eight acres of land was this day produced in open court and duly proven by the oaths of James W. Russell and David Russell subscribing witnesses thereto, and ordered to be certified for registration.
Certified delivered

Ordered by the court that Herndon Harrilson be appointed overseer of the road leading from the town of Brownsville to Nixon's ware House on Big

(p. 65 con.) Hatchie river, in place of Green L. Harrilson, and the same hand, together with all others ordered to work thereon by this court work under him as such.
Issued 26th Sept.

Ordered by the court that an order made at the present term of this court, appointing Julius Sanders overseer of the road leading from Nixon's ware House in a direction to Summerville as far as this county line be and the same is hereby recorded.

Robert F. Smith)
    vs   ) Motion for a new trial-
Robt. G. Green)

On motion of the plaintiff by his attorney for a new trial, and on solemn argument being had thereon & by the Court here fully understood, it is considered by the Court that the motion be sustained.
execution issued 26th Septr.

The State)
  vs   )
Levi Richards)

This day came as well the State of Tennessee by A. B. Bradford esquire, Attorney General, as the defendant in his proper, and the defendant being solemly charged says that he is not guilty in manner and form as charged in the bill of Indictment & puts himself upon a jury of the country and the state doth the like and thereupon came a jury of good and lawful men to wit, Eli Farris, James W. Rupell, Thomas Thweatt, John Rogers, Henry Wooten, Green L. Harrison, Jonathan T. Nixon, Francis L. Dillard, Robert F. Smith, William W. Douthet (p. 66) Matthew Ray, Nathan Williamson who being elected tried and sworn well and truly to try the issue of traverse upon their oath aforesaid do say that the defendant is guilty in manner and form as charged in the bill of Indictment. It is therefore considered by the court here that the said defendant make his fine with the State of Tennessee by the payment of five dollars and all costs and that he be taken etc.

The State of Tennessee)
    vs   ) Presentment for Gaming
Lee H. Burks)

This day came Alexander B. Bradford attorney-General who prosecutes on behalf of the state, and the defendant in his proper person, and the defendant being solemly charged says that he is not guilty in manner and form as charged in the said Bill of presentment and for his trial puts himself upon a jury of his country, and the solicitor General doth the like and thereupon came a jury of good and lawful men to wit, Herndon Haralson, Hiram Bradford, James Hollingsworth, L. H. Ellison, Edward T. Friend, William Lankford, James T. White, Thomas Rutherford, Thomas Rowland, Mason F. Johnston and Montin Monday who being elected tried and sworn well and truly to try the issue of traverse joined upon their oath aforesaid do say that the defendant is guilty in manner and form as charged in the bill of presentment. It is therefore considered by the Court here that the said defendant make his fine with the

(p. 66 con.) State of Tennessee by the payment of five dollars and all costs and he be taken etc.
Iss'd. 29th Sept. 1826

The State of Tennessee)   Presentment for Gaming
        vs   )
Robert Neale

    This day came the solicitor General who prosecutes on behalf of the state and the defendant in his proper person and the defendant being solemnly charged says that he is not guilty in manner and form as charged in the said bill of presentment and for his trial puts himself upon a jury of his country and the solicitor general doth the like and thereupon came a jury of good and lawful men to wit, Eli Faris, James W. Rupell, John Rodgers, William Lankford, James Hollingsworth, Francis L. Dilliard, Robert F. Smith, Allen H. Howard, James T. White, James Green, Edward T. Friend and Lewis H. Ellison who being elected tried and sworn well and truly to try the issue of traverse joined, upon their oath aforesaid do say that the defendant is guiltin in manner & form as charged in the bill of presentment. It is therefore considered by the Court here that the P. Defendant make his fine with the state of Tennessee by (p. 67) the payment of one dollar and all costs and that he be taken etc.
Issued

The State of Tennessee)   Bill of Presentment for issuing
       vs   )   Accepted Orders
Green B. Jamison   )

    This day came Alexander B. Bradford solicitor general who prosecutes on behalf of the state, and the Defendant in his proper person, and by consent of parties this case is continued until the next term of this court.
Bill

    This day personally appeared in open Court Green B. Jamison, Esquire, and it appearing to the satisfaction of the court that he is licensed to practice as attorney and counsellor at law he thereupon took the necessary oaths as attorney and counsellor prescribed by law, and is admitted to practice in this court.

    The Grand jury returned into court, and there being no further business before them, it is ordered that they be discharged from the present service, and any further duties as jurors during the present term of this Court.

State   )   Bill of presentment for issuing
   vs   )   accepted orders
Green B. Jamerson)

    In this case the defendant came into Court together with Alondus Gholson his security and acknowledged themselves to owe and be indebted to the state of Tennessee, that is to say the said Green B. Jameson in the sum of fifty dollars lawful money of the sd state, and the said Alondus Gholson in the sum of their goods & chattels lands and tenements respectively for the use of the said state; but to be void on condition that the above bound Green B. Jameson shall well & truly make his personal appearance at the next court of pleas and quarter sessions to be holden for the county of Haywood

(p. 67 con.) at the courthouse in the Town of Brownsville on the second Monday in December next to answer the state in a charge of issuing accepted. Orders contrary to the act of assembly and then and there stand to abide by and receive the Judgt. of said Court, and not depart there from without leave first had and obtained.

(p. 68)   State   )   A Bill of presentment for gambling
             vs   )
        John McWhite)

In this case the defendant came into Court together with Reuben Alphin his security and acknowledged themselves to owe and be indebted to the State of Tennessee that is to say, the said John McWhite in the sum of fifty dollars lawful money of the state; and the said Reuben Alphin in the sum of Twenty five dollars, to be levied of their goods and chattels land, and tenements respectfully for the use of the said state, but to be void on condition that the above bound John McWhite shall well & truly make his personal appearance at the next court of pleas and quarter sessions to be holden for the county of Haywood at the Courthouse in the town of Brownsville on the second Monday in December next to answer the state in a charge of gambling contrary to act of assembly, and then and there stand to abide by and receive the judgement of said court, and not depart therefrom without leave first had and obtained.
(Paragraph omitted in typed manuscript - errata on page 44a)

(p. 69)   State   )   A bill of indictment for gambling
             vs   )
        Robert Lucky)

In this case the defendant came into Court together with John Hardwick his security and acknowledged themselves to owe and be indebted to the state of Tennessee that is to say the said Robert Lucky in the sum of fifty dollars lawful money of the state and the said John Hardwick in the sum of twenty five dollars, to be levied of their goods and chattels lands and tenements respectfully for the use of the said state but to be void on condition that the above bound Robert Lucky shall well and truly make his personal appearance at the next court of pleas and quarter sessions to be holden for the county of Haywood at the courthouse in the town of Brownsville on the 2nd Monday in December next to answer the state in a charge of gambling contrary to act of assembly and then and there stand to abide by and receive the judgt. of said court and not depart therefrom without leave first had and obtained.

        State   )   A bill of presentment for gambling.
         vs   )
    Peter Lankford)

In this case the defendant came into court together with John Hardwick his security and acknowledged themselves to owe and be indebted to the state of Tennessee, that is to say the said Peter Lankford in the sum of fifty dollars, lawful money of the state, and the said John Hardwick in the sum of twenty five dollars to be levied of their goods and chattels lands and tenements respectfully for the use of the said state, but to be void on condition that the above bound Peter Lankford shall well and truly make his personal appearance at the next court of pleas and quarter sessions to be

ERRATA

(p. 68 con.)   State   )   A Bill of presentment for gambling-
                 vs   )
                 James Dorris   )

In this case the defendant came into Court together with Reuben Alphin his security and acknowledged themselves to owe and be indebted to the state of Tennessee that is to say, the said James Dorris in the sum of fifty dollars lawful money of the State, and the said Reubin Alphin in the sum of twenty five dollars, to be levied on their goods and chattels, lands and tenements respectfully for the use of the said state but, to be void on condition that the above bound James Dorris, shall well & truly, make his personal appearance at the next court of pleas and quarter sessions to be holden for the county of Haywood at the courthouse in the town of Brownsville on the second Monday in December next to answer the state in a charge of gambling contrary to act of Assembly, and then and there stood to abide by and receive the judgement of said Court, and not depart therefrom without leave first had and obtained.

(p. 69 con.) holden for the county of Haywood at the courthouse in the town of Brownsville on the 2nd Monday in December next to answer the state in a charge of gambling contrary to act of assembly and then and there stand to abide by and receive the Judgt. of said court and not depart therefrom without leave first had and obtained.

(p. 70)   State   )   A bill of presentment for gambling-
              vs   )
        John Hardwick)

In this case the defendant came into Court together with Edmond Richmond his security and acknowledged themselves to owe and be indebted, to the state of Tennessee, that is to say, the said John Hardwick in the sum of fifty dollars, lawful money of the state, and the said Edmond Richmond in the sum of twenty five dollars, to be levied of their goods and chattels lands and tenements, respectfully, for the use of the state but to be void on condition that the above bound.

John Hardwick shall well and truly make his personal appearance at the next court of pleas and quarter sessions to be holden for the county of Haywood at the courthouse in the town of Brownsville on the second Monday in December next to answer the state in a charge of gambling contrary to act of assembly and then and there stand to and abide by and receive the judgt. of said court and not depart therefrom without leave first being had & obtained.

State   )   A bill of presentment for gambling
  vs   )
Benjamin Noaks)

In this case the defendant came into court together with Edmond Richmond his security and acknowledged themselves indebted to the State of Tennessee that is to say the said Benjamin Noaks in the sum of fifty dollars, lawfull money of the state and the said Edmond Richmond in the sum of twenty five dollars to be levied on their goods and chattels land and tenements respectively for the use of the state but to be void on condition that the said Benjamin Noaks shall well and truly make his personal appearance at the next court of pleas and quarter sessions to be holden for the county of Haywood at the courthouse in the town of Brownsville on the second Monday in December next to answer the state in a charge of gambling contrary to the act of assembly and then and there stand to abide by and receive the Judgt. of said court and not depart without leave first being had and obtained.

(p. 71)   The court then adjourned until half after eight o'clock.
                                Rich. Nixon Char.
                                Blackman Coleman J. P.
                                L. McGuire

The court met according to adjournment Friday the 15th of September 1826

Robert Neal)   Slander
   vs   )
John Potter)

The plaintiff in this case has leave to take depositions generally

(p. 71 con.) by giving ten days notice in the county, Twenty days notice in the state and thirty days notice out of the state.

Robert Neal)   Slander
   vs   )
Thomas Potter)

The plaintiff in this case has leave to take depositions generally by giving ten days notice in the county, twenty days notice in this state and thirty days notice out of the state.

State   )   Gaming
   vs   )
Alexander Stewart)

The defendant* came into court and acknowledged himself to owe and be indebted to the state of Tennessee in the sum of fifty dollars to be void on condition that he as well and truly make his personal appearance before the court of pleas and quarter sessions for Haywood County on the first Wednesday after the second Monday in December next & not depart without leave of the court first had.

(p. 72)   State   )   Gaming
         vs   )
        A. Stuart)

John Hardwick acknowledges himself to owe and be indebted to the State of Tennessee in the sum of twenty five dollars to be void on condition that the said Stuart does well & truly make his personal appearance on the first Wednesday after the second Monday in December next and not depart without leave of the court first had.

State   )   Gaming in two cases
   vs   )
Lee H. Burks)

The def't. in these two cases acknowledges himself to owe & be indebted to the State of Tennessee in sum of one hundred dollars to be void on condition that he does well & truly make his personal appearance on the first Wednesday after the second Monday in December next & not depart without leave of the Court first had obtained. And Francis L. Dilliard acknowledges to be indebted as above in the sum of fifty dollars that the said Burks does appear as above required until discharged by law.

(p. 73)   On motion & petition filed, Levi Richards & Samuel Elliott have leave to keep an ordinary in the Town of Brownsville having given bond & security as the law directs and took the oaths prescribed by law.
Issue

State   )   Assault & Battery
   vs   )
Willis H. Burks)
*in this cause

(p. 73 con.)   The solicitor on part of the state & by assent of the court
a nolle prosequi be intend and that the county pay the cost.

The court adjourned untill court in course September 15th 1826
Blackman Coleman
Rich. Nixon Chair-
L. McGuire

(p. 74)   State of Tennessee
At a court of pleas and quarter sessions began and holden in and for
the county of Haywood at the Courthouse in the town of Brownsville on the
second Monday in December in the year of our Lord one thousand eight hundred
and twenty six it being the 11th day of   said month. Present the worshipful
Richard Nixon Chairman Jonathan T. Jacocks, Lawrence McGuire Esquires and
others their fellow justices of the peace John G. Carithers Shff. and
Britain H. Sanders clerk.

A bill of sale from Thomas White to William Moss for a negro woman
was this day produced in open Court and proven in part by the oath of
William Henderson a subscribing witness thereto and filed further probate.

A deed of Trust from Henry L. Gray to William Loving was this day produced in open Court and duly acknowledged and ordered to be certified for
registration.
Certified & De -

John D. Martin Esqr. attorney and counsellor at law appeared in open
court and took the necessary oath prescribed by law and admitted to practice
as such in this Court-

Edwin J. Osborn Esq. attorney and counsellor at law appeared in open
Court and took the oath to support the constitution of the United States
and the State of Tennessee-

This day the last will & testament of James Casby late of said county
Dec. was produced in open Court and duly proven by the oaths of D. W.Parrish
and W. W. Douthit subscribing witness thereto and ordered to be filed and
recorded. Whereupon Gabriel Minter the executor therein named appeared in
open court and qualified as such and entered into bond together with Joseph
Minter and Mathew Ray his security as the law requires.
It is therefore ordered by the Court that letters testamentary be issued to
the last Gabriel Minter executor accordingly-

On sufficient cause being shown it is ordered by the court that
Mathew Ray be ligenced to retail spirituous liquors for the term of twelve
months he having entered into hand and together with Reuben Alpin and
Robert T. Smith his securities as the law directs

(p. 75)   On sufficient cause being shown it is ordered by the court that
Henry L. Gray be licenced to retail spirituous liquors for the time of
twelve months he having entered into bond together with Blackman Coleman
and Mathew Ray his securities as the law directs.
Issued 11th Dec. 1826

Ordered by the court a majority of the acting justices being present
that William Morrison be appointed overseer of the road leading from

(p. 75 con.) Brownsville in a direction to Bolivar in place of Caleb Warren as far as where the same crosses the road known by the name of the McGuire road and that all the hands within the following bounds to wit, all east of the road leading from Brownsville to Haywood Bluffs and south of the road passing Richard Nixon's Esqr. and west of the 4th range and north of the McGuire road work under him as such in opening the same.
Issued

Ordered by the court a majority of the acting justices being present that county trustee pay to the commissioners of the town of Brownsville the sum of forty seven dollars and fifty cents it having been paid by the said commissioners to the printer for services rendered by advertizing etc. relative to sale of said town lots.
Iss'd to T. J. N.

A deed of Bargain and sale from Jane Casby to Mathew Figures was this day produced in open court and his hand writing duly proven by the oaths of Gabriel Minter and Joseph Minter there being no subscribing witnesses thereto, by whom the same could be proved.
Certified and del.

Ordered by the Court a majority of the acting justices being present that John G. Carithers Esq. Sherriff and collector be allowed the sum of fifty dollars for his ex oficio services, and that the county trustee pay the same which shall be good in the settlement of his account.
Iss'd. 18th Decr.

Ordered by the Court a majority of the acting justices being present that Alexander B. Bradford Esqr. solicitor be allowed the sum of fifty dollars for his ex oficio services and that the county trustee pay the same which shall be good in the settlement of his account.
Iss'd. 18th Decr.

Ordered by the court a majority of the acting justices being present that Britain H. Sanders Clerk be allowed the sum of forty dollars for his ex oficio services and the further sum of twenty five dollars for making out the tax lists, and that the county Trustee pay the same which shall be good in the settlement of his account.
Issue'd. 18th Decr.

(p. 76) Ordered by the court a majority of the acting Justices being present that John G. Carithers Esquire Sheriff and collector be allowed a credit with the county Treasurer for the year 1825 the sum of four hundred and seventy three dollars forty two cents it being the amount of taxes due on lands reported for said year and not sold for want of bidders.
Issued to Shff.

Ordered by the court a majority of the acting Justices being present that John G. Carithers Esqr. sheriff and collector be allowed a credit with the Treasurer of West Tennessee for the year 1825 the sum of one hundred and seventy two dollars and fifteen cents it being the amount of the taxes due on lands reported for said year and not sold for want of bidders.
Iss'd shff.

Ordered by the court a majority of the acting justices being present that Britain H. Sanders clerk be allowed the sum of sixty five dollars and eighty cents it being his fees on lands reported for the year 1825 and not

(p. 76 con.) sold for the want of bidders and that the county Treasurer pay the same out of any monies unappropriated unappropriated which shall be good on the settlement of his accounts.

Ordered by the court a majority of the acting justices being present that John G. Carithers Esqr. Sheriff and collector of the state and county tax of the county of Haywood for the year 1826 be allowed a credit of six months after the 1st Monday in January 1827, on the amount of four hundred and sixty one dollars one and 1/3 cents the amount of Taxes due to the State on lands for the present year which amount is unpaid by the respective owners of said land and the same will have to be reported for the taxes due thereon for said year, and it is further ordered that the clerk of this Court certify the same under his hand and seal to the Treasurer of West Tennessee.
Issd. Shff-

Ordered by the court a majority of the acting Justices being present that John G. Carithers Sheriff and collector of the state & county taxes of the county of Haywood for the year 1826 be allowed a credit of six months after the 1st Monday in January 1827 on the amount of twelve hundred sixty seven dollars and ten cents the amount of Taxes due the county on lands for the present year, which amount is unpaid by the respective owners of (p.77) said lands and the same will have to be reported for the taxes due thereon for said year, and it is further ordered that the Clerk of this Court certify the same under his hand and seal to the Trustee of this county.

James Russell this day produced the scalp of a wolf over the age of four months in open court and proved the killing of the same within the bounds of this county by his own oath having no other evidence whereby he could prove the same, it is therefore ordered that the clerk issue a certificate to the treasurer of West Tennessee accordingly.
Issued

A deed of Bargain and sale from John R. McGuire to Thomas J. McGuire for two hundred and thirty acres of land was this day produced in open court and duly proven by the oaths of Wm. C. Bruce and William H. Loving subscribing witnesses thereto and ordered to be certified for registration.
                                        Thomas J. McGuire

A deed of bargain and sale from Robt. Hughs to John R. McGuire for two hundred and thirty acres of land was this day produced in open Court and duly proven by the oaths of H . Harrelson & Green L. Harrelson subscribing witnesses thereto and ordered to be certified for registration.

A Deed of bargain and sale from John G. Carithers sheriff and collector of Haywood county to Thos. G. Nixon for six hundred and forty acres of land was this day produced in open Court and duly acknowledged and ordered to be certified for registration.
certified fees not paid

A deed of bargain and sale from John G. Carithers Sheriff and collector for the county of Haywood to Thos. G. Nixon for three hundred thirty two and one half acres of land was this day produced in open Court and duly acknowledged and ordered to be certified for registration.
certified-fees not paid

Ordered by the court a majority of the acting justices being present

(p. 77 con.) that Henry Wooten and the hands of David Hay, Joseph Lowry and all the hands from the range line dividing 5 & 6 for the distance of one mile east in addition to the former hands work under Laurance McGuire Esqr, overseer of what is called the McGuire road and that an order issue accordingly.
Iss'd.

(p. 78) Ordered by the court a majority of the acting Justices being present that Laurence McGuire, Nathan Bridgman, Alexander Roddy, Benjamin Noaks, Samuel P. Ash, Isaac Edwards, Griffeth Edwards, John Roddy, and James Fields be appointed a jury to view mark and lay of a road, begining at McGuire Ferry and run through the bottom of Hatchie River in such a direction to the summit of the high lands on the south side of said river so as to suit a road to branch off from thence to Memphis and to Summerville and to continue to mark out that part (or Branch) of the road leading from the same in the best direction to Summerville and make report of their proceedings to the next term of this court.
Issued

Ordered by the Court a majority of the acting justices being present that Bignal Crook be appointed overseer of the road from Joel Estes, Esqr. to Pains ferry and that his own hands, Henry Boothe's, James Crook's work under him as such-
Issued-

Ordered by Court that tomorrow until one o'clock be set apart for transacting county business and the same be advertized agreeable to law.

The court then adjourned until tomorrow morning 9 o'clock.
                              Rich. Nixon Chair.
                              Jona. T. Jacocks
                              L. McGuire

Tuesday the 12th day of Dec. 1826 the court met according to ajournment.

Ordered by the court that the clerk insert in this tax list for the present year four town lots in the name of Jonathan Jones, Senr-

The court then proceeded to the election of constable for the next ensuing two years, whereupon Julius Sanders was unanimously elected, who appeared in open court and took the necessary oath prescribed by law and took the necessary oath prescribed by law and entered into bond together with Reubin Alphin and John McWhite his securities as the law directs.

(p. 79) The court then proceeded to the election of constable in Captain Edward's company, whereupon after counting the votes Benjamin Noaks was declared duly and constitutionally elected for the ensuing two years, who entered into bond together with --- his securities and took the necessary oaths prescribed by laws.
1
Sufficient cause being shown to the court, it is ordered by the Court that James Dorris be exempt from serving as a juror to the present term.
2 Iss'd.

Ordered by the court a majority of the acting justices being present that John T. Turner be appointed overseer in place of James Maldin of the

(p. 79 con.) road leading from Brownsville to boliver from the McGuire road to Big Hatchie River and that all the hands south of the McGuire road east of range five and north of the river together with Odle Smith and   Ross be subject to work under him as such to keep the same in good repair.
3 issued

Ordered by court a majority being present that Eli Faris be appointed overseer of the new road leading from Brownsville to Jackson together with Charles White the present overseer and that they divide the said road and hands heretofore allotted to work on the same to suit themselves, together with the addition of Samuel Brown and hands, Henry McCoy & hands, William and Thomas Crutcher and hands who are subject to work under them agreeable to such division.
4 issued

Ordered by the court that Cater Freeman be appointed overseer of the road marked by a Jury of view appointed for that purpose leading from where the road leading from the town of Jackson to Harrisburgh crosses the county line at or near James L. Worthams commencing at the Forked deer river from thence with said mark to where they intersect the Jackson road near Col. Nixons and that he be authorized to call out all the hands north of the road leading from Brownsville to Jackson by said Nixon's and south of the said river to cut and open the same.
5 issued

Ordered by the Court that Wm. Alread be appointed overseer of the road marked by the jury of view appointed for that purpose leading from where the road leading from the Town of Jackson to Harrisburgh crosses the county line at or near James L. Worthams to Forked Deer river and that he be authorized to call out*all the hands north of said river from the county line to Fudges to cut out and open the same.
6 issued 1

Ordered by the court a majority of the acting justices being present that the county trustee pay to Jedediah Cusick the sum of fifty eight dollars as pr. certificate of commissioner filed it being for his services in clearing out the East end of Main Street which will stand good in the settlement of his account.
2 Iss'd 15th Dec.

A Deed of Bargain and sale from John G. Carithers Sheriff and Collector to Julius Sanders for fifteen hundred acres of land was this day produced in open court and duly acknowledged and ordered to be certified for registration.
Certified fee pd.

It appearing to the satisfaction of this court that the sum of twelve dollars and eighty three cents on lands improperly listed either by the overseer thereof or the surveyor gen'l- has heretofore been returned to the treasurer of West Tennessee in the aggregate amount as being due by the sheriff and collector to said Treasurer for the year 1824 over and above the amount actually due by the said sheriff and it also appearing to the court here that the same has by said sheriff been paid over to the said Treasurer. It is therefore ordered by the court that the same be entered of record and certified to the treasurer of West Tennessee that the same may be allowed said sheriff in his next settlement with said Treasurer
* (p. 80)

(p. 80 con.)   It appearing to the satisfaction of the court that a tract of land of one thousand acres was heretofore reported for the nonpayment of taxes for the year 1824 in the names of Joseph Bryan and J. Freeman and was sold for the same to Jonathan T. Freeman and was sold for the same to Jonathan T. Jacocks, and it also appearing to this court that there is no such tract of land in this county of Haywood. It is therefore ordered by the court that the said Jonathan T. Jacocks be allowed the sum of five dollars fifty one and one fourth cents (it being the amount paid by him which was due the county on said tract of Land to be paid by the county Trustee out of any monies in his hands not otherwise appropriated.
Issued April 30 1827 To T. G. Nixon

(p. 81)   It appearing to the satisfaction of the court that a tract of land for one hundred acres was heretofore reported for the non payment of Taxes for the year 1824 in the name of Joshua Newman, that the same was sold to Thomas G. Nixon, and it also appearing to the court that there is no such tract of land in this county. It is therefore ordered by the court that the sum of two dollars eighty nine and one fourth cents (it being the amount paid by him which was due the county on said tract of lands to be paid by the county trustee out of any monies in his hands not otherwise appropriated.
Issued April 30th 1827 To T. G. Nixon

It appearing to the satisfaction of the court that a tract of land for one thousand acres was heretofore reported for the non payment of Taxes for the year 1824 in the name of John McAllister, that the sum was sold to Thomas G. Nixon and Mathew Ray and it also appearing to this court that there is no such tract of land in this county. It is therefore ordered by the court that the said Thomas G. Nixon and Mathew Ray be allowed the sum of five dollars fifty one and one fourth cents (it being) the amount paid by them which was due the county on said tract of land) to be paid out of any monies in his hands not otherwise appropriated.
Issued April 30th 1827 To T. G. Nixon

It appearing to the satisfaction of the court that a tract of land for eight hundred and nineteen acres was heretofore reported for the non-payment of Taxes for the year 1824 and 1825 in the name of Jacob Lenard that the same was sold to Reubin Alfin & redeemed by Jno. A. Smith and it also appearing to this court, that there is no such tracts of land in this county. It is therefore ordered by the court that the said Jno. A. Smith be allowed the sum of eleven dollars seventy six cents (it being the amount paid by said Smith which was due to the county on said tracts of land for said years) to be paid out of any monies in his hands and otherwise appropriated.

It is ordered by the court that the following tracts of land now listed for taxation for the present year be stricken off the tax list it appearing to the satisfaction of the court that there are no such tracts of land in Haywood county to wit Bryan & Freman one thousand acres, Joshua Newman 100 acres John McAllister 1000 acres Jacob Leonard 819½ acres Evander McIver 640 acres.

(p.82)   John G. Carithers, sheriff of Haywood County makes return upon the writ of venire facias returnable to this court that he has summoned the person, therein named who were appointed by the court of pleas and quarter sessions of said county to serve as a jury at the present term of this court that is to say Benjamin Noaks, Berry Rucker, James Axley, Samuel Conner,

(p. 82 con.) Alfred Kennedy, James Barrington, William Hollingsworth, James Dorris, Robert Burns, Levi Goodman, Allen H. Howard, Benjamin Huckabee, Benjamin King, Alexander D. Gordon, Caleb Warren, Eli Jones, Julius Sanders, Jedediah Cusick, James Maulden, Robert T. Smith, John M. White, Thos. Rutherford, Matthew Ray, John Patton, John Hardwick & Peter Lankford, who are all free holders or house holders residents in sd. county over 21 yrs. of age; out of whom the following named persons, that is to say, Robt. Burns, foreman, John M. White, Alexander D. Gordon, Benj. King, Jedediah Cusick, Eli Jones, Caleb Warren, Matthew Ray, Benj. Huckabee, Thos. Rutherford, Allen H. Howard, Peter Lankford & Robt. T. Smith good & lawful men were drawn, elected sworn & charged as as agreed jury for the present term & having received their charge returned under the care of Cato Freeman & officers sworn to attend them to consider of the duties assigned them.

H . M. Rutledge assee)   Debt
       vs   )
William Johnston   )

     This day came the parties by their attornies and thereupon came a jury of good and lawful men to wit, James Maulden, Mason F. Johnson, Philip Koonce, Joshua Abstain, Henry Welch, Willie Woodard, John Marberry, Robt. A. Penn, Jonathan J. Nixon, William W. Douthit, James Elliot and Hiram Bradford, who being elected tried and sworn the truth to speak upon the issued joined upon their oaths do say that the defendant hath not paid the debt of one hundred and three dollars and thirty nine cents in the declaration mentioned as the plaintiff by replying to the defendants plea in this behalf hath alledged, and do assess the plaintiffs damages by reason of the detention thereof to eight dollars be sides his costs. It is therefore considered by the court that the plaintiff recover of the defendant his debt aforesaid together with his damages aforesaid by the jury aforesaid in form aforesaid assessed and also his costs by him about his suit in this behalf expended, and the said defendant in mercy etc.
Ex. Issued 29th Dec.

(p. 83) State   )   Delinquent Juror
         vs   )
      B erry Rucker)

     Berry Rucker who was regularly summoned to attend this term to serve as juror as appears from the return of the venire by the Sheriff being solemnly called came not but made default- It is therefore considered that for such his neglect, he be fined the sum of five dollars unless he appear at the next term of this court and show cause if any he can why this judgment should be set aside.

State   )   Delinquent Juror
   vs   )
James Axley)

     James Axley who was regularly summoned to attend this term to serve as Juror which appears from the return of the venire by the sheriff, being solemnly called came not but made default. It is therefore considered that for such his neglect he be fined the sum of five dollars unless he appear

(p. 83 con.) at the next term of this court and show cause if any he can why this judgment should be set aside.

State   ) Delinquent Juror
  vs   )
Samuel Conner)

    Samuel Conner who was regularly summoned to attend this term to serve as Juror which appears from the return of the venire by the sheriff being solemnly called came not but made default. It is therefore considered by the court that for such his neglect he be fined the sum of five dollars unless he appear at the next term of this court and show cause if any he can why Judgment should be set aside.

State   ) Delinquent Jurors
  vs   )
Alfred Kenedy)

    Alfred Kenedy who was regularly summoned to attend this term to serve as Juror which appears from the return of the venire by the sheriff being solemnly called came not but made default. It is therefore considered by the court that for such his neglect he be fined the sum of five dollars unless he appear at the next term of this court and show cause if any he can why this judgment should be set aside.

(p. 84) State   ) Delinquent Jurors
       vs   )
    James Barrington)

    James Barrington a delinquent Juror who was regularly summoned to attend this term to serve as juror, which appears from the return of the venire facias by the sherriff being solemnly called came not but made default. It is therefore considered by the court that for such his neglect he be fined the sum of five dollars unless he appear at the next term of this court and show cause if any he can why this Judgment should be set aside.

State   ) Delinquent Jurors
  vs   )
William Hollingsworth)

    William Hollingsworth who was regularly summoned to attent this term to serve as Juror which appears from the return of the venire by the sheriff being solemnly called came not but made default. It is therefore considered by the court that for such his neglect he be fined the sum of five dollars unless he appear at the next term of this court and show cause if any he can why this judgment should be set aside-

State   ) Delinquent Jurors
  vs   )
Levi Guardner)

(p. 84 con.)   Levi Guardner who was regularly summoned to attend this term to serve as Juror which appears by the return of the venire by the sheriff being solemnly called came not but made default. It is therefore considered by the court that for such his neglect he be fined the sum of five dollars unless he appear at the next term of this court & show cause if any he can Judgment should be set aside-

State   )   Delinquent Juror
  vs   )
John Hardwick   )

John Hardwick who was regularly summoned to attend this term to serve as Juror which appears by the return of the venire by the sheriff being solemnly called came not but made default. It is therefore considered by the court that for such his neglect he be fined the sum of five dollars unless he appear at next court and show cause if any he can why this Judgment should be set aside-

(p. 85)   Robert T. Smith   )   Appeal
              vs   )
          Robert G. Green   )

This day came the parties by their attorneys and thereupon came a jury of good and lawful men to wit, James Maldin, Mason F. Johnson, Philip Coonts, Joshua Absten, Henry Welsh, Wily Woodward, John Marbury, Robert A. Pen, Jonathan J. Nixon, William W. Douthit, Samuel Elliot, and Hiram Bradford, who being elected, tried and sworn the truth to speak on the matters in dispute between the parties, on their oaths do say they find the matter in dispute in favor of the plaintiff, and assess plaintiffs damages for the non payment of the note sent on, to seventy one dollars fifty seven cents.
Issued
It is therefore considered by the Court the the plaintiff recover of the defendant, and on motion of Plaintiff by his attorney of Joseph P. Wimberly defendants security in the appeal, the said sum of seventy one dollars fifty seven cents, together with his costs in this behalf expended etc.

Ordered by the court a majority of the acting justices being present that John G. Carithers Esquire Sheriff and collector of the state and county Tax for the present year be allowed a credit in his next settlement with the treasurer of West Tennessee the sum of five dollars sixty four cents the amount returned in the aggregate amount of the tax costs for the year 1826 on lands improperly listed and stricken from the tax list and that the clerk issue a certificate accordingly.
Issued Shff.

Ordered by the court a majority of the acting Justices being present that John G. Carithers sheriff and collector of the state and county tax for the year 1826 be allowed a credit in his next settlement with the county Trustee the sum of fifteen dollars fifty & ½ cents the amount returned in the aggregate amount of the Tax list for the present year on lands improperly listed and stricken from the tax list and that the clerk issue a certificate accordingly.
Issued Sheriff

(p. 86)   Court adjourned until tomorrow nine o'clock

B. Coleman J.P.
Richard Nixon Cha.
Jon. T. Jacocks

Wednesday morning December 13th 1826. The court met according to adjournment-
Issued

This day Ralings Henderson produced in open court the scalp of a wolf over the age of four months and proved the killing of the same within the bounds of Haywood County by his own oath he having no other evidence whereby he could prove the same- It is therefore ordered by the Court that the clerk certify the same to the treasurer of West Tennessee accordingly-

```
Silas Locke        )   Debt
    vs             )
John & Wm. Johnston )
```

This day came the parties by their attorneys and thereupon came a jury of good and lawful men to wit James Maldin, John Potter, Samuel Elliot, John Hardwick, Francis L. Dilliard, Robert A. Penn, Benjamin Rowland, German Seawell, Henry Welsh, Thomas Rowland, Edward T. Friend, and Mansfield Ware, who being elected tried and sworn the truth to speak upon the issue joined upon their oaths do say that the defendant hath not paid the debt of fifty seven dollars and thirty three cents in the declaration mentioned as the plaintiff by replying to the defendants plea in that behalf hath alledged and do assess the plaintiffs damages by reason of the detention thereof to three dollars and twenty four cents besides his costs. It is therefore considered by the court that the plaintiff recover of the defendant his debt aforesaid together with his damage aforesaid by the Jury aforesaid in form aforesaid assessed and also his costs by him about his suit in this behalf expended and the defendant in mercy etc. Issued 28th Dec. 1826

```
(p. 87)   J. & G. Sutherland )   Debt
                 vs
          Robert A. Penne
```

This day came the parties by their attornies, and thereupon came a jury of good and lawful men to wit James Maulden, John Potter, Samuel Elliot, John Hardwick, Francis L. Dillard, Benjamin Rowland, German Seawell, Henry Welsh, Thomas Rowland, Edward T. Friend, Mansfield Ware and Mathew Figures who being elected tried and sworn the truth to speak upon the issues, joined upon their oaths do say that the defendant hath not paid the Debt of two hundred and twenty dollars in the declaration mentioned as the plaintiffs by replying to the Defendants plea in that behalf hath alleged and do assess the plaintiffs damages by reason of the detention thereof to six dollars eighty seven and a half cents.

It is therefore considered by the court that the plaintiff recover of the defendant his debt aforesaid together with his damages aforesaid by the jury afordsaid in form aforesaid assessed and also his costs by him about his suit in this behalf expended and the defendant in mercy etc. From which judgment the defendant hath prayed and obtained an appeal to the next circuit Court of Haywood County he having given bond to prosecute the same- Assess'd.

(p. 87 con.)   Richard W. Nixon)   Appeal
                     vs   )
              Allin H. Howard)

This day came the parties by their attorneys and thereupon came a jury of good and lawful men to wit, James Maldin, John Potter, Samuel Eliot, John Hardwick, Francis L. Dillard, Benjamin Rowland, German Seawell, Henry Welsh, Thomas Rowland, Edward T. Friend, Mansfield Ware, and Herndon Harrelson who parties being elected tried and sworn to try the matters in dispute between them upon their oaths do say that the defendant hath not paid the debt of forty three dollars eighty nine and three fourth cents in the
Issued

It is therefore considered by the court that the plaintiff recover of the defendant his debt aforesaid by the jury aforesaid in form aforesaid assessed and also his costs by him about his suit in this behalf expended and the defendant in mercy etc.

(p.88)   State of Tennessee)   Presentment for Gaming
                   vs   )
              James Dorris   )

This day came as well the state of Tennessee by the attorney general as the defendant in his proper person and the said defendant being solemnly charged, saith that he is guilty in manner and form as charged in the bill of presentment, and puts himself upon the grace and mercy of the court. It is thereupon considered by the court that the defendant make his fine with the state of Tennessee by the payment of five dollars and all costs in this behalf expended, and that the defendant be taken etc.
Issued

                 State of Tennessee)   Presentment for Gaming
                         vs   )
                  Peter Lankford   )

This day came Alexander B. Bradford attorney general who prosecute in behalf of the state and the defendant in his proper person and the defendant being solemnly charged says that he is not guilty in manner and form as charged in the bill of presentment, and for his trial puts himself upon a jury and his country, and the solicitor general doth the like and thereupon came a jury of good and lawful men, to wit, James Maldin, Samuel Elliot, Francis L. Dilliard, Benjamin Rowland, German Seawel, Thomas Rowland, Edward T. Friend, Mansfield Ware, Herndon Harrelson, Henry Welsh, James T. White and Jonathan Nixon who being elected tried and sworn well and truly to try the issue of Traverse joined upon their oaths aforesaid do say that the defendant is guilty in manner and form as charged in the bill of presentment. It is therefore considered by the Court here that the defendant make his fine with the State of Tennessee by the payment of the sum of five dollars and all costs and that he be taken etc.
Issued

                    State   )   Presentment for Gambling
                       vs   )
              Alexander Stewart)

In this case came John Hardwick and acknowledged himself to owe and be indebted to the state of Tennessee in the sum of twenty five dollars,

(p. 88 con.) lawful money of the state to levied of his goods and chattels lands and tenements for the use of the state but to be void on condition that Alexander Stewart shall well and truly make his personal appearance at the (p. 89) next court of pleas and quarter sessions to be holden for the county of Haywood at the courthouse in the town Brownsville on the second Monday in March next to answer the state in a charge of gambling then and there stand to abide by and perform the Judgment of said court and not depart therefrom without leave first being had and obtained.

State of Tennessee)   Presentment for Gaming
      vs   )
Lee H. Burks   )

      This day came Alexander B. Bradford attorney general who prosecutes in behalf of the state and the defendant in his proper person and the defendant being solemnly charged says that he is not guilty in manner and form as charged in the bill of presentment and for his trial puts himself upon a jury and his country and the solicitor general doth the like and thereupon came a jury of good and lawful men to wit, James Mauldin, Samuel Elliot, Francis L. Dillard, Benjamin Rowland, German Seawell, Thomas Rowland, Edward T. Friend, Mansfield Ware, Herndon Harrelson, Henry Welsh, James F. White and Jonathan J. Nixon who being elected tried and sworn well and truly to try the issue of Traverse joined upon their oaths aforesaid do say that the defendant is guilty in manner and form as charged in the bill of presentment. It is therefore considered by the court here, that the defendant make his fine with the state of Tennessee by the payment of five dollars and all costs and that he be taken etc.
Iss'd.

State of Tennessee)   Presentment for Gambling
      vs   )
Benjamin Noaks)

      This day came Alexander B. Bradford attorney general who prosecutes in behalf of the state and the defendant in his proper person and the defendant being solemnly charged says that he is not guilty in manner and form as charged in the bill of presentment and for his trial puts himself upon a jury and his country and the solicitor general doth the like and thereupon came a jury of good and lawful men to wit James Maldin, Samuel Elliot, Francis L. Dillard, Benjamin Rowland, German Seawell, Thos. Rowland, Edward T. Friend, Mansfield Ware, Herndon, Harrelson, Henry Welch, James T. White and Jonathan J. Nixon who being elected tried and sworn well and truly to try the issue of traverse joined upon their oaths aforesaid do say that the defendant is guilty in manner and form as charged in the bill of Presentment. It is therefore considered by the court here that the defendant (p. 90) make his fine with the State of Tennessee by the payment of five dollars and all costs, and he be taken etc.
Issued

State of Tennessee)   Presentment for gambling
      vs   )
John McWhite   )

      This day came as well the State of Tennessee by the attorney general as the defendant in his proper person and the said defendant being solemnly charged saith that he is guilty in manner and form as charged in the bill of (p-90con.) presentment and puts himself upon the grace and mercy of the court. It is therefore considered by the court that the defendant make his fine with the state of Tennessee by the payment of five dollars and all costs in this behalf expended and that the defendant be taken etc.

It appearing to the satisfaction of the court that an entry no.797 made in the name of Mark R.Cockrill for 500 hundred acres of land has been heretofore improperly listed, as it should have been three hundred and twenty acres instead of 500. It is t erefore ordered by the court that the same be altered as such, on the tax list for the year 1826, and that the sheriff and collector receive the taxes accordingly and it is further order- ed that the clerk of this court certify the same to the treasurer Haywood County that the said John G.Carithers Sheriff and collector be allowed a credit of thirty three cents in his next settlement.
Listed

Court adjourned until tomorrow morning nine o'clock.

B.Coleman J.P.
Joel Estes
Rich. Nixon Cha-

Thursday December 14th 1826 the court met according to adjournment

(p-91) The State of Tennessee)
vs) Writ of Sciri Facias
Amos Chambers)

The defendant having been duly warned & not appearing tho solemnly called, on motion of the State by Alexander B .Bradford esquire attorney General, it is considered by the court here that the State of Tennessee may have execution against the said defendant for five hundred dollars in the writt of Scire fac ias aforesaid specified according to the form & effect of his recognizance therein mentioned, and also that the said state recover against the said defendant her costs by her expended in suing forth and prosec uting this writ and that the said defendant in may be taken etc.
Iss'd

The State of Tennessee)
vs) Writ of Sciri Facias
James Chambars)

The defendant hawing been duly warned and not appearing tho solemnly called on motion of the State by Alexander B.Bradford esquire, attorney General, it is considered by t he court here that the State of Tennessee may hav e execution against the said defendant for two hundred & fifty dollars in the writ of Scire facias aforesaid speciffedied, according to the form and effect of his recognizance therein mentioned and also that the said state recover against t he said defendant his costs by her expended in suing forth and prosecuting this wtit, and that the said defendant may be taken etc.
Issued

(p-91con.) The State of Tennessee)
                    vs   )   Writ of Scire facias
            Benjamin McDonald   )

    The defendant being duly warned and not appearing though solemnly
called, on motion of the State by Alexander B. Bradford Esquire attorney
general It is considered by the court here (p-92) that the state of
Tennessee may have execution against the s aid Defendant for two hundred
and fifty dollars in the writ of Scire facias aforesaid specified according to the form and effect of his recognizance therein mentioned, and also
that the said state recover against the said defendant his costs by him
expended in suing forth and prosecuting this writ and that the defendant
may be taken etc.
Issued

State of Tennessee)
            vs   )   Presentment for gambling
John Hardwick   )

    This day came as well the state of Tennessee by the attorney general
as the defendant in his proper person and the said defendant being solemnly
charged saith that he is guilty in manner and form as charged in the b ill
of presentment and puts himself upon the grace and mercy of the court
Issued Shff.

    It is therefore considered b y the court that the defendant make
his fine in the state by the payment of five dollars and all costs in this
behalf expended and that the defendant be taken etc.
Issued Shff.

The State of Tennessee)
            vs   )   Presentment for Gambling
Robert Lucky   )

    In this case came Mathew Figures and acknowledged himself t o owe
and be indebted to the state of Tennessee in the sum of fifty dollars
lawful money of the State of Tennessee to be levied of his good and chattels lands and tenements for the use of the State to be void on condition
that Robert Lucky shall well and truly make his personal appearance at
the next court of pleas and quarter sessions to be holden for the county of
Haywood at the courthouse in the town of Brownsville on the 2nd Monday
in March next to answer the State of Tennessee in a charge of gaming then
and there stand to abide by and perform the Judgement of said court, and
not depart therefrom without leave first being had and obtained.

(p-93) John Hardwick   )
        E.T.Friend   )
            vs   )   Certiorari
        Matthew Figures)

    On motion of the defendant to dismiss the certiorari in this cause &
upon solemn argument being had thereon and by the court here fully understood, it is considered by the court that the motion be sustained , and
upon motion of the defendant by his attorney the judgement of the justice
below is affirmed against the said John Hardwick & E.T.Friend and Edmond
Richmond their security in the certiorari & the Deft in mercy etc.
Issued

(p-93con.) The Grand jury returned into open court under the care of the
officer sworn to attend them, the following presentments, that is to say
a bill of Presentment against William Sawyers for gambling a bill of
presentment against Thomas Stokely for gambling and a Bill of presentment
against John Young for gambling all of which bill were signed by the jury
who returned to consider of further business.

A Deed of Bargain and sale from A.D.Murphy by his agent Robert Hughs
to Joel Estis for eleven hundred acres of land was this day produced in
open court and duly proven in part by the oath of Edward T.Friend and ordered to be filed for further probate

Certified Del'd & Register
Jonathan P.Hardwick use   )
of Joel W.Hardwick   )   Original attachment in Debt
Hudson Morris   )

This day came the plaintiff by his attorney and it appearing to
the satisfaction of this court that all proceedings in this cause having
been stayed six months agreable to an order of the June term last of this
court and publication having been made for three succesive weeks in the
Jackson Gazette published in the town of Jackson, Tennessee, the last
of which publication was made at least two months before the present term
of this court notifying the said defendant to appear at the present term of
this court and replevy his property attached and plead to issue or demur
otherwise Judgment final would be entered against him and the defendant being solemnly called to come in replevy the property attached & plead to
issue or demur, came not but made default. It is therefore considered by
the court here that the spaintiff recover of the defendant the sum of four
thousand (p-94) seven hundred and sixty five dollars the debt in the
declaration mentioned together with the further sum of ǿf three hundred
and forty nine dollars damages for the detention of the same, also his
costs by him ab out his suit in this behalf expended, and the said, Defendant in merc y. And it is further ordered by the court, on motion of the
plaintiff by his attorney that a writ of vendition exponas issue to the
sheriff of Haywood County commanding him to sell property levied by virtue
of the attachment aforesaid to satisfy the debt damages and costs aforesaid-

A Deed of Bargain and sale from A.D.Murphy by his agent Robert Hughs
to Joel Estes for nine hundred acres of land was this day produced in open
court and proven in part by the oath of Edward F.Friend a subscribing
witness thereto and ordered to be filed for further probate-

A Deed of Trust from Lee H.Burks to Francis L.Dillard was this day
produced in open court and duly acknowledged and ordered to be certified
for registration.

Ordered by the court that Joel Estes in Capt. McGuires Company
Charles Wortham in Capt. Blacwells Company James L. Wortham in Capt.
Fudges Company Nicholas T.Perkins in Capt. Curray's Company and Lawrence
McGuire Esquires in Captain Edwards Company be appointed to take lists of
Taxable property & polls for the year 1827 & make return of their respective
lists to the insuing March term of this court.
Issued 1st Jany. 1829

It is ordered by the court that the following persons be summoned to
attend at the next court of Pleas and quarter sessions of Haywood court

(p-94con.) then and there to serve a grand or petit jurors as the case may be to wit Samuel Elliott, Thomas Potter, James W.Russell, John Williams, Francis L.Dillard , Clement T.Walker, John Marbury, Henry Wooten Philip A Bruce, Eli Farris, William Morris, Joseph Murphy (p-95) Henry Womble, Robert Hammill, James Russell, Robert A.Penn, John Rodgers, Thomas G .Nixon Lee H.Burks, Tobias C.Henderson, William C.Bruce, John T.Majors, Thomas White, Mason F.Johnson, Matthew Figures, & John T.Turner and that avenire Facias issue accordingly & it is further ordered that Benjamin Noax & Wyatt F.Tweedy be summoned to attend it said court as constables etc. Issued

The State of Tennessee   )
        vs   )
Francis Chinag   )

By the knowledge and direction of the court, a nole proseque is entered and upon motion of the attorney general it is ordered by the court that the trustee of Haywood County pay all legal costs in this behalf expended etc.

James Cosby   )
    vs   )
B.H.Sanders   )

This day came the said plaintiff by his attorney and saith that he intends no further to prosecute his said action against the Defendant. It is therefore considered by the court here that the Defendant go hence with out day and recover against the said plaintiff his costs by him about his defence in this behalf expended

Peter Young   )
    vs   )
Arch'd. Brazeal)

This day came the said plaintiff by his attorney and saith he intend no further to prosecute his said action against the said Defendant. It is therefore considered by the court here that the defendant go hence without day & recover against the said plaintiff his costs by him about his defence in this behalf expended etc.

(p-96) The Grand jury returned into court & returned a presentment against John M.Smith for gaming- A presentment against Sam'l Copeland esq. for an assault & battery, a presentment against Osborn Wallace, for gaming and an Indictment against Robert A.Penn & Willis Holland for an affray & an Indictment against Green B.Jamison for an assault & battery & retired to consider of further business

It appearing to the satisfaction of the court that notice has been given by our surveyor L.McGuire to the respective courts of pleas and quarter sessions for the Counties of Tipton & Gibson of his being appointed a commissioner to run and mark the lines in conjunction with commissioners from the said counties between this county and those and that the courts have failed to appoint persons to aid in runing the same therefore it is ordered that our said commissioner shall after the 15th day of March next proceed to run, measure, and mark the said lines between this county and

(p-96con.) the said counties of Tipton and Gibson be first giving thirty days
notice in the Jackson Gazett of the time and place of Commencement on the
lines of either county and that the said commissioner or the clerk of this
court shall cause a copy of this order to be laid before the next succeeding
court of each of said counties
1 copy issued

(p-97) Thomas Stokely acknowledged himself to be indebted to the state of
Tennessee in the sum of fifty dollars to be levied of his goods & chattels,
lands, and tenements but to be vvoid on condition that he make his personal
appearance the next term of Haywood County Court to answer a charge of the
state against him for gambling & not depart without leave of the court.

Caleb Warner acknowledges himself to be indebted to the State of
Tennessee in the sum of twenty five dollars to be levied of his goods and
chattels , lands and tenements but to be void on condition that Thomas Stokely
do well & truly make his personal appearance at the next term of this court to
answer a charge of the State against the said Thomas Stokely & he shall not depart without leave of this court.

Court adjourned untill court in cause.

B.Coleman J.P.
Rich. Nixon Cha-
L.McGuire

(p-98)   State of Tennessee
At a court of pleas and quarter sessions began and held for the
County of Haywood at the court house in the town of Brownsville of the 12th day
of March 1827. Present the worshipful Blackman Coleman, Jonathan T.Jacocks
and Lawrence McGuire Eaqrs and others their fellow Justices of the peace.

A Deed of bargain and salefrom Isaac Koonce to David S.Nunn for 2 two
hundred and forty acres of land was this day proved in open court and acknowledg@
ed, which has been heretofore proven in part and is ordered to be certified
for Registration
certified and dec'd.

A Deed of bargain & sale from the commissioners of the town of
Brownsville to Jesse Brown for a certain town lot which is known & designated
by its number 138 was this day produced in open court & was acknowledged by
a majority of the said commissioners & ordered to be certified for
registration.

A Deed of Bargin and sale from the commissioners of the town of Brownsville
to Littleberry Mauldin for a certain town lots which are known and disignated
in the plan of said town by their numbers 77-90-5 was this day produced in open
court and duly acknowledged by a majority of the said commissioners and ordered
to be certified for registration.

A deed of Bargain and sale from Doctor James Cosby to Francis S.Coxe for
a certaintown lot in the town of Brownsville which is known and disignated in
the plan of said town by its number 6- was this day produced in open court and
was proven by the oath of Britain H.Sanders and T.J.McGuire and ordered to be
certified for registration

(p-98con.) certified & del'd

A Deed of bargain and sale from the commissioners of the town of Brownsville to James Mauldin for three certain lots or parcels of land which are known and designated in the plan of said town by their numbers 63-150-14 (p-99) was this day produced in open court and duly acknowledged by a majority of the commissioners and ordered to be certified for registration-

A Deed of bargain and sale from the commissioners of the town of Brownsville to Bryant H.Kirksey for two certain town lots which one known and designated in the plan of said town by their numbers 83-85 was this day produced in open court and acknowledged by a majority of the commissioners and ordered to be certified for registration

A Deed of bargain and sale from the commissioners of the town of Brownsville to the Trustees of the Methodist Church for one hundred and thirty seven poles and four tenths of a pole and a fraction was this day produced in open court and duly acknowledged by a majority of the commissioners and ordered to be certified for Registration.
certified & del'd register

This day Charles Howard produced in open court a wolf scalp over the age of four months and proved the killing of the same within the bounds of Haywood County and by his own oath he having no other evidence whereby he could prove the same it is therefore ordered by the court that the clerk certify the same to the treasurer of West Tennessee accordingly.
Iss'd. 26 March 1827

This day Rollings Henderson produced in open court the scalp of a wolfe over the age of four months and proved the killing of the same within the bounds of Haywood County by his own oath he having no other evidence whereby he could prove the same it is therefore ordered by the court that the clerk certify the same to the Treasurer of West Tennessee accordingly-
Iss'd 26th

This day James Henderson produced in open court a wolf scalp over the age of four months and proven the killing of the same within the bounds of Haywood County by his own oath he having no other evidence whereby he could prove the same. It is therefore ordered by the court that the clerk certify the same to the Treasurer of West Tennessee accordingly
Iss'd

(p-100) This day Wiatt F.Tweedy produced in open court a wolf scalp over the age of four months and proved the killing of the same within the bounds of Haywood County by the oath of Rollings Henderson it therefore ordered by the court that the clerk certify the same to Treasurer of West Tennessee accordingly-
Iss'd to R.Henderson March 26th 1827

This day Charles Wortham who was appointed to take lists at Taxable property and poles in Capt. Fudges Company, made his return of the same.

(p-100ccn.) An sufficient cause being shown it is ordered by the court that John M.Miller be licenced to keep an ordinary at his own house in the town of Brownsville for the term of twelve months be having complyed with the requisitions of the law.

On Sufficient cause being shown it is ordered by the court that James Brown be licensed to keep an ordinary in the town of Brownsville at his house he having complyed with the reguisitions of the law.

Ordered by the court the stock mark of James H.Brigham as follows to wit a slit in each ear be recorded-

The petition of E.Roddy and William Hannon praying the division of some land, therein mentioned was this day presented to the court and upon the reading of the same it is ordered by the court to be received and the following persons be appointed commissioners to partition and divide the same, and to make return thereof, according to law, to wit John Murray, Benjamin Booth, Charles White Charles Wortham, James Wortham and Azariah Thompson.
Issued

This day came into open court Matthew Ray, Gideon Pace, Oliver B. Wood, and Daniel Cherry and produced a commission from the governor of the state of Tennessee appointing them justices of the Peace in and for the County of Haywood in this State, who thereupontook the necessary oaths and qualified according to law as justices-
Iss'd

(p-101) The Inventory of James Cosby was this day returned into court and ordered to be registered.

Ordered by the court a majority being present that Andrew Hammel be appointed overseer over that part of the Key Corner road leading from Brownsville to Simon Turner in place of F.Lamoin former overseer-
Issued 27th March 1827

Ordered by the court a majority ofthe acting justices being present that agreeable to a former order Charles White & Elli Faris overseer of the new road leading from the town of Brownsville to Jackson have divided the hands as follows viz. Eli Farris, Farris as hands as agreed Philip A.Bruce, Garret P.Grisham, Jas. W.Seat, Joseph Murphy, L.D.Womble, Henry McCoy, W.Barry, J.R.Lee _____ C.Whites hands

Issued 27th March 1827

James Henderson, Joshua Kelly, Vincent Harralson, Tobias Henderson, Bowen Reynolds, Thos Crutcher, Sameul Brown _____
Col. Joseph T.Harralson nominated nominated in place of Charles White.
Iss'd 27th March 1827

The court then proceeded to Ellect a constable in Capt. Malcomb, Johnsons company whereupon after counting out the votes Samuel D.Wood was duly and constitutionally declared to be elected who entered into bond together with Oliver Woods and Joel Pace his securities and took the (p-101con.) necessary oaths prescribed by law.

Occupant claim was this day produced in open court by Alexander Stewart founded on no. Entry 1945 for 200 acres—which is ordered to be certified for registration
Issued & Del.

Ordered by the court a majority of the acting justices being present that William Fitzgerald be appointed overseer west of Richland Creek & East of the sixth range line and that they be subject to work under him as such—
Iss'd 27 March 1827

Ordered by the court a majority being present that William Jackson be appointed overseer of the road from Madison County line to the Ferry at Estanaula & that the following hands work under him as such viz; all the hands east of the main fork of Jeffers Creek from where it crosses the county line to its junction with Big Hatchie (p-102) thence up said river to said line and with said line to the beginning.
Iss'd 27 March 1827

Ordered by the court a majority of the acting justices being present petition being filed it is ordered by the court that Lawrence McGuire, H.Harralson,Guidian Pace, Henry Pace, Jas.Traytor, William Fitzgerald, Thos. Blythe, John Elliott, Oliver Woods, be appointed a jury to review to Mark out the road from Brownsville to Bolivar and make return of their proceedings to the next county court.
Iss'd. 27th March 1827

William Sherian was this day appointed guardian for Jarrott Shearin Henry Shearian, Joseph Shearian & Hugh Shearian who entered into bond together with Charles Wortham & T.Shearian his securities as the law direct the Inventory of the property of John Koonce deceased was this day produced in open court and ordered to be recorded.

Occupant claim was this day produced in open court by Berrycroft by virtue of Entry no 1943 dated the fifth day of May 1826 founded on certificate no containing 100 acres was this day proven in part and ordered to be registered for further probation.

A Bill of sale was this produced in open court Will R.Wortham and duly proven by the oaths W.F.Tweedy, William Shearian and ordered to be recorded for registration.
certified

Ordered by the court that John G.Carithers sheriff and collector of The State and county tax for the years 1824,1825, & 1826 be allowed a credit of sixty eight dollars and seventy two cents with the county Treasure in his settlement for the year 1826 for taxes overpaid—
Iss'd the 20th March 1827

The court by admr. set apart until tomorrow 11 o'clock to do county business—

The court then adjd until 9 o'clock tomorrow Morning—

(p-103) State of TTennessee Haywood County, Tuesday March 13, 1827
court met pursuant to adjournment . Present the worshipful Richard
Nixon Dan'l. Cherry Blackman Coleman, Esq. Justices of the peace of
said county.

Rich. Nixon Char-
Daniel Cherry J.P.
B.¢.Coleman J.P.

        On motion
and petition being filed it is ordered by the court a majority of the
acting justices being present it is ordered by the court that William
Jackson James Malden, Capt. Gordon, Parson Biggs Jesse L. Kirk, Robert
S.Williams Joseph Harralson be appointed jurors of review to mark and
lay off a road from Brownsville to Estaraula
  Issued
        Ordered by the court a majority of the acting justices being
present that the order issued in December Term appointing Lawrence
McGuire, Nathan Bridgman, Alexander Roddy, Benj. Noakes, Samuel P.Ashe,
Isac Edwards, Grifith Edwards, John Roddy and James Fields juror of view
to mark and lay off a road from McGuires Ferry through the bottom of
Hatchie river to the summit of highland on the south side of said river
in a direction to Memphis and Summerville whereupon it is ordered by the
court that the same be and is hereby received.
Iss'd 27 March 1827

        Ordered by the court that the order heretofore made to lay out
and mark a road leading from Brownsville to Harrisburgh be renewed and
that Richard Taylor, John Williams, Hardy L.Blackwell, Francis M.Wood
and Samuel Conyers be appointed a jury of view.
Iss'd 27th March 1827

        Ordered by the court a majority of the acting justices of the Peace
being present that the hands hereafter to work on the road leading from
Harrisburgh to the county line of Gibson in a direction to Trenton shall
be in the following bounds Biggs at Harrisburgh in the road leading to
Jackson all the hands on the north side of said road to the Gibson line
with said line west to the Hurricane with the same to the old road passing by Thos. Thweats to Harrisburgh including sd Thwats hands and that
Hardy L.Blackwell is appointed overseer on the end next Harrisburgh and
that Charles Wortham Esq. & Daniel Cherry Esqr. divide the hands between
him and Azh. Thompson & the distance that each shall work.
Issd 27th 1827

(p-104) Ordered by the court that Isaac Wood be appointed overseer on
the road leading from Harrisburgh to Jackson in the place of Edward
Good resigned and all the hands on the south side of said road to work on
it.
Iss'd March 27, 1827

        Ordered by the court a majority of the acting justices being present
that a jury of view be appointed to mark and lay out a road leading from
Harrisburgh on a direction to Bolivar to the county line and that Robert
Burns, John P.Majors, Joshua Abston, Stephen Booth and James Henderson be
appointed for that purpose.
Iss'd 27th March 1827

(p-104con.) This day James L.Wortham who was appointed to take a list of Taxable property and poles in Capt- Fudges Company made his return of the same.

Tuesday morning Mason F.Johnson discharged as a juror by the court.

Samuel P.Ash appeared in open court and agreeable to commission took the necessary oath prescribed by law as a justice of the peace of Haywood County

Ordered by the court that all persons who have failed to list their lands or other property be released from the payment of double taxes who may apply to the sheriff and collector of the County of Haywood due for the year 1826 and pay the single taxes and cost which may have accrued thereon if they apply during the present term.

Ordered by the court that the taxes be and remain as they were heretofore.

Ordered by the court that the order heretofore made to lay out and mark a road leading from Brownsville to Harrisburg be renewed and that Richard Tailor, John Williams, Hardy L.Blackwell, Frances M.Wood and Samuel Conyers be appointed a jury of view.
Issued

(p-105) John G.Carithers sheriff of Haywood County makes return of the following venire facias to wit at a court of pleas and Quarter sessions began and held for the County of Haywood at the courthouse in the Town of Brownsville on the second Monday in December A.D.1826 present the worshipful Richard Nixon, Blackman Coleman and Lawrence McGuire Esquires

It is ordered by the court that the following persons good and lawful men in each being a free white male citizen of the County of Haywood of the age of twenty one and a house holder to wit Samuel Elliot, Thos. Potter, James W.Russell, John Williams, F.L.Dillard, Clemen T.Walker John Marberry, Henry Wooten, Philip A. Bruce, Eli Farris, William Morris, Joseph Murphy, Henry Womble, Robert Hammet, James Russel Robert A.Penn John Rodgers, Thomas G.Nixon Lee H.B urks, Tobias C. Henderson William C. Bruce John T. Majors, Thomas White, Mason F.Johnson, Mathew Figures, and John T.Turner be sumoned to attend at the next term of this court then and there to serve as grand and petit jurors as the case may be Wyatte F. Tweedy and Binj. Noakes be summoned to attend at said court as constables

Test B.H.Sanders Clk-

To the sheriff of Haywood County greeting you are hereby commanded to summons the aforesaid persons to serve as jurors at the next court of pleas and quarter sessions to be held at the next court of pleas and quarter sessions to be held at the courthouse in the Town of B rownsville on Tuesday after the second Monday in March next and this they shall in no wise omit under the penalty prescribed by law and have you then and there this to wit witness Britain H.Sanders, clerk of our said court at office the 2nd Monday in December A.D.1826 and 51st. year of American Independence

B.H.Sanders, clk-

(p-105con.) By virtue of this venire facias on which was the following return to wit, I have proceeded to summon all the within named persons as grand and petit jurors except William Morris and such persons so summoned are inhabitans of said county and of the age of twenty one years and are free holders or house holders of said county

Jno.G.Carithers,Shff.

(p-106) A Deed of bargain and sale from Daniel Mading and Sarah Dyer for 675 acres of land to Carey Felts was this day produced in open court and proven by Blackman Coleman and Daniel Cherry subscribing witness thereto and is ordered to be certified for registration.

A Deed of bargain and sale from T.H.Taylor for a lot in the Town of Brownsville no. 2 to J.S. and James Smith was this day produced in open court and proven in part by Mason F.Johnston one of the subscribing witnesses thereto and filed for further probate.
Certified

It is ordered by the court there being a majority of the justices present that a precinct election be and is hereby established at the house of Oliver B.Wood esquire of this county, living on the south side of Hatchie River, for the purpose of electing a Governor of the State members to the Congress of the United States and Senators and Representatives in the state legislature of this State.

Ordered by the court that James Clark,John Roddy,Lewis _____ Griffith Edwards Nathan Bridgeman,Isaac Edwards, Benson and Samuel P.Ashe be appointed a jury to view and mark out a road thro the County of Haywood in a direction from Bolivar to Covington so as to Correspond with the road as now cut through Hardeman County in a direction from Bolivar to Covington and that they make report of their proceedings to the next court. Iss'd 27 March 1827

Ordered by the court that Thos.Thweat, Danl.Cherry, Edward Good, John Parker senior,Joel Parker *senior/Joel/Parker/* be appointed a jury of view to mark and lay out a road from where the road leading from (p-107) Nashes Bluffs to Jackson intersects the Haywood County line so as to meet the road leading from Jackson to Nashes Bluff the nearest and best way- Iss'd 27th March 1827

Out of the venire returned to the court the following named persons good and lawful men viz- John Williams foreman Harry Womble,John T.Majors James W.Russell, Thomas Murphy, Samuel Elliot, John Rodgers,Tobias C. Henderson, Clement T.Walker,Thomas Potter, John Marberry,Thomas White & William C.Bruce were drawn elected and sworn as a grand jury for the present term and after receiving their charge retired under the care of Wiatt F. Tweedy an officer sworn to attend them to consider of them presentment.

Matthew Figures,Eli Pharis and Francis F.L.Dillard were released from serving as jurors at the present term.

(p-107con.)Burrell Hunter   )
                    vs   )   Appeal
        Allen H.Howard   )

        This day came the parties by their attornies and thereupon came a
jury of good and lawful men to wit   James Russell, John T.Turner, Thomas
G.Nixon, Henry Wooten, Phillip Bruce, Isaac D.Edwards, Jonathan J.Nixon,
Robert A.Penn, William Weddle John B. Fudge, Lewis Powers and Francis
Lamain, who being elected tried and sworn well and truly to try the matters
in dispute upon their oaths do say they find for the plaintiff and do
assess his damages to twenty one dollars and forty five cents besides his
costs . It is therefore considered by the court that the plaintiff recover
of the said defendant (and on motion) of William W.Douthit and Thomas
Rutherford his securities in said appeal the said sum of twenty one dollars forty five cents the damages afore said by the jury aforesaid in form
aforesaid assessed and his costs by him about his suits in this behalf expended and the said defendant in mercy etc.
Issued 22nd March 1827

(p-108) James Smith   )
                    vs   )   Appeal
        Green B.Jameson)

        This day came the parties aforesaid by their attornies and thereupon
came a jury of good and lawful men to wit   James Russell, John T.Turner,
Thomas G .Nixon, Henry Wooten, Philip Bruce, Isaac D.Edward, Jonathan J.
Nixon, Robert A.Penn, William Widdle, John B.Fudge, Lewis Powers, and
Frances Lamoin who being elected tried and sworn well and truly to try the
matters in dispute upon their oaths do say they find the matters in dispute in favor of the plaintiff and do assess his damages to thirty eight
dollars and ninety three cents besides costs. It is therefore considered
by the court that the said plaintiff recover of the said defendant and on
motion of James W.Russell his security in said appeal the said sum of thirty
eight dollars and ninety three cents the damages aforesaid by jury aforesaid
in form aforesaid assessed and his costs by him about his suit in this behalf
expended and the said defendant in mercy.
Issued 22nd March 1827

        James W.Russell)
            vs   Debt
        Matthew Ray   )

        This day came the said parties by their attornies and thereupon came
a jury of good and lawful men to wit John Potter, John T.Turner, Thomas J.
Nixon, Henry Wooten, Philip Bruce, Isaac H.Edwards, Jonathan J.Nixon,
Robert A.Penn, William Weddle, John B.Fudge, Lewis Powers and Francis
Lamoin who being elected tried and sworn the truth to speak upon the issues
joined upon their oaths do say the find the issues in favor of the plaintiff
and that the defendant hath not paid the balance of the debt of twenty nine
dollars and seventy six cents in the declaration mentioned and that he
hath no set off and do assess the plaintiffs damages by reason thereof to
eight dollars and fifty one cents besides costs. It is therefore considered
by the court that the said plaintiff recover of the said defendant the debt
aforesaid together with the damages aforesaid by the jury aforesaid in form
aforesaid assessed and his costs by him about his suit in this behalf expended etc.

(p-109) Ordered by the court a majority of the acting justices that the Tax for the present year be and remain in all respects upon all property and polls, and for all purposes as they were laid in this county for the preceeding year (1826, and that the clerk marke out his tax list accordingly-

The court then adjourned until tomorrow morning nine o'clock.

                    Rich Nixon Char
                    Joel Estes
                    Matthew Ray

        Wednesday morning March the 14th 1827 the court met according to adjournment, present the worshipful Richard Nixon, Joel Estes, & Mathew Ray Justices of the peace of Haywood County and others their fellow Justices.

        This day was produced in open court a deed of bargain and sale from Benjamin Rouland, to Levi Gardner for two town lots known and designated in the plan of the Town of Brownsville by their numbers 47, and 103, and duly acknowledge and ordered to be certified for registration Del. the owner

        A Deed of Bargain and sale from William W.Douthit to John M.Miller two town lots in the Town of Brownsville known and designated in the plan of said town by their numbers 56, and part of lot 111 was this day produced in open court and duly proven by the oaths Reubin Alfin and William H. Henderson subscribing witnesses thereto and ordered to be certified for registration.

        A Deed of Bargain and sale from Mathew Figures to Francis Lamoin for one half acre of land was this day produced in open court and duly proven by the oaths of William H.Henderson and D.M.McLeon subscribing witness thereto and ordered to be certified for registration.
certified and del'd

        A Deed of Trust was this day produced in open court between Preston G.Hodges of the first part and Edmund Richmond of the second part and Joel Estes all of the County of Haywood and a State of Tennessee certified

(p-110) And proved by the oaths of M.P.Estes and A.M.Estes subscribing witnesses thereto and ordered to be certified for registration.

State of Tennessee)
           vs   )   Presentment for Gaming
Alexander Stewart   )

        This day came Alexander B.Bradford who prosecutes on behalf of the state and the defendant in his proper person who being assigned and open his assignment plead not guilty and puts himself the county and the said Alexander B.Bradford solicitor general doth the like, and thereupon came a jury of good and lawful men that is to say Philip Bruce,Benjamin Rowland, Alondus S.Gholson, Francis Lamoin, Philip Koonce,George Watts, John Potter Nelson Heartgrove, Albert M.Estes, Eli Pharis,James Russell (p-110con.) and John Osment who being elected tried and sworn the truth to speak upon the issue of traverse joined upon their oath, do say they cannot agree whereupon by consent of the said defendant and solicitor General and with the assent of the court John Potter one of the jurors here in was withdrawn on a mistrial intend whereupon this cause is continued until the next term of this court.

Robert Neal)
     vs   ) Slander
John Potter)

This day came the parties by their attorneys and thereupon came a jury of good and lawful men that is to say, Thomas G .Nixon, Philip Bruce James Russell, Henry Wooten, Jonathan J.Nixon Robert A.Penn, William Weddle Mason F.Johnson John T.Turner James T.White, John Osment & Eli Pharis who being elected tried and sworn the truth to speak upon the issues joined upon this oaths do say they cannot agree, whereupon by consent of parties Thomas G.Nixon one of the jurors is withdrawn and a mistrial is entered herein and his cause is continued until the next term of this court.

(p-111) State of Tennessee)
               vs   ) Presentment for Gaming
        Robert Lucky   )

This day came Alexander B.Bradford solicitor General who prosecutes on behalf of the state and with the assent of the court enters a nolli prosqui hereon, on condition that Matthew Figures appearance bail of the said Defendant will assume all costs which have acrud on this prosecution together with the policitor General fee. Whereupon the said Matthew Figures of his attorney comes into open court and confessed judgement for the costs in pursuance of the above condition. It is therefore considered by the court that the state recover of the said Matthew Figures the costs aforesaid by him herein confessed and that he may be taken etc.
Issued 22nd March 1827

State of Tennessee)
        vs   ) Presentment for Issuing charge Bills
Green B .Jamerson   )

This day came Alexander B.Bradford who prosecutes on behalf of the state and with the assent of the court enters a Nolli Prosequi herein, on condition that Alondus S.Gholson appearance bail of said defendant will assume all costs which have occurred on this prosecution together with the solicitor Generals fee. Whereupon the said Alondus S.Gholson comes into court in his own proper person and and confesses judgement for the costs in pursuance of the above condition. It is therefore considered by the court that the State recover of the said Alondus S.Gholson on the costs aforesaid by him herein confessed and that he may be taken etc.
Fee pd. the clerk.

State of Tennessee)
        vs   ) Presentment for Gaming
Lee H.Burks   )

(p-111con.) This cause is continued until the next term of this court by consent of Defendant and solicitor General with the assent of the court—

State of Tennessee)
  vs   ) Presentment for Gaming
Thomas Stokely)

  This day came Alexander B.Bradford who prosecutes on behalf of the state and the defendant in his proper person & the cause is continued until next court on affidavit of the Defendant.

(p-112) State of Tennessee)
      vs   ) Presentment for Gaming
    John Young)

  This day came Alexander B.Bradford solicitor General who prosecutes on behalf of the state and Defendant in his proper person who being arraigned upon this arraignment pleads guilty and puts himself upon the grace and mercy of the court. It is therefore considered by the court that the said Defendant make his peace with the state for his offence by the payment of one dollar fine and all costs in and about said prosecution, and that he may be taken etc.
Issued 23rd March 1827

State of Tennessee)
  vs   ) Presentment for Gaming
Osborn Wallace)

  This day came Alexander B.Bradford solicitor General who prosecutes on behalf of the state and with the assent of the court enters a nolli prosequi herein on condition that William R.Hess appearance bail of said Defendant will assume all costs which have accrud on this prosecution together with the solicitor Generals fee. Whereupon the said William R. Hess comes into open court and confesses Judgment for the costs in pursuance of the above condition. It is therefore considered by the court that the state recover of the said William R.Hess the costs aforesaid by him herein confessed, and that he may be taken etc.

State of Tennessee)
  vs   ) Presentment for Assault & Battery
Samuel Copeland)

  This day came the solicitor general who prosecutes on behalf of the state, and the sd defendant in his proper person, and pleads guilty in manner and form as charged in the bill of presentment. It is therefore considered by the court that for such his offence he pay a fine of fifty cents and the costs of this prosecution, and that he may be taken etc.
Issued 22nd March 1827

  The Grand jury returned into open court under the care of an officer, the following bills of presentment that if to say, a Presentment against Stephen S. Childress & Jourdon Hansbrough for Gaming; A Presentment against Francis L.Dillard, Edward Harris Thomas J.McGuire and David W.Parrish for gaming and a presentment against Jourdon Hansbrough for an assault and (p-112con.) Battery.

(p-113) Parrish & McAlovan)
    vs   )   Debt
  Henry L.Gray)

On motion of the plaintiffs by their attorney. It is ordered by the court that the plaintiff have leave to amend his writ herein so as not to charge the nature of the action by paying the costs of the amendment.

Robert Williams)
  vs   ) Case
Nathan Bridgemond)

This day came the said parties by their attornies and the plaintiff dismisses his suit herein and by agreement of said parties the costs are to be equally divided against the plaintiff and defendant. It is therefore considered by the court that the plaintiff recover of the said defendant one half of the costs by him about his suit in this behalf expended, and that the said Defendant recover of the said plaintiff the other equal half of the cost incurred in said suit and that the said plaintiff & defendant be in mercy etc.

William B.Miller esquire this day appeared in open court and took the necessary oaths prescribed by law, and was admitted to practice as an attorney and cousellor at law in this court-

This day came John G.Carithers Esqr. sherriff and collector of the state and and county tax and makes report in the words and figures following- To wit

State of Tennessee)
)
Haywood County)
       March Term 1827

I,John G.Carithers Sheriff and collector of the public taxes for the County of Haywood, do hereby report to court the following tracts of land and town lots as having been given in for the Taxes for the year 1826, That the Taxes thereon remain due and unpaid, and that the respective owners or claimants thereof, have no goods or chattels within my county on which I can Distrain (p-114) for said Taxes to wit-

NAME	No Acres	District	Range	Section	No.of Entry or grant	Water Course	Town lots	No. T Lots
n.)								
illiam	640	10	5	9	1137			
lfred	480	"	6	8	996	B.H.		
g Martin								
.	500	"	6 ?	6	418	"		
mas	57	"	5	8				
Robert	640	"	6	6	275			
omas	1000	"	5	8	Gt 272			
eorge	629	"	6.7	968			3	
oseph	2795		5.6	8	805			
Anthony								
	428		5.6	9	587	F D.		
Nathan	1000		394	7	808	B.H.		
Nathan	800		4	7				
ephen	4		4	6 &7	1127			
Joseph	1000		4.	9	Part of Grant No. 407			
William	500		6	6	259	B.H.		
Robert J.	1000	10	1	6	1740			Part of Lee Sullivan 2000 A.T.
Darling	640	10	4.5	8	838			
ohn	583	"	6	6	397			
Arthur	640	11	1	6	593			
John								
.	935	"	1	6	453			
er, Benj	1250	10	4	11				
& Polk	500	11	2	5.6	207			
William	500	10	4	10	190	F D		
	500	"	6	9	564			
y Thomas	500	"	4	7	77			

OWNERS NAME	No Acres	District	Range	Section	No. of Entry or grant	Water course	Town lots	No. T Lots
(p-114con.)								
Dyre Joel Hs. of	2510	"	5	11				Granted to B.Smith
Same	1000	"	6	9	part of a ten thousand Granted to B.Smith			
Ewing, Alexander								
C.	640	"	4.5	9	E313 F.D.			
Edmondson Samuel	390	11	2	9	359			
Same	390	"	1	9	125			
Ewing, Alexander	200	10	4	9	526			
Same	380	"	4	9	525			
Same	900	10	5	9	528			
Same	308	10	4	9				
(p-115)								
Flowers, Benj.	120	10	4	9	1809	F.D.		
Flowers, David	1660	10	5 & 6	7 &8	2140	B.H.		
Freeman, I.&J.H.								
Bryant	1000	11	1	9 &10	808	FD		
Fort, Elias	428	11	2	6	465	"		
Gerrard Charles	640	10	3	7	483	"		
Graves, Wm.B.	1500	10	5	7 & 8	2149	B.H.		
Greer, Joseph	1500	10	5	8	2147	"		
Green Hays	1500	11	1	9	407	F.D.		
Green J.S.&								
W.B.Sims	125	10	6	9				
Hart, James	1920	11	2	6	748	B.H.		
Hoard, Wm.	2000	10	4	9	506	F D		
Hightower, Richard	18	10	6	6	552			
Hart, Anthony	434	11	2	7	230	B.H.		
Hays, O.B.	210	11	1	6				
Hughs, Robert	840	10	5.6	7.8	2140			P. of Grant 298
Hamilton, Andrew								3

76

NAME	No Acres	District	Range	Section	No. of Entry or grant	Water course	Town lots	No. T Lots
on.)								
ary							2	
,Wm.	144	10	3.4	7		B.H.		
Mathew	185	10	4	11	256	F.D.		
, John	230	10	4	9	970	F.D.		
	1000	10	4	8.9	1507	F.D.		
nry	45	10	5	8.9	1331	F.D.		
,Thos.	1555	10	5.6	8		B.H.		
hard H.	135	10	4	10		F.D.		
,Jacob	819½	11	3	6		B.H.		
hn	2128	10					6	
	10	10	4	6				
	531/3	10	5	7	1817			
,Robt.	640	10	6	6	1116	B.H.		
,Sugars	160	10	6	8	996	B.H.		
,Jacob	341	10	5	8	542	F.D.		
John	640	10	5	6	656	B.H.		
	1000	11	2	10.11	597	F.D.		
	100	10	6	8				
.& B.								
	70	10	6	8	1322	B.H.		
nd,John	3	10	4	10	1796	B.H.		
nry	1684	11	2	9	690	B.H.		
Hugh D	419	10	5	10	733	F.D.		
Edward	640	11	2	9.10	572	F.D.		
,John	1000	10			155			
J.H.	220	10	6	9				
,John	274	10	4	10	931	F.D.		
,Jno.W.	500	10	4	8	319	B.H.		
	360	11	1	8				
omas	1434	10	5	6	406	B.H.		
	500	10	4	7	77	B.H.		
	500	10	4	7				
s,Abner	1500	10	6	8	2175	B.H.		

OWNERS NAME	No Acres	District	Range	Section	No. of Entry or grant	Water course	Town lots	No T lots
(p-116con.)								
Parker,John	15	10	4	10	1439 / 1493	F.D.		
Persons,John	2500	11	1	6	266	B.H.		
Rice,John	3000	11	1	8	2205			pt of a 5000 A. Tract
Reese,Solomon							1	
Ringlet,James	57	10	5	8				pt. of Dokes 2000
Rhodes,Tyre	263	10	5	9	790			
Robertson,James	666 2/3	10	6	6 & 7	428			
Smith,Benjamin	1250	10	4	11	632	F.D.		
Stewart,David	400	10	4	9	527	F.D.		
Sims,Walter B.	213½	10	6	9	530	B.H.		
Smith,Richard	640	10	4	6	1133	B.H.		
Stublefield, Clement	228	10	5	5	364	B.H.		
Steed,Jessee	1035	10	5	7 & 8	308			
Sulivan,Lee	1000	11	1.2	6	275	B.H.		
Scruggs,John	500	11	1	6	164			
Simms,Walter B.	60	11	1	6		B.H.		
Shelton,David	3000	10	5.6	10.11		F.D.		
Scudder,P.J.	1000	10	5	9		F.D.		
Taylor,Thos.H.	545	10	5.6	8		B.H.		
Turner,Simon T.	507	10	4	8				
Totten,Benjamin	450	10	4.5	10	195	F.D.		
Terrell,John	640	10	4	8	968			
Tate,Mark A.	640	10	5.6	6	1085	B.H.		
Todd,George	200	10	4	8	320	part of a 1000 acre track		
(p-117)								
Valch,Adrian	5000	11	1.2	7.8	278	B.H.		

AME	No Acres	District	Range	Section	No.of Entry or grant	Water course	Town lots	No. T lot
n)								
on,Benjmin	640	10				F.D.		
	640	10						
.W.	2756	10	4	7	704	B.H.		
	1000	10	4	7	1608	B.H.		
obt.	1875	10	4.5	11	447	F.D.		
,W.W.	172½	10	4	10	344	F.D.		
	1456	10	4	10	775	F.D.		
eorge	83	10	5	10	112	F.D.		
,Sam'l H.	1000	10	5	9	787	F.D.		
,SAML H								
r	1000	10	6	6	213	B.H.		
,John	1000	10	5	7-8	1259	B.H.		
ivens	640	10	4	10	179	"		
&Tisdale	640	11	1	9	355	F D		
,R.W.	176	10	5	11	735	F D		
John L.	6140	10	6	11	403	F D		
	1400	11	1	11	407	F D		
	4617	11	1	10	400	F D		
Mary	5796	11	1	10.11	413	F D		
	2786	10			part of grant 410			
	2393	11	1	11	part of grant 407			
Jas.								
	7606	11	2	11	412	F D		
	5000	11	1	11	414	F D		
	5592	10	1	10	415	F D.		
	3496	10	6	10	410	F D		
	6934	10	6	11	411	F.D.		

(p-117cpn.) Whereupon it is considered by the court that judgement be an a that the same is hereby entered against the aforesaid tracks of land in the name of the state for the amount of the Taxes costs and charges due severally thereon for the year 1826 and it is ordered by the court that said several tracks of land on so much thereof as shall be sufficient of each of them to satisfy the said taxes costs and charges be sold as the law directs-

The court then adjourned until tomorrow nine o'clock-

B.Coleman J.P.
Rich. Nixon Char.
L.McGuire

(p-118) Thursday Morning March the 15th 1827 the court met accordingly to adjournment, present the worshipful Richard Nixon, Blackman Coleman, and Lawrence McGuire, Esquires and others their fellow justices-

Nicholas T.Perkins, Guardian to Nancy M J.P.Turner and Simon T. Turner returned on account of the disbursements and receipts of their respective estates for the year 1826 qualified to by said guardian and ordered it be recorded.

A Deed of bargain and sale from Thomas H.Tailar to Thomas Rutherford for two acres and sixteen poles of land adjoining the town of Brownsville, was this day produced in open court and the execution thereof duly proven by the oaths of Richard Nixon and Thomas Potter subscribing witnesses thereto and ordered to be certified for registration. Certified & delivered

State of Tennessee)
    vs   ) Presentment for Gaming
Jourdan Hansbrough)

This day came Alexander B.Bradford solicitor General who prosecutes on behalf of the state and the Defendant in his proper person, and saith that he will not contend, that he is guilty in manner and form as charged in the said bill of Presentment and puts himself on the grace and mercy of the court. It is therefore considered by the court that the said defendant for such his officers be fined the sum of five dollars, and that he pay the costs of this prosec ution and he may be taken etc- paid clerk

State of Tennessee)
    vs   ) Presentment for an assault and Battery
Jourden Hansbrough)

This day came A.B.Bradford solicitor General who prosecutes on behalf of the state and the defendant in his proper person and saith that he will not contend, but that he is guilty of the assault & Battery in manner and form as charged in the said Bill of presentment and puts himself on the grace and mercy of the court. It is therefore considered by the court that the said Defendant for such his offence be fined ~~fined~~ the sum of one dollar and he pay the costs of this prosecution, and that he may be taken.

(p-118con.) Issued 22nd March 1827

(p-119) State of Tennessee   )
                         vs   )   Presentment for Gaming
          John M.Smith   )

    This day Alexander B.Bradford who prosecutes on behalf of the state
and the Defendant in his proper person and says that he will not contend,
but that he is guilty in manner and form as charged in the bill of Presentment and puts himself upon the grace and mercy of the court. It is there-
considered by the court that the said Defendant for such his offence he be
fined the sum of five dollars and that he pay the costs of this prosecution
and that he may be taken etc.
Issued 22nd March 1827

State of Tennessee   )
          vs   )   Presentment for an Assault & Battery
Green B.Jamerson   )

    This day came Alexander B.Bradford solicitor General who prosecutes
on behalf of the state and the said Defendant being solemnly called came
not whereupon by consent of the solicitor General and with the assent of
the court a Nolli Prosequi is entered herein on condition that John G.
Carithers who stands as special bail for the said Defendant will assume
all costs and thereupon the said John G.Carithers comes into open court
and assumes all costs incured in and about prosecution, according to the
term of said condition. It is therefore considered by the court that the
state recover of the said John G.Carithers the costs aforesaid by him herein confessed, and that he may be taken etc.

State of Tennessee   )
          vs   )
Robert A.Penn & Willis   )   Motion to Dismiss Presentment for an affray-
Holland   )

    This day came Alex ander B.Bradford solicitor General who prosecutes
on behalf of the state, and the defendants in their proper persons, and
thereupon the motion of the Defendants to quash the presentment herein,
being, argued , and by the court fully understood. It is considered by
the court that the said Presentment be quashed and that the county pay
the costs of this prosecution.
(p-120)
State of Tennessee)
          vs   )   Presentment for Gaming
Francis L. Dillard)

    This day came Alexander B.Bradford who prosecutes on behalf of the
state, and the said defendant in his proper person, and says that he will
not contend, but that he is guilty in manner and form as charged in the
said bill of of Presentment and puts himself upon the grace and mercy of
the court. It is therefore considered by the court that the said Defendant for such his offence be fined the sum of one dollar and that he pay
the costs of this prosecution & that he may be taken etc.
Issued 22nd March 1827

(p-120con.) State of Tennessee)
                vs   )   Presentment for Gaming
      Thomas J.McGuire   )

     This day came Alexander B.Bradford solicitor General who prosecutes
on behalf of the state, and the said defendant in his proper person and
says that he will not contend but that he is guilty in manner and form
as charged in the said bill of Presentment and puts himself upon the grace
and mercy of the court- It is therefore considered by the court that the
said Defendant for such his offence be fined the sum of five dollars and
that he pay the costs of this prosecution and that he may be taken etc.

State of Tennessee)
           vs   )   Presentment for Gaming
David W.Parrish   )

     This day came Alexander B.Bradford who prosecutes on behalf of the
state and the Defendant in his proper person and says that he will not
contend, but that he is guilty in manner and form as charged in said
bill of presentment and puts himself upon the the grace and mercy of the
court. It is therefore considered by the court that the said Defendant
for such his offence be fined the sum of five dollars and that he pay the
costs of this prosecution, and that he may be taken etc.
Issued 22nd March 1827

     The Grand jurors this day returned into court under the care of
their officer a Presentment against John M.White and Thomas Stokely for
Gaming by matching with dollars.

(p-121)   State of Tennessee)
                vs   )   Presentment for Gaming
      Edward Harris   )

     This day came Alexander B.Bradford solicitor General who prosecutes
on behalf of the state, and the said Defendant in his proper person, and
says he will not contend with the state but that he is guilty in manner
and form as charged in the said bill of Presentment and puts himself on
the graces and mercy of the court- It is therefore considered by the
court, that the said Defendant for such his offence be fined the sum of
five dollars and that he pay the costs of this prosecution and that he
may be taken
Issued 22nd March 1827

Asa Biggs   )
        vs   )   Trespass with force and arms.-
John Hardwick   )

     This day came the said parties by their attornies & thereupon came
a jury of good and lawful men to wit Thomas G.Nixon, John T.Turner, James
Russell, Philip Bruce, John A.King, Robert T.Smith Monroe P.Estes, Henry
Wooten, Robert A.Penn, William Sherron, John McWhite and Allen Howard,
who being elected tried and sworn well and truly to try the issue joined
upon their oaths do say that they find the issue joined in favor of the
plaintiff, that the defendant is guilty of the trespass assault and Battery
as the plaintiff hath in his declaration complained against him, and do

(p-121con.) assess the plaintiffs damages to one dollar besides his costs. It is therefore considered by the court that the plaintiff recover of the said Defendant his damages aforesaid by the jury aforesaid assessed and his costs by him about his suit in this behalf expended and that the said defendant may be taken etc.
Issued 22nd March 1827

Winston Harvy for the use of)
John McWhite)
     vs)   Debt
Henry L.Gray & Thos.J.Smith)

This day came the said parties by their attornies and thereupon came a jury of good and lawful men, to wit, Thomas G.Nixon, John T. Turner, James Russell, Philip Bruce, John A.King, Robt.T.Smith, Monroe P.Estes, Henry Wooten, Robert A.Penn, Wm. Sherron, John M.C.White and Allen, Howard, who being elected tried and sworn the truth to speak upon the issue joined in favor of the plaintiff that the Defendant have not paid the balance of the debt of one hundred and thirty nine dollars and ninety three cents as the plaintiff by replying to the Defendants plea on that behalf hath alledged, and do (p-122) assess the plaintiffs damages by reason of the detention of the same to five dollars and forty two cents besides his costs. It is therefore considered by the court that the plaintiff recover of the said defendants the debt aforesaid together with the damages aforesaid by the jury aforesaid in form aforesaid assessed, and his costs by him about his suit in his behalf expended and the said defendants in mercy etc.
Issued 22nd March 1827

Robert Neal)
    vs)   Slander
Thomas Potter)

By consent of the parties and with the assent of the court it is ordered by the court that the parties have leave to take depositions generally by giving each other twenty days notice of the time and place if taking the same within the state, and thirty days without the state; and that this cause be continued on affidavit by his paying the costs of the present term, until the next term of this court.

Ordered by the court that John Read, William Stoddert, Blackman Coleman, Richard Nixon, Wm. H.Laving, and William R.Hess Esquires be and they are hereby appointed a committee to draft rule for the Government of this court and the bar thereof and that they make report to the next term of this court.

Ordered by the court a majority of the acting justices being present that a former order for cutting out the road from Brownsville in the County of Haywood to Bolivar be renewed and it is further ordered that Harmon Frazier be appointed overseer south of the same from McGuire Road and north of Big Hatchie River & that all the hands south of what is called the McGuire road & north Hatchie be compelled to work therein-
Issued 22nd March 1827

And it is further ordered that William Fitzgerald be appointed overseer south of Big Hatchie River to Haywood County line and that all

(p-122con.) the hands west of Richland Creek and East of the sixth
Range line be compelled to work under him as such
Iss'd 22nd March 1827

(p-123) John G.Carithers Sheriff and collector of the state and county
Tax this day makes report to court in the words and figures following
State of Tennessee)
    vs   ) March Term 1827
Haywood County   )

       I,John G.Carithers Sheriff and collec. of the public Taxes of
said county do hereby report to court the following tracts of land and
town lots as not being listed for taxation for the year 1826, that the
taxes on the same have not been paid and that the respective owners are
liable to double taxes (to wit)

AME	No of Tr.	Dist	Range	Sec	Water course	No. of Entry or grant	No. of T.lot	No of the lots in the plan of the town of Brownsville
n)								
hn	4000	10				116		
T.	1000	10				60		
	1000	10				90		
Ths.							1	2
David etc.							1	12
rton							2	11 & 28
Robert							4	125,143,137,& 149
s.J.							2	19 & 35
ohn	4000	10				116		
.7.	1000	10				60		
	1000	10				90		
Ths.							1	2
David							1	12
rton							2	11 & 28
Robert							4	125,143,137 & 149
s.J.							2	19 & 35
ob H.							1	7
eph W.							3	10,33 & 32
ttleberry							2	29 & 37
Jno.T.							4	49,93,101 & 97
tephen							1	76
uncan							2	4 & 122
on, Ths.							1	94
B.							1	8
mos							1	31
hn							2	38 & 42
Reuben							1	81
Bryant							1	79
sse							1	138
n,Ths.							9	148,131,128,92,87,99 95,120,124
llen							4	47,103,107,98
,William							3	55,60,& 57
.							1	48

OWNERS NAME	No of Tr	Dist	Range	Sec	Water course	No.of Entry or grant	No. of T.lot	No of the lots in the plan of the town of Brownsville
(p-123con.)								
Williams Stith							1	88
Martin Joshua							1	91
Champ H.							2	96 & 126
Skurlock,Beverly							1	129
Hutchinson,Wilson							1	26
McWhite,Jno.							1	69
	6000						55	$172.50

(p-124 A) Whereupon it is considered by the court the judgement be and the same is hereby entered against the aforesaid tracks of land in the name of the state for the amount of the Double taxes cost charges due severly thereon for the year 1826 and it is ordered by the court thatsaid severial tracts of land or so much thereof do shall be sufficient of each of them to satisfy the said taxes cost and charges be sold as the law directs.

Mathew Ray   )
    vs   )
Green B .Jenson)

    This day came the plaintiff by his attorney wherefore the Defendant being solemnly called to come and replevy his property plead a demur came not but made default it is therefore considered by the court that the plantiff recover against the defendant the amount of his debt whereof he hath complained an oath by his attachment prayed and obtained but because it is not known to the court what is the amount of said debt let a Jury of good and lawful men came and find the same and therefore came a jury of good and lawful men to wit, Thomas G.Nixon, John T.Turner, James Russell, Philip Bruce,John A.King, Robert T.Smith, More P.Estes,Henry Wooten Robert A.Penn, William, Sherrin John M c White & Allen H.Howard, who being elected tried and sworn the truth of and upon the premises to speak upon their oaths say they find that the defendant is indebted to the plaintiff the sum of ninety one dollars & seventy five cents it is therefore considered by the court that the plaintiff recover against the defendant his debt aforesaid found as aforesaid together with his costs and about his suit in this behalf expended and it is further ordered by the court that the property heretofore attached as appears by the officer re - turn besubject to the satisfaction of the judgment of this court in this behalf made the defendant in mercy & etc.

    A Deed of bargain and sale from Thomas H.Taylor to James Smith was this day produced in oppen court and proven by the oaths of Mason F. Jhonston and Thomas Rutherford the subscribing witness thereto and ordered to be certified for Registration

(p-124 B) This day a Deed of B argain and sail from Egbert H.Shepperd, Jas.H.Shepperd, Sally Grove (formerly Sally Sheppard) John Rogers and Margarete Rogers (formerly Margarette Sheppard) Susan J.Hay (formerly Susan J.Shepperd and Samuel P.Ash in right of his wife Mary B .Ash (former- ly Mary B .Shepperd) to William Shepperd one of the _____ thereto and the same was acknowledged by Susan Hay, in open court, to be her act and deed and that she freely and willingly signed,sealed and delevd. the same (being seperate and apart from her husband) when examined

    This day a deed of release from David Hay and Susan Hay to Jno. Rodgers and his wife and Jas. Henry Shepperd, and the same was in open court acknowledged by Susan Hay one of the parties thereto seperate and apart from her husband, to be her act and deed and that she had freely and willingly signed, sealed and delev 'd the same-

(p-125) This day an instrument of writing purporting to be a power of atty. from Egbert H.Shepperd, Jas.H.Shepperd, Sally Grove, Jno.Rodgers and Margaret Rodgers (formerly Margarete Shepperd) Susan J.Hay, (formerly Susan J.Shepperd and Samuel D.Ashe in sight of his wife Mary B.Ashe formerly Mary B.Shepperd, to John Scott Esq. or Dr. Edward Shurdwick, and the same (p-125con.) was acknowledged in upen court by Susan J.Hay one of the parties thereto seperate and apart from her husband to be her act and deed, and that she had willingly signed, sealed and del'd the same.

Ordered that this court be adjourned untill tomorrow morning untill nine o'clock.

Rich.Nixon Ch
Saml.D.Ashe J.P.
Matthew Roy

Friday morning 16 day of March 1827
The court met according to adjournment
Present the worshipful Richard Nixon,Samuel D.Ashe, Nicholas T. Perkins and other their fellow Justices.

Ordered that the Sheriff of this County summon the following persons as Jurors to our next Circuit Court to be held for this county on the fourth Monday of June next, to wit

1.Samuel P.Ashe Esq.	11.John N.Roddy
2.Olliver B.Woods	12.Joshua Abstain
3.Gideon Pace	13.Henry McCoy
4.Richard Nixon	14.Lewis Fascue
5.Jonathan T.Jacocbs	15.Simon Turner
6.Lawrence McGuire	16.Tho. D.Nixon
7.Nicholas T.Perkins	17.Herndon Haralson
8.Joel Estes	18.Matthew Roy
9.Charles Wortham	19.John Marbery
10Dan'l. Cherry	20.Hyram Bradford

(p-126)21.Francis L.Dilliard	24.James Smith
22.Mason F.Johnson	25.Thomas Thweatt
23.Henry Welsh	26.Tobias Henderson

Ordered by the court that the following persons be summoned by the Sheriff as Jurors to next court to wit.

1. John Taylor	14.Samuel Elliott
2. Richard Taylor	15.Robert Roddy
3. William Weddle	16.Jas.W.Russell
4. Robert Burns	17.Thos.Rutherford
5. Vincent Haralson	18.John Potter
6. Samuel Sampson	19.Phillip Koontz
7. Samuel Brown	20.Levi Gardiner
8. Jonathan Hollowell	21.John Rodgers
9. James Henderson	22.Archibald McNeal
10.Griffith Edwards	23.Alex.D.Gorden
11.Nelson Hargrove	24.Thos.Crutcher
12.Robert Hamill	25.Bignell Crook
13.Francis Lemoin	26.John T.Turner

On motion of James Smith by his counsel and it appearing to the satisfaction of the court that German Sewell had been taken under acasa which issued from a justices judgment, and he having given bond and security for his personal appearance agreably to the act of the assembly of 1824, for the benefit of insolvent debtors, and failing to attend to (p-126con.) surrender himself according to law. It is ordered by the court that judgment for the sum of $3.75 debt cost 50¢ together with all further cost and interest that may accrue be rendered against the said Sewell and Thos Stokely his security-and that they may be taken etc. ex isd   127

Ordered by the court that James Hart be released from the payment of taxes on the following tract of land to wit no. Entry 748 in 11th district, range 2nd section 6th for 1920 acres for the year 1826,

It appearing to the satisfaction of the court that Jno.C.McLemore having paid the same to the shff. of Tipton County- and that Jno. G. Carithers shff. & collector be allowed a credit it with the Trustee of this county for the same.

```
(p-127) William A.Johnson   )
              vs             )
        Henry L.Gray         )
        Thos.J.Smith
```

On motion of the plaintiff by his attorney,it appearing that a Fi Fa has issued against the goods & chattels,lands and tenements of said defendants by a justice of the peace and it appearing to the satisfaction of the court, by the officers endorsement that there was no personal property of the said Debts: to be found within his Bailwick whereof, to destrainto make the said plffs. debt, costs etc. and it further appearing that a levy had been made upon this following town lots lying in the Town of Brownsville known and distinguished upon the plan of said town by no.49 it is ordered by the court upon application of the ptffs attorney aforesaid that the same be condemned for the said ptffs debt etc. and that the sherriff, sell the same as the law directs. Iss'd the 22nd March

```
Richard W.Nixon )
     vs         )
Henry L.Gray    )
```

On motion of the ptff. by his atty. it appearing that a Fifa had issued against the goods and chattels,lands and tenamants of said Deft. by a justices judgment and it appearing to the satisfaction of the court by the officers endorsement that there were no personal property of the said Deft. to be found within his bailwick whereupon to levy to make the said Ptffs debt costs etc. and it further appearing that a levy had been made upon the following town lots to wit. Nos 19 and 35 lying and being in the Town of Brownsville and so known as per plat of said town and it is ordered by the court upon application of ptffs. atty. aforesaid that the same be condemned for said ptffs. debt etc. and that the shff. of this county proceed to sell the same according to law.

```
Rich'd W.Nixon   )
     vs          )
                 )
Thos J.Smith and )
Henry L.Gray     )
```

(p-127con.) On motion of plff. by his attorney it appearing that a fifa
had issued against the goods and chattels, lands and tenements of the said
Defts of a justice of the peace and it appearing to the satisfaction of
the court, by the officers endorsement therein that there was no personal
property of the said Deft. to be found   (p-128) within his bailwick
whereupon to levy to make the said pltiff. debt cost etc. and it further
appearing that a levy had been made upon the following lots lying and
being in the town of Brownsville and know as Lots Nos. 19 and 35 as per
plat of said town, and it is ordered by the court that the same be condemned for the payment of said Pltiff debt etc and that the shff. of this
county be ordered to sell the same according to law.
Issued 22nd March 1827

John McWhite)
     vs   )
Henry L.Gray)

        On motion of the Pltiff. by his atty. it appearing to the court
that a fifa had issued against the goods, chattels, land & tenements of
said deft. by a justice of the peace & it appearing to the satisfaction
of the court by the officers endorsement therein that there was no personal property of said Deft. to be found within his bailawick whereupon
to levy to make the said ptffs. debt, cost etc. and it further appearing
that a levy had been made upon the following town lots lying and being
in the town of Brownsville known a Lots No.26. 18 and 35 as per plat of
said town and it is ordered by the court that the same be condemed for the
payment of pliff. debt, cost etc- and that the Shff. of this county be
ordered to sell the same according to law.
Iss'd 22nd March 1827

Matthew Ray)
     vs   )
Henry L.Gray)

        On motion of the ptliff by his atty. it appearing to the court
that a fifa had issued against the goods chattels lands & tenements of sd.
defendant by a justice of the peace and it appearing to the satisfaction
of the court by the officers endorsement thereon that there was no personal
property of said Deft to be found within his bailawick whereupon to levy
to make the said Pltiffs debt cost and it further appearing that a levy
had been made upon the following Town lots lying and being in the town of
Brownsville known as Lots nos. 19-26 and 35 as per plat of said Town; and
it is ordered that the same be condemed for the payment of pltiff debt
cost etc. and that the shff. of this county be ordered to sell the same
according to same.

 Jas .W.Russell)
     vs   )
Matthew Ray   )

        The pltiff. having rec'd a judgment at a former day of this term_____

the Defn. to which judgment the Defr. prays an appeal to the Circuit
Court holden for this county; and it appearing to the court that the
said Defr. having entered into bond with good security, the same is
allowed.

(p-129) Ordered by the court that Rich'd Nixon & Herndon Haralson be appointed commissioners to settle with the different officers of Haywood County according to act of Assembly.

Ordered that this court be now adjourned untill court in course.

> Rich'd Nixon Char
> Sam. P. Ashe
> Blackman Coleman

State of Tennessee)
)
Haywood County Court)

June Term 1827

At a court of pleas and quarter sessions began and holden in and for said county of Haywood at the courthouse in the town of Brownsville on the second Monday in June in the year of our Lord one thousand eight hundred and twenty seven it being the 11th day of said month, Present the worshipful Richard Nixon, Lawrence McGuire and Blackman Coleman Esquires and others their fellow Justices of the peace, John G.Carithers Sheriff and Britain H.Sanders clerk.

A Platt and certificate of survey for two hundred acres of land lying in this county, on the waters of the south fork of Forked Deer River in the ninth Section and sixth range, entered by Preston G.Hodges as an occupant claim was this day produced in open courts and the assignmet therein from the said Preston G.Hodges to Thomas Brown for the same duly acknowledged by the said Hodges and ordered to be so certified-certified & Delivered A.B.Bradford June 11th 1827

A Deed of Bargain and sale from David Jarrett to Richard Nixon for four hundred and eighty acres of Land was this day produced in open court and duly proven by the oaths of Jonathan J.Nixon and J.H.Nixon subscribing witnesses thereto and ordered to be certified for registration-

(p-130) A Deed of bargain and sale from Richard Nixon to David Jarrett for four hundred and eighty of land was this day produced in open court and duly proven by the oaths of Jonathan J.Nixon and J.H.Nixon subscribing witnesses thereto and ordered to be certified for registration

A Deed of Bargain and sale from Julius Sanders to Edmund Richmon and John W.Cook for eight hundred acres of land was this day produced in open court and duly acknowledged and and ordered to be certified for registration-

Ordered by the court that the clerk receive the tax of all such persons as may apply during the present term and insert them on the list for the present year.
Issd

This day Felix G.Miller produced in open court the scalp of a wolf over the age of four months and proved the killing of the same by his own oath he having no other evidence whereby he could prove the same, is therefore ordered by the court that the clerk certify the same to the Treasurer of West Tennessee accordingly-
Iss'd

Ordered by the court that the following named persons be appointed

(p-130con.) judges to hold the next ensuing election, to elect a
Governor, representatives to Congress, and member to the state Legislature
in the different precints as follows to wit, Daniel Cherry, Thomas Thweet
and Charles Wortham Esquire (at Thos. Thweets) Richard Nixon, Lawrence
McGuire and Joel Estes Esquires (at Brownsville Oliver B.Woods Esqr.
Malcomb Johnston and Joel Pace Esquire (at Woods Samuel P.Ash, Lewis
Foscue and Griffith Edwards (at Ashes)
Issd 27th June 1827

Ordered by Court that the order made at the March Term authorizing
the division of the lands mentioned in the petition of E.Roddy and
William Hannor be now renewed and that the commissioners therein mentioned have until the next Term of this court to make their return
Issued

On sufficient cause being shown- It is ordered by the court that
Alvan Bingham be licenced to keep an ordinary at his new dwelling house
for the term of twelve months he having entered into bond as the law
directs.

Ordered by the court that David Allen be appointed overseer of the
road leading from Brownsville in a direction of Bolivar in place of
William Morrison as for as where the same crosses the road known by the
name of the McGuire road and that (p-131) Hied. Allen, Edward Allen,
James Scott Jo Scott Turner Smith's three hands and William A.Morison
work under him as such in keeping the same in repair agreeable to law.
Iss'd 27 June

On motion of Joel Pace to be released as security of Samuel D.
Woods constable, It is ordered by the court that he be accordingly
released therefrom, and that the said Samuel D.Woods have leave to come
forward during the present Term and give other security as the law directs

Ordered by the court that Thursday next on a part thereof be set
apart for the purpose of transacting county business and that the clerk
advertise the same.

Ordered by the court that James Clark be appointed overseer to
cut and open the road from Fayette County line to Big Muddy Creek and
that all the hands within this county on the East side of said creek,
and south of Big Hatchie River work under him as such.
Iss'd 27th June 1827

Ordered by the court that Lewis Fascue be appointed overseer to cut
and open the road from Big Muddy Creek to Tipton County line and that all
the hands on the west side of said Creek and south side of Big Hatchie
river living within this county work under him as such.
Iss'd 27th June

Ordered by the court that administration of all and singular the
goods and chattels, rights and credits of Jesse Jackson deceased be
granted to Elizabeth Jackson widow of said Dec'd who thereupon entered
into an acknowledged bond with James Jackson and Jesse Jackson her securities in the penal sum of four hundred dollars conditioned according
to Law and took the oath of administratrix.

(p-131con.) Issued

The court proceeded agreeable to notice to the election of
constable in Captain Estes Company, whereas after counting out the
votes Maleche Jackson was declared duly and constitutionally elected for
the two succeeding years who entered into bond together with his securities and took the necessary prescribed by law

(p-132) Ordered by the court that Enoch Cox, William Boze, and Dulaney
Whitenerst be appointed commissioners to set apart and allot to Elizabeth
Jackson widow of the late Jesse Jackson Deceased one years provisions.
Issued

Ordered by the court that James Story and Elias Roddy be appointed
in addition to a former Jury of view to lay of and mark a road from
McGuires ferry in a direction to Summerville and Memphis as for as our
county lines the former order being hereby renewed, and that they make
report of their proceedings to the next term of this court.
Issued 27 June 1827

The court then adjourned until 9 o'clock tomorrow morning-

                                Rich'd Nixon Cha
                                L McGuire J.P.
                                Matthew Ray J.P.

Tuesday morning the court met according to adjournment Present
the worshipful Richard Nixon, Lawrence McGuire and Jonathan T.Jacocks,
Esquires and others their fellow Justices of the peace.

John G.Carithers, sheriff of Haywood County makes return of the
writ of venire facias returnable to this court, that he has summoned
all the persons therein named except Samuel Brown, Jonathan Hollowell,
and James Henderson who were appointed ~~who were appointed~~ by the
county court of said county ~~court of said county~~ to serve as a jury at
the present term of this court, that is to say-
John Taylor, Richard Taylor, William Weddle Robert Burns, Vincent
Harralson, James Sampson, Samuel Brown, Jonathan Hollowell, James
Henderson, Griffeth Edwars, Nelson Hargrove, Robert Hamill Frances
Lamoin, Samuel Elliott, Robert Roddy, James W.Russell, Thomas Rutherford
John Potter, Phillip Koonce. Levi Guardner, John Rodgers, Archibald
McNeal, Alexander D.Gordan, Thomas Cutcher, Bignal Crook, John T.Turner,
be summoned to attend at the next term of this court then and there to
serve as grand or petit Jurors as the case may be-

                    Test B.H.Sanders,Clk.

State of Tennessee to the sheriff of Haywood County Greeting;
your are hereby commanded to summon the aforesaid persons to serve as
Jurors at the next court of pleas and quarter sessions to be held at the
courthouse in the town of Brownsville on Tuesday after the second Monday
in June next and this they shall in no wise omit under the penalty
prescribed by law and have you then and there this writ, witness Britain
H.Sanders clerk of our (p-133) said ~~said~~ court at office the second

(p-133con.) Monday in March 1827 and fifty first year of American Independence.

B.H.Sanders,Clk

By virtue of the within venire facias to me directed I have proceeded to summon all the within named persons to serve as grand & petit jurors except Samuel Brown, Johnathan Hollowell, & James Henderson and such persons so summoned are inhabitants of said county and of the age of twenty one years and are house holders of or freeholders of said county.

Jno. G.Carithers, Shff.

Out of the venire facias returnable to this court the following named persons good and lawful men viz Vincent Harralson, foreman Francis Lamoyn, James Sampson John Potter Robert Hammell William Weddle, Archibald McNeal, Robert Burns, James W.Russell, Nelson Hargrove,Thomas Rutherford, Thos. Crutcher and Levi Guardner were drawn elected tried and sworn, and after receiving their charge retired and the care of Reuben, Alphin constable sworn to attend thereof to consider of presentments.

Robert Neale   )
     vs   ) Slander
Thomas Potter   )

This day came the parties by their attorneys and thereupon came a jury of good and lawful men, to wit, Richard Taylor, Phillip Koonce, Alexander D.Gordan, John Rodgers, John A.King, Thomas Stokely, Benj. Rowland, William C.Bruce, James R.Alphin, James Axley, John A.King, and John Williams, who being elected tried and sworn the truth to speak upon the issue Joined upon their oaths do say that the defendant is not guilty as in pleading he hath alledged, therefore it is considered by the court the plaintiff take nothing by his bill but for his false clamour be in mercy etc and that the said defendant go thereof without day and recover against said plaintiff his costs by him about his defence in this behalf expended.
Issued 19th July 1827
(p-134)
Robert Neale   )
     vs   ) Slander
John Potter   )

This day came the parties by their attorneys and thereupon came a Jury of good and lawful men (to wit) Richard Taylor, Phillip Koonce, Alexander D.Gordon, John Rodgers, John A.King , Thomas Stokely, William C.Bruce, James R.Alphin James Axley, John A.King, Mansfield Ware and Nathan Williamson who being elected tried and sworn the truth to speak upon the issue joined upon their oaths do say that the defendant is not guilty as in pleading he hath alledged Therefore it is considered by the court here that the plaintiff take nothing by his bill bill but for his false clamour be in mercy etc. and that the said defendant go therefore without day and recover against said plaintiff his cost by him about his

(p-134con.) defence in this behalf expended.
Issued 19th July 1827

Nathaniel Williamson)
    vs   )   Assault and Battery
Green B.Jamerson   )

    This day came the parties by their attorney and thereupon came a
jury of good and lawful men (to wit) Richard Taylor, Phillip Koonce,
John Rodgers, Alexander D.Gordon, John A.King, Thomas Stokely, William
C.Bruce, James R.Aplin, James Axley, John A.King Mansfield Ware & Henry
Wooten, who being elected tried and sworn the truth to speak upon the
issue joined on their oaths do say they find the issues in favor of the
Plaintiffs *damages by reason of the grievances in the declaration mentioned to two Dollars fifty cents. It is ther fore considered by the court,
that the plaintiff recover of the Deft. the damages aforesaid assessed,
and also his costs in this behalf expended etc.
Issued 30th June 1827

John D Martin assee)
    vs   )   Debt
Blackman Coleman   )

    This day came the plaintiff by his attorneys in proper person, who
acknowledgeth the plaintiffs action and confesses judgment for one hundred
and ten dollars seventy seven cents therefore with the assent of the
plaintiff it is considered by the court that the said plaintiff recover
as the said defendant the said one hundred and ten dollars and seventy
seven cents and his costs by him in this behalf expended and the defendant
in mercy etc.
Iss'd 29th June 1827
(p-135) Charles R.Abbot   )
         vs   )   Debt
      Blackman Coleman   )

    This day came the plaintiff by his attorney and the defendant in
proper person who acknowledgeth the plaintiff Debt for two hundred and
four dollars and seventy eight cents & confesses judgment for the same
therefore with the assent of the plaintiff it is considered by the court
that the said plaintiff recover against the said defendant the said two
hundred and four dollars and seventy eight cents, confessed as aforesaid
and his costs by him in this behalf expended and the defendant in mercy
etc from which judgment the defendant hath prayed and obtained an appeal
to the Circuit Court he having entered into bond as the law directs.
Transct made out 27th July 1827

    This day Daniel Cherry Esquire produced in open court the scalp of
a wolf over the age of four months and proved the killing of the same by
his own oath he having no other evidence by whom he could prove the same.
It is therefore ordered by the court that the clerk certify the same to
the treasurer of West Tennessee accordingly.
Issued June 13th

    James Axley a Juror summoned to attend at our last Decr. court,
this day came into court and on oath having made a sufficient excuse,
It is ordered by by the court his fine be remitted, and that he be also
* and assess the Plaintiffs

(p-135con.) exonorated from the paym't of the cents thereof.

Thomas & Jno. Potter)
   vs   )
Gab'l. Minter Excr. of) Assumset
James Cosby Dec'd)

   This day came the parties by their attornies and thereupon came a
jury of good and lawful men that is to say, John T.Turner Robert T.Smith,
Alexander D.Gordon, Benjamin Rowland, John B.Fudge, Thomas J.McGuire,
James Jackson, Robert Penn, James Hammill, John R.McGuire, John Mitchell,
Jonathan J.Nixon who being elected tried and sworn the truth to speak upon
the issues joined upon their oaths do say they find the issue in favor of
the defendant that he hath fully administered all and singular the goods
and chattels of the said decedant in his hands to be administered before
the bringing of this writ, or the said Defendant- (p-.136) and the plea
of non assumpit they find in favor of the plaintiff, that dec'd did assume
in manner and form as the said plaintiff hath explained, and assess the
plaintiff, hath alledged damages to two hundred and thirty six dollars
and nineteen cents therefore it is considered by the court that the said
plaintiff recover against the said Defendant his damages aforesaid in form
aforesaid assessed and his and costs by him about his suit in this
behalf expended, to be levied of the goods and chattels of the said
decedant when sufficient thereof shall come to the hands of the said
Defendant to be administered and the said Defendant in mercy etc.
Issued 17th Dec. 1827

Richard W.Nixon)
   vs   ) Debt
Francis L.Dillard)

   This day came the parties by their attorneys and thereupon came a
jury of good and lawful men (to wit, John T.Turner, Robert T.Smith,
Alondus Gholston Benjamin Rowland, John B.Fudge, Thomas J.McGuire, James
Jackson, Robert A.Penn, James Hammill, John R. McGuire, John Mitchell &
Jonathan J. Nixon who being elected tried and sworn to try the matters on
dispute upon their oaths do say that the defendant hath not paid the debt
of Eighty dollars in the declaration mentioned as the plaintiff by replying
to the defendants plea hath alledged and do assess the plaintiffs damages
by reason of the detention thereof to two dollar and forty cents besides
costs. It is therefore considered by the court that the plaintiff recover of the defendant his debt aforesaid together with his damages
aforesaid by the jury aforesaid in form aforesaid assessed and all his
costs by him about his suit in this behalf expended and the defendant in
mercy etc- and on motion of the defendants execution stayed by consent of
the ptffs. attorney until the first day of January 1828.

Parrish & McAlovan)
   vs   ) Debt
Henry Wooten   )

   This day came the parties by their attorneys and thereupon came a
Jury of good and lawful men to wit, John T.Turner, James Jackson, Robert
T.Smith, Alondus Gholston, Benjamin Rowland, John B.Fudge, Thomas J.McGuire

(p-136con.) James Jackson, Robert A.Penn, James Hammill, John R.McGuire
John Mitchell, & Jonathan J.Nixon who being elected tried and sworn to
try the matters in dispute upon their oaths do say that the defendant
hath not paid
Issued 15th Oct. 1827

(p-137) the debt of fifty five dollars in the declaration mentioned as q́s
the plaintiff by replying to the defendants plea hath alledged and do
assess the plaintiffs damages by reason of the detention thereof to one
dollar and ten cents besides costs. It is therefore considered by the
court that the plaintiff recover of the defendant his debt aforesaid
together with his damages aforesaid in form aforesaid by the Jury aforesaid assessed, and also his costs by him about his suit in this behalf
expended, and the defendant in mercy etc. execution stayed by consent of
the plffs. attorney ninety days.

  The court then adjourned until tomorrow nine o'clock.

        Rich'd Nixon cha-
        Dan'l Cherry
        L.McGuire

  Wednesday morning June 13th 1827 the court met according to
adjournment present the worshipful Richard Nixon, Lawrence McGuire,
and Daniel Cherry Esquires and others of their fellow Justices of the
peace.

  The petition of John Windsor Joseph Windsor, John Tapscott,
Thomas Windsor, Craven Boswell, and Newman Windsor, praying the division
of same lands therein mentioned was this day presented to the court and
upon the reading of the same it is ordered by the court to be received
and that the following persons be appointed commissioners to partition
and divide the same (to wit Lawrence McGuire Esqr. Herndon Harralson, Wm.
H.Henderson, A.D.Gordon, and Britain H.Sanders and make return thereof
to the next term of this court according to law.

State of Tennessee)
  vs   ) Presentment for Gaming
Lee H.Burks   )

  This cause is continued on the affadavit of Alexander B.Bradford
solicitor General until the next term of this court-

(p-138) State of Tennessee)
     vs   Presentment for Gaming
  Alexander Stewart)

  This day came Alexander B.Bradford solicitor General who prosecutes
on behalf of the state, and moves the court that a nolle prosequi be
entered in this cause whereupon with the assent of the court it is entered
according-
  It is therefore considered by the court that the said Defendant
go hence with out day and recover of the state his costs by him about his
defence in this behalf expended whereupon it is ordered by the court that
the county pay the costs of this prosecution.

(p-138con.) State of Tennessee)
                  vs   ) Presentment for Gaming
          Thomas Stokely   )

This day came A.B.Bradford solicitor general who prosecute in behalf of the state and the defendant in his proper person & the Defendant being solemnly charged sayeth he is not guilty in manner and form as charged in the bill of presentment and for his trial puts himself upon a jury and his country and the solicitor general doth the like and therefore came a jury of good and lawful men to wit Richard Taylor, Philip Koonce, A.D.Gordon, John Rodgers, John T.Turner, Robert A.Penn, Andrew Hammill, Nathan Williamson, Green L. Harralson John Mitchell, John B.Fudge and William C.Bruce, who being elected tried and sworn well and truly to try the issue of traverse joined upon their oaths aforesaid do say that the defendant is guilty in manner and form as charged in the bill of presentment it is therefore considered by the court that the defendant make his fine with the State of Tennessee by the payment of the sum of five dollars and all costs and that he be taken etc.
Issued 30th June 1827

State of Tennessee)
        vs   )
John McWhite &   ) Presentment for Gaming
Thomas Stokely   )

This day came Alexander B.Bradford solicitor general who prosecute on behalf of the state (p-139) and moves the court that a nole proseque be entered in this court whereupon with the assent of the court it is ordered accordingly. It is therefore considered by the court that the said defendant go hence without day and recover of the state his costs about his defence in that behalf expended whereupon it is ordered by the court that the county pay the costs of this prosecution.

Francis L.Cox   )
      vs   )
Mathew Figures &   )
Francis L.Dillard   )

On motion of the plaintiff by his attorney it appearing that a fifa had issued against the good and chattels land and tenements of the Deft. by a justices judgment, and it appearing to the satisfaction of the court by the officers endorsement that there were no personal property of said defendant to be found within his bailwick whereupon to levy to make the said plff. debt costs etc and it further appearing that a levy had been made on the following town lots to wit No. 70 & 80, lying and being in the town of Brownsville and so known as pr plat of said Town and it is ordered by the court an application of the plff. attory. aforesaid that the same be condemned for said plaintiffs debt etc. and that the sheriff of this county proceed to sell the same agreeable to law.
Issued 26th June 1827

(p-139con.) Francis L.Cox   )
           vs   )
     Mathew Figunes &   )
     Francis L.Dillard)

     On motion of the plaintiff by his attorney it appearing that a
fifa had issued against the goods and chattels lands and tennents of the

defendant by a justice Judgment and it appearing to the satisfaction
of the court by the officers indorsement that there were no personal
property of said defendant to be found within his bailwick whereupon to
levy to make the sd. plaintiff costs & etc. and or further appearing
that a levy had been made on the* town lots (to wit) No. 70 & 80 lying
and being in the town of Brownsville and so known as pr plat of said
town and it is ordered by the court on application of the plffs.(p-140)
attorney aforesaid that the same be condemned for said plaintiffs debt
etc etc and that the sheriff of this county proceed to sell the same
agreeable to law.
Issued June 30th 1827

Peter Landford)
    vs   ) Assault & Battery
John McWhite   )

     This day came the parties by their attorneys and thereupon came
a jury of good & lawful men (to wit) Richard Taylor, Phillip Koonce,
A.D.Gordon, John Rodgers, John T.Turner, Robert A.Penn, Nathan
Williamson, John Mitchell, John B.Fudge Robert T.Smith , Thomas J.
McGuire, Benjamin Rowland, who being elected tried and sworn the truth to
repeat upon the issues joined upon the oath do say they find the issues
in favor of the plaintiff and do assess the plaintiffs damages in the
declaration mentioned to six and one fourth cents. It is therefore
considered by the court that the plaintiff recover of the defendant the
damages aforesaid assessed and also his costs in this behalf expended
etc.
Issued June 30th 1827

Parrish & McAlovan)
     vs   ) Debt
Henry L.Gray   )

     This day came the parties by their attorneys and thereupon came a
jury of good and lawful men to wit, Richard Taylor, Philip Koonce, John
Rodgers, John T.Turner, Robert A.Penn Nathan Williamson, John Mitchell,
John B.Fudge, Robert T.Smith, Thomas J.McGuire, Benjamin Rowland, John
A.King who being elec ted tried and sworn by the matters in dispute upon
their oaths do say that the defendant hath not paid the debt of ninety
two dollars and forty three cents in the declaration mentioned as the
plaintiff in replying to the defendants plea hath alledged and do assess
the plff. damages by reason of the detention thereof to two dollars and
seventy three cents besides cost. It is therefore considered by the
court that the plaintiff recover of the said defendant his debt aforesaid
together with the damages aforesaid inform aforesaid, by the jury aforesaid assessed and his costs by him about his suit in this behalf expended
and the defendant in mercy etc.
 Issued 30th June 1827
* following

(p-140con.) Slater & Hicks)
      vs   )   Debt
   Joel Parker   )

    This day came the parties by their attorney and thereupon came a jury of good and lawful men, to wit,
Issued 2nd July 1827

(p-141) Richard Taylor, Phillip Koonce, John Rodgers, John T.Turner, Robert A.Penn, Nathan Williamson, John Mitchell John B.Fudge, Robert T. Smith, Thomas J.McGuire Benjamin Rowland, John A.King, who being elected tried and sworn upon their oaths do say that the defendant hath not paid the debt of one hundred and nine dollars and fifty nine cents in the declaration mentioned as the plaintiff in replying to the defendants plea hath alledged and do assess the plaintiff damages by reason of the detention thereof to fifteen dollars and thirty four cents besides costs. It is therefore considered by the court that the plaintiff recover of the said defendant his debt aforesaid together with his damages aforesaid in form aforesaid by the jury aforesaid assessed besides his costs in this behalf expended and that the defendant in mercy etc.
Iss'd 2nd July 1827

Hiram Bradford   )
   vs   )   Debt
Samuel Elliott   )

    This day came the parties by their attorneys and thereupon came a jury of good and lawful men to wit Richard Taylor, Phillip Koonce, John Rodgers, John T.Turner, Robert A.Penn, Nathan Williamson, John Mitchell, John B .Fudge, Robert T.Smith, T hos. J.McGuire, Benjamin Rowland and John A.King who being elected tried & sworn upon their oaths do ssay that the defendant hath not paid the debt and damages of Eighty one dollars and seventy four cents in the declaration mentioned as the plaintiff in replying to the defendants plea hath alledged, besides costs

    It is therefore considered by the court that the plaintiff recover of the said defendant his debt aforesaid in form aforesaid by the jury aforesaid assessed besides costs in this behalf expended and that the defendant in mercy etc.
Transcript made out 27 July 1827

    John Hardwick a juror who was regularly summoned to attend as such at a former term of this court this day came into court and made his excuse upon oath for his non attendance which being satisfactory. It is therefore ordered that he be released from the fine and costs heretofore impossed in consequence thereof.

(p-142) James Stalcup   )
     vs   )
   Nimrod Axley, Thomas   )   Certiorari motion to dismiss
   Stokely and James Darris   )

    This day came the parties by their attornies and thereupon the matters of law arising upon the plaintiffs motion to dismiss the

(p-142con.) certiorari herein having been argued and fully understood
by the court here it is the opinion of the court that the same be dismissed. It is therefore dismissed by the court that the plaintiff recover
the said Nimrod Axley Thomas Stokely and James Darris and on motion a
John Hardiwick and William R.Hess their securities in the certiorari the
sum of forty five dollars twelve and a half cents the amount of the
justices judgment below and twelve and a half percent interest per annum,
thereon from the vendition of said judgment up to the present time, and
his costs by him about his suit in this behalf expended etc. and the said
defendant in mercy etc.
Issued the 22 June 1827

        The court then adjourned until tomorrow hine o'clock-

                                        Rich Nixon Char.
                                        L.McGuire
                                        Danl. Cherry

        Thursday morning June the 14th. 1827 the court met according to
adjournment present the worshipful Richard Nixon, Daniel Cherry and
Lawrence McGuire Esquires and others their fellow justices of the peace
etc.

(p-143) Ordered by the court a majority being present that Robert Burns
John P.Majors, Joshua Abstain, Stephen Booth, James Henderson, Daniel
Cherry esquire and Richard Taylor be appointed a jury to view mark and
lay of a road from Harrisburgh in a direction to Bolivar as for as the
county line and majority of them make report to the next term of this
court.
Iss'd the 14 June

        Ordered by the court that Richard Taylor and John Williams be ap-
pointed overseers of the road leading from the town of Brownsville to
Harrisburgh, and that all the hands north of the road leading from
Brownsville to Jackson by the way of Richard Nixons and south of the
Forked deer river to Madison County line together with Nelson Hargrove
and hands George Watts and hands John McWhite and hands Robert A.Penns
hands Thomas Stokely Robert Hammell, James Darris, James Axley, Robert
Axley, Nimrod Axley and Tobias Lowery, work on said road, Richard Taylor
overseer to work to the north side of a field of Williams, and J.Williams
from there to Harrisburgh and that Richard Taylor and Daniel Cherry Esqr.
divide the hands between the said overseer; also Densmore on Cockern in
addition work under them as such-
Iss'd 27th Jun 1827

        Ordered by the court that John Brown be released from the payment of
the double tax on four thousand acres of land reported for the year
1826 he having paid the single tax on the same.

State of Tennessee   )
        vs   )   Delinquent Juror
Robert Roddy   )

(p-143con.) Robert Roddy who was regularly summoned to attend at this term to serve as a Juror which appears by the return of the venire by the sheriff being solemnly called come not but made default. It is therefore considered by the court that for such his neglect he be fined the sum of five dollars, unless he appear at the next term of this court and show cause if any they can why this Judgment should be set aside.
Issued 29th August

State of Tennessee   )
    vs   )   Delinquent Juror
Bignal Crook   )

Bignal Crook who was regularly summoned to attend at this term to serve as a juror which appears by the return of the venire by the sherriff, being solemnly called (p-144) came not but made default. It is therefore considered by the court that for such his neglect he be fined the sum of five dollars unless he appear at the next term of this court if any he can why this judgment should be set aside.
Issued

The Grand Jury returned into court the following presentment etc. to wit, a presentment vs John R.McGuire for Tipling a presentment vs Thomas Stokely and James Haggard for gaming a presentment vs. Wm. R.Hess & Thomas J.McGuire for an affray an indictment vs Jorden Hansborough for an assault and battery and there appearing no further business they are are accordingly discharged from further service

William Lamb ptff   )
    vs   )   Covenant
John Marbery deft   )

This day came the plaintiff aforesaid by his attorney and the Defendant though solemnly called came not but made default. It is therefore considered by the court that the plaintiff recover of the Defendant such Damages as he has sustained by reason of the breach of covenant in the declaration mentioned but because those damages are unknown it is commanded the sheriff that he cause a jury to come here etc. to enquire of those Damages at the next term of this court-

William Lamb ptff   )
    vs   )   Covenant
John Marberry Dept   )

This day came the plaintiff aforesaid by his attorney and the Defendant though solemnly called came not but made default. It is therefore considered by the court that the plaintiff recover (p-145) of the Defendant such Damages as he has sustained by reason of the breach of covenant in the declaration mentioned but because those Damges are unknown it is commanded the sheriff that he cause a jury to come here etc to enquire etc at the next term of this court-

The Jury of view heretofore appointed to mark and lay a road from McGuires ferry in a direction to Memphis and Summerville makes report that they have performed the duty assigned them and recommend the opening of the same whereupon it is ordered by the court that the road as marked be received and that Samuel P.Ashe be appointed overseer of the same and

(p-145con.) that he call on and work the hands on the south side of
Big Hatchie river and west of of Big Muddy Creek and that all the
hands which now work on the road from Brownsville to McGuires ferry as
live in the 11th District assent in opening and cutting the same through
the Hatchie bottom—
Issued June 27th 1827

William Arnold ptff.   )
      vs   )   Assumpsit
John R. and Thos. J.McGuire Deft)

     This day Robert L.Smith who was the special bail of the said
Thomas J.McGuire in this cause surrendered to the court the body of the
said Thomas J.McGuire in discharge of his bond for his appearance
whereupon Wm. H.Henderson came into open court, and acknowledged himself
indebted to the said William Arnold in the sum of eight hundred dollars
conditioned that the said Thomas J.McGuire shall pay and satisfy such
judgment as shall be rendered against him herein by this court or render
his body on satisfaction of the same

     An Indenture of apprenticeship between Richard Nixon chairman of
the court of pleas and quarter sessions of Haywood County, and John
Hardwick of said county, binding William Conner to the said John Hardwick
until his the said William twenty first year was duly acknowledged
(p-146) in open court by the said Richard Nixon chairman and John
Hardwick and ordered to be recorded.

Broadwater Matney)
      vs   )   Certiorari motion to Dismiss
Henry L.Gray   )

     This day came the parties by their attornies and thereupon the
matters of law arising upon the plaintiffs motion to dismiss herein being
argued by counsel learned in the law, and by the court fully understood
it is the opinion of the court that the law is for the plaintiff. It is
therefore considered by the court here that the plaintiff recover of
the said defendant and on motion of Thomas J.Smith his security in the
certiorari the sum of fourteen dollars and fifty cents the amount of the
justices judgment below together with six per cent per annum interest
thereon from the vendition of said judgment up to the present time and
his costs by him about his suit in the behalf expended and the said Defend-
and in mercy etc.

William A.Johnston)
      vs   )   Certiorari motion to Dismiss
Benjamin Noaks   )

     This day came the parties by their attorneys and thereupon the
matters of law arising upon the plaintiff motion to dismiss herein being
argued by council learned in the law and by the court here fully understood, it is the opinion of the court that the law is for the plaintiff.
It is therefore considered by the court here that he the plaintiff recover of the said defendant and on motion of Thomas J.Smith his security
in the certiorari the sum of thirty seven dollars and forty five cents
the amount of the justices judgment below together with six pr.cent per
annum entered thereon from the rendition of sd. judgment up to the

(p-146con.) present date and his costs by him about his suit in this behalf expended and the said defendant in mercy etc.
Issued 22 June 1827

William W.Douthit)
vs) Certiorari motion to dismiss
Henry Wooten)

This day came the parties by their attorneys (p-147) and thereupon the matters of law arising upon the plaintiffs motion to dismiss herein being argued by council learned in the law and by the court fully understood it is opinion of the court that the law is for the plaintiff. It is therefore considered by the court here that the plaintiff recover of the said defendant and (on motion) of John Murray his security in the certiorari the sum of thirty five dollars sixty two and one half cents the amount of the Justices Judgment below together with six per cent per annum interest from the rendition of said Judgment up to the present time and his costs by him about his suit in that behalf expended and the said defendant in mercy etc.
Issued 3rd July 1827 written in the margin.

On motion and petition filed . It is ordered by the court a majority being present that Malcomt Johnston, Oliver B.Woods, Gideon Pace, Joseph Shaw, John Blythe, William Fitzgerald and James Clark be appointed a Jury to view lay off and mark a road the nearest and best way from Estaraula in a direction to Covington and make report of their proceeding to the next term of this court
Issued 27 June 1827

Berry Dearing)
vs) Case
Benjamin Noaks)

The parties this day came into court and agree that all the matters and things in dispute between them them be submitted to the arbitration of Joel Estes Esqr. and Samuel P. Ashe Esqr. who may have the liberty to call in a third person as umpire should they not agree, that they make they their return of their decision at the next term of this court and that return be made a rule of this court—

Ordered by the court that the following named persons be summoned by the Sherriff to serve as jurors to our next courty court to wit—

No 1 Samuel Conyers	12 John Roddy
2 John Sanderlin	13 Thomas Potter
3 William Johnston (senr)	14 Robert T.Smith
4 William Hollingsworth	15 Frances L.Dillard
5 Francis M.Wood	16 Mansfield Ware
6 James F.Wortham	17 James Malden
7 John Williamson Senr.	18 Eli Jones
8 Henry Welsh	19 Thos.G.Nixon
9 William Shearrin	20 Thomas West
10 James Clark	21 Mason F.Johnston
P-148)	22 Henry McCoy
11 Isaac Edwards	23 Samuel Brown

(p-148con)

24 John McWhite

25 Willis Holland

26 Ezekiel Blacksher

and

Cato Freeman and as constables to attend said court

Issued 3rd July 1827

State	)	
vs	)	Presentment for Gaming
John M.Smith	)	

State	)	
vs	)	Presentment for assault and battery
John Rutherford	)	

State	)	
vs	)	Judgment or scifa
Amos Chambers	)	

State	)	
vs	)	Judgment or scifa
James Chambers	)	

State	)	
vs	)	Judgment or scifa
Benjamin McDonald	)	

Executions having been in the above cases and severally returned by the sherriff of this county no property found and it appearing to the satisfaction of the court that the costs incurred cannot be made out of the respective defendants, it is ordered by the court that the county pay the costs of said prosecutions and that receipts of the respective claimants shall be good vouchers in the hands of the Trustee of Haywood County in the settlement of his accounts-

(p-149) On the notion of William R. Hess who was bail for the appearance of Osburn Wallice at the suit of the State of Tennessee for an indictment vs the said Wallice, at the March term of this court; and the said Wallice having made default in his personal appearance whereby the said Wm. R.Hess became liable to the state of Tennessee to the judgment of the said court whereupon the said Hess, by the consent of the court they had assumed and took upon himself the payment of all costs etc. and it now appearing to the satisfaction of the court that the said W.R.Hess has well and truly paid and satisfied the full am't of all the costs etc. aforesaid It is ordered by the court that the said W.R.Hess recover of the said Wallace the sum of $17.50 the am't of cash aforesaid, and that the said Wallice may be taken etc.

The court then adjourned until tomorrow 9 o'clock

Rich'd Nixon Char
Matthew Ray J.P.
L.McGuire

(p-149con.) Friday morning June 15th 1827 the court met according to adjournment present the worshipful Richard Nixon, Lawrence McGuire and Mathew Ray Esquires and others their fellow justices of the peace-

A Deed of Bargain and sale from Robert Hughs to Herndon Haralson for four hundred and seventy acres of land was this day produced in open court and duly acknowledged and ordered to be certified for registration

Hiram Bradford)
    vs   ) Debt
Samuel Elliott)

Samuel Elliott the defendant in this case appeared in open court and prayed an appeal Circuit Court from a judgment entered on a former day of the present term which is granted he having entered into bond as the law directs-

The court then adjourned until court in course.

                              Rich'd Nixon Char
                              Matthew Ray
                              L.McGuire

(p-150 State of Tennessee
        At a court of pleas and quarter sessions began and holden for the county of Haywood at the courthouse in the town of Brownsville on the second Monday in September in the year of our Lord one thousand eight hundred and twenty seven it being the 10th day of said month present Daniel Cherry, Lawrence McGuire, Gideon Pace and Jonathan T.Jacocks, Esquires and others their fellow justices of the peaceeJohn G.Carithers Sheriff by his deputy Reuben Allphin and Britain H.Sanders clerk-

Ordered by court that Henry Welsh be licenced to keep an ordinary at the house of Hiram Bradford in the town of Brownsville for the term of twelve month he having complied with the requistions of the law.
Iss'd

Ordered by the court that Samuel Elliott be licenced to keep an ordinary at his house in the town of Brownsville the term of twelve months complied with the requsitions of the law.
Iss'd

A Deed of Bargain and sale from John L.Wheaton to Cornelius Buck for four hundred acres of land was this day produced in open court and duly proven by the oaths of Samuel Edney and Alfred Kennedy subscribing witnesses thereto and ordered to be certified for registration

A Deed of Bargain and sale from George W.Hockly Exr. by his agent Wm. H.Henderson to Wm. Patton for one hundred and five acres was this day produced in open court and duly acknowledged and ordered to be certified for registration.
certified & Del'd

Ordered by the court that Benjamin King's stockmark be recorded as follows, to wit, a cross and a slit in the right ear and a morbit in the (p-150con.) left.

A Deed of Bargain and sale from Eli Jones, to Joseph Curray for one hundred acres of land was this day produced in open court and duly acknowledged and ordered to be certified for registration. Certified & del'd

(p-151) Ordered by court a majority of the acting justices being present that Richard Taylor be appointed overseer of the road leading from Brownsville to Harrisburgh as for as the north side of a field called Williams and that Thos. Stokely, Robert Hammil, Wm. H.Lovings hands, Cap't Hargroves hands, John McWhite and George Watts be subject to work under him as such in keeping the same in repair-
Iss'd 19th Septr.

Ordered by court a majority of the acting justices being present that John Williams be appointed overseer of the road leading from Brownsville to Harrisburgh from the north side of a field called Williams to Harrisburgh and that Ichabod Herrins hands, John Williams , Quinny Graddy, James Nimrod, three Robt Axley, James Darris, John Morgan, John Y.Taylors hands, and Howell Taylors be subject to work under him as such in keeping the same in repair
Iss'd 19th Sept.

Ordered by court a majority of the acting justices being present that Wm.H.Henderson register be allowed the sum of ten dollars and fifty cents for registering eight deeds of trust for lots in the town of Brownsville and that the county trustee pay the same out of any monies not otherwise appropriated which shall be a good voucher in the settlement of his accounts

Ordered by court a majority of the acting justices being present that Robert Burns be appointed overseer of the road leading from Harrisburgh in a direction to Bolivar as far as this county line and that all the hands residing east of the road leading from Col.Richard Nixons to Harrisburgh (except Wm.Weddle, Levi Guardner, Wm. Terrel, Jonathan T.Jacocks, Elick Bryan, and Wm. Baricroft, and north of the section line road together with the hands of Bowen Reynolds, Charles White, Thomas Crutcher Vincent Haralson, Tobias Henderon, Joshua Kelly, James Henderson, Fifer Kelly and Jedediah Cusick be subject to work under him as such in opening the same-
Issued, 19th Septr.

Turner Shearrin one of the securities to the bond of Wm. Sharrin guardian being under age at the time of signing the same having now arrive at the age of twenty one years come into open court and acknowledged the same-

(p-152) On motion of E.Roddy and Wm. Hanner by their attorney. It is ordered by the court that the order for partition in this case be extended and that John A.King be substituted in place of Benja- Boothe one of the commissioners, and that John Murray be stricken out of the order, who was in the former order-and that they make report of their proceedings to the next term of this court-
Issued

(p-152con.) Thomas G.Nixon who has been summoned as a juror to attend at this term is exonorated thereform by order of the court-

Ordered that the clerk of this court receive lists of taxable property & poles for the present year from those who have failed to give in until the first day of October next together with the taxes due thereon for the said year and pay the same over to the sheriff and collector.

Ordered that Hardy L.Blackwell be appointed overseer of the road leading from Harrisburgh to the county line in a direction to Trenton in place of Azariah Thompson (resigned) and that all the hands east of the range line that runs near Charles Worthams Esqr. work under him as such on said road.
Issued 12 Septr.

On motion and petition filed   It is ordered by the court,Britain H.Sanders, Nelson Hargrove, George Watts, John Marbery, Henry McCoy, Alexander D.Gordon , Herndon Haralson or any five of them be appointed a jury to view mark and select a road the nearest and best way from the town of Brownsville in a direction to Fulton and Covington so far as may be expedient to make one road answer for both places, and from the point where they should separate to mark a road of continuance into either of said roads as the case may be as for as this county line and make report of their proceedings to the next term of this court-
Iss'd 19th Sept.

Charles Wortham Esquire one of the numbers of this court handed in his resignation as such which is accordingly received-

A Deed of Bargain and sale from Henry A.Powell to Wm. H.Henderson for one hundred and forty eight acres of land was this day produced in open court and duly acknowledged and ordered to be certified for registration
certified

(p-153) On motion and petition filed, it is ordered by the court a majority of the acting justices being present that Lawrence McGuire Esqr Julius Sanders, Green L.Haralson, James Clark, Robert Sanders, Thomas West, Henndon Haralson, Angus Colquehoun, Gideon Pace Esqr. Wm. Balch or any five of them be appointed a Jury of view to lay off and mark a road in continuation from Brownsville so as to cross Hatchie River at the best place near the bluff or Nixon landing and extend the same to Fayette County line on a direction to Summerville and that they make report of their proceedings to the next term of this court.
Iss'd 19th Septr. 1827

Ordered by court a majority of the acting Justices being present that James Jackson Malichi Jackson, Jesse Jackson, Whitehurst and Enos Coxe, be added to the hands already allotted to Bignal Crook overseer of the road leading from Joel Esteses to Everytts or pains Ferry to assist in opening and keeping the same in repair
Iss'd 19th Septr.

A Deed of Bargain and sale from Jonathan Jones senr. to Wm. H.

(p-153con.) Henderson for three town lots no. 121, 119 & 94 was this day produced in open court and duly proven by the oaths of M.H.Bradford and James Smith subscribing witnesses thereto and ordered to be certified for registration.

A Deed of Bargain and sale from Julius Sanders, Edmond Richmond and John W.Cooke to Abraham Phillips for fifteen hundred acres of land was this day produced in open court and duly acknowledged and ordered to be certified for registration.
Certified

Ordered by the court a majority of the acting justices being present that Thos. G.Nixon be allowed the sum of seven dollars and twenty cents the amount of the county tax for the last two years paid for the taxes due on a tract of land formerly in the name of Robert Dennet It appearing to the satisfaction of the court that there is no such tract and that the county trustee pay the same out of any monies not otherwise appropriated which shall be good in the settlement of his accounts.
Iss'd

(p-154) Ordered by the court a majority of the acting Justices being present that Thomas G.Nixon be released from the payment of the state & county tax on six hundred and forty acres of land formerly in the name of Robert Dennit for the present year and that the sheriff and collector be allowed a credit for said amount.
Iss'd Feb. 8 ,

Ordered by the court that until twelve o'clock tomorrow be set apart for county business and that the same be advertised.

The court then adjourned until nine o'clock tomorrow morning

                              Danl Cherry
                              Gideon Pace
                              L.McGuire

Tuesday morning September 11th 1827 the court met according to adjournment . Present the worshipful Daniel Cherry, Lawrence McGuire, Gideon Pace and others their fellow Justices of the peace.

Ordered by the court that Henry Welsh and Mason F.Johnston jurors to the present term be exonorated and discharge from serving as such-

A Deed of B argain and sale from David Jeffreys to Johnathan Hallowell for two hundred and twenty four acres of land was this day produced in open court and duly proven by the oaths of John H.Brown and Aa Tison subscribing witnesses thereto and ordered to be certified for registration.
certified & Del'd

Ordered by court a majority of the acting justices being present that Malcomb Johnston, Dempsey Pace, Will Fitzgerald, Wm. Balch, Wm. Lawrence, Thomas Blythe, Benjamin Wilks or any five of them be appointed a jury to view mark and lay of a road, from this town to the town of

(p-154con.) Bolivar as far as this county line, turning out the new road now ordered to be viewed from this place to Summerville near Big Hatchie river on the south side and runing thence to Hardeman County line so as to meet the road on that line leading to Bolivar and make report of their proceeding to the next term of this court-
Iss'd 19th Septr.

(p-155) John G.Carithers Esquire sheriff by his deputy Reuben Allphin makes return of the venire facias returnable to the court that he has summoned all the persons therein named (except John Williams and James Clarke) who were appointed by our said county court to serve as Jurors at the present term of this court. That is to say Samuel Conyers, John Sanderlin, Wm. Johnston senr. Wm. Hollingsworth, Francis M.Wood, James F.Wortham, John Williams senr. Henry Welsh, William Shearrin, James Clark Isaac Edwards, John Roddy, Thos. Potter, James Maldin, Thos . G. Nixon, Mason F.Johnston, Samuel Brown, Willis Holland , Robert T.Smith Francis L.Dilliard, Mansfield Ware, Eli Jones, Thomas West, Henry McCoy John McWhite, and Ezekiel Blackshire be summoned to attend at the next term of this court on Tuesday after the second Monday on September next then and there to serve as grand or petit, Jurors as the case may be and that Cato Freeman be also summoned to attend this court as constable.

Test B.H.Sanders,Clk.

State of Tennessee
        To the sherriff of Haywood County greeting- You are hereby commanded to summon the aforesaid persons to serve as jurors at the next court of pleas and quarter sessions to be held at the courthouse in the town of Brownsville on the Tuesday after the second Monday in September next and this they shall in no wise omit under the penalty perscribed by law and have you then and there this writ, witness Britain H.Sanders clerk of our said court at office the 2nd Monday in June A.D.1827 and 51st year of American Independence

B.H.Sanders, clk-

Whereupon was the following indorsement (to wit) I have summoned all the within named persons except John Williams & James Clark, August 11th 1827

Reubin Alphin D.
Shff.

Out of the venire facias returnable to this court the following named persons good and lawful men viz, Thos. Potter foreman Willis Holland Samuel Conner, Wm. Johnston senr. Isaac Edwards, Francis, M. Wood, Samuel Brown, William Shearrin, John Roddy John McWhite, Eli Jones, Thos West, and James Maldin were drawn elected tried and sworn and after receiving their charge retired under the charge of Cato Freeman const sworn to attend them, to consider of presentments-

(p-156) Robert Hammil   )
            vs   ) Appeal
        Ezekiel Blackshire)

(p-156con.) This day came the parties by their attorneys and thereupon came a jury of good and lawful men, to wit George R.Watts, Julius Sanders, Clemment T.Walker , Nathan Williamson, Benjamin Rowland, John Sanderlin Robert T.Smith, John Rodgers, David Allen, Enos Coxe , Joseph Murphy and Harry Womble, who being elected tried and sworn to try the matters in dispute between the parties upon their oaths do say that they find the matters in dispute in favor of the ptff. and assess the plaintiff damages to nine dollars & twenty five cents-
Iss'd 21st Sept.

It is therefore considered by the court that the plaintiff recover of the defendant and on motion & Donald McLeod his securities in the appeal the debt aforesaid by the jury aforesaid in form aforesaid assessed and also his costs by him about his suit in this behalf expended and the defendant in mercy etc.

William Bevins)
        vs   ) Appeal
Francis Lemoyn)

This day came the parties by their attorneys and thereupon came a jury of good and lawful men to wit Julius Sanders Clemment T.Walker, Nathan Williamson Benjamin Rowland, John Sanderlin, Robert T.Smith John Rodgers, Joseph Murphy, David Allen Enos Cox Henry Womble and Thomas Rutherford who being elected tried and sworn to try the matters in dispute between the parties upon their oaths do say they find the matters in dispute in favour of the plaintiff and do assess his damages to nine dollars and thirty cents-
It is therefore considered by the court that the said plaintiff recover of the said defendant the sum of nine dollars and thirty cents the damage aforesaid by the jury aforesaid in form aforesaid assessed and his costs by him about his suit in this behalf expended and the defendant in mercy etc. from which Judgt. the deft. hath payed an appeal to the Circuit Court.
Benjamin Noaks constable this day handed in his resignation as such which was accordingly received
Transcript 13th Octr. 1827

The court then proceeded to elect a constable in Capt. Edwards company whereupon after counting the votes James Story was declared duly and constitutionally elected and entered into bond which John Roddy and Isaac Edward his securities and took the necessary oaths of office.

(p-157) This day Joshua Brunson produced in open court the scalp of a wolf over the age of four months and proved the killing of the same within the bounds of this county by his own oath he having no other evidence whereby he could prove the same- It is therefore ordered by the court that the clerk certify the same to the treasurer of West Tennessee accordingly,certified fee not paid,

J. Wilson)
    vs   ) Appeal
Wm.R.Hess)

This day came the parties by their attorneys and thereupon came a jury of good and lawful men to wit, Julius Samders, Clemment T.Walker,

(p-157con.) Nathan Williamson Benjamin Rowland, John Sanderlin
Robert T.Smith John Rogers Joseph Murphy   David Allen, Enos Coxe,
Harvy Womble and Thomas Rutherford who being elected tried and sworn to
try the matters in dispute between the parties upon their oaths do say
they find the matters in dispute in favour of the plaintif and do assess
his damages to sixteen dollars eleven eleven ½ cents besides costs   It
is therefore considered by the that the said plaintiff recover of the sd.
defendant and on motion of Britain H.Sanders his security in the appeal
s̶a̶i̶d̶/̶p̶l̶a̶i̶n̶t̶i̶f̶f̶/̶r̶e̶c̶o̶v̶e̶r̶/̶o̶f̶ ̶t̶h̶e̶ ̶s̶d̶/̶ ̶d̶e̶f̶e̶n̶d̶a̶n̶t̶ ̶&̶ ̶o̶n̶/̶m̶o̶t̶i̶o̶n̶ ̶o̶f̶/̶B̶r̶i̶t̶a̶i̶n̶/̶H̶/̶
S̶a̶n̶d̶e̶r̶s̶/̶h̶i̶s̶ ̶s̶e̶c̶u̶r̶i̶t̶y̶ ̶i̶n̶/̶t̶h̶e̶ ̶a̶p̶p̶e̶a̶l̶ the sum of sixteen dollars eleven
and a half cents the damage aforesaid by the Jury aforesaid in form
aforesaid   assessed and his costs by him about his suit in this behalf
expended and the defendant in mercy etc-
Iss'd 21st Sept.

Parrish & McAlovan)
         vs   ) Debt
Thomas Rutherford   )

        This day came the parties by their attorneys and thereupon came a
jury of good and lawful men (to wit, Benjamin King, Ezekiel Blackshire
George Ables, James Russell, Francis Lamoyn, Phillip Koonce, John R.
McGuire, Robert Hammel Delany White Nathan Bridgman John Storms and
Robert Warren who being elected tried and sworn to try the matters in
dispute upon their oaths do say that the defendant hath not paid the debt
of eighty dollars and forty four cents in the declaration mentioned as
the plaintiff in replying to the defendant pleas hath alledged and do
assess the plaintiffs damages by reason of the detention thereof to two
dollars and twenty five cents besides (p-158) costs. It is therefore
considered by the court that the plaintiff recover of the defendant his
debt aforesaid together with the damages aforesaid by the Jury aforesaid
in form aforesaid assessed and his costs by him about his suit in this
behalf expended and the defendant in mercy etc.
transcript 15 Oct. 1827

Parrish & McAlovan)
         vs   ) Debt
Thomas G.Nixon   )

        This day came the parties by their attorney and thereupon came a
jury of good and lawful men to wit Benjamin King Ezekiel Blackshire,
George Ables, James Russell, Frances Lamoyn, Phillip Koonce, John R.
McGuire, Robert Hammell Delany Whites Nathan Bridgmen, John Storms,and
Robert Warren who being elected tried and sworn to try the matters in
dispute upon their oaths do say that the defendant hath not paid the
debt of fifty six dollars and fifty seven cents in the declaration
mentioned, as the plaintiff in replying to the defendants plea hath alledged and do assess the plaintiffs damages by reason of the detention
thereof to one dollar sixty two and a half cents besides costs, It is
therefore considered by the court that the plaintiff recover of the said
defendant his debt aforesaid together with the damages aforesaid by the
jury aforesaid in form aforesaid assessed and his costs by him about his
suit in this behalf expended and the defendant in mercy etc. from which
judgment the defendant have prayed and obtained an appeal to the Circuit

(p-158con.) Court he having entered into bond as the law directs
Transcript 15th of Octor.1827

Wm.Stoddert to the use)
of J.Currin   )
       vs   ) Debt
Blackman Coleman

This day came the parties by their attorneys and thereupon came a
jury of good and lawful men to wit, Benjamin King, Ezekial Blackshire,
George Ables, James Russell, Francis Lemoyn, Phillip Koonce, John R.
McGuire, Robert Hammell. Delany Whites, Nathan Bridgmen, John Storms and
Robert Warren who being elected tried & sworn to try the matters in dispute upon their oaths do say that the defendant hath not paid the debt
of fifty eight dollars and seventy six cents in the declaration mentioned as the plaintiff in replying to the defendants plea (p-159) hath
alledged and do assess the plaintiffs damages by reason of the detention
thereof to eight dollars and forty six cents besides costs. It is therefore considered by the court that the plaintiff recover of the said defendant his debt aforesaid together with the damages aforesaid by the Jury
aforesaid in form aforesaid assessed and also his costs about his suit
in this behalf expended and the defendant in mercy etc-
Transcript 16th Octr. 1827

Parrish & McAlovan   )
       vs   ) Debt
Blackman Coleman   )

This day came the parties by their attorneys and thereupon came
a jury of good and lawful men to wit Benjamin King, Ezekial Blackshire
George Ables, James Russell, Francis Lemoyn, Phillip Koonce, John R.
McGuire Robert Hammill, Delany Whites Nathan Bridgmen, John Storms and
Robert Warren who being elected tried and sworn to try the matters
in dispute upon their oaths do say that the defendant hath not paid the
debt of seventy six dollars & nineteen cents in the declaration mentioned
as the plaintiff in replying to the defendant plea hath alledged and
do assess the plaintiffs damages by reason of the detention thereof to
one dollar and ninety cents besides costs. It is therefore considered by
the court that the plaintiff recover of the said defendant his debt aforesaid together with his damages aforesaid by the Jury aforesaid in form
aforesaid assessed and also his costs above his suit in this behalf
expended and the defendant in mercy etc.
Transcript 16th Octr. 1827

Henry M.Rutledge)
       vs   ) Covenant
Blackman Coleman)

This day came the parties by their attorneys and thereupon came
a Jury of good and lawful men, to wit) Benjamin King, Ezekiel
B lackshire, George Ables, James Russell Francis Lemoyn Phillip Koonce,
John R.McGuire, Robert Hammill, Denany White, Nathan Bridgmen, John
Storms, and Robert Warren who being elected tried and sworn the truth to
speak upon the issue joined upon their oaths do say that the defendant
hath not performed his covenant as on pleading he hath alleged and assess
the plaintiffs damages by reason   therein/ (p-160) of the non

(p-160con.) performance of the covenant in the said declaration
mentioned and they assess the plaintiffs damage one hundred and two
dollars and fifty cents besides costs. It is therefore considered by
*the court here that the plaintiff do recover against the defendant the
Jury aforesaid in form aforesaid assessed and his costs in this behalf
expended and the defendant in mercy etc.
Transcript 17 Octr. 1827

Mansfield Wane)
    vs   ) Debt
John R.Leigh)

    This day came the parties by their attorneys and thereupon came
a jury of good and lawful men, to wit, B enjamin King, Ezekial
Blackshire, George Ables, James Russell, Francis Lemoyn, Phillip Koonce
John R.McGuire, Robert Hammill Delany White Nathanl Bridgmen, John
Storms and Robert Warren, who being elected tried & sworn to try the
matters in dispute upon their oaths do say that the defendant hath not
paid the debt of one hundred dollars in the declaration mentioned as
the plaintiff in replying to the defendants plea hath alledged and do
assess the plaintiffs damages by reason of the detention thereof to
four dollars and fifty cents besides cost. It is therefore considered
by the court here that the plaintiff recover of the said defendant his
debt aforesaid together with her damages aforesaid by the Jury aforesaid
in form aforesaid assessed and also his costs by him about his suit in
this behalf expended, and the defendant in mercy etc. stayed by consent
of the plff. until the first day of January next-

William Lamb)
    vs   )
John Marbery)

    This day came the plaintiff by his attorney and thereupon came
also a jury of good and lawful men to wit, Benjamin King, Ezekial
Blackshire, George Ables, James Russell, Francis Lamoin, Phillip
Koonce, John R.McGuire, Robert Hammell, Delany White, Nathan Bridgmen
John Storms, and Robert Warren who being sworn deligently to inquire
of damage in this suit on their oaths do say that the plaintiff hath
sustained damages by reason of the defendants breach of covenant in the
declaration mentioned to one hundred and thirty dollars besides his
costs, therefore it is considered by the court that the plaintiff recover
against the said defendant one hundred and thirty dollars the damages
aforesaid by the jury aforesaid in (p-161) form aforesaid assessed
and his costs by him about his suit in this behalf expended and the defendant in mercy etc.
Iss'd 21th Septr.

William Lamb)
    vs   )
John Marbery)

    This day came the plaintiff by his attorneys and thereupon came a
jury of good and lawful men (to wit) Benjamin King, Ezekial Blackshire,
George Ables, James Russell, Francis Lemoyn, Phillip Koonce, John R.
McGuire, Robert Hammell, Delana Whites Nathan Bridgmen, John Storms and
* damages aforesaid by the

(p-161con.) and Robert Warren who being elected tried and sworn
deligenly to inquire of Damages in this suit on their on oaths do say
that the plaintiff hath sustained damages by reason of the defendants
breach of the covenant in the declaration mentioned to one hundred and
three dollars besides costs, Therefore it is considered by the court
that the plaintiff recover against the said defendant one hundred dollars
and three dollars the damages aforesaid by the jury aforesaid aforesaid
in form aforesaid assessed and his costs by him about his suit in this
behalf expended and the defendant in mercy etc.
Iss'd 21st Sept.

Robert A.Penn for)
the use of John T.)
Turner   ) Debt-writing obligatory files under the act
    vs   )
Francis L.Dillard) of assembly

        This day came the parties by their attornies and thereupon came
a jury of good and lawful men, to wit, Benjamin King, Ezekial Blackshire
George Ables, James Russell, Francis Lemoyn, Philip Koonce, John R.
McGuire, Robert Hammell Delany Whites. Nathan Bridgeman, John Storms
and Robert Warrer, who being elected tried and sworn the truth to speak
upon the issue joined open their oath do say that they find the issue in
favor of the plaintiff that the defendant hath not paid the balance of
the debt of one hundred and twenty two dollars in the said writing
obligatory mentioned as the plaintiff by replying to the defendants
plea hath alledged, and do assess the plaintiff damages to twelve dollars and eighty cents besides costs. It is therefore considered by the
court that the plaintiff recover of the said Defendant the debt aforesaid
together with the damages aforesaid by the jury aforesaid in for aforesaid
assessed and his costs by him about his suit in this behalf expended etc-
Transcript 18th Octr. 1827

(p-162) Truisdale & Smith)
            vs   ) Case
      Julius & Robert   )
      Sanders   )
      of the defendants

        Continued on Julius Sanders one of the defendants.

Wm. Arnold   )
    vs   ) Assumsit
John R.& Thos J.McGuire)

        Continued by consent 2nd day of the term

Robert Sanders   )
    vs   ) Case
James A.Moore & others)

        The death of James A.Moore one of the defendants suggested.

(p-162con.) Robert Williams)
              vs   )   Trespass on the Case
         Nathan Bridgman   )   Continued on affidavit
         of the plaintiff   )

Britain H.Sanders)
        vs   )   Assumsit
Bennet R.Butter   )   Continued as on affidavit of the plaintiff

      he paying the costs of this continuance

Wm. P.Gains & others)
        vs   )   Trespass on the case
Joel Estis   )

      Continued as on affidavit of the defendant

      The court then adjourned until tomorrow nine o'clock-
                              Dan'l. Cherry
                              Gideon Pace
                              L.McGuire

(p-163) Wednesday morning September 12th 1827 the court met according
to adjournment present the worshipful Lawrence McGuire, Daniel Cherry,
Gideon Pace Esquires-

Robert A.Penn for the   )
use of John T.Turner   )
        vs   )
Frances L.Dillard   )

      In this case the defendant hath prayed and obtained an appeal to
the Circuit Court of this county the having entered into bond as the
law directs.

Parrish & McAlovan)
        vs   )
Thos. Rutherford   )

      This day the defendant hath prayed and taken an appeal to th
Circuit Court of the county he having entered into bond as the law
      directs.

      Reubin Alphin constable produced bill of costs of forty three
dollars and eighteen and three fourth cents in open court and proved
by his own oath the justices of the same wherein the state of Tennessee
is plaintiff and Elijah Bradbery is defendant and it appearing that the
defendant was released, at the expence of the county- It is therefore
ordered by the court that the county trustee pay the same out of any
monies not othe wise appropriated which shall be good in the settlement
of his acts.
Issued 19th Septr.

(p-163con.)   State of Tennessee)
        vs   )
    James Haggard of   )   Continued as on affidavit
    Defts. council

State of Tennessee)
    vs   ) Continued by consent
Thos. J.Smith   )

State of Tennessee)
    vs   )
Stephen Childres) Pluris Capias issue to next term
)

Iss'd

State of Tennessee)
    vs   )
Jourdan Hansborough) Continued by consent

(p-164) A power of attorney from Wm. M Edwars to Benja W.Edwards was
this day produced in open court and duly acknowledged for the purposes
therein contained.

   A power of attorney from Wm. Fitzgerald to Obediah Fitzgerald
was this day produced in open court and duly acknowledged for the
purposes therein contained.

State of Tennessee)
    vs   )
William Sawyers)

   This day came Alexander B.Bradford who prosecutes in behalf of
the state and moves the court that a nole prosqui be entered whereupon
with the assent of the court it is ordered accordingly. It is therefore
considered by the court that the defendant go hence without day & recover
of the State of Tennessee his costs about his defence in this behalf
expended whereupon it is ordered by the court that the county pay the
costs of this prosecution.

The State of Tennessee)
     vs   )
  Lee H.Burks   )

   This day the defendant by his attorney and saith that he is
guilty in manner and form as charged in the bill of indictment, and
submits to the grace and mercy of the court. It is therefore considered
by the court that the defendant make his fine with the State of Tennessee
by the payment of five dollars & all costs & that he be taken etc.
Iss'd 21st Sept. 1827

State of Tennessee)
    vs   )
William R.Hess   )

   This day came the defendant in his proper person & being charged
saith that he is guilty in manner and form as charged saith that he is

(p-164con.) guilty in manner and form as charged in the bill of
Indictment and puts himself upon the grace and mercy of the court
It is therefore considered by the court that the said defendant make
his fine with the state of Tennessee of the payment of one dollar & the
costs in this behalf expended etc.
Iss'd 22nd Septr.

The State of Tennessee)
       vs)
Thomas J.McGuire)

    This day came the defendant by his attorney and being charged
saith that he is guilty in manner and form as charged in the bill of
Indictment and puts himself upon the grace and mercy of the court. It
is therefore considered by the court that the defendant make his fine
with the state by the payment of one dollar and all costs in this behalf expended & that he be taken etc.
Iss'd 22nd Septr.

(p-165) The State of Tennessee)
        vs
    John R.McGuire)

    This day came the defendant in his proper person being solemnly
charged saith that he is guilty in manner of form as charged in the
bill of Indictment & puts himself upon the grace and mercy of the
court. It is therefore considered by the court that said defendant
make his fine with the State of Tennessee by the payment of one dollar
& all costs in this behalf expended & that he be taken etc.
Iss'd 22nd Septr.

Berry Dearing)
    vs)
Benjamin Noake)

    Joel Estes & Samuel P.Ashe, the arbitrators to whom was referred
the matters in dispute between the parties ,this day returned their
award as follows Having been appointed by the court of pleas & quarter
sessions for Haywood County to settle the several accounts between the
parties B.Dearing vs Benjamin Noakes we have determined and settled that
there is a balance due Berry Dearing of twenty three dollars & seventy
four cents.
    In confirmation whereof it is considered by the court that the
said plaintiff do recover against the said defendant the said sum of
twenty three dollars and seventy four cents and all costs in this behalf
expended & the defendant in mercy etc.
Iss'd 21 Septr. 1827

(p-166) State of Tennessee
        vs)
    Benjamin Noakes & his)
    securities T.J. McGuire &) Copias ad satisfacidum
    Caleb Goodman

(p-166con.) Whereas a copias ad satisfaciendam issued from the court of pleas and quarter sessions of Haywood County, dated the 27th June, 1827, returnable to the present term of this court for the sum of twenty three dollars and eighty cents, against the body of the said Benjamin Noakes, which said writ is returned executed with a bond dated the 7th day of July 1827, for the personal appearance of the said Benjamin Noaks signed by the said Thomas J. McGuire and Caleb Goodmen and seated with their seals conditioned as the law directs in such case made and provided and the said Benjamin Noaks be called to make payment of the said sum of twenty three dollars and eighty cents surrender a schedule of his property or take the oath of insolvent debters, came not but made default- It is therefore considered by the court that the said plaintiff recover of the said Defendants the said sum of twenty three dollars and eighty cents the amount of the said capias and satisfaction and her costs by her about her suit in this behalf expended etc.
Iss'd 22 Sept. 1827

William Stoddart-)
of J. Currin)
    vs)
B. Coleman)

    The Defendant hath prayed & obtained an appeal to the Circuit Court, He having given bond & security to prosecute the same.

Parrish & McAlovan)
    vs)
B. Coleman)

    The defendant hath prayed & obtained an appeal to the Circuit Court. He having given bond & security etc.

Henry M. Rutletge)
    vs)
B. Coleman)

    The defendant hath prayed and obtained an appeal to the Circuit Court. He having given bond & security etc.

(p-167) State of Tennessee)
    vs)
    John Young) Capias Assatis-faciendum

    John Young the Defendant comes into open court and brings with him a schedule of his property which is ordered to be received and filed whereupon he makes oath that the said schedule contains full time time and perfect statement of all his worldly effects etc. according to the act of-1811 chapter 4th section 3d and in conformity with the provisions of the act of 1824 chapter 17 whereupon it is ordered that his body be released and because there is nothing contained in said schedule out of which any money can be made by sale- It is ordered by the court that the costs be paid by the county trustee out of any monies not otherwise appropriated.

(p-167con.) State of Tennessee)
                     vs   )   Ca Sa
)
        Peter Langford   )

Peter Langford comes here into open court and thereupon in discharge of his body took the oath made and provided for Insolvent Debtors whereupon it is ordered that his body be released from custody. It is therefore ordered by the court that the costs in this case be paid by the county trustee out of any publick monies in his hands not otherwise appropriated

Ordered by the court that Wilie Dodd have time given him until the next term of this court to pay the fine & costs assessed and accrued against him heretofore for trespass assault & Battery for which a Ca Sa has issued against his body returnable to this court.

Ordered by the court that John Roddy be appointed overseer of the road leading from Ashes Mill to Tipton County line and that him and Samuel P. Ashe overseer of the other road divide the hands between themselves.
Issued 19th Septr.

(p-168) Ordered by the court that Lewis Foscue be released from the payment of taxes for the present year and that he be striken from the Tax list.

This day Elizabeth Jackson administratrix of Jesse Jackson Dec'd. made return of an Inventory and an account of sales of said Dec'd which is accordingly received and ordered to recorded and filed.

Mansfield Wane)
      vs   ) Motion to Dismiss
Mathew Ray   ) Certiorari

On motions of the plaintiff to dismiss the certiorari and upon argument being had thereon, it is considered by the court here that the motion be sustained and on motion of the plaintiff, it is considered by the court here that the plaintiff recover against the Defendant his costs in this behalf expended etc.

It is ordered by the court that the following persons be summoned to attend at the next Circuit Court of Haywood County, then and there to serve as grand or petit jurors as the case may be to wit, Samuel P. Ashe, Joseph Murphy, Richard Nixon, Jonathan F.Jacocks, Daniel Cherry, David Allen, Henry McCoy, Robt. F.Smith, Alexander D.Gordon, James Malden, Robert Perry, Thomas Crutcher, Henndon Harrelson, Richard Taylor Isaac Koonce James Henderson, Joshua Abstain, Charles White Vincent Harralson, Bowen Reynolds Griffith Edwards William Morrison, John Marberry, Joseph Swift, Nicholas T.Perkins and Hyrum Bradford and that a venire facias issue accordingly and that James Story a constable be summoned to attend at said court as constable .

It is ordered by the court that Thomas G.Nixon, Philip Koonce, John Potter, Nelson Hargrove, George Able, James Jackson, Berry Deering, Jessee Jackson, Robert Hammell, Julius Sanders, Benjamin King, L.D.

(p-168con.) Womble, Eli Pharis, John Williams Senr. Levi Gardner, William Weddle, James H.Wortham, Jonathan Hollowell, William Jackson, Phillip A.Bruce, Harvy Womble, James Russell, Harman Frazier, John A. Key, James Scott, Nathaniel D.Lilly be summoned (p-169) to attend at the next court of pleas and quarter sessions of this county, then and there serve as grand or petit jurors as the case may be and that Cato Freeman be also summoned to attend at said court as constable.

The Grand jury returned into court a bill of presentment the State of Tennessee vs Herndon Harralson overseer of the road and there appearing no further business are discharged from further service.

Court adjourned until court in course.

B.Coleman J.P.
M.Ray, J.P.
L.McGuire

(p-170) State of Tennessee- At a court of pleas and quarter sessions began and held for the county of Haywood at the courthouse in the town of Brownsville on the second Monday in December in the year of our Lord one thousand eight hundred and twenty seven it being the 10th day of said month, present the worshipful Richard Nixon, Blackman Coleman, Nicholas T.Perkins, Lawrence McGuire, and others their fellow justices of the peace, John G.Carithers sheriff and Britain H.Sanders clerk-

A Deed of Bargain and sale from Archibald D.Murphy to Robert Hughs for five hundred acres of land was this day produced in open court and admitted to registration, it having the seal of the state of north Carolina thereon etc.

A Deed of Bargain and sale from Joseph T.Haralson to Richard T.Moore for one hundred acres of land was this day produced in open court and duly proven by the oaths of John P.Majors and Robert Burns subscribing witnesses thereto and ordered to be certified for registration.

On sufficient cause being shown to the court it is ordered by the same that William Lawrence be authorized to keep an ordinary at his house in the town of Brownsville for the term of twelve months he having entered into bond together with Reubin Alphin and Henry West his securities-

Ordered by court a majority being present that Blackman Coleman clerk of the Circuit Court of this county be allowed the sum of twenty dollars for Blank Books purchased etc. as pr. act. filed and that the county trustee pay the same out of any monies in his hands not otherwise appropriated which shall stand good in the settlement of his accounts Copy issued

Ordered by the court that letters of administration be granted to Mrs. Eliza H.Leigh (consort of the late John R.Leigh dead and Thomas G.Nixon, and that they have during this term to appear and give bond etc.

Ordered by the court that Andrew Hammels stock mark be recorded as follows to wit, a smooth crop of the left ear and a underbit in the right.

(p-170con.) Ordered by the court that the commissions heretofore appointed to divide the land of John Earle Dec'd between Roddy Hanner, & others, have until next term to make their report of said division it appearing to the satisfaction of court that the high water has prevented at the present term

(p-171) John T.Turner is this day appointed guardian to his wife Jane N.Turner (formerly Jane N.Fort) who gave bond and security as the law directs.

Benjamin Boothe this day produced in open court the scalp of a wolf over the age of four months and proved the killing of the same within the bounds of this county- It is therefore ordered by the court that the clerk certify the same to the treasurer of West Tennessee accordingly.
Issued, to D.C.

Ordered by court that Lawrence McGuire, Julius Sanders, Green L. Haralson, James Clark, Robert Sanders, Thomas West, Herndon Haralson, Angus Colquehaun, Gideon Pace, and William Balch or any five of them be appointed a jury of view to mark and lay of a road in continuation from Brownsville so as to cross Hatchie River at the best place near the bluffs or Nixons landing and extend the same to Fayette County line on a direction to Summerville and that they make report of their proceedings to the next term of this court.
Iss'd 20th Decr.

Ordered by the court that Malcomb Johnston, Demsey Pace, William Fitzgerald, Wm. Balch, Wm. Lawrence, Thomas Blythe and Benjamin Wilks, or any five of them be appointed a jury to view mark and lay of a road from this town to the town of Bolivar as for as this county line, turning out of the new road now ordered to be viewed from this place to summerville near big Hatchie River on the south side and runing thence to Hardeman County line so as to meet the road on that line leading to Bolivar and make report of their proceedings to the next term of this court-
Iss'd 20th Decr.

Ordered by the court that letters of administration be granted to Berry Dearing administrator on the estate of Travis Kindle, he having entered into bond together with John Roddy and John A.Key his securities as such in the penal sum of two hundred dollars

Ordered by the court that Hiram Bradford have letters of administration on the estate of Robert Penn Dec'd he having entered into bond together with William H. Loving and Robert Ferry his securities in the penal sum of ten thousand dollars

(p-172) Ordered by the court a majority of the acting justices being present that Alexander B.Bradford solicitor general be allowed the sum of fifty dollars for his exoficio services and that the county trustee pay the same out of any monies not otherwise appropriated-
Issued 14th decr.

Ordered by the court a majority being present that John G.Carithers

(p-172con.) sheriff be allowed the sum of fifty dollars for his exoficio services and that the county trustee pay the same out of any monies in his hands not otherwise appropriated.
Iss'd 14 Decr.

Ordered by court a majority being present that Britain H. Sanders clerk be allowed the sum of forty dollars for his exoficio services, and the further sum of twenty five dollars for making out Tax list and that the county Trustee pay the same out of any monies not otherwise appropriated.
Iss'd 14th Decr.

State of Tennessee	)	
vs	)	Delinquent
Bignal Crook	)	Juror, scifa

Ordered by the court that Bignal Crook who was heretofore summoned at June term 1827 to appear as a juror be released from the fine imposed he having having shown sufficient cause, and it is further ordered that the county pay the costs thereof-

Ordered by the court that clerk list Richard Hightowers lands for the present year as follows 73½ acres of land in the 11th District first range and sixth section & 95 acres in the 11 District first Range and sixth section-

Ordered by court that William A.Terrells stock mark be recorded as follows to wit, two under bits and two over bits in each ear.

A Deed of Bargain and sale from Daniel P.Perkins attorney in fact for John L.Wheaton for six hundred sixty eight and one fourth acres land, was this day produced in open court and duly proven by the oaths of Mathew Ray and John A.King subscribing witnesses thereto and ordered to be certified for registration.
Certified and delivered Registr

A power of attorney from George W.Hockly one of the executors of Patience Wescott dec'd to William H.Henderson was this day produced in open court and duly proven by the oaths of John Hardwick and John A. King subscribing witnesses thereto and ordered to be certified for registration.
certified and del'd. J.A.King

(p-173 A Deed of bargain and sale from Daniel P.Perkins attorney in fact for John S.Wheaton to Marcus Boyd for three hundred thirty one and three fourth acres of land was this day produced in open court and duly proven in part by the oath of John Young a subscribing witness thereto and ordered to be filed for further probit
certified & Dl.

On motion and petition filed it is ordered by the court a majority being present that Willis C.Holland, Julius Sanders, Allen H.Howard Delany Whitehurst, James Jackson Berry Deering and Nelson Hargrove, be appointed a jury to view mark and lay of a road leading from Paynes ferry on Big Hatchie River to intersect the road leading from McGuires ferry on Big Hatchie River to intersect the road leading from McGuires

(p-173con.) ferry to Brownsville at or near Berry Dearing and make
report of their proceedings to the next term of this court.
Iss'd 20th Decr.

A Deed of Bargain and sale from the commissioners of the town of
Brownsville to Henry Welsh for a certain town town lot known by its
number thirteen was this day produced in open court and duly acknowledged
and ordered to be certified for registered.

A power of attorney from John C.McLemore to William H.Henderson
was this produced in open court and duly proven by the oaths of William
R.Hess and Mathew Ray subscribing witnesses thereto and ordered to be
certified for registration.
certified

```
Winston Harvy to use of  )
John McWhite             )
          vs             )   Alias
Henry L.Gray and Thos.   )   Casa
J. Smith                 )
```

In this case came Henry L.Gray into open court and rendered the
following schedule in words and figures, to wit, one note on John M.
Smith for $60.00 one ditto on Richard W.Nixon for $10.87½ pr on account
on Thos. Stokely with whom there is to be a settlement to make for $60.
on account on John R.McGuire for $65.75 cents with whom there is also to
be a settlement, on account on Monroe P.Estes for $4.12½ cents a receipt
on Jno. G.Carithers for fifty four dollars in the hands of A.S.Gholson
$37.00 of which belongs to said Gholson on account on Samuel Copeland
for $73.00, debts on John Young (run away) $12. 37½ do Henry Wooten
$1.25 Harris $4.00 debts on James McLaughtin do on Robert Lucky $47.62½
debts on Joseph P.Wimberly $13.00 do on Robt. Wallace $1.50 a suit
pending in court between (p-174) the executons of James Cosby and
Henry L.Gray which if decided in my favor will be between sixty and eighty
dollars I think Decr. 10th 1827 signed H.L. Gray- and thereupon took
the oath in that case made and provided for the benefit of insolvent
debtors

Ordered by the court that a part of tomorrow be set apart for the purpose
of transacting county business.

The court then adjourned until tomorrow ten o'clock

                         B.Coleman J.P.
                         N.T.Perkins J.P.
                         Dan'l. Cherrys J.P.

Tuesday morning December the 11th 1827 the court met according to adjournment presentthe worshipful Blackman Coleman Nicholas T.Perkins and
Daniel Cherry Esquires and others their fellow Justices of the peace

Ordered by the court a majority being present that Britain H.
Sanders Nelson Hargrove, George Watts, John Marbery, Henry McCoy,
Alexander D.Gordon & Herndon Haralson or any five of them be appointed
a jury to view mark and select a road the nearest and best way from the
town of Brownsville in a direction to Fulton and Covington so far as

(p-174con.) may be expedient to make one road answer for both places
and from that point where they should separate to mark a road of continuance into either of said road as the case may be as for as the county
line and make report of their proceedings to the next term of this court.
Iss'd 20th Decr. 1827

Ordered by the court a majority being present that Daniel Cherry
Esqr. be allowed the sum of thirty seven dollars (for work done by Allen
H.Howard on the south end of Lafayette street, and that the county trustee
pay the same out of any monies not otherwise appropriated which shall be
a good voucher in the settlement of his accounts-
Iss'd

Ordered by the court that Nicholas T.Perkins be allowed the sum
of four dollars fifty two and a half cents it being the amount of the
county tax paid by him for a tract of land in the name of (p-175)
Oliver B.Hays for 249 acres. It appearing to the satisfaction of the
court that there is no such tract of land within this county, and that
the county treasurer pay the same out of any monies not otherwise appropriated, which shall be a good voucher in the settlement of his accounts.
Iss'd fees pd.

On motion and petition filed It is ordered by the court a majority
being that Alfred Kennady, Thomas Furgerson, John R.Williams, James Darris
John McWhite, Nimrod Axley, Thomas G.Nixon, Thomas Stokely or any five of
them be appointed a Jury to view lay of and mark a road from Brownsville
in a direction to Dyersburgh as for as the county line having respect to
a line to be run by Lawrence McGuire Esqr. who is hereby authorized and
appointed to run the same and make report of their proceedings to the
next term of this court.
Iss'd 20th Decr. 1827

Ordered by court that George Weddle (former guardian in Williamson
County) be appointed Guardian to Charles H.Prim and Logan D.Prim orphan
children of John Prim dec'd he having entered into bond in the penal sum
of one hundred and fifty dollars together with Levi Gardner and John McWhite
his securities as the law directs-

John G.Carithers sheriff of Haywood County makes return of the writ
of venire facias returnable to the present term in the words and figures
following to wit.
     State of Tennessee
     At a court of pleas and quarter sessions began and held for the
county of Haywood at the courthouse in the town of Brownsville on the
second Monday in September A.D.1827 present the worshipful Daniel Cherry,
Lawrence McGuire , Gideon Pace, Esq. and other their fellow Justices
John G.Carithers, Sheriff by his deputy Reuben Allphin and Britain H.
Sanders clerk. It is ordered by the court that the following persons
good and lawful men vis each being being a white male citizen of the age
of twenty one years and an inhabitant of Haywood County aforesaid, and
a householder (to wit Thomas G.Nixon, Phillip Koonce, John Potter,
Nelson Hargrove, George Ables, James Jackson, Berry Dearing, Jessee Jackson
Robert Hammell, Julius Sanders, Benjamin King, L.D.Womble, Eli Faris, John
Williams senr. Levi Gardner, William Weddle, James H.Wortham Jonathan
Hollowell, William Jackson, Phillip A.Bruce, Harvy Womble, James Russell

(p-176) Harmon Frazier, John A.Key, James Scott and Nathaniel D.Lilly
be summoned to attend at the next term of this court in Tuesday after
the second Monday in December next then and there serve as grand or
petit jurors as the case may be and that Cato Freeman be also summoned
to attend said court as constables-

                                Test B.H.Sanders clk-

        State of Tennessee
                To the sherif of Haywood County greeting- You are hereby
commanded to summons the aforesaid persons to serve as Jurors at the
next court of pleas and quarter sessions to be held at the courthouse
in the town of Brownsville on Tuesday after the second Monday in
December next and this they shall in no wise omit under the penalty prescribed by the law and have you then and there this writ witness Britain
H.Sanders, clerk of our said court at office, the second Monday in
September A.D. 1827 and 52nd year of American Independence.

                                B.H.Sanders, Clk.

        Upon the back of which said writ John G.Carithers sheriff and makes
the following indornment, to wit-
        By virtue of the within venire facias to me directed I have proceed-
ed to summons all the within named persons except Jessee Jackson, L.D.
Womble, William Weddle and Jonathan Hollowell and such persons as
summoned are inhabitants of said county and freeholders or householders
of said county and of the age of twenty one years.

                                John G.Carithers Shff.

        Out of which said venire facias returnable to this court the
following named persons good and lawful men vis Thomas G.Nixon foreman
Phillip A.Bruce, Nathaniel D.Lilly, Levi Gardner Eli Faris, Robert
Hammel , Harvy Womble, John Potter, Nelson Hargrove, James Russell,
Harmon Frazier, Benjamin King and Berry Dearing were drawn elected tried
and sworn and after receiving their charge retired (under the care of
Cato Freeman, constable sworn to attend them,) to consider of presentments

        George Ables and William Jackson who was regularly summoned to
attend as jurors to the present term, having an oath shown sufficient
case, they are exonorated from the present service, durin this term.

        The court adjourned untill tomorrow 9 o'clock

                                L.McGuire J.P.
                                Danl. Cherry J.P.
                                Jona. T.Jacoks J.P.

(p-177) Wednesday morning December the 12th 1827 the court met according to adjournment present the worshipful Daniel Cherry, Lawrence
McGuire, Jonathan T.Jacoks , Esquires and others their fellow justices
of the peace, sheriff and clerk present.

State of Tennessee)
        vs   )   Presentment for Gaming
Stephen Childres   )

(p-177con.) This day came Alexander B.Bradford solicitor genl. who prosecutes in behalf of the state and moves the court that a noli prosequi entered in this cause , whereupon with the assent of the court it is entered accordingly. It is therefore considered by the court that the Defendant go hence without day and recover of the state his costs by him about his defence in this behalf expended, whereupon it is ordered by the court that the county pay the costs of this prosecution.

State of Tennessee   )
  vs   )   Presentment
Thomas J.Smith)

   This case is continued by consent of the solicitor General A.B. Bradford who prosecutes in behalf of the state-

State of Tennessee)
  vs   )   Indictment
Jourdon M.Hansborough)

   This day came Alexander B.Bradford solicitor General who prosecutes in behalf of the state and the defendant in his proper person, who being solemnly charged sayeth he is not guilty in manner and form as charged in the bill of Indictment and for his trial puts himself upon a jury of his county and the solicitor General doth the like, and thereupon came a Jury of good and lawful men (to wit) James Jackson Julius Sanders, Thomas Rutherford, John T.Turner, Samuel Elliott, Alexander Kerksey, Jonathan Weaver, Thomas Fergerson, Benjamin Rowland, Andrew Wolf, Robert Sanders, and Monroe P.Estes, who being elected tried and sworn the truth to speak upon the issue of Traverse joined upon their oaths do say that the defendant is guilty in manner and form as charged in the bill of Indictment. It is therefore considered by the court that the defendant make his fine with the state of Tennessee by the payment of the sum of fifty cents and all costs, and that he be taken etc.
Transcript Issued 12th Jany. 1828

(p-178) State of Tennessee)
     vs   )   Presentment
   Herndon Harralson)

   This day came Alexander B.Bradford solicitor general who prosecutes in behalf of the state, and the defendant in the proper person who sayeth that he is guilty in manner and form as charged in the bill of presentment and puts himself upon the grace and mercy of the court It is therefore considered by the court that the said defendant make his fine with the State of Tennessee by the payment of the sum of one dollar and the costs of suit in this behalf expended, and that he be taken etc.

State of Tennessee)
  vs   )   Presentment
Thomas Stokely)

   This day came Alexander B.Bradford solicitor general who prosecutes in behalf of the state, and the defendant in his proper person who

(p-178con.) sayeth that he is guilty in manner and form as charged in the bill of prsentment and puts himself open the grace and mercy of the court. It is therefore considered by the court that the said defendant make his fine with the State of Tennessee by the payment of the sum of five dollars and the costs of suit in this behalf expended, and that he be taken etc.
Issued, 20th Decr. 1827

State of Tennessee)
    vs   ) Presentment for Gaming
James Haggard)

    This cause is continued by the consent of A.B.Bradford solicitor general who prosecutes in behalf of the state.

Gabriel Minter Exer.)
of James Cosby dec'd) Appeal
    vs   )
Henry L.Gray & M.)
H.Grey

    This day came the parties by their attorneys and thereupon came a jury of good and lawful men to wit, James Jackson Julius Sanders, John A.Key, Thomas Rutherford, Samuel Elliot, Alexander Kirksey Binjamin Rowland, Andrew Wolf, Robert Sanders Monroe P. Estes, Arthur F.McCain & John A.King, who being elected tried and sworn to try the matters in dispute between the parties upon their oaths do say they find the matters in dispute in favour of the defendant, and do assess (p-179) his damages to thirty nine dollars eighteen and three fourths cents besides costs. It is therefore considered by the court that the said defendant recover of the said plaintiffs the sum of thirty nine dollars eighteen and three fourth cents the damages aforesaid by the Jury aforesaid in form aforesaid assessed and his costs by him about his defence in this behalf expended and the plaintiff in mercy etc. Iss'd 27 Decr.

    Ordered by the court by the court that Hiram Bradford Mathew Ray, and James Smith be appointed commissioners to settle with Richard Nixon, Esquire county treasurer and John G.Carithers, sheriff of Haywood County for the year 1826 & 1827 agreeable to an act of assembly in that case made and provided and make report thereof to the next term of this court.

    Ordered by court that Herndon Haralson and Hiram Bradford be appointed to settle with the county and Circuit Court clerks agreeable to an act of assembly in that case made and provided.

William Arnold)
    vs   ) Assembly
John R.& Thos.J.McGuire)

    This cause is continued by the consent of the parties council

State of Tennessee)
    vs   ) Casa
Thomas Stokely)

(p-179con.) Ordered by the court that the defendant in this case have indulgence until the next term of this court for the payment of the same.

Gabriel Minter exor. of)
James Cosby dec'd   )
           vs   )   appeal
Henry L.Gray   )

This day came the parties by their attorneys and thereupon came a jury of good and lawful men to wit, James Jackson, Julius Sanders, John A.Key, Thomas Rutherford Samuel Elliot, Alexander Kirksey Benjamin Rowland, Andrew Wolf, Robert Sanders, Monroe P.Estes, Arthur F.McCain and John A.King who being elected tried and sworn to try the matters in dispute upon their do say they in favour of the (p-180) defendant Therefore it is considered by the court that the plaintiff take nothing of the defendant but for his false claims be in mercy etc. and that the Defendant go hence without day and recover of the plaintiff his costs by him about his defence in this behalf expended-

Trousdale & Smith   )
        vs   )   Case
Julius Sanders &   )
Robert Sanders

This day came the parties by their attorneys and thereupon came a jury of good and lawful men to wit James Jackson, John A.Key, Thomas Rutherford, Alexander Kirksey, Benjamin Rowland, Andrew Wolf, Monroe P.Estes, Arthur F.McCain, John A.King, William C. Bruce, Allen J. Barbee and Samuel Elliot who being elected tried and sworn to try the matters in dispute upon their oath do say that the defendant hath not paid the debt of one hundred and ninety eight dollars and seventy seven cents the ballance of the debt in the declaration mentioned as the plaintiff in replying to the defendants plea hath alleged and do assess the plaintiffs damages by reason of the detention thereof to eight dollars and seventy five cents besides costs. It is therefore considered by the court that the said plaintiff recover of the said defendant his debt aforesaid together with the damages aforesaid by the Jury aforesaid in form aforesaid assessed, and also his costs by him about his suit in this behalf expended and the defendant in mercy etc.
Transcript issued

Ordered by the court that John G.Carithers, sheriff and collector of the state and county taxes be allowed a credit with the county treasurer for the sum of six hundred and thirty five dollars twenty four and a half cents for lands reported for the year 1826 and not sold for the want of bidders, which said amount includes the sheriff & printers fee-
Iss'd Febry. 8th, 1828

Ordered by the court that John G.Carithers sheriff and collector of the state and county tax be allowed a credit with the treasurer of West Tennessee for the sum of sixty nine dollars and thirty two cents for lands reported for the year 1826 and not sold for the want of bidders.
Issued, 16th Feby.

(p-180con.) Ordered by the court that Britain H.Sanders clerk be allowed the sum of eighty four dollars for his fees on land reported for the year 1826 and not sold for want of bidders, and the county trustee pay the same out of any monies in his hands not otherwise appropriated which shall be good in the settlement of his accounts. Issued 15th Decr.

(p-181) A transfer on a plat and certificate from John H.Nixon to Caleb Warren for one hundred and seventy five acres of land was this day produced in open court and duly acknowledged and ordered to be certified accordingly.

The court then adjourned until tomorrow 9 o'clock

Matthew Ray J.P.
Jona. T.Jococks J.P.
L.McGuire J.P.

Thursday morning December 13th 1827 The court met accordingly to adjournment present the worshipful Richard Nixon, Lawrence McGuire Jonathan T.Jococks Esqr. and others their fellow justices of the peace sheriff & clerk.

Ordered by the court that letters of administration be granted to Thomas G.Nixon on the estate of John R.Leigh late of this county deceased, It appearing to the satisfaction of the court that the widow of said dec'd has relinquished her right thereto-whereupon the said Thos G.Nixon entered into bond together Richard Nixon and Jonathan J.Nixon his securities in the penal sum of twenty thousand dollars conditioned as the law directs and took the necessary oath of an administrator.

A transfer on the back of a plat and certificate, from Jonathan J.Nixon to Caleb Warren for fifty acres of land was this day produced in open court and duly acknowledged for the purposes therein contained and ordered to be certified for registration.

This day Hiram Bradford appeared in open court and took the necessary oath of administration on the estate of Robert A.Penn Deceased as prescribed by law.

This day Berry Dearing appeared in open court and took the necessary oath of an administrator on the estate of Travis Kindal dec'd as prescribed by law.

A power of attorney from William Kavanaugh to David Lane was this day produced in open court and proven in part by the oath of Alvin Bingham, and ordered to be filed for further probit Certified & del-

(p-182) On motion and petition filed. It is ordered by the court that Henry E.Turner Charles White, John T.Turner, Samuel Brown, Bowen Reynolds, Lewis Powers, James Maldin, and Nicholas T.Perkins or any five of them be appointed a jury to view lay of and mark a road the nearest and best way from Jeffreys bluff to Madison County line to intersect the McGuire road where the same crosses the said county line and make report of their proceedings to the next term of this court (p-182con.) Iss'd 20th Decr.

Robert Williams)
       vs   )   Trespass on the case
Nathan Bridgmen)

    This day came the parties by their attorneys and thereupon came a jury of good and lawful men to wit Julius Sanders John A.Key, James Jackson, Francis L.Dillard, Arthur F.McCain, John A.King, Samuel Elliot, Abraham Kirksey, Andrew Wolf, Thomas Rutherford, William C.Bruce, and Herndon Haralson who being elected tried and sworn the truth to speak upon their oath do say that the defendant is not guilty of the trespass as the plaintiff in replying to the defendants plea hath alledged. It is therefore considered by the court that the plaintiff take nothing of the defendant but for his false clamour be in mercy etc. and that the defendant go hence without day and recover of the plaintiff his costs by him about his suit in this behalf expended
Transcript the 10th Jany 1828

    From which judgment the plaintiff hath prayed and obtained an appeal to the Circuit Court of this county he having entered into bond as the law directs.

Britain H.Sanders)
    vs   )   Assumpsit
Bennet R.Butler)

    This day came the parties by their attorneys and thereupon came a jury of good and lawful men to wit, Benjamin Rowland, Monroe, P.Estes, Archibald McNeal, Jonathan J.Nixon, Simon Turner, Hermis Champ Francis S.Coxe, L.D.Womble, Caleb Warren, Lee H.Burks, Alexander Kirksey & William Stanford who being elected tried and sworn the truth to speak upon the issue joined on their oaths do say the defendant did assume upon himself in manner and form as the plaintiff against him hath complained, and they do assess the plaintiff damages by reason of the defendants nonperformance of the assumption (p-183) in the declaration mentioned to one hundred and one dollars twenty two and a half cents, besides costs, Therefore it is considered by the court that the plaintiff recover against the said defendant his damages aforesaid by the Jury aforesaid in form aforesaid assessed and his costs by him about his suit in this behalf expended and the said defendant in mercy etc-

Richard White)
    vs   )
William Butler &)   Case
others)

    This day came the parties by their attorneys and thereupon came a jury of good and lawful men to wit Benjamin Rowland, Monroe P.Estes, Archibald McNeal, Jonathan J.Nixon, Simon Turner, Hermis Champ, Francis S.Coxe, L.D.Womble, Caleb Warren, Lee H.Burks, Alexander Kirksey & William Stanford who being elected, tried and sworn to speak upon their oaths do say that the defendant hath not paid the debt of one hundred and seventy five dollars in the declaration. Mentioned
Issd 10 March

(p-183con.) as the plaintiff in replying to the defendants plea hath alledged, and do asses the plaintiffs damages by reason of detention thereof to ten dollars and seven cents besides costs. It is therefore considered by the court that the plaintiff recover of the said defendants his debt aforesaid together with the damages aforesaid by the Jury aforesaid in form aforesaid assessed and also his costs by him about his suit in this behalf expended and the defendant in mercy etc. and on the motion of the defendant by their attorney and with the assent of the plaintiffs attorney, it is ordered by the court that Julius Sanders one of the defendants in the above cause be released from said Judgment.
Iss'd 19th Dec. 1827

Parrish & McAlvran)
    vs   ) Debt
John Potter   )

    This day came the parties by their attorneys and and thereupon came a jury ofgood and lawful men to wit, Benjamin Rowland, Monroe P. Estes, L.D.Womble, Caleb Warren, Lee H.Burks Francis S.Coxe, Alexander Kirkey, Wm.Stanford, Archibald McNeale Jonathan J.Nixon, Simon Turner, & Hermis Champ, who being elected tried and sworn, the truth to speak upon their oaths do say that the defendant hath not paid the debt of seventy four dollars and seventy five cents in the declaration mentioned as the plaintiff in replying to the defendants plea hath alledged, and do assess the plaintiffs damages (p-184) by reason of the detention thereof to one dollar and seventy five cents besides costs, It is therefore considered by the court that the plaintiff recover of the said defendant his debt aforesaid together with the damages aforesaid by the jury aforesaid in form aforesaid assessed and also his costs by him about his suit in in this behalf expended and the defendant in mercy etc.
From which said judgment the defendant hath this day day prayed and obtained an appeal to the Circuit Court he having entered into bond as the law directs.
Transcript 10th Jany 1828

    Ordered by the court that John G.Carithers sheriff and collector be allowed a credit with the county treasurer for the sum of two hundred and eight dollars sixty eight and three fourth cents for lands and town lots reported for double tax for the year 1826 and not sold for want of bidders which said amount includes the sherriff and printers fees.
Iss'd Febry. 8th

    Ordered by the court that John G.Carithers, sheriff and collector be allowed a credit with the treasurer of West Tennessee for the sum of thirty seven dollars one and fourth cents for lands and town lots reported for double taxes for the year 1826 and not sold for want of bidders.
Iss'd Feb. 8th, 1828

    Ordered by court that Britain H. Sanders clerk be allowed the sum of fifty dollars and forty cents for his fees on lands and town lots reported for double tax for the year 1826 and not sold for want of bidders, out of any monies in his hands not otherwise appropriated

(p-184con.) which shall be good in the settlement of his accounts-
Iss'd

Thos. Carnahan)
    vs) Debt
John R.Leigh)

    This day came the plaintiff by his attorney and/attorney and say
that he does not any further prosecute his said suit and thereupon came
Thos.G.Nixon administrator of John R.Leigh dec'd by attorney and assumes
the payment of the costs in the above suit.

Mathew Figures)
    vs) Debt
Frances Lamoyn)

    This day came the parties by their attorneys (p-185) and thereupon
came a jury of good and lawful men to wit Benjamin Rowland, Monroe P.
Estes, Archibald McNeal, Jonathan J.Nixon, Simon Turner , Hermis Champ,
Francis S.Coxe, L.D.Womble, Caleb Warren, Lee H. Burks, Alexander Kirksey
and William Stanford who being elected tried and sworn the truth to speak
upon their oaths do say that the defendant hath not paid the debt of sixty
dollars in the declaration mentioned as the plaintiff in replying to the
defendants plea hath alledged, and do assess the plaintiffs damages by
reason of the detention thereof to one dollar and twenty cents besides
costs. It is therefore considered by the court that the plaintiff recover of the defendant his debt aforesaid together with the damages
aforesaid by the Jury aforesaid in form aforesaid assessed and his costs
by him about his suit in the behalf expended, and the defendant in
mercy etc.
Issued, Issued 31st Decr. 1827

State of Tennessee)
    vs) Indictment
Jourdan M.Hansborough)

    The defendant in this case has this day prayed and obtained an
appeal to the Circuit Court he having entered into bond as the law
directs.

    The grand jury returned into court the following presentment to
wit, The State of Tennessee vs Benjamin Wilson for tipling and retired
to consider of further presentments.

Wm. P.G rains & others)
    vs) Assumpsit
Joel Estes)

    This day came the parties by their attornes and on motion of the
defendant and satisfactory reasons shown to the court. It is ordered
by the court here that the defendant have leave to amend his pleadings
by filing the plea of lit off here tendered to the court on the payment
of the costs of this order. Whereupon this cause is continued until the
next term of this court.

    The court then adjourned until tomorrow ten o'clock.

(p-185)   Rich'd Nixon cha
                                           Sam P.Ashe
                                           L.McGuire J.P.

(p-186) Friday morning December 14th 1827 the court met according to
adjournment present the worshipful Richard Nixon, Lawrence McGuire,
Samuel P.Ashe, Esquires and others their fellow justices of the peace the
clerk and sheriff present.

        Ordered by the court that Francis L.Dillard be released from the
payment of the taxes on four and a half town lots in the town of Brownsville
amounting to three dollars thirty seven and a half cents, It appearing
to the satisfaction of the court that the same have been twice listed
and that the sheriff and collector be allowed a credit with the state and
county treasurers each one dollar sixty eight and three fourth cents
the amount of the state and county tax due severally thereon for the
year 1827.

        Ordered by the court that Mansfield Ware be released from the pay-
ment of the sum of Eleven dollars and forty cents the amount of the taxes
and costs and charges on a tract of land in the name of Nathan Roddie
for one thousand acres reported and sold for the year 1826, and purchased
by said Ware. It appearing to the satisfaction of the court that the
same has been improperly listed and otherwise paid for therefore it is
further ordered by the court that John G.Carithers sheriff and collector
be allowed a credit with the county trustee for the said amount of
eleven dollars and forty cents due for the year 1826.
Iss'd Febry. 1828

        The Grand jury returned into court the following presentment to
wit, The State of Tennessee vs John A.Key for Tipling and retired to
consider of further business.

        A Deed of bargain and sale from John G.Carithers sheriff and
collector to David Jeffreys and Nicholas T.Perkins for twenty two hundred
and fifty acres of land was this day produced in open court and duly
acknowledged for the purposes therein contained and ordered to the
certified for registration

John A. Key   )
     vs   )   Trespass on the Case
Benjamin Rowland   )

        This day came the parties by their attorneys and thereupon came
a jury of good and lawful men to wit. Julius Sanders, James Jackson,
Jonathan J.Nixons. Hermis Champ, Arthur F.McCain, William C.Bruce,
Archibald McNeale, John A.King, Alexander Kirksey, Phillip Koonce,
Herndon Haralson (p-187) and James Smith who being elected tried and
sworn the truth to speak, upon their oaths do say that the defendant is
not guilty of the trespass as the plaintiff in replying to the defendants
plea hath alledged It is therefore considered by the court here that
the plaintiff take nothing of the defendant but for his false clamour
be in mercy etc and that the defendant go hence without day and recover
of the plaintiff his costs by him about his defence in this behalf expended
iss'd 11th Jany 1828

(p-187con.)State of Tennessee)
          vs   )   Presentment
     John A.Key   )

    This day came the solicitor general who prosecutes in behalf of
the state, and the defendant in his proper person and being solemnly
charged sayeth that he is guilty in manner and form as charged in the bill
of presentment and puts himself upon the grace and mercy of the court.
It is therefore considered by the court that the said defendant make his
fine with the State of Tennessee by the payment of one dollar and all
costs in this behalf expended and that he be taken etc-
Iss'd 31th. Decr.1827

State of Tennessee)
          vs   )   Case agreed
William R.Hess   )

    On motion of the attorney Gen'l to compel said witness to answer
certain questions asked of him by the Grand jury this day came Alexander B.
Bradford with the state of Tennessee by the payment of one dollar and
all costs in this behalf expended and that he be taken etc.
Iss'd 31st Decr. 1827

State of Tennessee)
          vs   )   Case agreed on motion of the attorney
William R.Hess   )

    Gen'l to compel said witness to answer certain questions asked
of him by by the grand jury this day came Alexander B.Bradford solicitor
General who prosecutes on behalf of the state and the said defendant in
his proper person, and after argument had thereon, it is the opinion of
the court that the said motion be overuled. It is therefore considered
by the court that the defendant recover of the state his costs by him
about his defence in this behalf expended. To which opinion of the
court the solicitor General excepted and filed his bill of exceptions
which were signed and sealed by the court and made a part of the record,
and prayed an appeal in the notice of a writ of Error to the next Circuit
Court of this county and thereupon the said William R.Hess defendant came
(p-188) into open court and in proper person and waves all manner of
exception and agrees that this cause he argued at the Circuit Court of
this county to be holden in the town of Brownsville on the 4th Monday
of this instant upon the matters of law presented in said Bill of exceptions.

    The grand jury returned into court and there appearing no further
business they were dis discharged from further service during the
present year.

    Ordered by court t he amount of ten dollars and seventy seven
cents be deducted from the report of the sheriff for single taxes due
for the year 1826 which has been returned through mistake with N.T.
Perkins.

    The court then adjourned until tomorrow 9 o'clock.

(p-188con.)   Rich'd Nixon char
                                     Matthew Ray J.P.
                                     L.McGuire
                                     N.T.Perkins J.P.

        Saturday Morning December 15th 1827 the court met according to
adjournment present the worshipful Richard Nixon, Nicholas T.Perkins
Lawrence McGuire Esquires, and others-

Truisdale & Smith   )
        vs   )
Julius Sanders &   )   Judgment on a former day of the term
Robert Sanders   )
o̸f̸/t̸h̸e̸/t̸e̸r̸m̸

        From which Judgment the defendants hath this day prayed and
obtained an appeal to the Circuit Court of this county they having entered into bond as the law directs-

John A.Key   )   Judgh. for defendant on a former day of this term.
        vs   )
Benjamin Rowland   )

        From which Judgment the plaintiff hath this day prayed and obtained
an appeal to the Circuit Court of this county he having entered into bond
together with Alexander Kirksey and Joseph Findly his securities (one
of whom were sworn as to his s̸e̸c̸u̸r̸i̸t̸i̸e̸s̸ (̸o̸n̸e̸/o̸f̸ w̸h̸o̸m̸/w̸e̸r̸e̸ s̸w̸o̸r̸n̸ t̸o̸/h̸is
worth) as the law directs-

(p-189) Ordered by the court that John G.Carithers sheriff and collector
of the state and county tax for the county of Haywood for the year 1827
be allowed a credit with the treasurer of West Tennessee for the term of
six months (as prescribed by law after) the first Monday in January
next on the amount of four hundred and eighty four dollars seventy nine
and one fourth cents the amount of taxes due to the state on lands, which
amount is unpaid b y the respective owners thereof and the same will have
to be reported for said taxes thereon, for said year 1827, and it further
ordered by the court that the clerk of this court certify the same under
his hand and seal of office to the treasurer of West Tennessee accordingly.
Iss'd

        Ordered by the court that John G.Carithers sheriff and collector
of the state and county tax for the year 1827 be allowed a credit of
six months after the first Monday in January next with the county trustee
on the amount of fourteen hundred and fifty four dollars thirty eight
cents which is the amount of taxes due to the county of Haywood and unpaid by the respective owners thereof and will have to be reported for
said taxes, for said year 1827, and it is further ordered by the court
that the clerk of this court certify under his hand and seal the same
to the county trustee accordingly.
Issd.

        Ordered by the court that Samuel P.Ashe Oliver B.Woods, Nicholas
T.Perkins, Lowrence McGuire, Joel Estes, Mathew Ray, Richard Nixon,

(p-189con.) Jonathan T.Jococks, Daniel Cherry and Wilie Dodd, Esquires be appointed to take in lists of taxable property and poles within the limits of this county for the year 1828 and make return thereof to the next term of this court. Iss'd
Iss'd. (B)

It is ordered by the court that Allen H.Howard, Thomas Rutherford, Clemment T.Walker, John Rodgers, James W.Russell, Phillip Koonce, Alexander D.Gordon, John McWhite, John Allbright, William W.Man, Mason F.Johnston, Francis L.Dillard, Robert Perry, Thos G.Nixon, James Sampson, Samuel Elliott, Wm. C.Bruce, Herndon Haralson, Lewis Powers Samuel Brown, Henry H.Turner, Jonathan Hollowell, Thos. Potter, Francis Lemoyn,William Stanford and William Patton be summoned to attend at the next court of pleas and quarter sessions to be holden for Haywood County then and there to serve as grand and petit Jurors as the case may be, and that Reuben Allphin & Cato Freeman be summoned as constables to attend the same.
Iss'd

(p-190) Ordered by the court that John G.Carithers Esqr. be appointed to take special care of the courthouse.

The court then adjourned untill court in course.

Rich'd. Nixon Cha
N.T.Perkins, J.P.
L.McGuire J.P.

(p-191) State of Tennessee)
         Haywood County   ) Sct.

At a court of pleas and quarter sessions began and holden for the County of Haywood at the courthouse in the town of Brownsville on the second Monday, it being the tenth day of March in the year of our Lord, one thousand eight hundred & twenty eight & of the Independence of the United States the fifty second year- Present the worshipful Richard Nixon Daniel Cherry, Lawrence McGuire and Samuel P.Ashe.

Britain H.Sanders clerk & John G.Carithers,Sherriff.

Jesse L.Kirk this day produced here in open court a commission issued by his excellency Samuel Houston esquire, governor of the State of Tennessee appointing the said Jesse L.Kirk a justice of the peace for the county of Haywood & thereupon the sd. Jesse L.Kirk took the several oaths prescribed by law for justices of peace to take in this state.

It is ordered by the court that the county trustee of Haywood County refund to Jonathan Nixon the sum of five dollars twelve & one half cents, it being the amount due & paid to the county on one hundred & fifty nine acres of land, reported & sold in the name of David Joiner for 1825 & upon 274 acres of land reported & sold in the name of John Patrick for said year & upon 125 acres reported & sold in the name of J.S.Green & (p-192) William B.Lynn for said year upon the said Jonathan Nixon's producing to said trustee a certificate of the surveyor General that there are no such tracts of land in the county.
Iss'd 20th June 1828

138

(p-192con.) An Indenture of bargain and sale from Richard Nixon to
Caleb Warren for one hundred acres of land was this day acknowledged in
open court & ordered to be registered- Deed, certified & Delivered,

It is ordered by the court that John G.Carithers sheriff be allowed
a credit of three dollars by the county trustee & one dollar with the state
treasurer, on five hundred acres of land improperly entered in the name
of Clement T.Walker in Haywood County for the year 1827
Is'd

An Indenture of bargain from William Jackson to Samuel Townsend for
one hundred & forty four acres of land was this day acknowledged in open
court by said Jackson & ordered to be registered   Deed certified &Dl'd
Mr. Bullock,

It is ordered by the court that Alfred Kennady, Hardy L.Blackwell,
John Williams, Enos Novell, or a majority of them be appointed a jury of
view to mark and lay off a road from Bucks Ferry to the county line in a
direction to Rutherfords Mill a distance of three fourth of a mile or
perhaps one mile to meet a road from said mill in the direction, to
Bucks Ferry
Iss'd

Nimrod Axley produced here into open court the scalp of a wolf
over the age of four months within the county of Haywood and the necessary
oath, agreeably to the act of assembly, being made thereof it is ordered
by the court that the said Nimrod Axly be allowed the sum of three dollars, to be paid by the Treasurer of Western District & that a certificate
issue therefor.
Iss'd

(p-193) It is ordered by the court that the clerk of this court receive the amount of monies due the state and county for the year 1827
as a single tax from all persons whose property is listed for a double
tax for said year, provided the same is paid by the sitting of the court
on tomorrow or before the report of the sheriff-

An Indenture of bargain and sale from M.Spence to J.Stone for
one hundred & fifty acres of land was this day acknowledged in open
county said Spence & ordered to be registered. Deed, certified &
delivered

William A.Morrison produced here into court the scalp of a wolf
over four months of age and proved as the law directs that he killed the
same in this county. It is therefore ordered by the court that he be
allowed the sum of three dollars, to be paid by the Treasurer of the
Western District.

It is ordered by the court that the jury of view appointed at
the last term of this court to view and mark a road from Jefferies &
Perkins Bluff to the nearest point to intersect the McGuire road at the
county line be continued & have until the next term of the court to make
their report-
Iss'd

(p-193con.) Robert S.Wilkins and Thomas J.Blythe who were this day
elected constables for this county came into court, entered into bond
and security & took the oaths prescribed by law-

The commissioners appointed to settle with John G.Carithers esqr.
sheriff of Haywood County makes report to this court that they have done
the same, which is received & ordered to be recorded.

(p-194) It is ordered by the court that Lawrence McGuire, Jonathan T.
Jacocks, Wyatt F.Tweedy, Joseph Haralson, Charles White, Daniel Shaw,
Richard Taylor, or any five of them be and are hereby appointed a jury
of view to view and examine the Ferry now established by this court at
the town of Estonaula and the one now at this term petitioned for by
William H.Moore and make report to the next term of this court which of
the two will be of most public utility and which of the two should be
continued by this court.
Iss'd

It is ordered by the court that Hyram Bradford and Herndon Haralson
be and hereby appointed commissioners to settle with the clerk of the
Circuit and County Court of this County for the present year.
Iss'd

It is ordered by the court that Herndon Haralson be and is hereby
appointed commissioners for the County of Haywood to receive the
Academy Move in due to said county.
Iss'd

This day came into open court John A.King, Charles A.Wortham, &
James L.Wortham, Commissioners appointed by a former term of this court
to lay off and divide the hands mentioned in the petition for partition
of E.Roddy & William Hannon said commissioners having been duly sworn
according to act of assembly in such case made and provided and made
their report in writing under their hands & seals how they had divided
and apportioned the same amongst the different claimants. and it appearing
to the satisfaction of the court that notice of said petition had been
duly given according to law in the Jackson Gazette a paper printed in
town of Jackson at least six months preceeding the term at which said
petition was presented and filed. It is therefore ordered by the court
after duly inspecting said report of said commissioners that said report
be received and entered of record and certified for registration.
It is therefore considered by the court that the said petitioned pay the
costs in and about this behalf expended and that Fieri Facias issue
accordingly and it is further ordered that Charles Wortham a commission
be allowed twelve dollars John A.King, commissioner thirty dollars
James Wortham a commissioner ten dollars & Azariah Thompson a commissioner
six dollars (James L.Wortham allowance to the use of F.S.Cox,)

(p-195) It is ordered by the court that John G.Carithers esquire
sheriff, be allowed a credit in his settlement with the county trustee
the sum of twenty six dollars and sixty four cents, and also with the
treasurer of West Tennessee of Eight dollars & Eighty eight cents on
four thousand four hundred thirty acres of land entered in the name of
James Walker it appearing satisfactorelly to this court that the same

(p-195con.) had been listed twice for the year 1827-
        Iss'd

    Court adjourned until tomorrow nine o'clock

                    Jesse L.Kirk J.P.
                    Oliver Woods J.P.
                    J.L.Worthas J.P.

    Tuesday morning March 11th 1828

    Court met pursuant to adjournment present Jesse L.Kirk, Oliver
B.Woods & James L.Wortham esquires, Justices-

    Icabod Herrin produced into court two wolf scalps over the age of
four months and proved as the law directs the killing of the same in
the county of Haywood. It is therefore ordered by the court that he be
allowed the sum of three dollars each, to be paid by the treasurer of
the western district-
Iss'd. fee pd. to B.H.S-

    Deed of Bargain and sale from John G.Carithers sheriff to James
Freeman & Hugh B.Robison for six hundred & forty acres of land was this
day acknowledged in open court & ordered to be registered.

(p-196) Deed of bargain & sale from John G.Carithers shff. to Jonathan
Nixon for four hundred acres of land was this day acknowledged in open
court and ordered to be registered.

    Deed of bargain & sale from John G.Carithers sheriff to Jonathan
Nixon for two thousand five hundred acres of land was this day acknowledg-
ed in open court & ordered to be registered
Certified & Del'd

    Reubin Alphin and Jordan M.Haresborough who were on yesterday
elected constables for this county, came into court, entered into
bond with security and took the oaths prescribed by law-

    John G.Carithers was this day duly & constitutionally elected
sheriff & collector for this county for the ensuing two years, who
entered into bond & security & took the several oaths prescribed by law.

    Samuel Green has permission to change the road running near his
house, beginning at or near the section line running thence east with
his fence & to intersect the old road at or near the second _____
east of his plantation

    Deed of Gift from Richard Nixon to Thomas G.Nixon for one hundred
acres of land was this day acknowledged in open court & ordered to be
registered
Certified & del'd

    It is ordered by the court that James W.Green be allowed the sum
of six dollars twelve & one half cents for work done on the courthouse,

(p-196con.) to be paid out of any unappropriate money in the hands of
the county trustee
(Iss'd. and del'd. to Jourdan M.Hansborough the 2nd day of April 1828
fee pd.

(p-197) It is ordered by the court that Benjamin Wilkes Joel Pace____
Fitsgerald , Oliver B.Woods, John M.Hale and Thomas J.Blythe or a majority
of them be appointed a jury to mark out a road from Estanaula in a direction to Covington*about Big Muddy Creek-
Iss'd.

It is ordered by the court that John G.Carithers shff be allowed
a credit with the state and county for five hundred acres of land improperly listed for taxation for 1827 in the name of Thomas Polk-
Iss'd.

It is ordered by the court that the taxes for the present year be
the same as heretofore laid for the year 1827 and that an additional tax
of twelve and one half cents on each hundred acres of land be taxed for
the purpose of raising a fund for the purpose of building bridges,,
repairing roads etc.

It is ordered by the court that Jesse L.Kirk be permitted to turn
the road leading from Estanaula to Jackson about one hundred yards, it
being round his new ground provided he does it with his own hands, &
when done to be received by the overseer of the present road.

It is ordered by the court that Lawrence McGuire, Charles White,
Thomas G.Nixon, David Jeffers and N.T.Perkins, the late commissioners of
the town of Brownsville be allowed two dollars per day for each & every
day they served as such (p-198) to wit Lawrence McGuire, thirteen
days, Charles White fourteen days, Thomas G.Nixon fifteen days, David
Jeffers six days and Nicholas T.Perkins twenty days
Iss'd to N.T.Perkins, Iss'd to T.G.Nixon, Issd to N.T.O. for Chas
White, Isd. to Lawrence McGuire , D.Jefferies issd to N.T.Perkins

It is ordered by the court that the sheriff of this court report
to this court all the lands which have been heretofore reported and not
sold together with the report which he is to make to this court.

It is ordered by the court that Samuel P.Ashe, Daniel Cherry,
Jesse L.Kirk, Richard Nixon & Blackman Coleman be and hereby appointed
commissioners to receive the monies arising from the tax laid for the
purpose of building Bridges etc. and that they be and are hereby
authorised to appropriate the same in such manner as they may judge with
best advance the interest of the county.

It is ordered by the court that the jury of view appointed to
view a road from B rownsville to the county line in a direction to
Dyersburg at the last term of this court be continued together with the
surveyor heretofore appointed and that they make report to the next term
of this court.
Iss'd.

John G.Carithers esquires Sherriff of Haywood County makes return
* to intersect the road leading from Bolivar to Covington

(p-198con.) of the venire facias returnable to this court, which is as
follows to wit

State of Tennessee
        At a court of pleas and quarter sessions began and held for
the County of Haywood at the courthouse in the town of Brownsville on the
second Monday in December 1827, it being the tenth day of said month
present the worshipful Richard Nixon, Nicholas T.Perkins and Lawrence
McGuire esquire It is ordered by the court that the following persons
good and lawful men (viz) each being a white male citizen of the age of
twenty one years and a householder to wit, Allen H.Howard Thomas Rutherford
Clement T.Walker, John Rodgers, James W.Russell, Phillip Koonce,
Alexander D.Gordon, John McWhite, John Albright, William W. Mann.

(p-199) Mason F.Johnson, Francis L.Dillard, Robert Perry, Thomas G.Nixon
James Sampson, Samuel Elliott, William C.Bruce, Herndon Harralson, Lewis :
Powers, Samuel Brown, Henry H.Turner, Jonathan Hollowell, Thomas Potter
Francis Lamoin, William Stanford and William Patton, be summoned to
attend at the next term of this court on Tuesday after the second Monday
in March next & there to serve as grand or petit jurors as the case may be
and that Reubin Alphin and Cater Freeman be summoned to attend said court
as constables

                        Test B.H.Sanders,Clk.

(p-199) State of Tennessee
        To the sheriff of Haywood County, Greeting
You are hereby commanded to summon the aforesaid persons to serve as
jurors at the next court of pleas and quarter sessions to be held at the
courthouse in the town of Brownsville on Tuesday after the second Monday
in March next and this they shall in no wise omit under the penalty
prescribed by law. Herein fail not and have you then and there this
writ - witness Britain H.Sanders, clerk of our said court at office the
second Monday in December 1827 and 52 year of American Independence.

                        B.H.Sanders,Clk.
upon the back of which said writ is the following endorsement came to
hand this 28th of December 1827 Jno. G.Carithers,Shff. By virtue of the
within venire facias to me directed I have proceeded to summon all the
within named persons except James Sampson, Samuel Brown, and Jonathan
Hollwell, and such   (p-200) persons so summoned are free holders or
householders of said county except William Stanford & of the age of twenty
one years.
                        Jno. G.Caruthers Shff.

        The following persons were drawn elected, sworn and charged as a
grand jury for the present term to wit, William W.Mann, foreman Thomas
Potter, Allen H.Howard, Francis Lamoin, Henry H.Turner, John Rogers, W.C.
Bruce, Robert Perry, Lewis Powers, William Patton, James W.Russell,John
Albright and ClementF. Walker, & retired to consider of presentments

        It is ordered by the court that Robert S.Wilkins, Alexander W.
Cartney,_____Bigham, James Bigham, Henry Sullivan be appointed a
jury of view to mark and lay off a road from Estanaula the nearest and
best way to intersect the road to Brownsville and make report to next
court.

(p-200con.) Iss'd

It is ordered by the court that Isaac Wood, Newman Parker Foster Parker, Robt. Biles, Caleb Miller, D.M.McIver, & James Burton be and are hereby appointed a jury to view and mark a road from James L. Worthams Ferry to the county line in a direction to Trenton & make report to our next court.
Iss'd.

In obedience to the requistions of the act of assembly A.B. Bradford esqr. attorneyGen'l called on the clerk of this court to produce here to court his receipts for the public monies due to the Treasurer of West Tennessee & to the county trustee of this county, when the clerk established the following

Nashbille February 23nd 1828 Received of Britain H.Sanders clerk of Haywood County court three hundred and seventy seven dollars, seventy five cents Being the amount of State tax by him collected for the year ending first day of October 1827 agreeably to a statement made by Messrs. Haralson & Bradford as commissioners for said county for said year 1827.

Thos. Crutcher
Treasurer

(p-201) State of Tennessee)
    Haywood County)

This day received of Britain H.Sanders the clerk of the County Court of Haywood aforesaid the sum of twenty three dollars in full(as by examination agreeably by the commissioners appointed for that purpose by the court) It being the amount due from said clerk to said Trustee for the year ending the first day of October 1827 this 1st day of March 1828-

Rich'd Nixon cty.
Tres.

William W.Gaines &)
Robt V.Mays   )
   To   )
Joel Estes   )

This day came the said parties by their attornies & thereupon came also a jury of good and lawful men, to wit, Thomas Rutherford, Thomas G.Nixon, Herndon Haralson, Francis L.Dillard, Samuel Elliott, S̸a̸m̸u̸e̸l̸/ E̸l̸l̸i̸o̸t̸t̸, Philip Koonce, John McWhite, Caleb Warren, Levi Gardner, John Osburn, Berry Derin, and Archibald McNeal who being elected, tried & sworn the truth to speak upon the issue joined, upon their oaths aforesaid do say that they find the issues in favour of the plaintiff & assess their damages to one hundred & thirty two dollars and thirty two cents besides costs.
Iss'd 28th March 1828 for cost,

It is therefore considered by the court here that the said plaintiffs do recover against the said defendant the damages aforesaid by the jury in (p-201con.) form aforesaid assessed & the costs in this behalf expended.

(p-202) William A.Akin   )
                vs   )   Debt
        Bowen Reynolds   )

    This day came the said parties by their attornies and thereupon came also a jury of good and lawful men to wit, Thomas Rutherford,Thomas G.Nixon, Herndon Haralson, Francis L.Dillard, Samuel Elliott, Philip Koonce, John McWhite, Caleb Warren, Levi Gardner, John Osburn, Berry Derin and Archibald McNeal, who being elected tried and sworn well & truly to try the issues joined between the parties upon their oaths do say they find the issues in favour of the plaintiff & assess his damages to twenty four dollars and sixty cents. It is therefore considered by the court that the plaintiff do recover against the said Defendant two hundred and ten dollars the residue of the debt in the declaration mentioned and the damages aforesaid by the Jury assessed , and the costs in this behalf expended & the defendant in mercy-
Paid the same day

    Isaac L.Moody-   )
            vs   )
    Preston G.Hodges and   )
    Richard W.Nixon   )

    This day came the said parties by their attornies, and thereupon came also a jury of good and lawful men, to wit, Thomas Rutherford, Thomas G.Nixon, Herndon Haralson, Francis L.Dillard, Samuel Elliott, Phillip Koonce, John McWhite Caleb Warren, Levi Gardner, John Osburn, Berry Derin and Archibald McNeal who being elected tried and sworn the truth to speak upon the issue joined upon their oaths aforesaid do say that the said defendants have not kept and performed their covenants as the said plaintiff in replying hath alledged, and they assess the said plaintiff, damages by reason thereof to one hundred and thirty one dollars and fifty cents, besides costs.

    It is therefore considered by the court that the said plaintiffs do recover against the said Defendants the damages aforesaid by the jury in form aforesaid assessed & the costs in this behalf expended etc. Iss'd 28 March 1828

(p-203) Edwin H.Childress)
                vs   )   Debt
        Jesse L.Kirk   )

    This day came the said parties by their attornies and thereupon came also a jury of good and lawful men to wit, Thomas Rutherford Thomas G.Nixon, Herndon Haralson, Francis L.Dillard, Samuel Elliott, Philip Koonce, John McWhite, Caleb Warren, Levi Gardner, John Osburn, Berry Derin & Archibald McNeal, who being elected, tried and sworn the truth to speak upon the issues joined upon their oath aforesaid do say that the defendant hath paid thirty one dollars, part of the debt of one hundred and fifty four dollars in the declaration mentioned, and that the residue of the debt remains wholly unpaid, and they assess the

(p-203con.) plaintiffs damages by reason of the detention of the residue
of the debt in the declaration mentioned to fifteen dollars and twenty
five cents besides cost. It is therefore considered by the court that
the plaintiff do recover against the said defendant residue of the debt
aforesaid of one hundred & nineteen dollars & the Damages aforesaid by
the jury assessed & the costs in this behalf expended-
Transcript Issued 25th day of March 1828

Robert Reaves &)
Alexander Brown)
        vs   )   Debt
Charles Watts   )
        vs
Charles Watts

    This day came the said parties by their attornies & thereupon
came a jury of good and lawful men to wit, Thomas Rutherford, Thomas G.
Nixon, Herndon Haralson, Francis L.Dillard, Samuel Elliott, Philip
Koonce, John McWhite, Caleb Warren, Levi Gardner, John Osburn, Berry
Derin and Archibald McNeal who being elected, tried & sworn well and
truly to try the issue joined between the parties upon their oaths aforesaid do say that the (p-204) Defendant hath not paid the debt of six
hundred and twenty nine dollars and ninety two cents as the plaintiff in
declaring hath alledged, and they assess the plaintiffs damages by reason
thereof to twelve dollars and fifty nine cents ,besides costs
    It is therefore considered by the court here that the said plaintiffs
do recover against the said defendant the Debt aforesaid in the declaration
mentioned & the damages aforesaid by the jury assessed and the costs in
this behalf expended etc.

Parish & McAlovan)
        vs   )   Debt
Francis L.Dillard)

    This day came the said parties by their attornies & thereupon came
also a jury of good & lawful men to wit   Thomas Rutherford,Thomas G.
Nixon, Herndon Haralson, Caleb Warren, Samuel Elliott, Phillip Koonce,
John McWhite, Caleb Warren, Levi Gardner , John Osburn, Berry Derin &
Archibald McNeal who being elected tried and sworn well & truly to try the
issue joined upon their oaths do say that the defendant hath not paid the
Debt of one hundred & fourteen dollars & sixty seven cents in the declaration ,mentioned as the plaintiff in declaring hath alledged & they assess
the plaintiffs Damages by reason of the detention of that debt to one
dollar & seventy one cents besides costs-

Execution Iss'd 28th March 1828

    It is therefore considered by the court here that the said plaintiff
do recover against the said Defendant the Debt aforesaid together with
the Damages aforesaid by the Jury assessed & the costs in this behalf expended etc. From which judgment the defendant hath prayed & obtained and
appeal to the Circuit Court of this County. He having given bond & security
therefore.
Iss'd/28th March 1828/

(p-205)   Parish & McAlonan) Certiorario
                 vs   )
          Thomas Potter   )

This day came the Defendant Thomas Potter, in his proper person
into open court & saith that he intends no further to prosecute his said
writ of certiorario and Dismisses the same, and assumes to pay all costs
in this behalf expended-
It is therefore considered by the court here that the said plaintiffs
recover against the said Defendant the costs in this behalf expended etc.
Iss'd

Nicholas T.Perkins guardian for Simon T.Turner makes his report is
such to this court as the law directs which is ordered to be recorded.

Nicholas T.Perkins former guardian for Nancy M.J.P.Turner makes his
report to this court which is ordered to be recorded.

Blackman Coleman was this day appointed & qualified as a Deputy
clerk of this court.

The State of Tennessee)
        vs   )
Alexander D.Gordon   )

Alexander D.Gordon who was regularly summoned to attend this court
to serve as a juror which appeares by the return made upon the venire
facias returnable to this court was this day solemnly called, came not
but made default. It is therefore considered by the court that he be fined
in the sum ofnfive dollars and a Sciri facias issue returnable to the next
term of this court.
Iss'd

It is ordered by the court that Richard Nixon, Samuel McGuire &
Blackman Coleman be appointed to settle with N.T.Perkins, Guardian for
Nancy T.& Simon T.Turner & make report to next court.

(p-206) This day came into open court Herndon Haralson, Lawrence McGuire
and Alexander D.Gordon commissioners appointed to lay off and divide the
lands mentioned in the petition for partition of Thomas Windsor Newman
Windsor, Joseph Windsor, John Windsor Craver Bosweal, and John Tapscot,
said commissioners having been duly sworn according to act of assembly
and make them report in writing under their hands & seals how they had
divided and apportioned the same among the different claimants.
It is therefore ordered by the court that the same be received and
entered of record and certified for registration. And it is considered
by said court that said petitioners pay all costs in this behalf expended
and that Fieri facias issue therefor- And it is further ordered that
Herndon Haralson a commissioner be allowed the sum of three dollars
Lawrence McGuire four dollars and A.D.Gordon three dollars.

Richard Nixon was this day duly & constitution elected county
trustee of this county for the ensuing two years who gave bond & security.

(p-206con.) Court adjourned until tomorrow morning nine o'clock.

Rich. Nixon, Chr
Dan'l Cherry
Sam. P.Ashe

Wednesday morning 12th March 1828, court met according to adjournment.

Harmis Champ vs John McCrory, Levi Gardner, This day came the Plaintiff by his attorneys and the Defendant Levi Gardner, being solemnly called came not, but made default. It is therefore considered by the court that the plaintiff recover against the defendant seventy five dollars in the declaration mentioned and one dollar and fifty cents damages for the detention thereof and his costs in this behalf expended etc. and thereupon came a jury of good and lawful men, to wit Thomas Rutherford, Thomas G.Nixon Herndon Haralson, Francis L.Dillard, Samuel Elliott, Phillip Koonce, and John McWhite, Caleb Warren, Allen M.Howard, John Osbern, Berry Derin , and Archibald McNeal who being elected, tried and sworn well and truly to try the issue joined between the plaintiffs and John McCrory the other defendant upon their oath do say the defendant John McCrory hath not paid the debt of seventy five dollars the debt in the declaration mentioned and assess his damages by reason thereof to one dollar and fifty cents and the damages aforesaid by the jury in form aforesaid assessed & the costs in this behalf expended.
(Issued 27th March 1828)

(p-207) On motion it is ordered by the court that William R.Hess,Hyram Bradford, & Herndon Harralson, be & are hereby appointed to lay off to Mrs. Eliza H.Leigh, widow of the late John R.Leigh Esq. of this county, one years provision agreeably to the act of assembly in such case made & provided & make report to the next term of this court.
Issd-

Edwin H.Childress)
    vs   )
Jesse L.Kirk   )

The defendant being dissatisfied with the judgment rendered against him at this term hath prayed & obtained an appeal to the Circuit Court which is granted. He having given bond & security therefor.

Hermis Champ   )
    vs   )
McCrory & Gardner)

The defendant John McCrory being dissatisfied with the judgment heretofore at this term rendered against the defendants hath prayed & obtained an appeal to the Circuit Court He having given bond & security therefor.

The State of Tennessee)
    vs
Thomas J.Smith   )

This day came as well the State of Tennessee by A.B.Bradford esqr.

(p-207con.) attorney General as the Defendant in his proper person and the sd Defendant being solemnly charged saith he is not guilty in manner & form as charged in the bill of Indictment. And by the knowledge & direction of the court, a nole prosequi is entered.

(p-208)   The State of Tennessee)
                    vs   )
          James Haggard

This day came as well the State of Tennesseeby Alexander B.Bradford attorney General as the defendant in his proper person and the defendant being solemnly charged saith he is not guilty in manner & form as charged in the bill of Indictment and thereupon came also a jury of good and lawful * to wit, Herndon Harrelson, Francis L.Dillard, Samuel Elliott, Caleb Warren John P.Majors, John G.Jones, Benjam Boothe, John Osburn, Alexander McNeal, Thomas West, Jonathan J.Nixon & Rawlin Patram who being elected tried & sworn well & truly to try the issue of travers upon their oath aforesaid do say that the defendant is guilty in manner & form as charged in the bill of Indictment. It is therefore considered by the court that the Defendant make his fine with the State of Tennessee by the payment of five dollars & all costs & that he be taken etc.

Alexander D.Gordon who was arrested by virtue of a States warrent issued by Richard Nixon esquire a justice of the peace of this county upon the oath of Asa Biggs, this day came into court and acknowledged himself indebted to the State of Tennessee in the sum of five hundred dollars, to be levied of his goods & chattels, lands & tenements, but to be void on condition that he the said Alexander D.Gordon shall well & truly keep the peace toward all the good people of the County of Haywood and particularly towards the said Asa Biggs until the next term of this court.
And thereupon came also into open court Reubin Alphin and John McWhite and acknowledge themselves each indebted to the State of Tennessee in the sum of two hundred and fifty dollars to be void on condition that the said Alexander D.Gordon shall well & truly keep the peace of the State toward all the good people of the County of Haywood & particularly towards Asa Biggs untill the next term of this court. And it is ordered that the said Alexander D.Gordon payable costs in this behalf expended and that Fieri facias issue thereupon.

(p-209) Abraham Kirksey   )   Trespass
                    vs   )
          Archibald McNeal   )

This day came the said parties by their attornies and thereupon came also a jury of good and lawful men, to wit, Thomas Rutherford, Herndon Harrelson Samuel Elliott, Philip Koonce, John McWhite, John G.Jones, Robert T.Smith, John Kee John P.Majors, Berry Derin & Nelson Hartgrove, William Lorance who being elected, tried and sworn well and truly to try the issue joined upon their oaths aforesaid do say that they find the issue in favour of the plaintiff & assess his damages to twenty five dollars, besides costs. It is therefore considered by the court that the said plaintiff do recover against the said Defendant the Damages aforesaid by the jury assessed & the costs in this behalf expended & the defendant in mercy etc.
Transcript 25th March 1828
 *men

(p-209con.) The Defendant being dissatisfied with the Judgement hath prayed & obtained an appeal to the Circuit Court. He having given bond & security therefor.

Edwin H.Childress)
     vs   )   Debt
Andrew Hammil   )

     This day came the said parties by their attornies and thereupon came a jury of good and lawful men to wit, Thomas Rutherford, Herndon Harelson, Samuel Elliott, Philip Koonce, John McWhite, William Larance John G.Jones, Robert T.Smith, John Kee John P.Majors, Berry Derin, & Nelson Hartgrove, who being elected tried and sworn well and truly to try the issue joined, upon their oath aforesaid do say that the defendant hath paid all the Debt in the declaration mentioned except the sum of one hundred & forty one dollars, eighty seven & one half cents, and they assess the plaintiffs damages by reason of the detention of the residue of that debt to seven (p-210) dollars and eighty three cents besides costs. It is therefore considered by the court here that the said plaintiff do recover against the said defendant one hundred and forty one dollars, eighty seven & one half cents, the residue of the in the declaration mentioned and the damages aforesaid by the Jury in form aforesaid assessed and the costs in this behalf expended & the defendant in mercy etc. Issued 28th March 1828

     Deed of bargain & sale from John G.Carithers sheriff of Haywood County to Thomas G.Nixon for six hundred and forty acres of land was this day acknowledged in open by the said John G.Carithers, sheriff as aforesaid to be his act of deed & ordered to be registered.

     Deed of bargain and sale from Francis L.Dillard to James Mauldin for one hundred & twenty acres of land was this day acknowledged in open court by said Francis L.Dillard to be his act & deed & ordered to be registered.

     Thomas G.Nixon administrator of John P.Leigh dec. makes return of the amount of sales etc. of said estate, which is ordered to be recorded.

     Nicholas T.Perkins, Guardian to Simon T.Turner, makes known to this court his resignation as guardian aforesaid- And thereupon and John T. Turner was appointed guardian for the said Simon T.Turner who entered into bond in the penal sum of eight thousand dollars with Hyram Bradford and Henry H.Turner his securities.

John Potter   )
     vs   )) Sci fa
Thomas J.McGuire)

     The Defendant being duly warned and not appearing tho solemnly called on motion of the plaintiff by his attorney it is considered by the court that the plaintiff may have execution against the said Defendant for seventeen dollars fifty three and three (p-211) fourth cents, the costs in the writ aforesaid specified according to the form and effect of his recognizance therein mentioned and also that the plaintiff recover against the said Defendant his costs by him expended in sueing forth and

(p-21 con.) prosecuting this writ and the said Defendant in mercy
etc.
(Execution 28th March 1828)

```
        Thomas Potter   )
             vs         )  Sciri Facias
        Thomas J.McGuire )
```

The defendant having been duly warned and not appearing tho
solemnly called, on motion of the plaintiff by his attorney it is considered by the the court that the plaintiff may have execution against
the said Defendant for twenty nine dollars seventy eight and three fourth
cents the costs in the writ aforesaid specified, according to the form &
& effect of his recognizance therein mentioned, and also that the said
plaintiff do recover against the said defendant his costs by him expended
in sueing forth and prescuting this writ, & the said defendant in mercy
etc.
Execution 28th March 1828

Daniel Cherry prayed & obtained leave to keep a ferry the south
fork of the Forked deer river, at Harrisburg & entered into bond &
security.

Court adjourned until tomorrow morning nine o'clock.

```
                        Dan'l. Cherry
                        N.T.Perkins
                        L.McGuire
```

(p-212) Thursday morning March 13th 1828 court met pursuant to adjournment. Present Daniel Cherry, N.T.Perkins, Lawrence McGuire, & Sam'l. P.
Ashe esqrs. Justices

```
Francis Lamoin      )
        vs          )  Appeal
Nicholas T.Perkins  )
```

This day came the said parties by their attornies and thereupon
came also a jury of good and lawful men to wit Thomas Rutherford,
Thomas G.Nixon Samuel Elliott, Herndon Haralson, Philip Koonce,
Franc is L.Dillard, John McWhite, Arthur F.McCain, Jullus Sanders,
Archibald McNeal, John A.King, and William Lawrence, who being elected
tried and sworn well & truly to try the matters in dispute between the
parties, upon their oaths do say they find for the Defendant & assess his
damages to ten dollars besides costs.
Ex. Issued 29th March 1828
It is therefore considered by the court that the said defendant
recover against the s aid plaintiffs the damages aforesaid by the jury
assessed etc.

Hyram B radford admr. of Robert A.Penn makes return of the amount
of sales of said estate, which is ordered to be recorded.

Deed of bargain & sale from Thomas H.Taylor by Matthew Ray his
attorney to Hyram Bradford for five acres, sixty six poles & twelve
twenty fifths of a pole was this day acknowledged in open court by said

(p-212con.) Matthew Ray & ordered to be certified for registration.
Fees pd. B.H.S.

Deed of conveyance from Thomas H.Taylor by Matthew Ray his attorney
to Robert Perry three acres fifty eight and twelve twenty twenty fifths
of a poles of land was this day a acknowledged in open court by said
Matthew Ray attorney as aforesaid & ordered to be registered.

(p-213) Deed of conveyance from William W.Kavanaugh to John Oneal for
one hundred and fifty acres of land was this day proved in open court
by the oath of Daniel Cherry one of the witnesses thereto.

It is ordered by the court that Francis M.Wood, Charles Wortham,
Daniel Cherry, William Johnson senr, John R.Roddy, Samuel P. Ashe,
Lewis Fascue, Lawrence McGuire, Richard Nixon, Nicholas T.Perkins, T.
Jacocks, Oliver Woods, Richard Taylor, John Williams, Daniel Shaw,
Bignal Crook, Charles White, Thomas Crutcher, Vincent Haralson, Jesse
L.Kirk, Simon Turner, James Hart, Doctor Edward Davie, David Hay,
Stephen Booth senr. Joshua Abstain, be summoned to attend at the next
Circuit Court then & there to serve as grand or petit jurors as the
case may be and also that Jordan M.Hansborough be summoned to serve at
said court as constables.
Iss'd

Deed of conveyance from Thomas H.Taylor by his attorney to Samuel
Elliott for two acres & 85 poles of land was acknowledged in open court
& ordered to be registered.
Certified & Del'd fees pd. B.H.S.

It is ordered by the court that Herndon Haralson and Hyraim
Bradford be and are hereby appointed commissioners to Little Richard
Nixon county trustee and John G.Carithers sherriff of this county for
the present year.
Iss'd

It is ordered by the court that Herndon Haralson, Thomas G.Nixon
John Potter, Mansfield Ware, Joseph Murphy, Nathaniel D.Lilly, John
Andrews, John Marberry, L.D.Womble, J.P. Majors, William Johnson senr.
Nelson (p-214) Hartgrove, Benjamin Weaver, Joseph Curry, Richard
Moore, Ephraim Stanfield, James Henderson, Thomas Hughes Levi Gardner,
Archibald McNeal, John McWhite Jordan Hollowell, Samuel Brown Thomas
Forest, William Weddle and Philip Koonce be summoned to attend as
jurors at the next term of this court as jurors- and that Reubin Alphin
and Thomas J.Blythe be summoned as constables-
Issd.

The State of Tennessee)
        vs   )
James Haggard   )

This day came as well the State of Tennessee by Alexander B.
Bradford esquire attorney General, as the Defendant in his proper person
and the defendant being solemnly charged saith he is not guilty in manner
and form as charged in the bill of Indictment- and thereupon came also
a jury of good and lawful men, to wit, Samuel Elliott, Francis L.

(p-214con.) Dillard, Philip Koonce, Thomas Rutherford, William
Lawrence, John T.Turner, Mason F.Johnson, Nelson Hartgrove, John Potter
John McWhite, Archibald McNeal, James R.Apling who being elected,
tried and sworn well and truly to try the issue of traverse upon their
oath do say that the defendant is guilty in manner and form as charged
in the bill of Indictment

It is therefore considered by the court that the Defendant make
his fine with the State of Tennessee by the payment of five dollars &
he be taken.
Issd.

The State   )
      vs   )
Stephens S.Childress)

This day came as well the State of Tennessee by A.B.Bradford esqr.
attorney General and the defendant being solemnly charged says he is
guilty in manner and form as charged in the bill of Indictment & puts
himself upon the grace and mercy of the court. It is therefore considered by the court that the Defendant make his fine with the state by
the payment of five dollars and all costs & the defendant in mercy etc.
Iss'd

(p-215) The following justices they being a majority of the court
to wit Richard Nixon, Nicholas T.Perkins, Samuel P.Ashe, Lawrence
McGuire, Daniel Cherry, Matthew Ray, & Blackman Coleman, and the vote
being taken as required by the act of 1827 it is unanimously agreed and
so voted for by each of said justices that the jurors for the present
year both for the Circuit of County Courts of this county be allowed
the sum of one dollar each for each day they may serve as such-

The State of Tennessee)
      vs   )
Francis L.Dillard   )

This day came as well the State of Tennessee by Alexander B.
Bradford esquire attorney General, as the said Defendant in his proper
person, and the defendant being charged saith he is guilty in manner and
form as charged in the bill of Indictment and puts himself upon the
grace & mercy of the court. It is therefore considered by the court
that the Defendant makes his fine with the state by the payment of five
dollars & all costs and that he be taken etc.
Iss'd

Mansfield Wane assee   )
      vs   )
Joel H.Dyer, executor of   )
Robert H.Dyer, dec'd & John G.Carithers)

This day came the plaintiff by his attorney & saith he intends no
further to prosecute his suit against the said Defendants. It is therefore considered by the court that the Defendants go hence without day
and recover against the said Plaintiff their costs about their defence
in this behalf expended
Satisfied

(p-215con.) Benjamin Rowland)
          vs   )
     Benjamin George)

This day came the plaintiff by their attorney & saith he intends no further to prosecute his suit against the Defendant. It is therefore considered by the court that the Defendant go hence without day (p-216) and recover against the plaintiff his costs in this behalf expended etc.

John Carithers esquires, sheriff and collector of the public Taxes for the County of Haywood this day made in open court a report in the following words and figures, to wit-

State of Tennessee)
Haywood County   )   March Term 1828

I, John G.Carithers sheriff and collector of the public taxes for said county report to court the following tracts of land, Town lots etc as having been given in for the taxes for the year 1827- that the taxes thereon remain due and unpaid and that the respective due owners or claimants thereof have no goods or chattels within his county on which he can destrain for said taxes the wit

Owners names	No.of acres	Dist.	Ran.	Sec.	No.of EorG	T.lot	Water course
Anderson, John	200	10					
Allread, William	3	"	4	10			
Aanderson, Daniel	640	"	4	10	E.684		
Anderson, Walker	1000	"	4	10	" 685		
Anderson, George	640	"	5	9	552		
Ashbrook, Moses	80	"	5	8			
Arthur William	480		5	9	1137		
Brown Peter	500	10			307		
Brown, Thomas	1000	"	5	7&8	2193		
Same	125	"	5	8	2191		
Baldridge Alford	640	"	4	8	906		
Branch, Joseph	2295	"	5.6	8	805		
Bledsoe Anthony, heirs of	428	"	5&6	9	587		
Barret Robert W.	50	"	6	6	2180		
Baker, Robert	50	"	6	6	2181		
Bond Eaton	100	"	4	7	2283		
Brown James	420½	"	6	8	1801		
Same	2875		4&5	7 &8	1803		
Bowers George	629	"	6	6"7	968		
Brown John	1000	"	"	"	"		
Brown John	1000	"	5	7&8	G.271		
Boyler, Nathan	800	"	4	7			
(p-217)							
Canady,John	240	11	2				
Cockrell Mark R.	490	10	4	10	E153		
Same	286	"	5	9	"302		
Same	117½	"	5	9	"570		
Same	320	"	5	9	"797		

(p-217con.) Owners Names	No.of acres	Dist	Ran.	Sec.	No.of EorG	T.lot	Water course
Calwell James	200	"	5&6	11	Ct.155		
Crawford,Wm.W.	320						
Chester,Robert J.	100	11	1	6	1740		
Cobbs,Robt.L.	50	10	5	9	703		
Same	345	"	6	8.9	1796		
Childress,John Repts of	935	11	1	6	453		
Carpenter Benj.	1250	10	4	11			
Dyson Eqilla	660	10	4	7pt	E589		
Denson,William	360	10	5	11	776		
Dixon, William	500	4	4	10	E190		
Doughtery,Thos.	500		4	7	77		
Douthit,Wm.W.					1		
Dobson Mathew	250	11	2	6			
Dixon William	500	10	6	9			
Same	500	10	4	6			
Same	50	"	3&4	10			
Ewing,Alexander C.	640	10	4&5	9	E5313		
Ewing,Alexander	200	"	4	9			
Same	380	"	4	9	525		
Same	900	"	5	9	528		
Edmonson,Samuel	390	"	1	9	359		
Same	390	"	1	9	125		
Flowers,Benj.	120	10	4	9	1809		
Flowers David	1660	10	5&6	7&8	Gr298		
Fowler Silavanus	400	"	455	9	950		
Freeman Green	200	"	4	9	2249		
Figures Mathew	3/4					2	
(p-218)							
Green A.Hays	1000	11	1	9	407		
Goodlow Marthy E.	117½	10	5	11			
Green,William H.of	200	"	4	8	320		
Givins & Wells	512	"	4	10	179		
Goff Andrew	75	"	6	9	477		
Graves,William B.	1500	"	5	7&8	2149		
Greer Joseph	1500		5	8	2147		
Green J.S.& W.B.Sims	125	11	6	9	0		
Hays O.B.	750	11	1	6	57		
Same	215	"	1	6	328		
Same	227	10	5	9	325		
Same	265	11	1	6	357		
Same	320	10	5	9	799		
Henderson,Thos.	640	10	4&5	9	516	9	
Hodges Preston G.	200	10	6	9	1958		
Harelson Silas	50	10	5	6	2222		
Harnelson Thos.B.	50		5	6	2223		
Henderson Robt	150		4	8	2270		
Harris Western	200		6	11	2368		
Hart James	1920	11	2	6	748		
Hart Anthony	261½	10	5	10			
Same	434	11	2	7	230		
Houston Robt.	80	10	5	11			
Joiner Matthew	185		4	11	256		
Johnston Kane	640	11	1&2	9&10	685		

(p-218con.) Owners Names	No. of acres	Dist	Ran	Sec.	No. of EorG	T.lot	Water course
Johnston Geo.	600	10	6	8	1255	part of Gt290	
Johnston Geo.M.	400		6	8	1255	part of Gt.290	
Jones Calvin	560		5	9	514		
Jones Henry	45		5	8	1331		
Jones Edmund	786		5&6	10	G406	part of B.S.3000	
King, Thomas	640		6	6	245		
Moore Robt C. paid	200	10	5	6	1936	Tax pd Shff.	
McClure,Wm.	150		5	6	2229		
McCampbell heirs of (p-219)	4757/1010	6	8		G291	part of 5000	
Same	502½	11	1	8	G295	part of 5000	
Same	540	10	6	8	"282		
Same	675	"	5	7	"294		
Same	240	"	5	7	294		
McNairy & others	317		4&5	10			
McLemore Robt	640	10	6	6	1116		
McLemore Sugars	160		6	8	996		
McNairy John	500		4&5	10	115		
McIver John	640		5	6	656		
Same	1000	11	2	9&10	497		
Same	100	10	4	10			
Same	1000	11	2	10&11	597		
Moore William	660	10	4	7	Gt.275		
Murry J.B.Gholston	70		6	8	1322		
McNary,Butler & Phillips	5000	11	1	9	629		
McOree J.Heirs of	640	11	1	6			
Same	180	"	1&2	9	261		
McLellon John	3	10	4	10	E1796		
McKen Griffith	640	11	1	6	"155		
Same	100	"	1	6	383		
Neal Henry Heirs of	1684	11	2	9	690	Big Hatchie	
Newton Edward	640	11	2	9&10	572		
Overton, John	1000	10			Gt155		
Overton Thomas Heirs of	1000		5	8	Gt272	granted to T.Brown	
Patrick John	274		4	10	931		
Polk Ezekiel	500	10	6	6&7	652		
Philpot John W.	500	"	4	8	319		
Same	360	11	1	8			
Polk Thomas	1434	10	5	6	406		
Same	500	"	4	7	77		
Same	500		4	7			
Read John &others	200	10	5&6	11			
Rice John	1046	10	6	8	Gt287	Balance of 5000 a T	
Same	5000	11	1	7&8	E2199		
Same	5000		1	7&8	E300		
Same	22963/4		1	8	2205	part of 5000A T	

(p-220)Owners Names	No.of acres	Dist	Ran.	Sec.	No.of EorG	T.lot	Water course
Same	2728		1&2	8	2210	part of 5000 a.t.	
Ringlet James	57	10	5	8			
Robison James	666 2/3	10	6	6&7	428		
Smith Thomas J.						3	
Skillan James	100	10	4	9	2312		
Searcy Robert	7312/1010		6	8&9	part of Gr.R.5000's		
Same	801½	10	6	8&9	Gt282		
Same	482	"	5	7&8	"294		
Same	240	"	5	7	294		
Same	284	11	1	8	295		
Scudder Phillip J.	1000	10	5	9	328		
Simms Walter B.	60	11	1	6			
Smith Benjamin	1250	10	4	11			
Smith Richard	640	10	4	6	1133		
Smith Sidney P.						2	
Subblefield Climart	228	10	5	6	364		
Steed Jesse	1035	10	4	7&8	Gt308		
Sullivan Lee	100 0	11	1&2	6	275		pd.clerk$9.90
Shrophire David						6	
Tisdale James,Heirs of	7606	11	2	11	Gt412		
Same	5000	"	1	9	"414		
Same	5592	10	6	10	"415		
Same	3496	10	6	10	"410		
Same	6934	10&11	6	10	"411		
Tisdale & Wheaton Heirs	12	10					
Same	640	10	1	9	E355		
Totten Benj	450	10	4&5	10	195		
Terrill John	640	10	4	8	968		
Tate Mark A	640	10	5&6	6	1085		
Wilkes Benjamin	50		4	6	2254		
Walker Green H	89½		4	6	2386		
Wilkes Benj	50		4	6	2392		
Wescot Patience	2539½	10	5&6	8&9	Gt282		
Same	1756	10	5	8	"287		
Same	2231	10	5&6	7&8	"294		
Same	1368	11	1	8&9	"295		
Same	2848	10&11	6&1	8&9	"291 (part of Gt.291		
Walker Jacob	512	10	5	11	E469		
(p-221)							
Wheaton John L.	6140	10	6	11	Gt403		
Same	1400	11	1	11	"407		
Same	4617	11	1	10	"400		
Wheaton Mary	5796	11	1	10&11	"413		
Same	2786	10&11	1&2	10	"410		
Same	2393	11	1	11	"407		
Warner Marrs	85	10	5	8			
William J.H.	1000	10	6	6	E219		
Williams Samuel H.	800	10	5	9	787		
Windsor John	1000	10	5	7&8	1259		
Williams R.W.	176	10	5	11	735		

(p-221con.)Owners Names	No.of acres	Dist.	Ran.	Sec.	No.of EorG	T.lot	Water course
Walker Alford M.	20	10	4	6	2405		
Yarby John	600					1	
Iss'd 10 May 1828							

Whereupon it is considered by the court that Judgment be and the same is hereby entered against the aforesaid several tracts of land in the name of the State of Tennessee for the amount of the taxes ,costs charges severally due thereon for the year 1827- And it is further considered by the court that the said several tracts of land or so much thereof as shall be sufficient of each of said tracts to satisfy the taxes costs of charges be sold as the law directs etc.

On motion it is ordered by the court that William R.Hess,Francis L.Dillard & Manfield Ware be and are hereby appointed to lay off & set apart to Mrs. Carolina Penn widow of the late Robert a Penn one years provision agreeably to act of assembly etc & make report to next court

(p-222)Nicholas T.Perkins guardian   )
        vs   )
    Benjamin Rowland and   )
    Hiram Bradford admr of   )   Indebt
    Robert A.Penn dec'd   )

This day came the plaintiff, by his atty. and the said Defts. being solemnly called came, not but made default. It is therefore considered by the court that the said plaintiff recover against the said Deft. Benj. Rowland debt of $85 together with one dollar and eight cents for the detention thereof; and it is further considered by the court that the said Pltiff . against the said Deft. H.Bradford admr. as aforesaid the said sum of $85. and the damages aforesaid to be levied of the goods and chattels rights and credits of the said Decedent in his hands to be administered when so much thereof shall come to his hand to be administered. and in mercy etc
Issued vs Rowland 13 May 1828

Seth Whitlay use of   )
Levi Gardner   )
     vs   )   Attachment
George McCray   )   In Debt

This day came the plaintiff by his atty. and it appearing to the satisfaction of the court that the Deft is not an inhabitant of this state- It is ordered by the court that all proceedings in said cause be stayed six months and that publication be made thereof for three successive weeks in the Whig and Bannera paper published in the town of Nashville, State of Tennessee, the last of which publication shall be made at least two months before the September term next of this court, notifying him the said Deft. to appear in this court on or before the 2nd Monday of Sept. next replevy his property attached & plead to issue or demur otherwise judgment final will be entered against him-

158

(p-222con.) Iss'd 3rd May

Ephriam Roddy)
vs   )   Attachment
Wilson Nesbitt)   In assumpsit

This day came the plaintiff by his attorney and it appearing to the
satisfaction of the court that the Deft is not an inhabitant of this state
It is ordered by the court that all proceedings in said cause be stayed
six months, and that publication be made thereof for three successive
(p-223) weeks in the whig and Banner assesser published in the Town of
Nashville state of Tennessee, the cost of which publication shall be
made at least two months previous to the next September term of this
court, notifying him the said Deft. to appear in this court on or before
the 2nd Monday of September next replevy his property attached & plead
to issue or demur otherwise judgment final will be entered against him.
Issued 5th May

Ephrain Roddy)
vs   )   Garnishment
John Roddy   )

This day came the Plaintiff by his attorney and it appearing to
the satisfaction of the court that said Defendant has been regularly
garnished, in the case of said Plaintiff against one Wilson Nesbitt,
and he being solemnly called, came not, but made default; It is therefore ordered by the court that a conditional judgment be entered against
said deft. for the sum of $500.00 so together with cost and that a
sciri facias issue to said Deft. requiring him to appear here at the next
term of the court holden on the 2nd Monday June next and show cause if
any he can why final judgment should not be entered of against him in
the final herein of said attachment.
Sci F.Iss'd

Eli J.McClun)
vs   )   In Debt
William Weaver)

This day came the plaintiff by his attorney and says that he will
no further prosecute his said suit, It is therefore ordered by the
court that the Deft. go hence sine die, and that he recover his cost
about his defence in this behalf expended.

(p-224) Joseph Spence)
vs   )   In Debt no 3
James H.Walker)

By consent of the parties by their attornies, leave is granted the
Deft. to put in the plea of non 1st factrum at the next term of this court.

Francis S.Coxe)
vs   )   Assumsit
Hiram Bradford)

On motion of the Plaintiff, by his attorney leave is granted the
plaintiff to take depostions generally by giving 20 days notice within

(p-224con.) the state and 40 days without

James L.Wortham has permission to keep a public Ferry on the South Fork of the Forked Deer River, who gave bond & security.

It is ordered that John G.Carithers Sheriff of this county be allowed a credit with the state treasurer for the sum of sixty five & one half cents on a tract of three hundred & fifty acres in the name of John McDonald improperly listed & also for the sum of one dollar & ninety seven cents with the county trustee on said tract, and also that the sheriff be allowed the sum of one dollar, twelve & one half cents with the State Treasurer on six hundred acres of land in properly reported in the name of Nathan Roddy, as also with the jurther sum of two dollars, thirty seven & one half cents with the county treasurer on said tract of land-
Issd

Court adjourned untill tomorrow nine o'clock-

> Rich'd Nixon Cha
> L.McGuire
> Matthew Ray

Friday morning 14 March 1828 court met pursuant, to adjournment present R.W.Nixon, Lawrence McGuire, S.P.Ashe and N.T.Perkins esqrs. Justices .

(p-225 omitted

(p-226) It being represented to this court that the family of Daniel Parker of this county are enterely destitue of the means of a support & are truly objects of charity, It is therefore ordered and requested by this court Jordan M.Hansborough make provision with some suitable person to furnish said family with necessonies & provisions until the next term of this court, at which time this court will make a suitable allowance, and it is further ordered that the said Jordan M.Hansborough have here on the first day of the next term of this court the said Damiel & family to be disposed of as to the court may____ meet.

G.Jarrad Grisham assee	)
of Hyram Bradford	)
vs	)
Ezekiel Blackshire &	)
Thomas West	)

The Defendant Ezekiel Blackshire who was taken by virtue of a writ of capias ad satis faciendum at the instance of the plaintiff issued by Matthew Ray esqr. a justice of the peace of this county to satisfy the sum of twenty seven dollars & fifteen cents obtained before said Ray on the 10th day of February 1828, & who entered into bond, with the said Thomas West as his security to appear at this term to render a schedule or take the insolvent debtors oath as required by act of assembly was this day solemnly called to come into court as he was bound to do come not, but made default, and the said Thomas West being also

(p-226con.) solemly called to come into court & bring with the body of
the said Ezekiel came not nor does (p-227) he bring here the body of
the said Ezekiel. It is therefore considered by the court here that
the said plaintiff recover against the defendants the said sum of twenty
seven dollars & fifteen cents, & the costs in this behalf expended etc.
Isd.

John Kinsey was this day bound as an apprentice to John Wiatt, to
learn the art, mistery and trade of a taylor, who entered into indentures

Matthew Ray prayed and obtained a license to keep an ordinary at
his house in the town of Brownsville, who into bond and took the oath
prescribed by law.

John G.Carithers esquire Sheriff- and collector of the public
taxes for the county of Haywood makes report to this court in the words
& figures following to wit

State of Tennessee)
Haywood County   )   March Tenn 1828

I John G.Carithers sheriff and collector of the public taxes of
said county do hereby report to court the following tracts of land and
town lots as not being listed for taxation for the year 1827-that the
taxes on the same have not been paid and that the respective owners are
liable to double taxes, to wit

Owners Names	No.of acres	Dist.	Ran.	Sec.	No.of EorG	T.lot	No.of lots
Brown John	4000	10			Gt116		
Lewis William T.	1000	10			G.60		
Same	1000	10			"90		
Williamson Thomas's Heirs						1	no.94
Hord William	2100	10	4	9	E.500		
Clanton Robert						4	no's 125,143, 137,49
Bryant John T.						4	No.49,93, 101,97
Bryant Stephen						1	No.70
Warrner Amos						1	No.31
Talbott & Bryant						1	No.79
Crutcher William						3	No.55,60,57
Scurlock,Beverly						1	No.129
Hermis Champ						1	"96
Hutcheson Wilson						1	"26

Iss'd 10th May 1828
(p-228) Whereupon it is considered by the court that that Judgment be
and the same is hereby entered up against the aforesaid several tracts
of land and town lots in the name of the State of Tennessee for the

(p-228con.) amount of Double taxes costs and charges severally due thereon for said year 1827 and it is ordered by the court that said several tracts and town lots, or so much thereof each as shall be suffi- cient to satisfy the taxes, costs and charges be sold as the law directs.

Court adjourned until court in course.

> Rich'd Nixon Char-
> L.McGuire
> Matthew Ray

(p-229) State of Tennessee)
            Haywood County   ) Set

At a court of pleas and quarter sessions began and holden for the County of Haywood at the courthouse in the town of Brownsville on the second Monday it being the ninth day of June A.D. 1828. Present the worshipful Richard Nixon, Lawrence McGuire, Daniel Cherry, Esquires and others their fellow justices of the peace John G.Carithers, sheriff and Britain H.Sanders Clerk-

It is ordered by the court that Hyram Bradford, James Smith ,& Herndon Harralson be & are hereby appointed commissioners to settle with James Malden administrator of Bryant H.Kirksy deceased & make report thereof to this court.
Iss'd

A power of attorney from Thomas G.Nixon of this county to Thomas Turner of Plymoth of the State of North Carolina was this day acknowledged in open court by said Thomas G.Nixon & ordered registered to be certified Delivered to Thos.G.Nixon

It is ordered by the court that the county part of the tax on a tract of land entered in the name of James Whitsett of one hundred & thirty nine acres for the years 1824 & 1825 be refunded to said Whitsitt or to Daniel Cherry his agent. It appearing satisfactorilly to this court that there is no such tract of land in the county a majority of the acting Justices being present to wit.

Ayes   )   Ayes
)
J.P.Ashe   )   O.Woods
Dan'l Cherry   )   Joel Estes
L.McGuire   )   J.L.Wortham
J.T.Jacocks   )
J.L.Kirk   )

(p-230) It is ordered by the court that the clerk of this court receive lists of Taxable property & polls from such as may not have given in for the present year, until the next term of this court, and at the same time receive the tax due thereon and pay the same over to the sheriff of this county, taking his receipt therefor - And it shall be the duty of said clerk to furnish the county trustee & the State treasurer with the amount thereof.

(p-230con.) Upon the petition of Hyram Bradford administrator of the estate of Robert A.Penn deceased, late of said county, setting fourth that there are not sufficient assets that has or will come into his hands to be administered to pay the Debts due by said estate & therefore prays this court to grant him leave to sell one of the negroes of said estate named Alsey for the purpose of satisfying the Debts of said estate. It is therefore ordered by the court that the said Hyram Bradford, administrator as aforesaid, be authorised to sell said slave for the purposes aforesaid.

Reubin Allphin constables in Cap't. Elliott company this day handed the court his resignation as such which was accordingly received-

A Deed of bargain and sale from George W.Hockly executor of J. Wescot, by his atto. Wm. H. Henderson to John Rodgers for thirty six acres of land was this day produced in open court , and duly acknowledged and ordered to be certified for registration

(p-231) A Deed of Bargain and sale from John C.McLemore and William Stoddert by Wm. H.Henderson their attorney to Wm. C.Russell for one hundred thirty three & three fourth acres of land, was this day acknowledged in open court by said William in open court by said William H. Henderson to be his act & deed & ordered to be registered.

John W.Wortham records the ear mark of his stock thus a cross & split in the left ear, and a swallow fork in the right.

Eli Faris records the ear mark of his stock thus , a crop off the right ear & an underbit in the same.

A Deed of conveyance from Charles Wortham to James F.Wortham for one hundred & ten acres of land was this day acknowledged in open court by the said Charles Wortham & ordered to be registered .
Certified & Dld.

William Shearin Guardian for Henry Shearin, Hugh Shearin & Joseph Shearin orphans of Jarret Shearin dec'd makes return of the amount of said orphans estate & account , which is ordered to be registered.

A Deed of Bargain and sale from Joel Dyer to Lewis & William Bowling for one hundred acres of land was this day produced in open court and duly proven by the oaths of Henry L.Gray and Samuel Elliott subscribing witnesses thereto and ordered to be certified for registration.
Certified & Deld.

A Deed of bargain and sale from Richard White to Joseph B.Findley for one hundred and sixty acres of land in the Arkansas Territory was this day produced in open court and duly proven by the oaths of Samuel Elliot and Henry L.Gray subscribing witnesses thereto and ordered to be certified for registration.
Certified & del'd

It is ordered by the court that the following persons be added to the Jury of view heretofore appointed to view & mark a road from Estanaula

(p-231con.) in a direction to Brownsville to wit, David Drake & Samuel Blackman, James Malden, & Vardeman, Halsel (p-232) Matthew Ray esqr. one of the Justices of the peace of this county makes known to this court his resignation as such which is accepted.
Issd

Matthew Ray & Joel L.Abstain was this day appointed constables for the county who gave bond & security & took the oaths prescribed by law

It is ordered by the court there being a majority of the justices present, that Henry Turner, Charles White, John T.Turner Samuel Brown Bowen Reynolds, Lewis Powers, James Malden, and Vincent Haralson or any five of them be appointed a jury of view to view and mark a road the nearest and best way from Jeffers Bluff to Madison County line to intersect the McGuire road where the same crosses the said county line & make report to the next term of this court.
Iss'd. 23rd June.

Jordan M.Hansborough is appointed constable to attend this court in the room & stead of Thos. J.Blythe.

The commissioners appointed to settle with James Malden administrator of Bryant H.Kirksey Dec'd make report to this court that they have done the same which is ordered to be recorded.

(p-233)   State of Tennessee)
                    vs   )
           Alexander D.Gordon)

Upon the affidavit of the defendant it is ordered by the court that the five assessed against him at the last term court of five dollars for his non attendance as a juror, be set aside on the payment of costs.
The court adjourned until tomorrow nine o'clock-

                              Richd. Nixon cha-
                              L.McGuire
                              Jessee L.Kirk J.P.

Tuesday morning June 10th 1828 present
Court met according to adjournment present the worshipful Richard Nixon, Lawrence McGuire, Jesse L.Kirk & others, their fellow justices.

Thomas G.Nixon, admr. of John R. Leigh Deceased makes return to this court of an additional return of the sales of said estate which is ordered to be recorded.

Deed of Conveyance from Joseph B.Findly to William Lawrence for 160 acres of was this day produced in open court and duly acknowledged by said Findly to be his act and deed and ordered to be certified for registration
Certified & Deld,

John G.Carithers sheriff of this county makes return of the venire facias returnable to this term in the woods and figures following towit

(p-233con.) State of Tennessee
At a court of pleas and quarter sessions began and
held for the county of Haywood at the courthouse in the town of
Brownsville on the 2nd Monday in March 1828 it being the 10th day of said
month ,present the worshipful Richard Nixon, Daniel Cherry, Lawrence
McGuire and Samuel P.Ashe Esquires. It is ordered by the court that the
following persons good and lawful men viz, each being a white male citizen
of the age of twenty one years and a householder (p-234) to wit
Herndon Haralson, Thomas G.Nixon, John Potter, Mansfield Wane, Joseph
Murphy, Nathaniel, D.Lilly, John Andrews, John Marbry, Larinzo D.Womble
John P.Majors, William Johnston Jr. Nelson Hargrove, Benjamin Weaver,
Joseph Curry, Richard Moore, Ephraim Stanfield, James Henderson, Thos.
Hughs, Levi Guardner, Archibald McNeale, John McWhite, Jonathan Hollowell
Samuel Brown, Thomas Forrest, William Weddle, and Phillip Koonce, be
summoned to attend at the next term of this court on Tuesday after the
second Monday in June next then and there to serve as grand and petit
Jurors as the case may be and that Reubin Allphin and Thomas J.Blythe be
summoned to attend said court as constables.

Test B.H.Sanders, clk.

State of Tennessee
To the sheriff of Haywood County greeting. You are hereby commanded
to summon the aforesaid persons to serve as jurors to the next court of
pleas and quarter sessions to be held at the courthouse in the town of
Brownsville on Tuesday after the second Monday in June next, and this
they shall in no wise omit under the penalty prescribed by law herein
fail not and have you then and there this writ, witness Britain H.
Sanders clerk of our said court at office the second Monday in March 1828
and 52 years of American Independence

B.H.Sanders, clk.

Upon the back of which said venire facias John G.Carithers, shff.
has made the following indorsement to wit,

By virtue of the within venire facias I have proceeded to summon
all the within named persons to serve as jurors except Joseph Curry &
Thomas Thweatt and such persons so summoned are inhabitants of said
county and are free holders or householders of said county.

Jno. G.Carithers, Shff.

The following persons were drawn elected charged and sworn as grand
jurors for the present term, to wit, James Henderson foreman, Archibald
McNeal, Ephraim Stanfield, John Marbury, William Johnston, senr. Richard
Moore, Thomas Hughs, Phillip Koonce, Thomas G.Nixon, Samuel Brown, Nelson
Hargrove, (p-235) John P.Majors, & John Potter retired under the care of
an officer sworn to attend them, to consider of presentments.

The commissioners appointed to lay off one years provision for
Eliza Leigh widow of John R.Leigh dec'd makes report that they have done
the same, which is ordered to be recorded-

(p-235con.) The commissioners appointed to lay off one years provision for Lucy C.Penn, widow of Robt. A.Penn dec'd makes report that they have done the same, which is ordered to be recorded.

Matthew Arnold)
       vs   ) Motion
William Lawrence)

    On motion of the plaintiff by his attorney, and it appearing to the satisfaction of this court that the said plaintiff did on the twenty first day of May 1828, obtain a judgment against the said Defendant before Jesse L.Kirk esquire, a justice of the peace of this county, for the sum of twenty eight dollars & all lawful costs. That an execution issued thereon which came duly into the hands of F.J.Blythe a constable of said county, who hath made return thereon as follows "Levied May 27th 1828 on a tract of land of seventy four acres, lying in Haywood County on the waters of Bear Creek 5th range & 6th section adjoining a tract of 957 acres belonging to McGimpsey levied on as the property of sd. Lawrence, there being no personal property of his on which to levy in this county. It is therefore ordered by the court that a writ of venditional exponas issue to cause said land so levied on as aforesaid to be sold to satisfy the debt & costs aforesaid & the costs about the motion in this behalf expended etc.
Iss'd

    Herndon Haralson & John Andrews, two of the jurors summoned on the venire facias to this court, are excused from serving as such.

(p-236) Peck & Cockram)
          vs   ) Motion
    William Lawrence)

    On motion of the said plaintiffs by by their attorney and it appearing to the satisfaction of this court, that the said plaintiffs did on the day of recover a Judgment against the said defendant before Oliver Woods esquire a justice of the peace of this county for the sum of Eleven dollars, fifty six & one fourth cents & all legal costs. That an executive issued thereon which came duly into the hands of T.J.Blythe a constable of this county who hath made return thereon as follows "Levied may 27th, 1828 on a tract of land of Seventy four acres lying in Haywood County on the waters of Bear Creek 5 range 6 section adjoining a tract of 957 acres belonging McGimpsey, levied on as the property of said Lawrence. there being no personal property of his on which to levy in this county. It is therefore ordered by the court that a writ of venditioni Exponas issue to cause said land so levied on as aforesaid to be sold to satisfy said judgment & costs aforesaid & the costs about the motion in this behalf expended etc.
Issd.

John Elliott)
     vs   ) Motion
William Lawrence)

    On motion of the plaintiff by his attorney and it appearing to the satisfaction of this court that the said plaintiff did on the 21st day

(p-236con.) of May 1828 obtain a Judgment against the said Defendant before Jesse L. Kirk esquire a Justice of the Peace for this county for the sum of six dollars & fifty cents & all legal costs. That an execution issued thereon which came into the hands of T.J.Blythe a constable of said county who hath made return thereon as follows, to wit, Levied May 27, 1828 (p-237) on a tract of land of seventy four acres lying in Haywood County on the waters of Bear Creek 5 range & 6 Section adjoining a tract of 957 acres belonging to McGimsey levied on as the property of said Lawrence, there being no personal property of his which to levy on in this county. It is therefore ordered by the court that a writ of venditioni exponas issue to cause said land, so levied on as aforesaid to be sold to satisfy the Debt & costs aforesaid & the costs about the motion in this behalf expended
Iss'd.

William Balch   )
    vs   ) Motion
William Lawrence)

     On motion of the said plaintiff by his attorney and it appearing to the satisfaction of this court that the said plaintiff did on the 21st day of May 1828 obtain a Judgement against the said defendant before Jesse L.Kirk esquire, a justice of the peace of this county for the sum of thirty five dollars and costs of suit. That an execution issued thereon which came duly into the hands of T.Blythe, a constable of this county who hath made return thereon, as follows, to wit, Levied May 27th 1828 an a tract of land of seventy four acres, lying in Haywood County, on the waters of Bear Creek 5th range & 6th section adjoining a tract of land of 957 acres belonging to McGimsey, Levied on as the property of said W.Lawrence there being no personal property of his on which to levy in this county. It is therefore ordered by the court that a writ of venditioni exponas issue to cause said land, so levied on as aforesaid to be sold to satisfy the Judgment and costs aforesaid & the costs about the motion in this behalf expended etc.
Iss'd

(p-238) William Arnold   )
          vs   )
)
    John R.& Thomas J.)
    McGuire   )

     This day came the said plaintiff by his attorney & saith that he intends no further to prosecute his said suit against the said defendants. It is therefore considered by the court here that the said Defendants go hence without day & recover against the said plaintiffs their costs by them about their defence in this behalf expended etc.

John L.Jetton (use of)
Isaac Jetton   )
    vs   )
John G.Carithers   )

     Continued on of the Defendant & leave granted him to take the Deposition of William Mitchell Jr. of Rutherford giving the plaintiff

(p-238con.)
twenty days notice.

Robert Sanders   )
        vs   )
Benjamin Lynn administrator)
of J.H.Moore,Charles M.Logwood)
Julius Sanders   )

    This day came the said parties by their attornies & whereupon came
also a jury of good and lawful men, to wit John McWhite, Nathaniel D.
Lilly, Lorenza D.Womble, William Weddle, Benjamin Weaver, Joseph Murphy,
John Hollowell, Levi Gardner, John Andrews, Samuel Elliott, Cato
Freeman, and William Lawrence, who being elected, tried & sworn well &
truly to try the issue joined upon their oath aforesaid do say they find
the issues in favour of the Defendant Lynn adm. as aforesaid & the
Jurors aforesaid upon their oaths aforesaid do further say that they find
the issues joined between the said plaintiff & the said Defendants
Charles M.Logwood & Julius Sanders, in favour of the said plaintiff and
they assess the plaintiffs damages by reason thereof to two hundred &
thirteen & eighty two cents besides costs. It is therefore (p-239)
considered by the court here that the said plaintiff do recover against
the said Benjamin Lynn, administrator as aforesaid the said Benjamin Lynn
administrator as aforesaid the said sum of two hundred & thirteen
dollars & eighty two, the damages aforesaid to be levied of the goods
and chattels, rights & credits of the said intestate when so much thereof
shall come into the hands of the said administrator to be administered
not subject to the satisfaction of prior judgments and it is further
considered by the court that the said plaintiff do recover against the
said Defendants Charles M.Logwood & Julius Sanders the damages aforesaid
by the jury inform aforesaid assessed & the costs in this behalf expended
to be levied of their proper goods & chattels land & tenements & the
said defendants in mercy etc.
Fifa issued

Joseph Spence   )
        vs   ).
James H. Walker)

    This day came the parties aforesaid by their attornies & there-
upon came also a jury of good and lawful men,to wit, John McWhite,
Nathaniel D.Lilly, Lorenza D.Womble, Benjamin Weaver, Joseph Murphy,
Jonathan Hollowell, Levi Gardner, Mansfield Ware, Samuel Elliott,
Cato Freeman, William Lawrence & Nathan Williams, who being elected,
tried & sworn well & truly to try the issue joined between the parties
upon their oath aforesaid do say they find the issue joined in favor
of the plaintiff & assess his damages to Eleven dollars & seventeen
cents besides costs. It is therefore considered by the court that the
said plaintiff recover against the said Defendant one hundred and fifty
nine dollars and sixty three cents the Debt in the declaration mentioned
and the damages aforesaid by the Jury aforesaid assessed & the costs
in this behalf expended etc. From which Judgment the Defendant prayed
 & obtained an appeal to the next Circuit Court of the County, which is
granted, he having given bond & security to prosecute the same.

(p-240) Francis S.Coxe   )
        vs   )
        Hyram Bradford Adm. ofRobert A.Penn) Assumpsit

(p-240con.) This day came the said parties by their attornies and thereupon came of Robert A.Penn came also a jury of good & lawful men, to wit, John McWhite Nathaniel D.Lilly, Lorenza D.Womble, Benjamin Weaver, Joseph Murphy, Jonathan Hollowell, Levi Gardner, Mansfield Ware, Samuel Elliott, Cato Freeman, William Lawrence & Nathan Williamson who being elected, tried & sworn well & truly to try the issue joined upon their oath aforesaid do say they find the issue in favour of the plaintiff & as assess his damages to ohe hundred & twenty one dollars forty eight and three fourth cents, besides costs. It is therefore considered by the court here that the said plaintiff do recover against the said defendant the damages aforesaid by the jury in form aforesaid assessed & the costs in this behalf expended to be levied of the goods & chattels, rights & credits of the said intestate in the hands of said administrator to be administered and the defendant in mercy etc. whereupon on the progress of this cause , the defendant by his council filed bill of exceptions, which is prayed to be signed, sealed & enrolled made a part of the record of this suit which is accordingly done.
Transcript issued

Jordan M.Hansborough)
      vs   )
William Lawrence   )

This day came the said plaintiff in his proper person & suit that he intends no further to prosecute his action against the said Defendant It is therefore considered by the court that the said Defendant go hence without day & recover against the said plaintiff his costs by him about his defence in this behalf expended etc.
costs pd.

(p-241) William L.Duncan)
        vs   )
   William Lawrence)

This day came the said plaintiff by his attorney & saith he intends no further to prosecute his suit against the said defendant, and thereupon came also the said Defendant & assumes upon himself to pay all costs in this behalf expended etc.
Fifa issue

James Smith assee)
)
    vs   )
William Weddle)

This day came the said parties by their attornies & thereupon came also a jury of good & lawful men to wit, John McWhite, Nathaniel D.Lilly, Lorenza D.Womble, Benjamin Weaver, Joseph Murphy, Jonathan Hollowell, Levi Gardner, Mansfield Ware, Samuel Elliott, Cato Freeman, William Lawrence, & Nathan Williamson, who being elected tried and sworn well and truly to try the issue joined upon their oaths aforesaid do say that the Defendant hath not paid the Debt of ninety four dollars twenty nine & three fourth cents in the declaration mentioned as the plaintiff in replying hath alledged, and they assess the plaintiffs damages by reason of the detention thereof to two dollars & twenty cents, besides,

(p-241con.) costs. It is therefore considered by the court that the plaintiff do recover against the said defendant the Debt aforesaid in the declaration mentioned and the Damages aforesaid by the jury assessed & the Defendant in mercy etc
Transcript (issued)

John Bevill   )
    vs   )
Robert Sanders   )

    This day came the said parties by their attornies & thereupon came also a jury of good & lawful men to wit, John McWhite, Nathaniel D.Lilly Lorenza D.Womble, Benjamin Weaver, Joseph Murphy, Jonathan Hollowell, Levi Gardner, Mansfield Ware, Samuel Elliott, Cato Freeman, (p-242) William Lawrence & Nathan Williamson, who being elected tried and sworn well truly to try the issue joined upon their oaths aforesaid do say that the defendant hath not paid the Debt of Sixty dollars forty, one & a fourth cents in the declaration mentioned as the plaintiff in replying hath alledged & they assess the plaintiffs damages by reason of the detention of that debt to one dollar & fifty cents, besides costs. It is therefore considered by the court that the said plaintiff do recover against the said Defendant the Debt aforesaid in the declaration mention & the damages aforesaid by the jury assessed & the costs in this behalf expended & the said Defendant in mercy etc.

Ezekiel Blackshire)
    vs   ) Case
Robert Hammell   )

    Continued on affidavit of the defendant

Julius Sanders   )
    vs   ) Appeal
Sidney P.Smith   )

    Continued as an affidavit of Defendant

Joseph Spence   )
    vs   ) Debt
James H.Walker   )

    Continued by consent of the parties

Thos. Potter assee)
    vs   ) Debt
Mathew Ray   )

    Continued on affidavit of the Defendant

James Stevens   )
    vs   ) Trespass
Malcomb Johnston)

    Continued of affidavit of this Defendant

(p-242con.)   George Stalcups   )
                    vs   )   Debt
              Wm.C.Russell   )

Continued as on affidavit of the defendant and leave granted to
ament the pleadings by the payment of the costs of said amendment.

(p-243) George Stalcup   )
                   vs   )   Debt
          William C.Russell)

Continued as on affidavit of the Deft. and leave granted to amend
the pleadings by the payment of the costs of said amendment-

Ephraim Roddy   )
        vs   )   Sci fa
John Roddy   )

Continued alias sci fa to issue

Ephraim Roddy   )
        vs   )   Atto
Wilson Nesbit   )

Continued by consent

Seth Whitley to use   )
of Guardner   )
        vs   )   Attachment
George McCrory   )

This day came plaintiff by his attorney and sayeth that he intends no further to prosecute his attachment against the said defendant.
It is therefore considered by the court that the said defendant go hence
without day and recover against the said plaintiff his costs by him
about his defence in this behalf expended & etc. Fifa issued,

Court adjourned until tomorrow morning nine o'clock.
Fifa iss'd.

                              Rich'd. Nixon
                              Dan'l Cherry
                              Sam. P.Ashe
                              Jesse L.Kirk

Wednesday morning June the 11th 1828

The court met according to adjournment present the worshipful
Richard Nixon Samuel P.Ashe, Jesse L.Kirk, and others their fellow
justices

A Deed of bargain and sale from Archibald D.Murphy by Benjamin A.
Rainey his attorney in fact to Robert Russell for two hundred & thirty
five acres of land was this proved in open court by the oaths of
Herndon Haralson & Jordan M.Hansborough witnesses thereto & ordered to

(p-243con.) be registered
Certified & del'd. fee pd.

(p-244) Francis S.Coxe)
        vs)
    Hiram Bradford adm.)
    of Robert A.Penn

    The Defendant being dissatisfied with the Judgment rendered
againsthim rendered, hath prayed & obtained an appeal in the nature of
a writ of Error to the next Circuit of this County which is granted,he
having given bond & security to prosecute to the same.
Issued

Rodoh Horton)
   vs)
Samuel P.Ashe)

    This day came the said defendant in his proper and saith he can-
not gainsay the said plaintiffs action against herein and acknowledged
judgment for the sum of five hundred and fifty five dollars and twenty
cents, & costs of suit. It is therefore considered by the court that
said plaintiff recover against the said Defendant the said sum of five
hundred and fifty five dollars & twenty cents, and the costs in this behalf expended etc. and by agreement between the parties execution is
stayed till March term of this court 1829.

Joseph Ables & B.Derin)
      vs)
Jesse Kemp)

    On motion of the defendant by his attorneys leave is granted the
said defendant to take the deposition of John M.Chelton of Weakly
County on giving the adverse party ten days notice.

    A transfer of a Platt & certified of survey from William Barcroft
to John Murry for 100 acres of lands the executorss of which has been
proved heretofore by Blachman Coleman was this day again produced in
open court and proved by the oath of Elisha Bryeans another witness therein
& ordered to be certified.

(p-245) George Stalcup)
      vs)
   William C.Russell)

    On motion of the defendant by his attorney, leave granted the
said defendant to take the deposition of Reubin S.Brown & Benjamin H.
Young on giving twenty days notice.

George Stalcup)
   vs)
William C.Russell)

    On motion of the Defendant by his attorney leave is granted the
said defendant to take the deposition of Reubin S.Brown & Benjamin
H.Young on giving days notice.

(p=245con.) Ezekiel Fuller   )
               vs   )
         Jonathan R.Burlison)

This day came the said plaintiff by his attorney and the said defendant being solemnly called came not but made default, nor does he prosecute his said appeal. It is therefore considered by the court here that the said plaintiff do recover against the said defendant & on motion against James A.Burlison his security in the appeal, the sum of ten dollars and fifty cents, the amount of the Judgement before the Justice of the peace, with twelve & one half per cent interest thereon from the 12th day of April 1828, the date of the Judgement below, up to this day & his costs in this behalf expended etc.
Iss'd.

(p-246) Ezekiel Fuller   )
             vs   )
        Johnathan R.Burlison)

This day came the said plaintiff by his attorney and the defendant being solemnly called come not but made default, nor does he prosecute his said appeal. It is therefore considered by the court that the said plaintiff do recover of the said defendant and on motion against James A.Burlison his security in the appeal the sum of seven dollars and fifty cents, the amount of the Judgment before a Justice of the peace with twelve and one half pr. cent interest thereon from the 12th day of April 1828 up to this day and his costs in this behalf expended & etc.
Fifa iss'd.

Ezekial Fuller   )
      vs   )
Jonathan R.Burlison)

This day came the said plaintiff by his attorney and the defendant being solemnly called come not but made default, nor does he prosecute his said appeal.

It is therefore considered by the court that the said plaintiff do recover against said defendant and on motion against James A.Burlison his security in the appeal the sum of ten dollars and twenty cents, the amount of the Judgment before the Justice of the peace with twelve and one half per cent interest thereon from the 12th day of April 1828 up to this day and his cost in this behalf expended etc.
Fifa issued.

John Bevill   )
      vs   )
Robert Sanders)

The defendant in this case being dissatisfied with the judgment of court heretofore entered, hath prayed and obtained an appeal to the Circuit Court of this county he having entered into bond to prosecute the same.
Iss'd.

```
(p-246con.) John Harris(use    )
            of John Hendrick)  )
                   vs          )
            Lawrence McGuire   )
```

This day came the said Defendant in his proper person & saith he cannot gainsay the said plaintiff action against him & confesses judgment for the sum of one hundred and thirty four dollars and fifty three cents, besides costs. It is therefore considered (p-247) by the court here that the said plaintiff do recover against the said Lawrence McGuire (for the use of the said John Hendrick the said sum of one hundred & thirty four dollars ʌʌʌ and fifty three cents, and the costs in this behalf expended etc.

Deed of bargain & sale from Thomas H.Taylor by Matthew Ray his attorney in fact, to Mansfield Ware for two acres & one hundred & eleven poles of land was this day acknowledged in open court and ordered to be registered.
Certified & Del'd

The Grand Jury came into court & there appearing no further business for their consideration were discharged & proved two days attendance each as also the following jurors two days each to wit John McWhite, Nathaniel D.Lilly, Lorenza D.Womble, Benjamin Weaver, Joseph Murphy, Jonathan Hollowell, Levi Gardner, Mansfield Ware-

```
The State of Tennessee    )
           vs             )
Thomas Ferguson           )
```

This day came as well the State of Tennessee by A.B.Bradford esquire attorney General, as the Defendant in his proper person & the Defendant being solemnly charged saith he is guilty in manner & form as charged in the bill of the Indictment & puts himself upon the grace & mercy of the court. It is therefore considered by the court that the defendant make his fine with the State of Tennessee by the payment of seven-dollars & fifty cents all costs, and that he be taken & Blackman Coleman & William R.Hess agree to go security & that execution issue jointly against them Fifa
issd.

```
E.H.Childress            )
     vs                  )
B.Coleman & D.Madding    )
```

Leave is granted by the plaintiff attorney to the defendants, with the Circuit Court of this County to file his pleas etc-

```
(p-248) E.H.Childress      )
              vs           )
         B.Coleman,D.      )
       Mading & C.Madding  )
```

Leave is granted by the plaintiff attorney to the Defendants (p-248con.) till the next Circuit Court of this county to file their pleas.

James King was this day bound as an apprentice to John Potter to learn the art, mistery & trade of a carpenter who entered into indentures.

The State   )
    vs   )
Benja. Wilson)

By the knowledge & direction of the court a nole prosequi is entered & on motion it is ordered that the county trustee pay all legal costs.

The State   )
    vs   )
Martin G.Frazier)

By the knowledge and direction of the court a nole prosequi is entered & an motion it is ordered that the county trustee pay all legal costs

F.L.Dillard   )
    vs   )
Eli McChung   )

Continued on affidavit of Matthew Ray-

Joseph R.Ray)
    vs   )
R.P.T.Stone   )

Continued by the court-

Court adjourned until tomorrow morning nine o'clock.

                Joel Estes
                L.MCGuire
                Jesse L.Kirk

Thursday Morning June 12th 1828, court met according to adjournment. Present the worshipful Joel Estes, Lawrence McGuire Jesse L. Kirk, & others their justices.

(p-249) Ordered by the court that Benjamin Wilks, Demsey Pace, Malcom Johnston, James Taylor John Elliott, John B.Elliott, William Balch, Jonathan Burlison, John McHabe, Oliver B.Woods, Elisha Arnold, Thomas J.Blythe, or any five of them be appointed a jury of view to view and mark a road leading from Estaraula in a direction to Covington to intersect the Bolivar road east of Big Muddy Creek and report to the next term of this court
(Issued 23rd June)

It is ordered by the court that an order made at the last term of this court appointing a Jury of view to view and mark a road

(p-249con.) from Brownsville in a direction to Dyersburg be renewed
and the same commission & surveyors be & are again appointed for that
purpose
Iss'd 23rd.

Deed of Conveyance from Stephen Bryan & John T.Bryan to Hiram
Bradford for two town lots in Brownsville was this day proved in open
court by the oath of M.H.Bradford, one of the witnesses thereto also
by Simon Turner or ordered to be registered.

It is ordered by the court that the county part of the Tax
on 640 acres of land reported & sold in the name of Eward Newton for
the years 1825 & 1826 to Thomas J.McGuire, amounting to seven dollars
& eight cents be refunded to said McGuire it appearing satisfaction of
this court that there is no such land in this county. The following
Justices being on the bench & the ayes & noes being taken thereon.

Ayes
James L.Wortham   And it is further ordered that the same
Saml. P.Ashe   be paid by the county trustee of this county
Richd. Nixon   out of any unappropriated money in his
Lawrence McGuire   hands.
Jesse L.Kirk   Issued
Dan'l Cherry

(p-250) It is ordered by the court Mansfield Ware, William Barcroft,
Elisha Bryan, Robert Roddy, Griffith Edwards, Anderson Brit Charles
Wortham, Robert Perry, Giles Mattett, John T.Turner, Henry H.Turner,
Henry H.Turner   Benjamin Wilkes, Joel Pace, Alvin Bigham, Walker
Wilson, David Stanly, James Maulden, John Carlton, Robert Robison,
Tobias C.Henderson, Eli Jones, John Link, John McFarland, John Sanderlain
William Shearin Thomas Thweatt be summoned to attend at the next term
of this court, then & there to serve as grand or petit jurors as the
case may be, and that Jordan M.Hansborough & Joel Abstain be appointed
constable to attend said court-
Issued.

Sarah L.Dyer was this day appointed Guardian for Joel S.Charles
C.James M.Cornelia J.& Sarah Ann Dyer, minor heirs of Joel Dyer dec'd
who gave bond & security etc.

(p-251) Deed of Conveyance from Wilds Cook to George W.Hockly for
833 acres of land was this day produced in open court & proved by
the oaths of Jordan M.Hansborough & Reubin Alphin, witnesses there
& ordered to be registered.

Deed of conveyance from David Stwart to John C.McLemore,
James   and James Caruthers for twenty five acres of land was
this day proved in open court by theoaths of Herndon Haralson & William
H.Haralson witnesses thereto & ordered to be registered.

Deed of Conveyance from John G.Carithers Sheriff to Gray
Huckaby for twelve hundred and fifty acres of land was this day ac-
knowledged in open court by said Carithers and ordered to be registered
Certified etc.

(p=251con.) Deed of Conveyance from John G.Carithers sheriff to Gray Huckaby for 180½ acres of land was this day acknowledged in open court. and ordered to be registered
Certified etc.

A Deed of bargain and sale from David Jeffreys and Nicholas T. Perkins to Archibald D.Murphy for seven hundred and fifty acres of land was this day produced in open court and duly proven by the oaths of James H.Walker and Jas. Sampson subscribing witnesses thereto and ordered to be certified for registration.

It is ordered by the court that Hiram Bradford, Robert Perry, James Smith, Henry Welch, Mason F.Johnson, Francis L.Dillard & Britain H.Sanders be appointed a jury of view to view the Jackson road as for as one mile from the town of Brownsville & mark out a road from thence East of Taylors field, to intersect the Bolivar road within four miles of this town.
Iss'd.

(p-252) It appearing to the satisfaction of the court by the affidavit of Richard Nixons exhibited & sworn to in open court, that John R. Leigh esquire, late of said county, now deceased, did in his life-time make a last will & testament, which he, the said Nixon believes is now in the hands of Peter Mattett of the state of North Cumberland County with whom it was deposited by the deceased in his life time. It is therefore ordered by the court that a commission issue to the said county of Cumberland & state aforesaid in order that said last will & testament may be properly & legally certified to this court record.

It is ordered by the court that Nathan Gooch be released from the county Tax, to wit four dollars, in a stud horse listed for taxation for 1828, there being a majority of the Justices present & the ayes & noes being taken to wit ayes, Jesse L.Kirk, Joel Estes, Blackman Coleman, Sam'l. P.Ashe, Richard Nixon, Lawrence McGuire and N.T.Perkins

Ordered by the court that Reubin Alphin a constable of Haywood County, Tennessee pay over to Berry Deering administrator of Travis Vindle deceased twenty one dollars which he collected as an officer of William H.Henderson. The said Alphin having given a receipt for the collection of said money to one Rodah Horton.

It is ordered by the court that Charles White, Vincent Harralson, Lawrence McGuire, James Sampson , Daniel Shaw, Blackman Coleman, James H.Walker & Benjamin Wilkes or a majority of them be & are hereby appointed to view the road proposed to pass at or near Estanaula at which is called the upper Ferry. That they also view the road crossing at Murrys ' Ferry & ascertain (p-253) which is the best and will condunce most to the Public convenience at which of the two places a public convenience at which of the two places a public Ferry should be granted & established. That a correct survey of Murrays one acre tract be made by Lawrence McGuire, & that they a report of all their proceedings & of all things relative thereto to our next court.
Issued.

(p-253con.) James Smith assee)
                   vs   )
         William Weddle   )

    The defendant being dissatified with the judgment rendered against him hath prayed & obtained an appeal to the next Circuit Court of this county he having given bond & security to prosecute the same.
Iss'd

    Court adjourned until tomorrow morning nine o'clock-

                             Rich'd Nixon cha
                             Sam P.Ashe
                             L.McGuire

    Friday morning June 13th 1828

    Court met according to adjournment . Present the worshipful Richard Nixon, Sam'l P.Ashe & Lawrence McGuire esquire Justices.

    John Murry, who at the March term of this court 1826 obtained an order & permission to establish a ferry at Murry's bluff on Hatchie river entered into bond & security

    Ordered by the court (that a former order made by this court be renewed) to wit. It is ordered by the court that Simon Turner, James Hammell, James Sanders , Edward West, Thomas G.Nixon, Clemment T.Walker, David Thomison, & Andrew Hammell be appointed a Jury to view, mark and lay of the ballance of the road leading from Brownsville to the Key Corner commencing at the bridge on Meredian Creek where the said road now crosses, to Dyer County line to intersect the road from the Key Corner line at the said line and make report thereof to the next term of this court.
Iss'd.

(p-254) Ordered by the court that Lawrence McGuire, Herndon Haralson, Richard Nixon, B.Coleman, B.H.Sanders, James Carlton, James C.Hart, and Thomas G.Nixon be and are hereby appointed a jury of view to view asertain in what way all or any of the roads lying west and north of the town of Brownsville shall come into said town and it shall be the duty also of said Jury to view all or any of said roads and ascertain if the said roads run on the best and most elligible ground to the several places to which said roads are intended to run, and said jury are particulary required to examine the McGuire road as for as links or thereabouts, and report whether any and if any what alteration should be made in that road, all of which they shall report to next court.
Issd.

J.R.Ray   )
    vs   )
R.P.T.Stone)

    This day came the said plaintiff by John Read his attorney & saith that he intends no further to prosecute his attachment against (p-254con.) the said defendant. It is therefore considered by the court that the said Defendant go hence & recover against the said plaintiff his costs in this behalf expended etc.

It is ordered by the court that Berry Derin Rev. _____Lanier
_____Matthews John Link, Jessee Jackson, John G.Jones & Parson Boyce or any five of them be appointed a jury to lay off a road from or about Berry Dearins to the Tipton County line in a direction to Covington & report to next court.
Iss'd.

(p-255) It is ordered by the court that all those who may give in lists of taxable property & polls under the order made at this term between this & the next term of this court and also all who may have given in at this time shall shall be released from the double tax.

Court adjourned until court in course.

Rich'd Nixon Cha.
L.McGuire
Sam. P.Ashe

(p-256) State of Tennessee)
       Haywood County) Sct.

At a court of pleas and quarter sessions, began & holden for the county of Haywood at the courthouse in the town of Brownsville on the second Monday in September 1828 it being the 8th day of said month. Present the worshipful Samuel P.Ashe, Jonathan T.Jacocks & Lawrence McGuire esquire, Justices etc.

Hyram Bradford, Mason F.Johnson, B.H.Sanders, James Smith, and Robert Perry, Commissioners appointed to view to the Jackson road as for as one mile from the town of Brownsville & to mark out a road from thence East to Taylors field, to intersect the Bolivar road within four miles of this town make their report as follows "In persuance to the within order we the undersigned report that the Bolivar road run with the Jackson road to the one mile tree and from thence in a direction to intersect the present road to Bolivar at the south west corner of Mrs. Smiths field as marked believing the ground to be more suitable than where the present road runs equally as near & every respect more advantageous to the public.

Deed of conveyance from Robert Carithers to Jedediah Cusick for one thousand acres of land was this day proved in open court by the oaths of Joshua Kelly & Newton M.Cusick subscribing witnesses thereto & ordered to be certified for registration.

Deed of conveyance from Francis Lamoin to Pane P.Kelly for certain piece or parcel of ground therein mentioned, was this day acknowledged in open court by said Francis Lamoin to be his act & deed and ordered to be certified for registration.

(p-257) Rawlings Henderson this day produced into open court the scalp of a wolf over the age of four months & proved by the oaths of Sephen

(p-257con.) Howard the killing of the same in this county within less than twelve months past- It is therefore considered by the court (there being a majority of the justices present) that he be allowed the sum of three dollars to be paid by the Treasurer of the western district.
Iss'd.

James B. Powell this day produced into open court the scalp of a wolf over the age of four months and proved by his own oath that he killed the said wolf within this county within less than twelve months past. It is considered by the court (there being a majority of the justices present) that he be allowed the sum of three dollars, to be paid by the treasurer of the western District.
Iss'd.

James Darris produced here into open court the scalp of a wolf over the age of four months & proved as the law directs the killing of the wolf in this county within less than twelve months past. It is ordered by the court (there being a majority of the Justices present) that the said James Darris be allowed the sum of three dollars to be paid by the treasurer of the western District.
Iss'd.

Bill of sale from Daniel Smith to Aaron T. Brooks for a negro woman named Jane, a child named Sarah, a boy named Jim and a girl named Sylvia was this day acknowledged in open court by the said Daniel Smith & ordered to be certified for registration.

Bill of sale from Daniel Smith to William Jackson for two negroes, to wit, a girl named Mary and a boy named George was this day acknowledged in open court by said Daniel Smith & ordered to be certified for registration.
Certified & Del 'd.

Deed of conveyance from Samuel Dickins to Ferry & Bilbro for two hundred acres of land was this day proved in open court by the oaths of David Jeffreys and Thomas Crutcher, witnesses thereto & ordered to be certified for registration.

(p-258) Deed of conveyance from Rawling Henderson to John Nunn for one hundred acres of land was this day acknowledged in open court by said Henderson to be his act and deed and ordered to be certified for registration.

Deed of conveyance from John Jackson to James Jackson for fifty acres of land was this day produced in opencourt & proved by the oath Aaron T. Brooks & William Jackson witnesses thereto & ordered to be certified for registration.
Certified & Deld.

Deed of conveyance from Jedediah Cusick to Joshua Kelly for one hundred & sixty three acres of land was this day acknowledged in open court ordered to be certified for registration.

The Jury of view appointed at the June term of this court 1828

(p-258con.) to view, mark and lay off the balance of the road leading
from Brownsville to the Key Corner commencing at the Bridge on Meredian
Creek wherethe said road now crosses to Dyer County line, so as to
intersect the road from the Key Corner at said line make report that
they have done the same which is received by the court.

Charles White, Vincent Haralson Lawrence McGuire, James Sampson,
Daniel Shaw, Blackman Coleman, James H.Walker and Benjamin Wilkes
who were at the last term appointed a jury of view to view the road
proposed to pass at or near Estaraula at what is called the upper
Ferry, that they also view the road crossing at Muray's ferry & ascertain
which is the best and will conduce most to the Public convenience at
which of the two places a public Ferry should be granted and established
etc. make report to this court as follows to wit, We, the jurors appointed by the within order have on this 28th July 1828 proceeded to the
examination of the duties assigned us, and after having made the survey
as required and upon a full and fairexamination of the whole subject
are clearly and decidedly of the (p-259) opinion that is to say, a
large majority of the Jury, that the upper Ferry should be the one
established by the worshipful the county court of Haywood County , it
being the one, in the opinion of the majority of the jury that will most
conduce to the public interest
                                        Signed
                                        Blackman Coleman

James H.Walker, Benj. Wilkes, James Sampson, Charles White,
Lawrence McGuire, & Vincent Harralson.

Whereupon it is considered by the court that William H.Moore
be permitted to keep a Ferry at what is called the upper Ferry at the
town of Estanaula in this county an his giving bond & security as the
law directs and thereupon the said William H.Moore entered into bond
with Joshua Abstain and Thomas J.Blythe his securities and thereupon
John Murry by his attorney appeared in court & prayed to be made a
part to the cause which is granted, and thereupon the said John Murry
being dissatisfied with the opinion of the court, prayed and obtained
an appeal to the Circuit Court of this County he having given bond
and security to prosecute the same.

Upon petition it is ordered by the court (there being a majority
of the justices present) that the road heretofore established from the
town of Brownsville to James Worthams Ferry on the South fork of the
Forked deer river be discontinued.

William A.Morrison this day produced in open court the scalp of
two wolves under the age of four months, and he having made oath that
he killed the same in the county of Haywood within the last twelve
months, it is ordered by the court that he be allowed the sum of four
dollars to be paid by the treasurer of the western district. A
majority of the justices being present-
Iss'd.

(p-260) It appearing to the satisfaction of this court that Joel
Furgerson late of said county is dead and hath made no last will &
testament, and Thomas Furguson having applied to this court for letters

(p-260con.) of administration on said plate and he having given bond & security for the same, to him they are granted.

It is ordered by the court that Thomas Furguson administrator of Joel Furgerson decd. have leave to sell the perishable property of the estate of said Joel Furgerson dec'd and make report to this court.

It is ordered by the court (there being a majority of the acting justices present and the ayes & noes being taken) that Julius Sanders, corner of this county be allowed the sum of five dollars for his services in summoning to an inquest over the body of_____ Atchison, to be paid out of any unappropriated money in the hands of the county trustee also the further sum of ten dollars to be paid out poor funds of this county when collected- Five dollars of this claim issued to Henderson pr. verbal order the other to F.S.Coxe

It is ordered by the court (there being a majority of the justices present and the ayes & noes being taken,) that Thomas and John Potter be allowed out of the poor funds of the county when collected the sum of four dollars for a coffin furnished for _____ Atchison dec'd. Issued

Court adjourned until tomorrow nine o'clock.
Iss'd.

Rich'd. Nixon, Cha-
Jesse L.Kirk
Sam. P.Ashe, J.P.

(p-261)   Tuesday morning 9th of September 1828

Court met pursuant to adjournment Present the worshipful Richard Nixon, Jesse L.Kirk, Samuel P.Ashe, and others their fellow justices

John G.Carithers sheriff makes return of the venire facias returnable to this term in the words and figures following to wit.

State of Tennessee,
At a court of pleas and quarter sessions began and held for the county of Haywood at the court in the town of Brownsville on the second Monday in June 1828 it being the 10th day of said month present the worshipful Joel Estis Lawrence McGuire, Jesse L.Kirk and others their fellow justices. It is ordered by the court that the following persons good and lawful men viz, each being a white male citizen of the age of twenty one years and a house holder to wit Mansfield Ware, William Barcroft, Elisha Boyan , Robert Roddy, Griffeth Edwards, Anderson Brett, Charles Wortham Robert Perry, Giles Matette, John T. Turner, Henry H.Turner, Benjamin Wilks, Joel Pace, Alvin Bingham, Walker Wilson, David Stanly, James Maldin, James Carlton, Robert Robison Tobias C.Henderson, Eli Jones, Bird Link, John McFarland, John Sanderlin, William Shearin and Thomas Thweatt, be summoned to attend at the next term of this court on tuesday after the second Monday in September next then and there to serve as grand and petit Jurors as the case may be and that Jordan M.Hansborough and Joel Abstain be appointed constables to attend said court.

(p-261con.)   Test B.H.Sanders
                               Clk-

        State of Tennessee,
               To the sheriff of Haywood Counry greeting-
You are hereby commanded to summon the aforesaid persons to serve as
Jurors at the next court of pleas and quarter sessions to be held at
the courthouse in (p-262) the town of Brownsville on Tuesday after the
second Monday in September next and this they shall in no wise omit
under the penalty prescribed by law. Herein fail not and have you then
and there this writ witness Britain H.Sanders, clerk of our said court
at office the 2nd Monday in June 1828 and 52nd year of American
Independence.
                               B.H.Sanders,Clk.

        Upon the back of which venire facias John G.Carithers shff. has
made the following indorsement to wit By virtue of the within venire
facias to me directed. I have proceeded to summon all the within
named persons as Jurors except Henry H.Turner, David Stanley & Robert
Robertson and such persons so summoned are habitants of said county
and are householders.
                               Jno.G.Carithers,
                               shff.

        It is ordered by the court that the road cut out by Hiram
Bradford & Robert Perry , intersecting the Jackson road leading by Col.
Nixons west of Koonces be and the same is hereby established, and
that that part of the Jackson road from where the new road intersects
the same to Brownsville be & the same is hereby discontinued.

        Elias Roddy this day produced in open court the scalps of four
wolfs over the age of four months and proved the killing of the same
by his own oath he having no other evidence whereby he could prove the
same-
        It is therefore by the court that the issue a certificate
accordingly.
Issued 13th Noon.

(p-263) Cullin Andrews was this day appointed Guardian for Mary
Andrews, James Andrews, Jane Andrews, Harriet Andrews, Lemuel Andrews
and Sarah Andrews minor children of John Andrews who gave bond in the
sum of five thousand dollars with Herndon Haralson, John Marbury and
Matthew Ray as his security.

        It is ordered by the court that Francis S.Coxe, Blackman
Coleman Nelson Hargrove, Henry M.Coy, Lawrence McGuire, Herndon
Haralson, Britain H.Sanders, or any five of them be and are hereby appointed a jury to view the Estes road and the Fulton road and report to the
next term of this court whether the said two roads should not be consolidated & if they are of the opinion that they should, to report to said
court at what point they should be brought together.
Iss'd

        It is ordered by the court that Daniel Shaw, Samuel Brown, Charles
White, Bowen Reynolds, Henry Turner, Jas. Sampson, Jas. H.Walker, &

(p-263con.) James Malden, be and are hereby appointed a jury of view
to view & mark from said Walkers to Jeffreys Bluff on Hatchie river
& make report to the next term.
Iss'd.

The following persons, good and lawful men of Haywood County
were elected, drawn sworn and charged as a grand Jury for the present
term, to wit.

James Malden Foreman

John T.Turner	James Carlton
Charles Wortham	Giles Matett
Anderson Brit	John Sanderlin
Robert Perry	Bird Link
William Barrycroft	Walker Wilson
	John McFarland &
	Tobias C.Henderson
	M.Ray, Constable

(p-264) Lawrence McGuire who was heretofore appointed to survey as
certain and mark the county lines of this county makes report to this
that he has done the same & produced here in open court a plan and
survey of said county which is received by the Court & ordered to be
recorded.

It is ordered by the court that Lawrence McGuire be allowed the
sum of one hundred dollars as a full compensation for his services
rendered in running out, surveying and marking the lines of Haywood
County to be paid out of any unappropriated money in the hands of the
county trustee (there being a majority of the justices present & the
ayes & noes being taken agreeably to act of assembly)
Copy issued

It is ordered by the court that the order heretofore made
appointing a jury of view to mark a road from the Brownsville landing
to the Fayette County line be renewed & issued accordingly
Iss'd.

It is ordered by the court that Joel Pace and Alvan Bingham,
jurors summoned on the venire facias returnable to this court each be
fined in the sum of five dollars for their non attendance as such, and
that a sciri facias issue severally against them
Sci fa

(p-265) Wyatt F.Tweedy who was at this term elected a constable in
Capt. Tweedy's company for this county this day came into court entered
into bond and security as the law directs & took the several oaths
prescribed by law.

John Jetton, to the use)   No. 1
of Isaac Jetton   )
     vs   )
John G.Carithers   )

(p=265con.) This day came the said parties by their attornies and thereupon came also a jury of good and lawful men, to wit, Robert Roddy, Eli Jones Thomas Thweatt, Mansfield Ware, William Shearin, Philip Bruce, Joseph Ables, Philip Koonce, William C.Russell, William Lawrence Thomas G.Nixon and Giles Bullock, who being elected tried and sworn well and truly to try the issue joined between the parties upon their oath aforesaid do say that the defendant hath paid all the debt in the the declaration mentioned except the sum of one hundred and thirty dollars and fifty cents and they assess the plaintiffs damages by reason of the detention of the residue of that debt to fifty two dollars and eighty five cents, besides costs.

It is therefore considered by the court that the said plaintiff do recover against the said Defendant the residue of the debt of one hundred and thirty dollars and fifty cents and the damages aforesaid by the jury assessed and the costs in this behalf expended and the said defendant in mercy etc.

(p=266) Ezekiel Blackshear)   No. 21
             vs   )
        Robert Hamil   )

This day came the said parties by their attornies and thereupon came also a jury of good and lawful men, to wit, Robert Roddy, Eli Jones, Thomas Thweatt, Mansfield Ware, William Shearin, Philip Bruce Joseph Ables, Philip Koonce, William C.Russell William Lawrence, Thomas G.Nixon, and Giles Bullock who being elected tried and sworn well and truly to try the issue joined between the parties upon their oaths aforesaid do say they find for the defendant. It is therefore considered by the court here that the defendant go hence without day & recover against the said plaintiff his costs by him about his defence in this behalf expended etc and thereupon the plaintiff by his attorney moved the court for a new trial.

On motion of Joel Pace it is ordered by the court that Walker Wilson, Reubin Golden, Malcomb Johnston Treston Patton, James Clark, Archibald Brazeal, Robert S.Wilkins, Thomas Clark Samuel Blackburn, A.T.Brooks, Thomas J.Blythe, and Robert Rinney be and are hereby appointed to assess what damages of any or to change the same if in their opinion it should be done ̸i̸f̸/̸a̸n̸y̸ ̸o̸f̸ ̸t̸o̸/̸c̸h̸a̸n̸g̸e̸ ̸t̸h̸e̸ ̸s̸a̸m̸e̸/̸i̸f̸ ̸i̸n̸/̸t̸h̸e̸i̸r̸/ ̸o̸p̸i̸n̸i̸o̸n̸ ̸i̸t̸/̸s̸h̸o̸u̸l̸d̸ ̸b̸e̸/̸d̸o̸n̸e̸ Joel Pace will sustain by the roads running through his plantation as marked by the Jury of view appointed to view a road leading from Estanaula in a direction to Covington and make report of their proceedings to next court.
Iss'd 25th Septr.

(p=267) It is ordered by the court that John R.Williams Hardy L. Blackwell, Cornelius Buck, Anderson Turpin, Alfred Kennaby , Thomas Fergerson & Eli Johnson or any five of them be appointed a jury of view to mark a way for them be appointed a jury of view to mark a way for a road from Bucks Ferry to meet a road leading from the Key corner in Dyer County to Jackson & make report to next court.
Iss'd.

The Jury of view appointed at the last term to view and mark a road from Estanaula the nearest and best way to intersect the road to

(p-267con.)   Brownsville, make report as follows to wit "The undersigned
agreeably to order of the court to view a road from Estanaula to
Brownsville report as follows, That we have viewed & marked said road
as follows, to leave Blackburnes on the right, thence to Mr. Sullivans,
thence to Mr.Blacks leaving him on the left, to go round David Jeffreys
field or improvement on one side or the other and thence to intersect
the Brownsville road as the mill road runs, about one & a half miles
from Malden north.

It is ordered by the court (there being a majority of the acting
Justices present) that Henry H.Turner, Charles White, John T.Turner,
Samuel Brown, Bowen Reynolds, Lewis Powers, James Mauldin, and Vincent
Haralson, or any five of them be appointed a Jury of view, to view and
mark a road the nearest and best way from Jeffreys bluff to Madison
County line to intersect the McGuire road where the same crosses the
said county line and make report to the next term of this court-
Iss'd.

Herndon Haralson, James C. Hart, James Carlton, Thomas G.Nixon
Britain H.Sanders & Blackman Coleman, who were at the last court
appointed to view the several roads lying west & north of Brownsville
& to report how said roads should be connected & brought into said town
made their report in writing which is received by the court & approved,
except as to the McGuire road.
(p-268)
The court then adjourned until tomorrow 9 o'clock.

                                    Dan'l.Cherry
                                    Joel Estes
                                    Jesse L.Kirk

Wednesday morning September 10th 1828.

Court met pursuant to adjournment Present Daniel Cherry, Joel
Estes and Jesse L.Kirk esquires Justices.

The State of Tennessee)
         vs   ) Sci Fa
Robert Roddy   )

On the affidavit of the defendant it is ordered by the court that
the fine heretofore assessed against him for his non attendance as a
juror be set aside on the payment of all costs & that execution issue
therefor.

Elisha Bryant this day came into open court and acknowledged
himself indebted to the State of Tennessee in the sum of five hundred
dollars to be void on condition that he the said Bryant shall keep the
peace of the state of Tennessee towards all the good people of the county
of Haywood for and during twelve months from this day & it is further
considered by the court that said Bryant pay all costs in this behalf
expended and that execution for issue therefor.

Thomas G.Nixon and William R.Hess each acknowledge themselves
indebted to the State of Tennessee in the sum of two hundred and fifty

(p-268con.) dollars but to be void on condition that Elisha Bryant shall well & truly observe and keep the peace of the state towards all the good people of this county for and during twelve months.

(p-269) E.Blackshear)
    vs   ) On a motion for a new trial
  Robert Hamil)

This day came the said parties by their attornies, and upon solemn argument being had thereon by council learned in the law, and by the court here fully understood it is considered by the court that the motion for a new trial be sustained.

The State of Tennessee)
    vs   ) Presentment
Samuel Whitehead)

This day came the defendant in his proper person and saith he is guilty in manner and form as charged in the bill of Indictment and puts himself upon the grace and mercy of the court-
  It is therefore considered by the court that the defendant make his five with the state by the payment of five dollars & all costs & that he be taken .

James Stephens)
   vs   )
M.Johnson)

This day came the said parties by their attornies and thereupon came also a jury of good and lawful men, to wit, Robert Roddy, Eli Jones Thomas Thweatt, Mansfield Ware, Benjamin Wilkes, Thomas Potter,Robert F. Smith, Samuel Elliott, Arthur F.McCain, Thomas Stokely, Berry Dorin, and William H.Patton who being elected, tried, and sworn well and truly to try the issues joined retired to consider of the duties assigned them and again returned into court and declared that they could not agree, and by consent of the parties and with the assent of the court Robert Roddy, one of the jurors of the jury aforesaid is withdrawn and the rest of the jurors from rendering their verdict are wholly discharged.

Julius Sanders)
   vs)
Sidney P.Smith)

Continued on affidavit of the defendant until the next term of this court.

(p-270) A Deed of relinquishment from Francis S.Coxe to Peter S. Du Ponceau for his interest in the estate of Tench Coxe Dec'd of Philadelphia Was this day produced in open court and duly acknowledged for the purposes therein contained and ordered to be so certified.

A bill of sale from Vincent Haralson to Nicholas T.Perkins for certain negroes, (namely) Isham, Chany and Judy & Tiller was this day produced in open court and duly acknowledged and ordered to be certified (p-270con.) for registration.

A bill of sale from Nicholas T.Perkins to Vincent Haralson for a certain negro man named Hanibal was this day produced in open court and duly acknowledged, and ordered to be certified for registration.

Nimrod Axley this day produced in open court the scalp of a wolf over the age of four month and made both as the law directs that he killed the same within the bounds of Haywood County. It is therefore ordered by the court that he be allowed the sum of three dollars to be paid by the treasurer of the western District.

Francis L.Dillard   )
        vs   )
Eli McClung   )

This day came the said parties by their attornies and thereupon came a jury of good and lawful men, to wit, William Shearin, Benjamin George, Amos Moore, John Keathly Sanford Perry, John D.Stamps, Joshua Abstain, James W.Russell, Marceau P.Estes, William Pace, Alexander Gordon and Joseph Ables who being elected, tried and sworn, well and truly to try the matters in dispute between the parties upon their oaths aforesaid do say they find for the plaintiff and assess his damages to twenty four dollars, twenty one & a half cents the amount of the Judgment rendered by the the Justices below.

(p-271) It is therefore considered by the court that the plaintiff do recover against the defendant & on motion against Matthew Ray his security in the appeal, the damages aforesaid by the Jury assessed, together with $12\frac{1}{2}$ per cent interest thereon from 11th of December 1827, the date of the judgment below up to this day & the costs in this behalf expended and the Defendant in mercy etc.

Thomas Potter assee   )
      vs   )
Matthew Ray   )

This day came the said parties by their attorneys and thereupon came a jury of good and lawful men, to wit, Robert Roddy, Eli Jones, Thomas Thweatt, Mansfield Ware, Benjamin Wilks, Wm. Shearin, Robert T. Smith, Samuel Elliott, Benj Arthur T.McCain, Thomas Stokely, Berry Dearing & William H.Patton who being elected tried and sworn well and truly to try the issues joined upon their oaths aforesaid do say that to try the issues joined/upon their the defendant has not paid the debt of sixty six dollars and forty cents mentioned as the plaintiff in replying hath alledged, and they assess the plaintiffs damages by reason of the detention thereof to two dollars and sixty five cents besides cost. It is therefore considered by the court that the plaintiff do recover of the said defendant the debt aforesaid mentioned, and the damages aforesaid assessed and the defendant in mercy etc.

Thomas G.Nison to use of   )
Mansfield Ware   )
vs   )
Archibald McNeal   )

(p-271con.) This day came the said parties by their attorneys and thereupon came a jury of good and lawful men, to wit, Robert Roddy, Eli Jones, Thomas Thweatt, Mansfield Ware, Benjamin Wilks, Thomas Potter Robert T.Smith, Samuel Elliott, Arthur F.McCain, Thomas Stokely, Berry Dearing and William H.Patton who being elected tried and sworn to try the issues joined, upon their oaths aforesaid do say that the defendant has paid all the debt in the declaration mentioned except the sum of one hundred and fifty five dollars and eleven cents the/ and they assess the plaintiffs damages by reason of the detention thereof to four dollars and sixty five cents besides costs, It is therefore considered by the court that the plaintiff do recover of the said defendant the ballance of the debt aforesaid together with the damages aforesaid by the Jury aforesaid assessed and the Deft in mercy etc.

(p-272) Rodah Horton   )
           vs   )
      Nathaniel Bridgemen)

This day came the said parties by their attorneys and thereupon came a jury of good and lawful men to wit Roddy Roddy Eli Jones, Thomas Thweatt, Mansield Ware, Benjamin Wilks, Thomas Potter, Robt. T. Smith Samuel Elliott, Arthur F.McCain, Thomas Stokely, Berry Dearing and William H.Patton, who being elected tried & sworn well & truly to try the issue joined upon their oath do say that the defendant hath not paid the debt of one hundred and five dollars in the declaration mentioned as the plaintiff in replying hath alledged, and they assess the plaintiffs damages by reason of the detention of that debt to three dollars & five cents, besides costs.

It is therefore considered by the court that the said plaintiff do recover against the said defendant the debt aforesaid in the declaration mentioned, and the damages aforesaid by the jury in form aforesaid assessed and the costs in this behalf expended & the defendant in mercy etc.

Jesse Powers assee etc   )
           vs   )
William C.Bruce   )
Phillip Bruce &   )
Joseph Murphy   )

This day came the said parties by their attornies and thereupon came also a jury of good and lawful men, to wit Robert Roddy, Eli Jones, Thomas Thweatt, Mansfield Ware, Benjamin Wilkes, Thomas Potter Robt. T.Smith Samuel Elliott, Arthur F.McCain, Thomas Stokely, Berry Dearing and William H.Patton, who being elected, tried and sworn well and truly to try the issue joined upon their oaths aforesaid do say that the defendant have not paid the Debt of seventy five dollars in the Declaration mentioned as the plaintiff in replying hath (p-273) alledged and they assess the plaintiffs damages by reason of the detention of that debt to three dollars besides costs. It is therefore considered by the court that the said plaintiff recover against the said defendants the debt aforesaid in the declaration mentioned and the Damages aforesaid by the jury in form aforesaid assessed & the costs in this behalf expended etc.

(p-273con.) Ephraim Roddy)
           vs   )   Attachment
     Wilson Nisbit)

This day came the plaintiff by his attorney, and the defendant
being solemnly called to come into court came not but made default. It
is therefore considered by the court here that the said plaintiff recover against the said Defendant the debt of five hundred dollars in
the declartion mentioned and his costs by him about his suit in this
behalf expended & the defendant in mercy etc.

(p-274) Ephraim Roddy)
          vs   )   On a Sci Fa on Guarnishment
     John Roddy   )

This day came the said plaintiff by his attorney and it appearing
to the satisfaction of this court that a writ of sciri facias had been
regularly issued from this court and duly served and the defendant not
appearing to show cause why the conditional judgment heretofore rendered
against him should be set aside. It is therefore considered by the
court that the said plaintiff may have execution against the said defendant for the said sum of five hundred dollars.

     Court adjourned until tomorrow morning nine o'clock-

                          Rich. Nixon Chr-
                          Jesse L.Kirk
                          Dan'l. Cherry

Thursday morning 11th September 1828

     Court met persuant to adjournment. Present the worshipful Richard
Nixon, Jesse L.Kirk, & Daniel Cherry esquires Justices.

Bane & Walker   )
     vs   )
James H.Walker   )

     This day came the said parties by their attornies & thereupon came
also a jury of good and lawful men to wit, Robert Roddy, Eli Jones,
Thomas Thweatt, Mansfield Ware, Benjamin Wilkes, Thomas Potter, Samuel
Elliott, Arthur F,McCain, Thomas Stokely, Berry Derin, William H.Patton,
& Robert T.Smith, who being elected tried and sworn well and truly to
try the issue joined between the parties, upon their (p-275) oaths
aforesaid do say that the defendant hath not paid the debt of one hundred
and thirty dollars and twenty cents in the declaration mentioned as the
plaintiff in replying hath alledged and they assess the plaintiffs
damages by reason of the detention of that debt to twenty dollars &
eighty three cents, besides costs.

     It is therefore considered by the court that the said plaintiff do
recover against the defendant the debt aforesaid in the declaration
mentioned and the damages aforesaid by the jury assessed and the costs
in this behalf expended & the defendant in mercy etc. From which Judgment
the Defendant hath prayed and obtained and appeal to the Circuit Court
of Haywood County he having given bond & security to prosecute the same-

(p-275con.) George Stalcup   )
                vs   )
        William C.Russell)

This day came the said parties by their atörnies and thereupon came
also a jury of good and lawful men, to wit, Eli Jones, Benjamin Wilkes,
Thomas Thweatt, William Shearin, Robert Roddy, Stephen S.Childress, Allen
J.Barbe, George Wills, Edward West, Arthur F.McCain, Archibald McNeal,
and Robert T.Smith who being elected tried and sworn well and truly to try
the issue joined, upon their oaths aforesaid do say that the defendant
hath not paid, the debt of one hundred dollars in the declaration mentioned
as the plaintiff in declaring hath alledged and they assess the plaintiffs
damages by reason of the detention of that debt to seven dollars and
twenty five cents besides costs. It is therefore considered by the court
that the plaintiff do recover against the defendant the debt aforesaid
with declaration and the damages aforesaid by the Jury assessed and the
costs in this behalf expended etc.

Skip of 276-277-278- 279

(p-280) George Stalcup   )
                vs   )
        William C.Russell)

This day came the said parties by their attorneys, and thereupon
came also a jury of good and lawful men, to wit Eli Jones, Benjamin
Wilkes, Thomas Thweatt, William Shearin, Robert Roddy, Stephen S.Childress
Allen J.Barbe, George Wills, Edward West, Arthur F.McCain Archibald
McNeal, and Robert T.Smith who being elected tried and sworn well and truly
to try the issue joined upon their oath aforesaid do say that the defendant
hath not paid the debt of one hundred dollars in the declaration mentioned
as the plaintiff in declaring hath alledged, and they assess the plaintiffs
damages by reason thereof to seven dollars twenty five cents besides
costs-

It is therefore considered by the court that the said plaintiff
recover against the said defendant the debt aforesaid in the declaration
mentioned, and the damages aforesaid by the jury assessed and the costs
in this behalf expended & the defendant in mercy etc-

A Deed of bargain and sale from Mary Shearin, William Shearin
and Turner Shearin to Thomas Shearin for an undivided share of land was
this day produced in open court and duly proven by the oaths of Charles
Wortham and James F.Wortham subscribing witnesses thereto and ordered to
be certified for registration.
Certified & Del'd.

(p-281) Francis L.Dillard)
                vs   )
        Eli McClung   )

The defendant being dissatisfied with the judgment and rendered
against him has prayed and obtained an appeal to the next Circuit Court
of this County, he having given bond & security to prosecute to the same.

(p-281con.) Henry M.Rutledge)
                    vs   )
             Blackman Coleman   )

This day came the said parties by their attorneys, and thereupon
came also a jury of good and lawful men to wit, Robert Roddy, Eli Jones,
Thomas Thweatt, Mansfield Ware, Benjamin Wilkes, Thomas Potter, Samuel
Elliott, Arthur F.McCain, Thomas Stokely, Berry Derin, William H.Patton
and Robert T.Smith who being elected, tried and sworn well and truly to
try the issue joined upon their oaths aforesaid that they find the issue
in favour of the plaintiff and assess his damages to one hundred and
two dollars and fifty cents, besides costs.

It is therefore considered by the court that the said plaintiff
do recover against the said defendant the damages aforesaid by the
jury in form aforesaid assessed, and the costs in this behalf expended
& the defendant in mercy.

Francis L.Dillard   )
       vs   )
William H. Henderson   )
John Hardwick

This day came the said plaintiff by his attorney and saith he
intends no further to prosecute his suit against the said defendants.
And thereupon came the said defendants and assume upon themselves to pay
all costs in this behalf expended. It is therefore considered by the
court that the said plaintiff do recover against the said defendants
the costs by them in this behalf assumed and the said defendants in
mercy.

Henry R.W.Hill & others   )
Executors of Joseph Branch   )
       vs   )
Blackman Coleman   )

This day came the said parties by their attornies & thereupon
came also a jury of good and lawful men, to wit Robert Roddy, Eli
Jones, Thomas Thweatt, Mansfield Ware, Benjamin Wilkes, Thomas Potter
Samuel Elliott, Arthur F.McCain, Thomas Stokely, Berry Derin, William
H.Patton, and Robert T.Smith, who (p-282) being elected, tried and
sworn well and truly to try the issue joined upon their oaths aforesaid
do say that the defendant hath not paid the debt of five hundred and
thirty dollars in the declaration mentioned as the plaintiff in replying
hath alledged, and they assess the plaintiff damages by reason of the
detention of that debt to twenty five dollars and seventeen cents, besides costs.
It is therefore considered by the court here that the said plaintiffs do recover against the said defendants the debt aforesaid in the
declaration mentioned and the damages aforesaid by the jury assessed
and the costs in this behalf expended.

The grand jury returned into court & returned an Indictment "the
State of Tennessee against Samuel Whitehead for an assault and battery
on the body of Joseph Curry" a true bill and there appearing no
further business for their consideration at this term were discharged

(p-282) Hermes Champ assee)
      (to the use of M.Ware))
           vs)
      Thomas G.Nixon admr)
      of John R.Leigh)

      This day came the said parties by their attornies & thereupon
came also a jury of good and lawful men, to wit, Robert Roddy, Eli
Jones, Thomas Thweatt, Mansfield Ware, Benjamin Wilkes, Thomas Potter
Samuel Elliott, Arthur F.McCain, Thomas Stokely, Berry Derin, William
H.Patton and Robert T.Smith who being elected, tried and sworn well
and truly to try the issue joined upon the oaths do say that that
the defendant hath not paid the debt of one hundred and nine dollars
and thirty one cents in the declaration mentioned, as the plaintiff
in replying hath alledged and they assess the plaintiffs damages by
reason thereof to two dollars and thirty six cents, besides costs. It
is therefore considered by the court that the said plaintiffs do recover against the (p-283) said defendant the debt aforesaid by the
jury assessed to be levied of the goods and chattels, rights &
credits of the said is _____ in the hands of said administrator to
be administered, if to much can be found in his hands to be administered,
and if not, then of the proper goods & chattels land & tenements of the
sd. defendant

      A Deed of bargain and sale from William W.Kavanaugh to John
Oneal for one hundred and fifty acres of land was this day again produced in open court and duly proven by the oath of Thomas Thweatt a
subscribing witness thereto and ordered to be certified for registration
it having heretofore at March term of our said heir proven in part by
Daniel Cherry and filed for further probit.

      A Deed of bargain and sale from William W.Kavanaugh to Henry A.
Powell for one hundred acres of land, which was heretofore at December
Term 1827 proven in part by the oath of Daniel Cherry, Was again this
day produced in open court and duly proven by the oath of Thomas Thweatt
a subscribing witness thereto and ordered to be certified for registration.

      A Deed of bargain and sale from John G.Carithers, sheriff of
Haywood County to Soloman Rease for three hundred and sixty five
acres of land was this day produced in open court and duly acknowledged
to be his act and deed and ordered to be certified for registration.

      A deed of bargain and sale from James Freeman to Richard T.Moore
for thirty acres of land was this day produced in open court and duly
proven by the oaths of Robert Burnes and Thomas Hughs subscribing
witnesses thereto and ordered to be certified for registration.

Hermes Champ assee)
(use of M.Ware)
      vs)
Thomas G.Nixon adm. of)
Jno. R. Leigh)

(p-283con.) The defendant being dissatisfied with the judgment rendered
against him hath prayed and obtained an appeal to the Circuit Court
of this county he having given bond and security to prosecute the same.

(p-284) Rodah Horton   )
       vs   )
Frances L.Dillard   )

      This day the said parties by their attorneys and thereupon came a
jury of good and lawful men to wit, Robert Roddy, Eli Jones, Thomas
Thweatt, Mansfield Ware, Benjamin Wilkes, Thomas Potter, Samuel Elliott,
Arthur F.McCain, Thomas Stokely, Berry Derin, William H.Patton and Robert
T.Smith, who being elected, tried and sworn well and truly to try the
issue joined between the parties , upon their oaths aforesaid do say that
the said defendant hath not paid the debt of sixty four dollars and fifty
cents in the declaration mentioned as the plaintiff in replying hath
alledged and they assess the plaintiffs damages by reason thereof to two
dollars and fifty eight cents besides costs. It is therefore considered
by the court that the plaintiff do recover against the said defendant the
*declaration mentioned and the damages aforesaid by the jury assessed and
the said defendant in mercy etc.

      It is ordered by the court that Richard Nixon, Daniel Cherry,
Joel Estes, Lawrence McGuire, Jonathan Jacocks, Nicholas T.Perkins ,
Jesse L.Kirk, Oliver Woods, Samuel P.Ashe, Francis M.Wood, David Hay
Vincent Haralson, Joshua Abstain, John R.Roddy, Francis S.Coxe, James
Crook, Richard Taylor, James Mauldin, Thos N.White, James Henderson,
Mansfield Ware, Giles Matette, James Carlton, James W.Russell, John T.
Turner and Wilson A.W.Mann be summoned to attend at the next term of the
Circuit (p-285) to be holden for this county then and there to serve
as grand or petit Jurors as the case may be and that Jourdan M.
Hansborough and Joel Abstain be appointed constables to attend said court.
Iss'd.

      It is ordered by the court that Herndon Haralson, Simon Turner,
Charles White, Bignal Crook, Cato Freeman, Daniel Shaw, Thomas G.Nixon,
John Williams, Henry H.Turner, Archibald McNeal, John Andrews, Robert
T.Smith, William Weddle, Benjamin Weaver, Julius Sanders, Henry McCoy,
Joseph Murphy Robert Perry, John Marbery, Berry Dearing, Allen J.Barbee
Stephen Childress, Nelson Hargrove, Thomas West, Joseph Curry, Richard
Moore, be summoned to attend at the next term of this court, then and
there to serve as grand and petit jurors as the case may be, and that
Joel Abstain and Jordon M.Hansborough constables be appointed to attend
said court.
Iss'd.

Francis/Dillard/   )
      vs   )
William H.Henderson &)
John/Hardwick   )

      This day came the said plaintiff by his attorney and saith he in-
tends no further to prosecute his suit against the said defendant, and
thereupon came also the said defendant and assumes upon himself to pay
all costs in this behalf expended etc Entered Heretofore written across
paragraph.
* debt aforesaid in the

(p-285con.) Archibald McNeal assee)
         vs   )
    Blackman Coleman   )

This day came the said parties by their attorneys and thereupon came a jury of good and lawful men to wit, Robert Roddy, Eli Jones, Thomas Thweatt Mansfield Ware, Benjamin Wilks, Thomas Potter, Samuel Elliott, Arthur F.McCain, Thomas Stokely, Berry Dearing, William H.Patton and Robert T.Smith who being elected tried and sworn well and truly to try the issue joined between the parties, upon their oaths aforesaid do say that the said defendant hath not paid the debt of one hundred and (p-286) forty three dollars and sixty cents in the declaration mentioned as the plaintiff in replying hath alledged, and do assess the plaintiffs damages by reason of the detention thereof to four dollars and thirty cents besides costs. It is therefore considered by the court that the plaintiff do recover against the said defendant the debt aforesaid in the declaration mentioned and the damages aforesaid by the jury aforesaid assessed, and the costs in this behalf expended, and the defendant in mercy etc.

George Thomison assee)
      vs   )
John Walling and   )
Caleb Swindle   )

This day came the said parties by their attorneys and thereupon came a jury of good and lawful men to wit, Robert Roddy, Eli Jones, Thomas Thweatt, Mansfield Ware, Benjamin Wilks, Thomas Potter Samuel Elliott, Arthur F.McCain, Thomas Stokely, Berry Dearing, William H. Patton & Robert T.Smith who being elected tried and sworn well and truly to try the issues joined between the parties upon their oaths aforesaid do say that the defendant hath not paid the debt of one hundred and five dollars in the declaration mentioned as the plaintiff in replying to the defendants plea hath alledged, and do assess the plaintiffs damages by reason of the detention thereof to three dollars and fifteen cents besides costs, It is therefore considered by the court that the said plaintiff do recover against the said defendant the debt aforesaid in the declaration mentioned and the damages aforesaid by the Jury in form aforesaid assessed and the costs in this behalf expended and the defendant in mercy etc.

Joseph Spence)
)
   vs   )
James Walker

Continued as on affidavit of the plaintiff.

(p-287) John ____ assee)
        vs   )
    John T.Turner   )

This day came the parties by their attorneys and thereupon came also a jury of good and lawful men to wit, Robert Roddy, Eli Jones, Thomas Thweatt, Mansfield Ware, Benjamin Wilks, Thomas Potter, Samuel Elliott , Arthur F.McCain, Thomas Stokely, Berry Dearing, William H.

(p-287con.) Patton, and Robert T.Smith, who being elected tried and sworn well and truly to try the issues joined between the parties upon their oaths aforesaid do say that the defendant hath not paid the debt of one hundred dollars in the declaration mentioned as the plaintiff in replying to the defendants plea hath alledged, and they assess the plaintiffs damages by reason of the detention thereof to eight dollars and fifty cents besides costs. It is therefore considered by the court that the said plaintiff do recover against the said defendant the debt aforesaid in the declaration mentioned together with the damages aforesaid by the Jury aforesaid assessed and the costs in this behalf expended and the defendant in mercy etc.

Acopy? of a decretal order made by the county court of Mecklenberg of of the State of Virginia in Chancery sitting under date of the 18th of February 1828 appointing ordering & decreeing John T.Taylor, & Richard Taylor trustees of under a deed of trust made & executed by John G. Baptist coveying to William Baptist & Joseph B. Clause two negroes, Hampton & Carey in trust for the bennefit of May Meredith & other purposes in said deed of trust mentioned in the place & stead of said John G. Baptist & Richard Taylor, was produced in open court duly certified according to law and ordered to be admitted to Registration.

A Deed of trust from Richard H.Baptist of Mecklinburgh County Virginia unto William R.Merdith, John Y.Taylor & Richard Taylor for certain personal property therein mentioned for the use & benefit of May Meredith was produced in open court duly certified & ordered to be admited to registration.

Thomas Potter assee)
    vs)
Matthew Ray)

    The defendant being dissatisfied with the Judgment rendered against him, hath prayed and obtained an appeal to the next Circuit Court of this county. He having given bond and security to prosecute the same.

(p-288) Jesse Powers assee)
    vs)
    William C.Bruce)
    Philip Bruce & Joseph Murphy)

    The defendants being dissatisfied with the judgment rendered against them hath prayed and obtained an appeal to the next Circuit of this county, they having given bond and security to prosecute the same.

Thomas H.Taylor)
    vs) On a Demurer
Francis S.Coxe)

    This day came the said, parties by their attornies and thereupon the matters of law arising upon the defendants demurer to the plaintiffs declaration being argued. It seems to the court that the said declaration and the matters therein contained are not sufficient in law to maintain the action of the plaintiff against the defendant . Therefore it is considered by the court that the said declaration be quashed and that the said defendant go hence without day and recover against the said plaintiff (p-288con.) his costs by him about his defence in this behalf expended etc. From which Judgment of the court the plaintiff prayed and obtained an appeal in the nature of a writ of Error to the next Circuit Court of this county. He having given bond & security to prosecute the same.

(p-289) George W.Hockly)
            vs)
    James Carlton)

This day came the Defendant in his proper person & saith that he cannot gainsay the said plaintiffs action for two hundred and forty nine dollars and sixteen cents, besides costs, and confesseth Judgment for the same- It is therefore considered by the court that the said plaintiff do recover against the said defendant the said sum of two hundred and forty nine dollars and sixteen cents, and the costs in this behalf expended & the defendant in mercy etc.

Samuel Edney)
    vs)   Certiorari
Broadwater Matney)

This day came the said defendant in his proper person and saith that he intends no further to prosecute his said certiorari and dismisses the same. It is therefore considered by the court that the plaintiff do recover against the said defendant & on motion against William Shearin & John Sanderlin his security in the certiorari the sum thirty five dollars seventeen & one half cents, the amount of the Judgment before the Justice of the peace, with 12 one half per cent interest thereon from 14th day of June 1828, the date of the Judgement of the Justice, up to this day and the costs in this behalf expended etc.

C.M.Phipps)
    vs)
B.Matney)

This day came the said B.Matney one of the defendants in his proper person and saith that he intends no further to prosecute his said certiorari and dismisses the same . It is therefore considered by the (p-290) court that the plaintiff recover against the said defendant and on motion against John Sanderlin, and William Shearin, his securities in the certiorari the sum of two dollars and ninety cents the amount of the judgment before the justice of the peace with twelve and one half percent interest thereon from the 14th day of June 1828 the date of the Judgment of the Justice up to this day and the costs in this behalf expended etc.

C.M.Phipps)
    vs)
Broadwaters Matney)

This day came the said deft. in his proper person and saith that he intends no further to prosecute his said certiorari and dismisses the same- It is therefore considered by the court that the plaintiff recover against the said defendants and on motion against John Sanderlin and William Shearin his securities in the certiorari the sum of five dollars sixty eight and three fourth cents the amount of the Judgment before the (p=290con.) Justice of the peace in the twelve and one half per cent interest from the 14th day of June 1828 the date of the Judgment of the Justice up to this day and the costs in this behalf expended.

C.M.Phipps   )
        vs   )
Broadwaters Matney)

This day came the defendant in his proper person and saith that he intends no further to prosecute his said certiorari and dismisses the same. It is therefore considered by the court that the plaintiff recover against the said defendant and on motion against John Sanderlin and William Shearin his security in the certiorari the sum of thirty one dollars and seventy five cents the amount of the judgment before the justice of the peace (p-291) with twelve and a half per cent interest from the ninth day of May 1828 the date of the Justice judgment up to this day and the costs in this behalf expended etc.

C.M.Phipps   )
        vs   )
Broadwater Matney   )

This day came the defendant in his proper person and saith that he intends no further to prosecute his said certiorari and dismisses his suit- It is therefore consedered by the court that the plaintiff recovered against the said defendant and on motion against John Sanderlin and William Shearin his security in the certiorari the sum of three dollars fifty cents fourth cents the amount of the Judgment before the Justice of the peace with twelve and one half percent interest from the 14th day June 1828 up to the present day and the costs in this behalf expended-

C.M.Phipps   )
        vs   )
Broadwater Matney   )

This day came the said defendant in his proper person and saith that he intends no further to prosecute his said certiorari and dismiss the same . It is therefore considered by the court that the plaintiff do recover against the said defendant and on motion against John Sanderlin and William Shearin his security in the certiorari the sum of three dollars sixty eight and three fourth cents the amount of the Judgment before the Justice of the peace with twelve and one half per cent interest from the 14th of June 1828 up to this and the costs in this behalf expended.

(p-292) Jonathan R.Burlison)
            vs   )
        Franklin Glenn &   ) Attachment for a Contempt
        William Balch   )

This day the Defendants whose bodies were attached for a contempt shown to this court for not obeying the process of this court were this day brought into court in the custody of the Sheriff, and upon motion of the defendants by John D.Martin their attorney and for reasons satisfactorilly appearing to the court it is ordered by the court that the said (p-292con.) attachment be dismissed and the defends discharged from custody and it is further considered by the court that the defends recover against the said Jonathan R.Burlison the costs in this behalf expended .

There appearing no further business for the consideration of the jury at this term were discharged and proved each three days attendance to wit, Robert Roddy, Eli Jones, Thomas Thweatt, Mansfield Ware, Benjamin Wilkes & William Shearin-

The court then adjourned until tomorrow 9 o'clock-

Rich. Nixon Cha.
N.T.Perkins J.P.
Joel Estes
L.McGuire

(p-293) Friday morning September 12th 1828

Court met according to adjournment present the worshipful Richard Nixon, Nicholas T.Perkins, Joel Estes and Lawrence McGuire esquires-

John Jetton to use of   )
Isaac Jetton   )
         vs   )
John G.Carithers   )

The defendant being dissatisfied with the Judgment of the court hath prayed and obtained an appeal to the next Circuit Court he having entered into bond to prosecute the same.

Edney & Phipps   )
       vs   ) Certiorari
Broadwater Matney   )

On motion of the plaintiffs by their attorney it is to dismiss the certioarar in this cause and upon solemn argument being had thereon and by the court here fully understood it is considered by the court here that the motion be sustained, and that the plaintiffs do recover against the said defendant and John Sanderline and William Shearin his security in the certioarari their costs in this behalf expended, and the said defendants in mercy etc. And upon motion of the said plaintiffs by their attorney, it is further considered by the court that a procedure issue to the Justice below to issue executions on the followling courses returned to the court in the writ of certioarari , to wit, Samuel Edney vs Broadwater Matney, C.M.Phipps vs Broadwarer Matney and James Burton, C.M.Phipps vs B.Matney and Wyatt F.Tweedy, C.M.Phipps vs Matney C.M.Phipps vs B.Matney . C.M.Phipps vs B.Matney and William Johnson Jr., and it is also further considered by the court that the Judgments heretofore taken at this time in the above several causes against the said Broadwater Matney & his said securities in the certioarari be set aside without costs.

(p-294) James Smith   )
             vs   )
         William Weddle)

(p-294con.) This day came the said plaintiff by his attorney and moved the court to dismiss the certioarari in this cause, and upon solemn argument being had thereon by council learned in the law, and by the court here fully understood, it is considered by the court here that the motion be sustained . It is therefore considered by the court here that the said plaintiff do recover against the said defendant & on*against Levi Gardner and John M.White his security in the certioarari the sum of forty one dollars & forty three cents, the amount of the Judgement before the Justice with 12½ per cent interest thereon from the 4th of March 1828 the date of the Judgement of the Justice, up to this day and the costs in this behalf expended etc.

William Downs   )
        vs   ) Certiorari
William Weddle   )

This day came the said plaintiff by his attorney, and moved the court to dismiss the certioari in this cause, and upon solemn argument being had thereon and by the court here fully understood, it is considered by the court here that the motion be sustained . It is therefore considered by the court that the said plaintiff recover against the said defendant and on motion against Levi Gardner, and John McWhite his security in the certioarari the sum of fifty nine dollars, sixty two & one half cents, the amount of the Judgement of the Justice, with 12½ per cents interest thereon from the 9th of January 1828, the date of the Judgement, up to this day and the costs in this behalf expended-

(p-295) Thos J.Rodgers   )
            vs   ) Motion
      Samuel Elliott   )

On motion of the said plaintiff by his attorney and it appearing to the satisfaction of this court that the defendant did on the 6th day of September 1828 recover a judgment against the said defendant before Richard Nixon esquire one of the Justices of the peace of this county for the sum of ten dollars and fifty cents & all legal costs. That an execution issued thereon which came duly into the hands of Mathew Ray a constable of this county who have made return thereon as follows came to hand September the 9th 1828 levied on one corner lot and house in the town of Brownsville No.4 there being no personal property to be found in my county. It is therefore ordered by the court that a writ of vendition exponas to issue to cause said lot so levied on as aforesaid to be sold to satsfy said Judgment and costs aforesaid and the costs about this motion expended.

Stith M.King   )
        vs   ) Motion
Samuel Elliott   )

On motion of the said plaintiff by his attorney and it appearing to the satisfaction of this court that the defendant did on the 6th day of September 1829 recover a judgment against the said defendant before Richard Nixon esquire one of the Justices of the peace of this county for the sum of sixty dollars and fifty cents and all legal costs

* motion

(p-295con.) That an execution issued thereon which came duly to the hands of Mathew Ray a constable of this county who hath made return thereon as follows, came to hand the 9th of Septr. 1828 levied on one house and lot in the town of Brownsville No. 4 there being no personal property to be found in my county. It is therefore ordered by the court that a writ of vendition exponas issue to cause said Lot so levied in as aforesaid to be sold to satisfy said Judgment and costs aforesaid and the costs about this motion.

Joe Ables & B.Dearing)
  vs   )
Jesse Kemp   )

   Continued on affidavit of the Deft

(p-296) William A.Johnston)
      vs   )
    Berry Dearing)

  This day came the said plaintiff by his attorney and moved the court to dismiss the certiorari in this cause, and by solemn argumant being had thereon by council learned in the law, and by the court here fully understood it is considered by the court here that the motion be sustained, It is therefore considered by the court here that the said plaintiff do recover against the said defendant and on motion against William Powell and John Hardwick his securities in the certiorari the sum of forty nine dollars and seventy nine cents the amount of the Judgment before the Justice with twelve and a half per cent interest thereon from the 5th of April 1828 the date of the Judgment of the Justice up to this day and the costs in this behalf expended.

Fox & Bourland)
  vs   )
Berry Dearing)

  This day came the said plaintiffs by his attorney and moved the court to dismiss the certiorari in this cause, and by solemn argument being had thereon by council learned in the law, and by the court here fully understood. It is therefore considered by the court here that the said plaintiffs do recover against the said defendant , and on motion against William Powell and John Hardwick his securities in the certiorari the sum of thirty eight dollars and seventy nine cents the amount of the judgment before the Justice of the peace with twelve and a half per cent interest thereon from the 1st day of December 1827 the date of the Judgment of the Justice up to this day and the costs in this behalf expended.

(p-297) Isaac L.Moody assee)
      vs   ) Sci fa
    Jonathan J.Nixon)

  This day came the said plaintiff by his attorney and saith that he intends no further to prosecute his said sciri facias against the said defendant. It is therefore considered by the court that the defendant go hence without day and recover against the said plaintiff his costs by him about his defence in this behalf expended etc.

201

(p-297con.) A Deed of bargain and sale from John G.Carithers sheriff
and collector of Haywood County to Robert J.Chester for two hundred and
eighty two acres of land was this day produced in open court and duly
acknowledged to be his act and deed and ordered to be certified for
registration.

A Bill of sale from John G.Carithers sheriff of Haywood County to
William B .Miller for a certain negro boy named Wilson was this day produced in open court and duly acknowledged and ordered to be certified
for registration.

An Indenture of bargain & sale from Dickson Givens of the county
of Lexington & State of Kentucky to Samuel Woods for three hundred and
forty two acres of land was this day produced in open court and and
duly proven by the oath of William H.Henderson one of the subscribing
witnesses thereto who also made oath that Guilford Wimberly the other
witness thereto became a subscribing witness to said deed in his presence
and that said Wimberly is an Inhabitant of the State of Kentucky all
of which is ordered to be certified for registration.

Archibald McNeal assee)
          vs   )
B.Coleman   )

The defendant being dissatisfied with the Judgment of the court
hath prayed and obtained an appeal to the next Circuit Court he having
given bond as the law directs to prosecute the same.

(p-298) Upon the Petition of Jonathan R.Burlison exhibitted and sworn
to in open court, setting fourth that he did on third of July 1828
obtain a judgement before Oliver Wood a justice of this County, against
William Balch for the sum of nineteen dollars and sixty five cents
That an prayed was prayed & granted to the county court by said Balch
and that the papers he believes have been lost or destroyed. He therefore prays that a certioarari issue to said Justice to bring up to
our next court the original papers if to be found, and if not a certified
copy thereof, which petition is granted by the court, and accordingly
ordered to issue.

Isaac L.Moody   )
          vs   )   On a Sciri Facias
Bignal Crook an appearance)
bail for Preston G.Hodges   )

The defendant Begnal Crook this day surrendered here in open court
the body of the said Preston G.Hodges in discharged of himself a
special bail, who is not prayed in custody of the sheriff by the plaintiff
but is discharged whereupon the Defendant is discharged from his recognizance, and it is ordered (p-299) that the suit be dismissed and that
the defendant pay to the plaintiff his costs.

Henry M.Rutledge   )
    vs   )
Blackman Coleman   )

(p-299 con.) The defendant being dissatisfied with the Judgment of
the court hath this day prayed and obtained an appeal to the next
Circuit Court he having given bond to prosecute the same-

The court then adjourned until court in course.

                                    Rich'd. Nixon Cha.
                                    L.McGuire
                                    B.Coleman

(p-300)   State of Tennessee)
            Haywood County   )   At a court of Pleas

        and Quarter sessions began & holden for the county of Haywood,
at the courthouse in the Town of Brownsville on the second Monday, it
being the Eight day of December A.D.1828, Present the worshipful
Richard Nixon, Joel Estes and Lawrence McGuire esquires and others
their fellow justices of the peace the clerk and sheriff present.

        A Deed of trust from Samuel Elliott to William R.Hess for certain
purposes therein mentioned, was this day proved in open court by the
oath of Herndon Haralson and Henry Welch , subscribing witnesses thereto
and ordered to be registered.

        Deed of conveyance from Henry Neal to John C.McLemore & J.Vaulx
for 426 & 2/3 acres of land in Tipton County, was this day proved in
open court by the oaths of Herndon Haralson and Lawrence McGuire witnesses thereto & ordered to be registered.

        Deed of Trust from John Potter to Thomas Potter for certain
articles therein mentioned, together with one half of a lot of ground
in the town of Brownsville was this day proved in open court by the
oaths of Blackman Coleman and William R.Hess, witnesses thereto and
ordered to be registered.

        It is ordered by the court that Charles Wortham, Dan'l Cherry
and James Wortham Jr. be and are hereby appointed to settle with Isaac
Koonce administrator of John Koonce deceased and make report to the next
term of this court

(p-301) It is ordered by the court that John G.Carithers, sheriff and
collector of Haywood be and is hereby allowed for his exofficio
services for the last year the sum of fifty dollars, (the following
Justices being on the bench and the ayes and noes being taken as the
law directs) to wit. B.Coleman, aye, Daniel Cherry aye, Lawrence
McGuire, aye, Jonathan T.Jacocks aye, Samuel P.Ashe aye. James L.
Wortham aye, Joel Estes, aye, to be paid by the county trustee out of
any unappropriated money in his hands.
Iss'd.

        It is ordered by the court that Alexander B.Bradford, Esquire,
attorney General, be allowed the sum of fifty dollars for his Exofficio
services for the last twelve months the ayes following Justices being
present to wit, Richard Nixon, Daniel Cherry, Lawrence McGuire, Joel
Estes, Samuel P.Ashe, James L.Wortham and Jonathan T.Jacocks, and the
ayes and noes being taken as the law directs, all of the said Justices

(p-301con.) voted in the affirmative to be paid out of any unappropriated money in the hands of the county trustee.
Issued

It is ordered by the court the Britain H.Sanders clerk of this
court be allowed the sum of forty dollars for his exofficio services for
the last twelve months, and the further sum of twenty five dollars for
making out and recording the tax lists to be paid out of any unappropriated money in the hands of the county trustee. The following Justices
of the peace being present and the ayes and noes being taken as the law
directs, ayes, Richard Nixon, Dan'l. Cherry, Lawrence McGuire, Joel
Estes, Saml. P.Ashe, James L.Wortham and Jonathan T.Jacocks.
Iss'd.

Joshua Abstain records the Ear mark of his stock thus, to wit,
a crop of the left ear and a swallow fork in the right ear.
Pd. to B.C.

(p-302) It is ordered by the court that Britain H.Sanders, clerk of
this court, be allowed the sum of Eleven dollars for a county Seal and
press for the same, to be paid by the county trustee out of any unappropiated monies in his hands the following Justices of the peace being
on the bench and the ayes and noes being taken as the law directs they
being a majority of the court to wit ayes Richard Nixon, Daniel Cherry,
Lawrence McGuire, Nicholas T.Perkins, Jonathan T.Jacocks, Joel Estes,
Samuel P.Ashe, James L.Wortham.
Is'd.

James Kinney was this day appointed a constable for this county
in Capt. Woods company who took the several oaths prescribed by law,
and entered into bond with Robert Kennady and Champion Blythe, his
securities.

John H.Freeman this day prayed and obtained a licence to keep an
ordinary at his now dwelling house in this county, who gave bond &
security & took the oaths prescribed by law.

Deed of Conveyance from James Caruthers, John C.McLemore and
James Vaulx to Benjamin Boothe for seventy five acres of land was this
day proved in open court by the oaths of Reubin Alphin & M.H.Bradford,
witnesses thereto and ordered to be registered.

A Power of attorney from William Dillon, Daniel Dillon, Samuel
Ross & his wife Mary Ross formerly Mary Dillon, and Sally Dillon,
John Albertson, Ruth Albertson,

John Tracey and Rachel Tracey to Nathan Dillon & Isaac Dillon
was this day proved in open court by the oath of Willis C.Holland , a
witness thereto and ordered to be certified.

(p-303) It is ordered by the court that the order heretofore made
appointing commissioners to view and consolidate the Fulton Road and
the Estes road be renewed, and that Henry Welch, Mansfield Ware and
Nichalos T.Perkins be added thereto as commissioners.
Iss'd.

(p-303con.) Noah W.Dill Esquire this day produced in open court a
license from the Hon. Thomas Stewart and N.W.Williams Judges etc
authorising him to practice law in the several court of this State and
the said Dill having taken the oaths required by law, he is authorised
to practice as such in this court .
Iss'd.

Court adjourned until tomorrow morning nine o'clock.

> Dan'l. Cherry
> Joel Estes
> Sam. P.Ashe
> Jesse L.Kirk

Tuesday morning December 9th 1828

Court met pursuant to adjournment. Present the worshipful
Daniel Cherry Joel Estes, Samuel P.Ashe & Jesse L.Kirk esquires
Justices.

```
Isaac L.Moody            )
      vs                 )
Jonathan J.Nixon         )      Sci Fa
special bail for Richard)
W.Nixon                  )
```

The defendant produced into court the body of the said Richard
W.Nixon, who is committed to the custody of the sheriff of this county
to remain in the common jail of the same until he shall have satisfied
the judgement in the writ of Sciri Facias mentioned whereupon the defendant is discharged from his recognizance , and

(p-304) Granville D.Searcy Esquire produced in court a licene from
the Hon. Jno. Catran, and W.E.Kennady Esqrs. Judges & authorising
him to practice law in the several cents in this State, and the said
Granville D.Searcy Esq. having taken the oaths prescribed by law , is
authorised to practice as such in this court-

John G.Carithers, Sheriff, makes return of the venire Facias, returnable to this court which is as follows to wit.

State of Tennessee
        At a court of pleas and quarter sessions, began and held
for the county of Haywood ,at the courthouse in the town of Brownsville
on the second Monday in September 1828 it being the 8th day of said
month. Present the worshipful Samuel P.Ashe, Jonathan T.Jacocks,
Lawrence McGuire and others their fellow justices. Clerk and sheriff
present. It is ordered by the court that the following persons, good
and lawful men, viz. each being a white male citizen of the age of
twenty one years and a house holder to wit, Herndon Haralson, Simon
Turner, Charles White, Bignal Crook, Cato Freeman, Daniel Shaw, Thomas
G.Nixon, John Williams, Henry H.Turner, Archibald McNeale, John Andrews
Robt Turner, Smith, William Widdle, Benja. Weaver, Julius Sanders,
Henry McCoy, Joseph Murphy, Robert Perry, John Marbury, Berry Dearing,
Allen J.Barbee, Stephen Childress, Nelson Hargrove, Thomas West,Joseph

(p-304con.) Curry, Richard Moore, be summoned to attend at the next
court. Then and there to serve as grand and petit Jurors as the case
may be and that Joel Abstain and Jourdan M.Hansborough constables be
appointed to attend said court.

Test B.H.Sanders,Clk.

State of Tennessee
       To the sheriff of Haywood County Greeting
You are hereby commanded to summons the aforesaid persons to serve as
Grand and petit Jurors as the case maybe at the next court of pleas and
quarter sessions to be held at the courthouse in the Town of Brownsville
on Tuesday after the second Monday in December next and this they (p-305)
shall in no wise omit under the penalty prescribed by Law,
Herein fail not and have you then and there this writ witness Britain
H.Sanders, clerk of our said court at office this second Monday in
September 1828 and fifty third year of American Independence.

B.H.Sanders Clk.

Upon the back of which said writ John G.Carithers sheriff of
Haywood County has made the following indorsements came to hand the
same day Issued-

J.G.Carithers, shff.

And also By virtue of the within venire facias I have proceded
to summons all the within named persons except William Weddle, Henry H.
Turner, Bignal Crook, John Marbery and Thos. West such persons so summoned are free holders or householders of said county-

J.G.Carithers shff-

The following persons, good and lawful men of the county of
Haywood, were elected, drawn sworn and charged as a grand jury for the
present term, to wit, Herddon Haralson Foreman, Nilson Hartgrove,
Robert Perry, Archibald McNeal, Joseph Murphy, Julias Sanders,
Benjamin Weaver, John Williams, Henry McCoy, Robert T.Smith, Stephen S.
Childress, Thos. G.Nixon, & Simon Turner Matthew Ray constable retired
to consider of the duties assigned them. (Benja. Weaver is below
Julius Sanders & S.S.Childress issued & maked recorded in page 10,
in the margin.)

Mathew/Ray/constable/

It isordered by the court that Cato Freeman, Richard Moore,
Joseph Curry and/ who were regularly and legally served summoned on the
venire facias as to this court, to serve as grand or petit jurors, as
the case might be be fined the sum of Five dollars for their non attendance as such, and that Sciri Facias issue according to law.
Sci Fa issd.

(p-306) Ezekiel Blackshire   )
                vs   )   Case No. 1
         Robert Hamel   )

(p-306con.) This day came the said parties by their attornies and thereupon came also a jury of good and lawful men, to wit, Valentine Sevier, Monroe P.Estes, John H.Freeman, Francis S.Coxe, Edward Matthews Tobias Hall, Benjamin Huckaby, Samuel Elliott, Joseph Baxter, Sanford Perry, Nathan Bridgeman and Robert Sanders, who being elected, tried & sworn well and truly to try the issue joined upon their oaths do say they find the issue in favour of the plaintiff and assess his damages to thirty dollars. It is therefore considered by the court that the plaintiff do recover against the defendant the damages aforesaid by the jury in form aforesaid assessed and the costs in this behalf expended, and the said defendant in mercy etc. The Defendant go being dissatisfied with the judgement rendered against him hath prayed and obtained an appeal to the Circuit Court of this county he having given bond and security therefor.

Ezekial Blackshire)
        vs   )
Robert Hamel   )

Alondus S.Gholson, who hath been summoned to appear and give evidence in behalf of the defendant in this cause, was this day solemnly called to come into court as he was bound to do, came not, but made default.

It is therefore considered by the court that the defendant recover against the said Alondus S.Gholson, the sum of one hundred and twenty five dollars and that a writ of Sciri Facias issue to the next term of this court to make known to the said Gholson why said judgment should not be made final against him etc.

(p-307) Upon petition it is ordered by the court that William H. Henderson, Thomas G.Nixon, Nicholas T.Perkins, Blackman Coleman,Jonathan T.Jacocks, and Mansfield Ware, or a majority of them be and are hereby appointed a jury of view to view and mark a road from the Town of Brownsville to the Tipton County line in a direction to Paynes Ferry & Covington etc. and said jury of view are hereby required also to view Estes road and report to the next court which of the two roads the one now contemplated to be cut out or the Estes road is the nearest and best, the said order having passed on the first day of the term when a majority of the Justices was present.
Issd.

The Jury of view appointed at the last term of this court to mark and lay off a road in continuation of a road from Brownsville to Nixons Ware house to Fayette County line in a direction to Summerville makes report to this court that they have done the same, which is ordered to be received by the court.

The court adjourned until tomorrow morning nine o'clock.

                              Joel Estes
                              Dan'l. Cherry
                              Jesse L.Kirk

(p-308) Wednesday morning, December 10th 1828

Court met pursuant to adjournment, Present the worshipful Joel Estes, Daniel Cherry, Jesse L.Kirk & others their fellow Justices.

Deed of conveyance from Elisha Bryant to John Murry for twenty one acres of land was this day acknowledged in open court by the said Bryant and ordered to be registered.

It is ordered by the court that the road as heretofore established by this court, and which has been cut out, leading from the town of Brownsville in a direction towards Bollivar be and is hereby established and continued as the public road, there being a majority of the acting Justices present.

Deed of Gift from David Glass to Nathan a Longly & Robertson Y. Longly for certain property in said deed mentioned was this day proved in open court by the oaths of John G.Carithers and Matthew Ray. Witnesses thereto and ordered to be registered.

It is ordered by the court that Caleb Miller, Foster Parker,Berry Rucker, Robert Boles Jr. William Boles, James L.Wortham & Benjamin W. Perry be appointed a jury of view to view and mark a road from Wortham Ferry to the Madison County line in a direction to Trenton.
Iss'd

It is ordered by the court the following justices being present, to wit, Jesse L.Kirk, Lawrence McGuire, Daniel Cherry, Nicholas T. Perkins, Jonathan T.Jacocks, Samuel P.Ashe and James L.Wortham (being a majority of this county and the ayes and (p-309) noes being taken as the law directs, all of which whom voted in the affirmative , that Thomas Potter, be allowed the sum of Ten dollars and fifty cents for repairs done to the courthouse, to be paid by the county trustee out of any unappropriated money in his hands.
Iss'd

It is ordered by the court the sheriff of this county at the proper term for reporting lands for the non-payment of Taxes, report all lands which have heretofore been reported by him and which were not sold for the want of bidders.

A Power of attorney from John G.Carithers and Matthew C.Carithers to Mary Carithers of for the sale and conveyance of a tract of land in Abberville district, South Carolina, was this day acknowledged in open court by said John G.and Matthew C.Carithers and ordered to be so certified.

It is ordered by the court that the order made at the last term of this court authorising the clerk of this court to receive taxes be, and the same is hereby recinded, and that the sheriff collect the single tax during this term.

It is ordered by the court that hereafter the Presinct, elections held on the north side of the south fork of Forked Deer river be held at Harrisburg instead of Thomas Thweatts the present place and that the (p-309con.) presinct established at the house of Samuel P.Ashe esqr. be so changed that the election be held at the cross roads on said Ashe's land.

(p-310) It is ordered by the court that the order made at the last term of this court for a jury of view to mark a road from Buck's ferry to intersect a road from the Key Corner be renewed and issued accordingly Issd.

John James this day produced in court the scalp of a wolf over the age of Six months, and proved,as the law directs , the killing of said wolf within Haywood . It is therefore ordered by the court,a majority of the justices being present, to wit, Jesse L. Kirk & Lawrence McGuire, Daniel Cherry, Nicholas T.Perkins, Jonathan T.Jacocks,Samuel P.Ashe, and James L.Wortham, ad. of whom voted in the affirmative that said John James be allowed the sum of three dollars, to be paid by the treasurer of the Western district.

Issued to D.Cherry

A Transfer of a Platt and certificate of survey from Caleb Warren to Phillip Koonce for fifty acres of land was this day acknowledged in open court and ordered to be registered.
50 pd. B.H.S.delivered

It is ordered by the court that the overseer of that part of the road leading from Jackson to McGuires Ferry which David Hay proposes to turn examine the same as cost by him and should he think it not to the injury of the public, to receive the same, and report accordingly to next court.
Iss'd. 19th Decr. To D.Hay

(p-311) The Grand Jury of the present term returned into court and returned a bill of Indictment against Nathan Bridgeman & Reese Porter for an affray,"a true Bill"andretired to consider of further business.

It is ordered by the court that the following justices of the peace be and are hereby appointed to take lists of Taxable property and poles in the following captains company for the year 1829, to wit Daniel Cherry esqr. in Worthams and Tweedy's companies, Nicholas T. Perkins, in Capt. Elliots company, Oliver Woods in Capt. Woods Company. Jesse L.Kirk in Captain Brooks company, Samuel P.Ashe in Captain Edwards company Jonathan T.Jacocks in Capt Curry's Company, Lawrence McGuire & Richard Nixon Generally and that orders issue accordingly Iss'd.

Deed of Conveyance from Thomas J.McGuire to James M.McGuire, for two hundred and thirty acres of land was this day proved in open court by the oaths of John H.Freeman and Christopher Freeman witnesses thereto and ordered to be registered.

Deed of Conveyance from Samuel Richardson to Lion Hunt for five hundred fifty one and one half acres of land was this day proved in open court by the oaths of Charles White and Stephen Terry,Witnesses (p-311con.) thereto and ordered to be registered.

It is ordered by the court a majority of the Justices being
present to wit Richard Nixon, Jesse L.Kirk, Samuel P.Ashe, Oliver Woods,
Lawrence McGuire, James L.Wortham, N.T.Perkins, Daniel Cherry, and the
ayes & noes being taken as the law directs, and each of said justices
voting in the affirmation, that Mansfield Ware, be allowed the sum of
Five dollars it being county part of the tax on 380 acres of land heretofore reported & sold for non payment of Taxes. It appearing to this
court that there was no such land in this county to be paid out of
any unappropriated money in the hands of the county trustee.
Iss'd.

(p-312) It is ordered by the court a majority of the Justices being
present to wit Richard Nixon Jesse L.Kirk, Lawrence McGuire, James
L.Wortham, Oliver Woods,Daniel Cherry & Nicholas T.Perkins, and the
ayes & noes being taken as the law directs, each justice voting in the
affirmative that Matthew Ray be allowed as a full compensation for
Guarding John Hardwick & for taking him from this county to the jail
in Jackson, the sum of Eighteen dollars and thirty two cents which
allowance is in full for the Guard summoned on that occasion, to be paid
by the county trustee out of any unappropriated money in his hands.
Iss'd.

The State of Tennessee)
          vs   ) Indictment for an affray
Nathan Bridgeman   )

This day came as well the State of Tennessee by A.B.Bradford
esqr attorney General, as the Defendant in his proper person, and the
defendant being solemnly charged saith that he is guilty in manner and
form as charged in the bill of Indictment and puts himself upon the
grace & mercy of the court. It is thereupon ordered by the court that
the Defendant make his fine with the State of Tennessee by the payment of
Ten Dollars & all costs in this behalf expended, and that the Defendant
be taken.

A Power of attorney from Sicilly W.McGraw to James Herndon for
the purposes therein mentioned was this day acknowledged in open court
by said Sicilly W.McGrain & ordered to be certified.
$1 pd. B.C.Delivered

(p-313) The State of Tennessee)
             vs   ) Indictment for an affray
         Reese Porter   )

This day came as well the State of Tennessee by A.B.Bradford
esquire attorney General as the defendant in his proper person, and
the defendant being solemnly charged saith that he is not guilty in
manner and form as charged in the bill of Indictment, and for his trial
puts himself upon the country and the attorney General doth the like
and thereupon came also a jury of good and lawful men to wit, Daniel
Shaw, Cato Freeman, Phillip Koonce, Mansfield Ware, John Wills Berry
Derin, James Russel, Samuel Elliott, Malcom Johnson, John Sevier,

(p-313con.) William Pace, and Francis Lamoin, who being elected, tried and sworn well and truly to try the issue of traverses upon their oaths do say that the defendant is not guilty in manner and form as charged in the bill of Indictment. It is therefore considered by the court that the defendant be released and go hence, thereof without day.

William Lawrence for the   )
use of John Caldwell   )
         vs   )
John R.McGuire,Thomas Stokely   )
& John McWhite securities   )
for Benjamin Noakes late a   )
constable of said county   )

Whereas it appears to the satisfaction of this court that said Benjamin Noaks as constable in & for the county of Haywood in the year 1827 during the time that he was constable & during the time that John R.McGuire, Thomas Stokely & John C.McWhite was his securities for the faithful performance of the duties of his said office & for the faithful receiving & paying over all monies by him collected by virtue of his said office, did receive & collect the sum of Forty Dollars, upon a Judgment recovered against Britain H.Sanders in favour of Green B. Jamison for the use of William Lawrence, & whereas it further appears to the satisfaction of this court that the interest in said Judgment has been transferring assigned & set over to John Caldwell, and it further appearing that notice has been duly served upon the above named John R. McGuire, Thomas Stokely & John C.McWhite that a motion would be made against them at the present term of this court as securities aforesaid for a Judgment for the amount of said sum of money received & collected as aforesaid by said Benjamin Noaks as aforesaid, which as it appears to this court has not been paid over by said Benjamin Noaks & which remains wholly due & unpaid. And now the parties on both sides appeared by their counsel & the counsel of the defendant opposing said motion after argument thereon & for reasons appearing to the court. It is considered by the court that the plaintiff recover against said defendant said sum of forty dollars besides his cost by him about his suit in this behalf expended.

(p-314) Rodah Horton   )
             vs   ) Garnishment
         Francis L.Dillard   )

This day appeared Thomas Rutherford upon the garnishment in open court to answer what is due & owing by him to the said Dilliard & what effects of sd. Dillards he knows of in the hands of other persons who answers and says upon oath that he is indebted to the said Dilliard in the sum of forty dollars, upon a judgment recovered by said Dilliard against him at the last July Term of the Circuit Court, of the County of Haywood by said Dilliard. It is therefor considered by the court that the said Rodah Horton recover of the said Thomas Rutherford the sum of forty dollars, acknowledged to be due & owing as aforesaid. And that said plaintiff recover of the sd. Dilliard, the costs about this garnishment in this behalf expended and the defendant in mercy etc.

It is ordered by the court that John G.Carithers esquire Sheriff

(p-314con.) and collector of this county be allowed a credit with
State treasurer of Tennessee for the sum of two hundred dollars and nine
cents for lands reported for the single tax & not sold for the want of
bidders for the year 1827, as also the further sum of Forty dollars and
eighty one cents in lands reported for the double tax for said year
1827 & not sold for the want of bidders, and that this shall be a good
voucher for said sherriff and collector in the settlement of his accounts
with said Treasurer, the following Justices of the Peace being a majority
of the court being on the bench and the ayes and noes being taken as the
law directs ayes Jesse L.Kirk, Esqr. Lawrence McGuire Esqr. Daniel Cherry
Esqr. Richard Nixon Esqr. Jonathan T.Jacocks, Esqr. James L.Wortham
Esqr. (p-315) Nicholas T.Perkins Esqr. and Samuel P.Ashe Esqr.
Issd.

It is ordered by the court that John G.Carithers, Sheriff and collector of this county be allowed a credit of six hundred Dollars & 27
cents with the County Trustee of this county for lands reported for
the single tax and not sold for the want of bidders for the year 1827.
As also the further sum of one hundred and twenty two dollars and forty
four cents on lands reported for the double tax for said year 1827
and not sold for the want of bidders and that this shall be a good
voucher for said Sheriff in his settlement with said Trustee a majority
of the Justices being present and the ayes and noes being taken as
the law directs to wit ayes Jesse L.Kirk, Lawrence McGuire, Daniel Cherry
Richard Nixon, Jonathan T.Jacocks, James L.Wortham, Nicholas T.Perkins
& Samuel P.Ashe Esqrs.
Issd.

Ordered by the court that John G.Carithers shff. and collector
of this county be allowed a credit with the State Treasurer of the
Western District for six months after the first day of January next
for the sum of two hundred and sixty three dollars twelve and one half
cents for lands to be reported for the year 1828
Iss'd.

A majority of the Justices being present and the Ayes and nos.
being taken as the Law Directs (to wit) Ayes Jesse L.Kirk, Lawrence
McGuire, Daniel Cherry, Richard Nixon, Jonathan T.Jacocks, James L.
Wortham, Nicholas T.Perkins and Samuel P.Ashe Esqrs.

Ordered by the court that John G.Carithers sheriff and collector
of this county be allowed a credit with the county trustee of this
county for six months after the first day of January next for the sum
of one thousand and thirty five dollars and ninety seven cents for
lands to be reported for the year 1828 a majority of the Justices being
present and the ayes & noes being taken as the law directs, Aayes,
Jesse L. Kirk, Lawrence McGuire, Dan'l. Cherry, Rich'd. Nixon, Jonathan
T.Jacocks, James L.Wortham Nicholas T.Perkins and Samuel P.Ashe Esqrs.
Is'd.

(p-316) Ordered by the court that Britain H.Sanders Esqr. clerk of
this court be allowed the sum of one hundred and twenty three dollars
and twenty cents for his fees as clerk on 88 tracts of land reported
for the single Tax for the year 1827- and not sold for the want of
bidders and also the further sum of sixteen Dollars and Eighty cents

(p-316con) on twelve tracts of Land and town lots reported for the double Tax for said year 1827, and not sold for the want of bidders to be paid by the County Trustee out of any unappropriated money in his hands not otherwise appropriated a majority of the acting Justices being presentand the ayes and noes being taken as the Law directs ayes Jesse L.Kirk, Lawrence McGuire, Daniel Cherry, Richard Nixon, Jonathan T. Jacocks, James L.Wortham, Nicholas T.Perkins and Samuel P.Ashe Esqr. Iss'd.

Bias Hall   )
    vs   )   Motion
William Butler   )

On motion of the Plaintiff by his attorney for a Judgement for money heretofore paid by the said Plaintiff for the said Defendant as his security upon a certain note executed by the said Defendant and the said Plaintiff as his security on the Eleventh of April 1826 and payable on the 25th of December-thereafter to Julius Saunders and by him assigned to Richard White which said note was for the sum of one hundred and seventy five Dollars and it approving to the satisfaction of the court that the said Richard White did on the 13th day of December 1827. Obtain a Judgement in this court for the sum of one hundred and Eighty five Dollars and seven cents Debt and Damages as also the further sum of seventeen Dollars and forty five cents costs of suit upon which Judgment the said Bias Hall hath paid the sum of one hundred and seventeen Dollars and a fifty five and one half cents and thereupon came a Jury of good and lawful men to wit Daniel Shaw, Cato Freeman, Philip Kounts, Mansfield Ware, John Wells, Berry Dearing, James Russell, Samuel Elliott Malcomb Johnson, John Severe, William Pace, Frances Lamoin (p-317) who being elected tried and sworn well and truly to enquire whether the said Plaintiff was secnity only for the said Defendant Butler in said note upon their oath aforesaid do say that the said Plaintiff Bias Hall was only security on said note for the said Defendant Butler- It is therefore considered by the court that the said Bias Hall do recover against the said Defendant Butler the said sum of one hundred and seventeen Dollars and fifty five and a half cents the amount hereto fore paid by him on the Judgement aforesaid as security for the said Defendant and his costs about his motion in this behalf expended and the Defendant in mercy.
Sci fa

Court adjourned until tomorrow morning nine o'clock.

                              Rich'd Nixon Cha
                              Dan'l. Cherry
                              Sam. P.Ashe

Thursday Morning December 11th 1828.

Court met according to adjournment Present Richard Nixon Daniel Cherry, & Samuel P.Ashe esquires, Justices

The State of Tennessee   )
        vs   )   Assault & Battery
Wyatt F.Tweedy   )

(p-317con)This day came as well the State of Tennessee by A.B.Bradford
esqr. attorney General, as the Defendant in his proper person, and
the Defendant being solemnly charged saith that he is not guilty in
manner and form as charged in the bill of Indictment, and for his trial
puts himself upon the country, and the attorney General doth the like
and thereupon came a jury of good and lawful men to wit. Sanford Perry
Samuel Elliott Joseph Baxter, Nathan Bridgeman Jonathan J.Nixon, Daniel
Shaw, Mansfield Ware, Allen J.Barbee, Cato Freeman Malcom Johnson, John
Hardwick, and Sidney P.Smith, who being elected tried & sworn well and
truly to try the issue of (p-318) of traverse upon their oaths aforesaid
do say that the Defendant is _ Guilty in manner and form as charged in
the Bill of Indictment and they assess the fine to Eighty five dollars
besides costs.

It is therefore considered by the court that the defendant make
his fine with the State of Tennessee by the payment of the fine aforesaid of Eighty five dollars and all costs in this behalf expended, and
that he be taken etc. and thereupon the Defendant moved the court for
a new trial and upon solemn argument being had thereon by the council
on each side, and by the court fully understood by the court that the
motion be overruled.

It is ordered by the court that Michael Henderson and hands
Zachariah Coleman, Daniel Coleman, John Nunn & hands & Francis Nunn
& hands work on the road under Thomas Furgerson as an overseer on the
road from Harrisburg to Buck's Ferry.
Is'd.

It is ordered by the court that the clerk of this court report
to this court the amount of taxes received by him up to this term

```
The State of Tennessee )
            vs         )
Joel Pace              )
```

Upon the affidavit of the defendant it is ordered by the court
that the fine heretofore assessed against the Defendant for his non
attendance as a Juror, be set aside on the payment of costs.

```
(p-319) Julius Sanders )
            vs         ) Appeal No. 2
        Sidney P.Smith )
```

This day came the said parties by their attornies, and there upon
came a jury of good and lawful men to wit John Wells, Jesse Kemp, John
Mott, James Russell, Samuel B.Green, John Johnston, John H.Freeman,
William Pace, Benjamin George Valentine Sevier, Giles Mallet and Cato
Freeman who being elected tried and sworn well and truly to try the
matters in dispute between the parties upon their oaths aforesaid do say
they find for the Plaintiff and assess his damages to nineteen dollars
and twenty five cents besides costs.
It is therefore considered by the court here that the said plaintiff
do recover against the Defendant the Damages aforesaid by the jury in
form aforesaid assessed and the costs in this behalf expended, and the
defendant in mercy, and thereupon the Defendant by his attorney moved

(p-319con.) the court for a new trial and upon argument being had thereon, and by the court here fully understood. It is considered by the court be sustained.

Holland White adm. of)
Wilson White dec'd.)
        vs) Debt 6
William R.Hess)

    This day came the said parties by their attornies, and thereupon came also a jury of good and lawful men, to wit, John Wills, Jesse Kemp, John Mott, James Russell, Samuel B.Green, John Johnston, John H.Freeman, William Pace, Benjamin George, Valentine Sevier, Giles Mattet and Cato Freeman who being elected tried and sworn well and truly to try the issue joined between the parties upon their oaths aforesaid do say that the Defendant hath not paid the Debt of (p-320) of two hundred and thirty seven dollars in the declaration mentioned as the plaintiff in declaring hath alledged and they assess the plaintiffs damages by reason thereof to Eighty two dollars and ninety five cents, besides costs. It is therefore considered by the court here that the plaintiff do recover against the said Defendant the Debt aforesaid in the declaration mentioned and the Damages aforesaid by the Jury in form aforesaid assessed , and the costs in this behalf expended & the Defendant in mercy etc.

    James Dorris this day produced in open court the scalp of a wolf over the age of four months and proved as the law directs that he killed said wolf in this county. It is therefore ordered by the court, there being a majority of the justices present that the said James Dorris be allowed the sum of three dollars to be paid by the Treasurer of the western District.

James Stephens)
    vs) Trespass No. 4
Macom Johnson)

    This day came the said parties by their attornies and thereupon came also a jury of good and lawful men, to wit, Daniel Shaw, Thomas Rutherford, Allen H.Howard, Benjamin Huckaby, Allen J.Barbee, William Powell, JohnA.Key, Joseph T.Harrelson, James Smith, Sidney P.Smith, John Wells and John Mott who being elected tried and sworn well and truly to try the issue joined, retired to consider of their verdict & returned into court and declared that they could not agree in the same, and by consent of the parties by their attornies & with the assent of the court Daniel Shaw one of the jurors of the jury aforesaid is withdrawn and the rest of the jurors from rendering their verdict are wholly discharged and by consent (p-321) of the parties by their attornies this cause is transferredto the next Circuit Court of this County, and that the said cause be set for trial on the first day of the term.

James Smith)
    vs)
Hiram Bradford Admr.)
of Robert A.Penn Dec'd

(p-321con.) This day came the said plaintiff by his attorney, and
thereupon came also a Jury of good and lawful men to wit, Daniel Shaw,
Cato Freeman, Phillip Koonce, Mansfield Ware, John Wells, Berry Dearin,
James Russell Samuel Elliott, Macom Johnson, John Sevier, William Pace,
and Francis Lamoin, who being elected tried and sworn well and truly to
try the issue joined upon their oaths aforesaid do say that they find
the issue in favour of the plaintiff and assess his damages to seventy
one dollars eighteen and one half cents besides costs.

It is therefore considered by the court that the said plaintiff
do recover against the said defendant the damages aforesaid by the jury
in form aforesaid assessed to be levied of the proper goods and chattels
rights and credits of the said intestate in the hands of the said administrator to be administered when so much and the costs in this behalf expended etc.

James Smith   )
     vs   )
Blackman Coleman)

This day came the said parties by their attornies and thereupon
came also a jury of good and lawful men, to wit, Daniel Shaw, Cato
Freeman, Phillip Koonce, Mansfield Ware, John Wells, Berry Dearin, James
Russell Samuel Elliott, Macom Johnson, John Sevier, William Pace and
Francis Lamoin who being (p-322) elected, tried and sworn well and truly
to try the issue joined upon their oaths aforesaid do say that the defendant hath not paid the debt of two hundred and fifty two dollars and
fifteen cents in the declaration mentioned as the plaintiff in declaring
hath alledged, and they assess the plaintiffs damages by reason thereof
to ten dollars and eight cents besides costs. It is therefore considered
by the court here that the said plaintiff do recover against the said
defendant the debt aforesaid in the declaration mentioned, and the
damages aforesaid by the jury assessed and the costs in this behalf ex-
pended-

James Smith   )
     vs   )
Blackman Coleman)

This day came the said parties by their attornies & thereupon came
also a jury of good and lawful men, to wit, Daniel Shaw, Cato Freeman,
Phillip Koonce, Mansfield Ware, John Wells, Berry Dearin, James Russell,
Samuel Elliott, Macom Johnson, John Sevier, William Pace and Francis
Lamoin who being elected tried and sworn well and truly to try the issue
joined upon their oaths oaths aforesaid do say that the defendant hath
not paid the Debt of two hundred and three dollars and nine cents in the
declaration mentioned as the plaintiff in declaring hath alledged and
they assess the plaintiffs damages by reason thereof to twenty three dollars and thirty cents. besides costs. It is therefore considered by
the court that the plaintiff do recover against the said defendant the
Debt aforesaid in the Declaration mentioned & the Damages aforesaid by
the Jury assessed & the costs in this behalf expended.

(p-323) John Wills   )
          vs   )   Assumpsit
     Caleb Warren & Richard Nixon)

(p-323con.) This day came the parties by their attorneys and thereupon came a Jury of good and lawful men to wit, Daniel Shaw, Cato Freeman, Phillip Koonce, Mansfield Ware, James Smith, Berry Dearing, James Russell, Samuel Elliott , Malcomb Johnston,John Sevier William Pace and Francis Lemoin who being elected tried and sworn well and truly to try the issue joined between the parties upon their oaths do say that the defendant hath not paid the Debt of Eighty five dollars in the declaration mentioned as the plaintiff in declaring hath alledged & they assess the plaintiff damages by reason thereof to four dollars and sixty seven cents besides costs.

It is therefore considered by the court that the plaintiff recover against the defendants the Debt aforesaid in the declaration mentioned and the Damages aforesaid by the jury assessed and the costs in the behalf expended. etc.

Wm. Armour trustee for the)
use of Matthew Watson assee)
of Richard W.Nixon)
    vs)
John Wills)

This day came the said parties by their attornies and thereupon came also a Jury of good and lawful men, to wit, Daniel Shaw, Cato Freeman, Phillip Koonce, Mansfield Ware, Berry Dearin, James Russell, Samuel Elliott, Macom Johnson, John Sevier, William Pace, Francis Lamoin, & James Smith who being elected, tried and sworn well and truly to try the issue joined upon their oaths do say that the said defendant hath not paid the Debt of Eighty five Dollars in the plaintiffs declaration mentioned as the plaintiff in declaring hath alledged, and they assess the plaintiffs damages by reason thereof to four dollars sixty seven & one half cents besides (p-324) costs. It is therefore considered by the court that the plaintiff recover against the Defendant the Debt aforesaid in the declaration mentioned and the Damages aforesaid by the Jury assessed & the costs in this behalf expended-

Joseph Spence)
    vs)
James H.Walker)

This day came the Defendant by his attorney and the plaintiff being solemnly called came not but made default, nor is his suit further prosecuted. Therefore on the prayer of the said Defendant it is considered by the court that he recover against the said plaintiff his costs by him about his defence in this behalf expended.

Court adjourned until tomorrow morning nine o'clock.

                    Rich'd. Nixon Chr
                    Jesse L.Kirk
                    Dan'l. Cherry
                    Sam. P.Ashe

Friday morning December 12th 1828.

(p-324con.) Court met according to adjournment. Present the worshipful Richard Nixon, Jesse L.Kirk, and Daniel Cherry esqrs. Justices.

Joseph Ables &)
B.Derin)
   vs)
Jesse Kemp)

    This cause is continued on the affidavit of the plaintiff with leave for Defendant to take the Deposition of John H.Clifton of Weakly County by giving the adverse party fifteen days notice.

The State of Tennessee)
      vs)
Wyatt F.Tweedy)

(p-325) A.W.Vanier assee of

     Francis S.Coxe)
        vs)
     William Henderson &)   Motion
     John A.King)

    On motion of the plaintiff by his attorney and it appearing to the satisfaction of this court that the said plaintiff did on the 12th day of April 1828 obtain a judgment against the said defendants before Matthew Ray, there as acting justice of the peace for said county for the sum of forty three dollars and seventy five cents damages besides costs of suit. That an execution issued on said judgement which came duly into the hands of Jordan M.Hansborough, a constable of this county, who be virtue thereof hath made return on said execution "Came to hand Levied on four town lots in the Town of Brownsville known and designated by numbers 133, 141, 139 & 145 on the plan of said Town, there being no personal property to be found in my county, It is therefore considered by the court here that a writ of venditioni exponas issue to cause said lots so levied on as aforesaid to be sold to satisfy the judgement aforesaid and the costs aforesaid, as also the costs in this behalf expended etc.

    The Grand jury returned into court & returned the following present-ment"to wit " The road leading from Brownsville to Jackson by Colol. Richard Nixons arm or pointers giving the direction The road leading from B'Ville to Jackson by Green Hills has no arm or pointers giving the direction- The road leading from Brownsville to Covington by Capt. Estices has neither mile marks or an arme or pointer giving the direc-tion and in otherwise in bad order.

    The road leading from Brownsville to Fulton has no arm or pointer giving the direction.

    The Road called the McGuire road leading from the fork near Berry Dearings up the river to where the same crosses the Brownsville road near Herndon Haralsons is neither (p-326) mile marked nor has an arm or pointer giving the direction and in otherwise is in bad order and that the East end of said road commencing at Gordon's Creek is also in bad (p-326con.) order, and the grand Jury further say that in their opinions, that part of said road commencing at the cross on the Brownsville road and leading down the forks near Berry Dearings is entirely useless and unnessary.

A power of attorney from John Hardwick to Lindsay Hardwick was this day produced in open court and duly acknowledged for the purposes therein contained and order to be so certified.

The Grand jury returned into court the follwoing bill to wit, That the streets and other public ground and highway within the limits of the town of Brownsville is now and has been for a long space of time out of repair and shamefully neglected to the great injury of the citizens of both Town and country and contrary to the statistics in such case made and provided.

The Grand Jury returned into court and there appearing no further business they were discharged from further services during the present term.

```
Edwin H.Childress          )
      vs                   )
Blackman Coleman           )   In - covenant on Demurer
Daniel Madding & Champness )
Mading                     )
```

This came the parties by their attornies and thereupon the matters of law arising upon the plaintiffs Demurer to the pleas of the Defendants herein to the plaintiffs declaration, being argued and fully understood by the court it is the opinion the court that the law is for the plaintiff. It is therefore considered by the court that the Demurer of the plaintiff to the pleas of the Defendant herein be sustained, and that (p-327) the plaintiff recover of the defendants such damages as he has sustained by reason of the breach of covenant in the said plaintiffs declaration mentioned and be cause those damages are unknown it is ordered by the court that the sheriff cause a jury of good and lawful men to be and appear at the next term of this court, to enquire the amount of such damages etc.

```
Julius Sanders )
      vs       )
Sidney P.Smith )
```

On a motion of the Defendant by his attorney for a new trial in this cause, and upon solemn argument being had thereon and by the court here fully understood, it is considered by the court that the motion be sustained.

```
The State of Tennessee )
         vs            )
Wyatt F.Tweedy         )
```

On motion of the defendant for a new trial in this cause, and upon solemn argument being had thereon and by the court here fully understood it is considered by the court that the motion be overruled.

(p-327con.) Deed of Conveyance from Levi Richards to Hiram Bradford
for two acres and Eighty five poles of land was this day proved in open
court by the oaths Herndon Haralson & Sanford Perry, witnesses thereto and
ordered to be registered.

It is ordered by the court that Richard Nixon and Herndon Haralson
be and are hereby appointed commissioners on the part of this county to
superintend the collection of the amount due this county by the county
of Madison for taxes collected by said county of Madison, and which by
the Solicitor of the state is directed - to be refunded to this county and
said commissioners are hereby authorised & required to use such means as
to them may appear meet for the collection and settlement of said claim
against the said county of Madison and report to next term.
Iss'd.

(p-328) It is ordered by the court that Samuel P.Ashe and Joel Estes
Esquires be and are hereby appointed commissioners on the part of this
county, to confer with such persons as may be appointed by the worshipful
the Justices of the court of Pleas and Quarter sessions of the County
of Tipton and to establish the lines between said county of Tipton and
Haywood County and to do all other acts and things relative to a just &
final establishment of said boundary line which to them may appear
just & right.

Edwin H.Childress   )
        vs   )
Blackman Coleman &   )
Daniel Mading   )

This day came the said plaintiff by his attorney and saith that
he intends no further to prosecute his suit against said Defendants.
It is therefore considered by the court here that the said Defendants go
hence without day and recover against the said plaintiff their costs by
them about their defence in this behalf expended.

Allen H.Howard   )
      vs   )
William Butler   )

Motion of the Plaintiff by his attorney for a Judgement for
moneys heretofore paid by him the said Plaintiff for the said Defendant
as his security upon a certain note of hand executed by said Defendant
and the said Plaintiff as his security on the 11th day of April 1826,
and payable on the 25th day of December thereafter to Julius Saunders
and by him assigned to Richard White which said note was for the sum of
one hundred and seventy five dollars and it appearing to the satisfaction
of the court that the said Richard White did on the 13th day of December
1827, obtain a Judgement in this court for the sum of one hundred and
eighty five dollars and seven cents Debt and Damages as also the further
sum of seventeen dollars and forty five cents costs of suit upon which
(p-329) upon which Judgement the said Allen H.Howard hath paid the sum
of one hundred and four dollars. And eighteen cents, and thereupon came
a Jury of good and lawful men, to wit, Daniel Shaw, Cato Freeman,
Sanford Perry, William H.Patton, James Russell, James Smith, Mason F.

(p-329con.) Johnson, Thomas Furgeson , Jesse Golden, John Wells,
Robert Perry., James Thompson who being elected tried and sworn well
and truly to say whether the said Plaintiff was security only for the
said Defendant Butler in said note upon their oath aforesaid do say that
the said plaintiff Allen H.Howard was only security on said note for
said Butler. It is therefore considered by the court that the said
Plaintiff Allen H.Howard do recover against the said Defendant Butler
the said sum of one hundred and four dollars and eighteen cents the
amount heretofore paid by him on the said Judgment aforesaid as security
for the said Defendant Butler and his costs about his motion in this behalf expended and the Defendant in mercy.

It is ordered by the court that that Thomas G.Nixon be released
from the Taxes on the following tracts of land for the present year to
wit, one tract entered in the name of G.Johnston for 600 acres, one
Tract of 400 acres in the name of G.M.Johnston, and one Tract of 640
in the name of William Terrell-

It is ordered by the court that John G.Carithers be allowed a
credit with the Treasurer of the western District for the sum of one dollar twelve and one half cents, the State Tax on six hundred acres of
land listed for Taxation for this year in the name of G.Johnston, also
seventy five cents the State Tax on four hundred acres of land entered
in the name of G.M.Johnstons and also the sum of one dollar and forty
cents the State tax on 640 acres of land entered in the name of William
Terrell. It appearing to the satisfaction of the court that there are
no such Tracts of land within the limits of this county a majority of
the acting Justices being present and the ayes and noes being taken as
the law directs ayes Jesse L.Kirk, Lawrence McGuire, Daniel Cherry,
Nicholas T.Perkins, Jonathan T.Jacocks, Samuel P.Ashe and James L.
Wortham Esquires.

(p-330) It is ordered by the court there being a majority present
that John G.Carithers, sheriff and collector be allowed the sum of nine
dollars eighty two and a half cents it being the county part of the Tax
on six hundred acres of Land listed for Taxation for the present year
in the name of G.Johnston, 400 acres in the name of G.M.Johnston and
640 acres in the name of William Terrell. It appearing to the satisfaction of the court that their is no such tracts of land within the limits
of this county. The ayes and noes being taken ayes Jesse L.Kirk,
Lawrence McGuire, Daniel Cherry, Nicholas T.Perkins, Jonathan T.Jacocks
Samuel P.Ashe and James L. Wortham esquires and that an order issue
accordingly.

Ordered by the court that Nicholas T.Perkins be refunded by the
county Trustee the sum of five dollars fifty two and a half cents it being the county part of the Tax on a Tract of land reported and sold in
the name of Ambros Goslin, it appearing that there is no such Tract of
land within this county, there being a majority of the Justices present
and the ayes and noes being Taken ayes Jesse L.Kirk, Lawrence McGuire,
Daniel Cherry, Blackman Coleman, Jonathan T.Jacocks, Samuel P.Ashe and
James L.Wortham esquires, and that an order issue accordingly.

Ordered by the court that Wm. R. Hess be allowed the sum of five (p-330con.) dollars and twenty five cents it being the county part of the tax on a tract of land heretofore sold for the Taxes in the name of Thomas Dougherty. It appearing to the satisfaction of the court that there are no such tract of within this county (p-331) there being a majority of the acting Justices present and the ayes and noes being taken ayes Jesse L.Kirk, Lawrence McGuire, Daniel Cherry, Nicholas T.Perkins, Jonathan T.Jacocks, Samuel P.Ashe and James L.Wortham esquires and that the county trustee pay the same out of any monies in his hands not other wise appropriated.

Ordered by the court that Richard Moore , James W.Russell, John Marbery, James Hart, John Potter, Edward West, Robert Hammell, Mansfield Ware, William Terrell, Lorenzo D.Womble, Eli Faris, Wilson A. W.Mann, William Weddle, Robert Burns, Samuel Elliott, Thomas Rutherford David Thomison, John H.Freeman, John McWhite, Littlelon Joiner, Bird Link, Phillip Bruce, Francis Lemoin Caleb Warren , Henry Welsh, and Allen H.Howard be summoned to attend at our next court of pleas and quarter session on Tuesday after the second Monday in March next then and there to serve as grand and petit jurors as the case may be and that

Issued 26th Jany 1829

A power of attorney from John Hardwick, Lindsay Hardwick of the State of Virginia Amherst County was this day produced in open court and duly acknowled and ordered to be certified.

```
(p-332) James Maldin  )
           vs         )
Abbott A.Tucker       )
```

This day came the plaintiff in his proper person and saith that he intends no further to his said suit against the defendant
It is therefore considered by the court the defendant go hence without day and recover against the plaintiff his cost by him about his defence in this behalf expended and that the plff. be in mercy.

```
Isaac L.Moody assee )
         vs         )
Johnathan J.Nixon   )
```

Richard W.Nixon who was at this term surrendered in open court by the Defendant as his appearance bail in Discharge of himself as such and who was prayed in custody is by the plaintiff by his attorney discharged from custody.

The court then adjourned until tomorrow 11 o'clock.

                              Richd Nixon Cha
                              J.L.Wortham
                              Sam.P.Ashe

(p-333) Saturday morning 11 o'clock the court met according to adjournment Present the worshipfull Richard Nixon, Samuel P.Ashe and James L.Wortham and others.

(p-333con.) Wm.Hill   )
                    vs   )
             Samuel P.Ashe   )   Assumpsit
             & David Hay   )

This day came the defendants and sayeth that they cannot gainsay
the said plaintiffs action against them for the sum of nine hundred and
eleven dollars and twenty three cents and confessed Judgment for the same
It is therefore considered by the court that the said plaintiff recover
against the said Defendant the said sum of nine hundred and eleven dollars and twenty three cents by them assumed in this behalf as also the
costs in this behalf expended whereof the plaintiff stays execution
until June term next of this court.

Deed of trust from Blackman Coleman to John G.Carithers for certain property and for certain purposes in said deed of trust mentioned
was this day produced in open court by the said John G.Carithers and
was duly proven in open court by the oaths of Jordan Hansborough and
William R.Hess subscribing witnesses thereto, and was ordered to be
certified for registered.

William Lawrence for   )
the use of John Caldwell   )
             vs   )
John R.McGuire, Thomas Stokely)
& Jno. McWhite   )

The defendant John McWhite being dissatisfied with the Judgement
rendered against them hath prayed & obtained an appeal to the Circuit
of this County, who gave bond and security to prosecute the same.

(p-334) Hiram Bradford this day prayed & obtained a Licence to keep
an ordinary at his now dwelling house in this town, who gave bond etc.

          Court adjourned till court in course.
                              Richd. Nixon Char.
                              Sam.P.Ashe
                              J.L.Wortham P.

(p-335) Blank-

(p-336) State of Tennessee)
          Haywood County)

At a Court of pleas & Quarter sessions began & holden for the
County of Haywood, at the court house in the Town of Brownsville on the
Second Monday in March, in the year of our Lord one thousand, eight
hundred and Twenty nine and of the American Independence the Fifty thirdyear
(it being the 9th of said month)

Present the worshipful, Richard Nixon, Daniel Cherry, Jonathan
T.Jacocks, Lawrence McGuire, Nicholas T.Perkins, Oliver Wood and James
L.Wortham esquires, Justices as also Samuel P.Ashe esq.

(p-336con.) It is ordered by the Court that John Ray be entitled to receive from the County Trustee for Haywood County the County part of the Tax, to wit, three Dollars and sixty cents, on 640 acres of land in the 10 District 4 Range, 6 section no. Entry 1133 which was sold in the year 1826 for the Taxes of 1825.

It appearing that the land lies in the County of Hardeman- The following Justices being present and the ayes & noes being taken- Ayes Richard Nixon, Daniel Cherry, Jonathan T.Jacocks L.McGuire Oliver Wood N.T.Perkins, James L. Wortham & Samuel P.Ashe which sum is to be paid out of any unappropriated money in the hands of the county Trustee.

(p-327)* It is ordered by the court that Samuel Green overseer of the Key Corner road from Brownsville to Meredian Creek, be allowed the following hands to work under him as such to wit- Ware-Russell, Thomas Green ____ Wise, ____ Lankford, _____ Walker ____ Holmon and ___ Williams Iss'd.

On Petition of Samuel Henderson it is ordered by the court that he have leave to turn the road leading from Brownsville to Worthams Ferry, so that the same shall run on the north side of his new ground field, provided he does the same at his own expense & put the same in good order Iss'd.

James B.Powell this day produced in open court the scalps of two wolves over the age of four months & and proved, as the law directs, the killing of the same within this county-
It is therefore ordered by the court there being a majority of the Justices present that he be allowed the sum of three dollars each, to be paid, by the Treasurer of the Western District.
Iss'd.

It is ordered by the court that Jesse L.Kirk esquire who was appointed to take lists of Taxable property & polls & make return to this court, have been leave to return the same at anytime within thirty days to the clerk of this court.

John Nelson this day produced in open court the scalp of a wolf over the age of four months, & proved the killing of the same in this County. It is therefore ordered by the court, a majority of the Justices being present, that he be allowed the sum of three Dollars, to be paid by the Treasurer of the Western District
Issued to J.Sevier

(p-328) William Shearin was this day appointed Guardian for Henry Shearin, Hugh Shearin & Joseph Shearin minor heirs of Jarrott Shearin deceased who gave bond & security in the penal sum of four thousand dollars.

On Indenture of bargain & sale from Thomas J.Smith to James S. Steele for a lot of ground in the Town of Brownsville, known and distinguished in the plan of said Town by number thirty five, was this day proved in open court by the oaths of Britain H.Sanders & Mansfield Ware, witness thereto and ordered to be certified for registration.

* Editor's note: Page 327, discrepancy of 10 pages is observed by manuscript copyist in original volume

(p-328con.) James F.Wortham was this day appointed constable for this
County in Captain Wortham's Company, who entered into bond with
Azariah Thompson and Charles Wortham his securities, and took the oath
prescribed by law.

Joseph Talbott   )
  vs   )
Reuben Golden   )

  This day Aron T.Brooks who was appearance bail for the said Defendant, this day surrendered here in open court the body of the said
defendant in discharge of himself as such . Wherefore it is considered
that the said Arron T.Brooks be and is hereby discharged from all responsibility.

(p-329) Mansfield Ware was this day appointed constable for this
County for Captain McDearmans Company who gave bond with William H.
Loving and Nelson Hargrove & Henry Welch his securities & took the oaths
prescribed by law.

  Ordered by the court that Wednesday next the 11th Instant, be
set apart, for county business and for electing a quorum court for
the present year-

  An Indenture of bargain & sale from Jesse Green to William S.
Lambert for four negroes, to wit, Dolly aged about thirty eight years
and her three children, Ezekiel aged eight, Mary three years and Betsy
nine months was this day produced in open court & the execution thereof
duly proved by the oath of J.S.Simms one of the witnesses, thereto
Bill Sale

  Daniel Cherry, Charles Wortham & James L.Wortham, commissioner
appointed to settle with Isaac Koonce administrator of John Koonce deceased, make report to this court that they have done the same, which
is ordered to be recorded.

  An Indenture of Bargain & sale from Blackman Coleman to William
Johnson for Five hundred & ten acres of land was this day acknowledged
in open court by said Blackman Coleman & ordered to be certified for
registration.
Deed

  John T.Turner, Guardian,*Simon T.Turner makes return of his
account as guardian to this court which is received by the court & ordered to be recorded.

  Upon the petition of William H.Moore it is ordered by the court
that he be permitted to keep a public Ferry on Hatchie River opposite
the Town of Estanaula, on the south side where the road from Jackson
through Estanaula to Somerville crosses the said river upon his giving
bond & security therefore & thereupon the said William H.Moore entered
into bond with Charles White as security-

(p-330) An Indenture of Bargain & sale from Alexander M.Kirksey to
Thomas White for one half of a cotton Gin & given thereto, was this
day acknowledged in open court by said Kirksey & ordered to be certified
*for

(p-330con.) for Registration.

William Shearin guardian forthe minor heirs of Jarrett Shearin makes return to this court of his settlement, which is received by the court & ordered to be recorded.

Court adjourned until tomorrow morning nine o'clock.

Rich'd Nixon Cha
L.McGuire
J.L.Wortham

(p-331) Tuesday Morning March 10th 1829

Court met in pursuance to adjournment Present the worshipful Richard Nixon, Lawrence McGuire, and James L.Wortham esqrs.

John G.Carithers esquire, Sheriff of Haywood County makes report of the Venire Facias returnable to this court which is as follows, to wit,

State of Tennessee

At a court of Pleas and Quarter sessions began and held for the County of Haywood on the second Monday in December in the year of our Lord 1826 it being the 8th day of December in said month present the worshipful Richard Nixon, Joel Estes and Lawrence McGuire esquires and others their fellow Justices of the peace. It is ordered by the court that the following persons good and lawful men, viz, each being a white male citizen of the age of Twenty one years and a householder to wit Richard Moore, James W.Russell, John Marberry, James Hart, John Potter, Edward West, Robert Hamil, Mansfield Ware, William Terrill, Larenzo D. Womble, Eli Faris, Wilson A.W.Mann, William Weddle, Robert Burns, Samuel Elliott, Thomas Rutherford, David Thompson, John H.Freeman, John McWhite, Littleton Joiner, Bird Link, Philip Bruce, Francis Lamoin Caleb Warren, Henry Welch, and Allen H.Howard, be summoned to attend at our next court of pleas and Quarter sessions on Tuesday after the second Monday in March next, then and there to serve as grand or Petit Jurors as the case may be,

Test
B.H.Sanders, Clk

(p-332) State of Tennessee
To the Sheriff of Haywood County, Greeting-
You are hereby commanded to summon the aforesaid persons to serve as Jurors at the next court of pleas & Quarter sessions to be held at the courthouse in the Town of Brownsville on Tuesday after the second Monday in March next, and this they shall in no wise omit under the penalty prescribed by law.
Herein fail not and have you then and there this writ, witness, Britain H.Sanders, Clerk of our said court at office in the Second Monday in December in the year of our Lord 1828, & 53rd year of American Independence.

B.H.Sanders, clk-

(p-332con.) upon the back of which said venire Facias, John G.Carithers makes the following return to wit.

By virtue of the within writ of venire facias to me directed I have proceeded to summon all t̸h̸e̸ ̸w̸i̸t̸h̸i̸n̸ ̸n̸a̸m̸e̸d̸ ̸p̸e̸r̸s̸o̸n̸s̸,̸ ̸e̸x̸c̸e̸p̸t̸ ̸J̸a̸m̸e̸s̸ ̸H̸a̸r̸t̸ the within named persons except James Hart, Robert Hamil, and Caleb Warner & such persons so summoned are free holders or house holders of said county.

Jno. G.Carithers,Shff.

The following persons good and Lawful men of Haywood County, were elected, drawn, sworn and charged as a grand jury for the present term, to wit, Henry Welch, foreman, John Marberry, Samuel Elliott, Littleton Joiner, Philip Bruce, John H.Freeman, Robert Burns, James Thompson, Eli Faris Edward West, William Weddle, Bird Link and Allen H. Howard who after having received their charge, retired to consider of the duties assigned them. Matthew Ray, constable sworn to attend the grand Jury.

(p-333) An Indenture of Bargain and sale from Jediah Cusick to Washington M Cusick for 399 acres of land was this day acknowledged in open court by said Jedediah Cusick & ordered to be certified for registration.
Deed

Julius Sanders)
    vs) Appeal No. 1
Sidney P.Smith)

This day came the said parties by their attornies and thereupon came also a jury of good and lawful men, to wit, William Terrill, James W.Russell, Francis Lamoin Sanford Perry, John Wynne, John P. Majors, Hermis Champ, James Boothe, William Barcroft, Richard Moore, John Potter and Thomas Potter who being elected, tried & sworn well and truly to try the matters in dispute, upon their oath aforesaid do say they find for the plaintiff and assess his Damages to Twenty dollars and fifty cents. It is therefore considered by the court here that the said plaintiff do recover against the said defendant & on motion against Richard Nixon security in an appeal the Damages aforesaid by the Jury in form aforesaid assessed and the costs in this behalf expended and the defendant in mercy etc.

An Indenture of Bargain and sale from William H.Henderson to Ichabod Herring for fifty acres of land was this day was duly produced in open court and the execution thereof acknowledged by the said William H.Henderson to be his act and deed and ordered to be certified for registration.
Deed

Joseph Ables &)
'B erry Dearin)
    vs) Case No. 2
Jesse Kemp)

(p-333con) This day came the said parties by their attornies and thereupon came also a jury of good and lawful men to wit, Joshua Abstain John Wells, Thomas G.Nixon, Thomas J.Dobyns, Caleb Warren, John G. Flowers, Josiah Abstain, Monroe P.Estes, John Gamble, William P.Young, Archibald McNeal and Giles Bullock who being elected tried and sworn well and truly to try the issue joined between the parties upon aforesaid do say that the Defendant is guilty in manner and form as the plaintiffs in declaring hath alledged, and they assess the plaintiffs damages to Forty five Dollars.

(p-334) And thereupon the Defendant by his cousel appeared and before the verdict of the Jury was recorded moved the court to enter a non suit, against the plaintiffs on the ground that this court had no jurisdiction of the cause, the amount being under the sum of fifty dollars, & the cause having been originally commenced in this suit and upon argument being had thereon by consent on both sides & by the court here fully understood it is considered by the court here that the motion of the defendant be overuled & the verdict of the jury be sustained. It is therefore considered by the court that the Plaintiffs recover against the said Defendant, the Damages aforesaid by the Jury assessed & the costs in this behalf expended etc.

Daniel H.Williams)
   vs   ) Debt No. 3
Stephen Howard)

   This day came the said parties by their attornies and thereupon came also a jury of good and lawful men to wit William Tyrrill, James W.Russell, Francis Lamoin, Sanford Perry, John Wynne, John Majors, Hermis Champ, James Boothe, William Barcroft, Richard Moore, John Potter and Thomas Potter who being elected, tried and sworn well & truly to try the issue joined between the parties, upon their oath aforesaid do say that the defendant hath not paid the debt of Seventy dollars in the note filed, as the said plaintiff in replying hath alledged, and they assess the plaintiffs damages by reason thereof to forty six dollars and twenty cents, besides costs. It is therefore considered by the court that the said plaintiff do recover against the said defendant the Debt aforesaid of seventy dollars, and the damages aforesaid by the Jury in form aforesaid assessed & the costs in this behalf expended and the Defendant in mercy.

(p-335) James Stalcup)
     vs   ) Debt No.8
   Jesse L.Kirk)

   This day came the said parties by their attornies and thereupon came also a jury of good and lawful men, to wit, William Tyrrill, James W.Russell, Francis Lamoin, Sanford Perry, John Wynne, John P.Majors, Hermes Champ, James Boothe, William Barcroft Richard Moore John Potter
* who being elected, tried and sworn well and truly to try the issue joined upon their oath aforesaid do say that the Defendant hath not paid the Debt of seventy five dollars in the plaintiffs declaration mentioned as the plaintiff in declaring hath alledged and they assess the plaintiffs (in/declaring/hath alledged/and/they assess/the/plaintiffs) damages by reason of the detention of that Debt to one dollar eighty
* & Thomas Potter

(p-335con.) seven & one half cents besides costs.

It is therefore considered by the court that the said plaintiff do recover against the said Defendant the Debt aforesaid in the Declaration mentioned and the Damages aforesaid by the Jury in form aforesaid assessed & the costs in this behalf expended & the defendant in mercy etc.

George W.Hockly)
    vs   ) No. 7
Bird Link   )

This day came the said parties by their attornies, and thereupon came also a jury of good and lawful men, to wit, William Tyrrill,James W.Russell, Francis Lamoin, Sanford Perry, John Wynne, John P.Majors, Hermes Champ, James Boothe, William Barcroft Richard Moore, John Potter, and Thomas Potter, who being elected, tried and sworn well and truly to try the issue joined upon their oath aforesaid do say that the Defendant hath not paid the debt of one hundred & thirty three dollars , thirty three and one third cents in the plaintiffs declaration mentioned, as the plaintiff in replying hath alledged and they assess the plaintiffs damages by reason of the detention of that Debt to four dollars besides costs.

It is therefore considered by the court (p-336) that the said plaintiff recover against the said defendant the Debt aforesaid in the Declaration mentioned and the Damages aforesaid by the jury assessed, and the costs in this behalf expended, and the defendant in mercy etc.

John Moore was this day appointed Guardian for Frank Hill minor heir of Edward Hill deceased who entered into bond and security.

George W.Hockley)
    vs   )
Bird Link   )

This day came the said parties by their attornies and thereupon came also a Jury of good and lawful men to wit, Joshua Abstain, John Wells, Thomas G.Nixon, Thomas J.Dabyns Caleb Warren, John G.Flowers, Josiah Abstain, Monroe P.Estes, John Gamble, William P.Young,Archibald McNeal, and Giles Bullock, who being elected tried and sworn well and truly to try the issue joined upon their oaths aforesaid do say that the Defendant hath paid all the debt in the declaration mentioned except two hundred & ninety two dollars, which sum remains due and unpaid and they assess the plaintiffs damages by reason of the detention of the residue of that Debt to twenty three dollars and ninety cents besides costs.

It is therefore considered by the court that the plaintiff recover against the Defendant,the residue of the Debt aforesaid & the damages aforesaid by the Jury assessee & the costs in this behalf expended etc.

(p-337) Rhoda Horton)
        vs   ) Sci Fa as bail for F.L.Dillard
      Mansfield Ware)

(p-337con.) This day came the Defendant in his proper person & saith that he cannot gainsay the plaintiffs cause of action against him for the Debt of sixty seven Dollars & eight cents in the writ of Sciri facias mentioned and two dollars & one cents interest thereon, as also the further sum of nine dollars & five cents the in said writ specified and agrees that said plaintiff may have execution against him for the same- Wherefore it is considered by the court that said plaintiff have execution of the judgement aforesaid by the defendant possessed as also for the costs in this behalf expended.

State of Tennessee)
  Haywood County)   March Term 1829

    I, John G.Carithers Sheriff and collector of the public Taxes for the county of Haywood makes report to court of the following tracts of land and town lots listed for taxation in said county for the year 1828 the taxes on which remain due and unpaid and that the respective owners or claimants thereof have no goods or chattels in said county on which I could destrain for the satisfaction of said Taxes for said year, To Wit:

Owners Names	No.Acres	Dist	Range	Sect.	No.Entry or Grant	Water course	No.Town Lots	Gen.Remarks
(p-337con.)								
Alred Williams	3	10	4	10		F.D.		
Armstrong Jas.S.	637	10	4	10	621	F.D.		
Bryant J.T.& Stephen Bryan								no.93
The Same							1-97	
Baldridge Alfred	640	10	4	8	E906			
(p-338)								
Bryan Stephen							1.76	
Campbell Wm.	500	10	6	6	E257	B.H.		
Cobbs Robt.L.	346	10	6	6	8&9			
Caldwell Nathaniel E.	428	11	2	6	E465			
Coleman Jos.H.	111	10	4	8	E408			part of Thos. Greers
Donell William	640	11	1	5&6	E17950	B.H.		
Dillard Francis L.	100	10	6	8	E805			part of Branch tract
Elliott,Samuel	272	10	5	8				part of Taylor tract
Same							no 1.4	
Garrett Daniel	274	10	4&5	10		F.D.		
Huckaby Gray	1000	10	6	6&7	E 428			
Same	180½	10	4	7&8	E985			
Same	1250	10	4	11	E632			part of 1500 acres
Same	400	10	5&6	8				
Hart James	1248	11	2	6	E748	B.H.		part of 2560 acres
Howard Meekes H.&John C.								
McLemore	640	10	4	8	E988			part of Francis Baldridged
Same	160	10	5	9	E1137			
Hughes Robert	124							part of G.258

Names	No.Acres	Dist	Range	Sect.	No.Entry or Grant	Water course	No.Town Lots	Gen.Remarks
con.)								
gs Hiram	2000	11	1	7&8	G291			
n Thomas	1500	10	5&6	8		B.H.		
James	57	10	5					part of Doaks tract
Donelson	2500	11						part of McLernores 5000
William	291½	11	2	7		B.H.		
Francis	5	10	5	8		F.D.		
unsford	366	10	4	9				
icholas	408	11	1c	9		B.H.		
e Thos.J.	230	10	5					Gt.258part Flowers
	640	11	2		E572			part of E. Newton
A.D.	758	10	6	7&8	G298			part of Harts
	500	10	6	8	G279			Part of A. Phillips
re,John C.	289 1/3	10	5	8	G294			part of J. Rice
e T.J.&							no1-20	
w Wm.	320	10	4	9	E527			
E.H.&E.A.	366 1/3	11	1	6	E275			part of Lee Sullivan
9)								
ham,Thos	1000	10	6	6	E1125			
ton,John	1000	10			G.155			
er Matthew	150	10	4	10				
on John	2500	11	1	6	E266	B.M.		
in Thos							1-19nto	
Green	181	10	4	7&8	E133			
or,Thos H.	530	10	6	8				part of Windsors 1000 A.
ot,John	225	10	5	7				part of Ditto
dor,John	150	10	5	7				

Owners Names	Acres	Dist	Range	Sect.	Entry or Grant	Water Course	Lots & No.	Remarks
(p-339con.)								
Yarboraugh, David	1620	11	2	9	G22,490			
Boyd Marais	331 3/4	11	1	10				pt of Gt 400
Colart,John	668 3/4	11	1	10				pt of Gt.400
Drake Robt. heirs of	1000	10	5 & 6	10 &11				pt of Gt. 128,Pt of Shelton's 3000
Hightower, Richard and heirs of	72 3/4	11	1	6				
Same	95	11	1	6				
Same	/95	11/	1	6				
Hays,A.C.	600	10						part of Walkers 5000
Henderson,Thos	640	10	4&5	9	E516			
Same							nol.99	
Same							1.87-	
Same							1.92	
Same							1.95	
Same							1.120	
Same							1.124	
Same							1.131	
Same							1.128	
Same							1.148	
Phillips Abraham	1000	10	6	8	G.307			
Shelton,James	2000	10	5&6	10&11				pt.of Gt. 128 pt of D. Sheltons 3000
Scudder Philip J.	1000	10	5	9	E328			
Simms,Walter B.	60	11	1	6				
Smith,Sidney P.							2	
Wheaton,Jno.L.	2216	11	1	10				pt of Gt.400

rs Names	Acres	Dist	Range	Sect.	Entry or Grant	Water Course	Town lots & No.	Remarks
39con.)								
inson, Wm.	1500	11	1	10				pt of Gt 400
ot,Patience								
s of	1368	11	2	9				pt of Gt 295
	2848	11	1	8&9				pt of Gt 291
	1700	10&11	6&7	8&9				pt of Gt 282
	1020	10	6	8&9				pt of Gt 287
	1881	10	6	7&8				pt of Gt 298
er James	4220	10	5	6&7	E635			
er James &								
s S.Walker	623	10	5	5&6	E403			
40)								
ain Joshua	200	10	4	9				
&								
dwick	1500	10	5	8	E2147	B.H.		
n Stephen	4	10	4	6&7	E1722			
ghton Thos	75							
Eaton	100	10	4	7	E2283			
Thomas	100	10	4	7				
e Kindle	"	"	"	"	"	"	no.1.6	
nson,John								
lliam	180	11	2	9	E359			pt of 390
g Alexander								
	640							
g Alexander	900							
	308							
	200							
ers David	1660	10	5,6	7,8	2288			
					E2140	B.H.		
Benj. &Andrew							no.1.113	
d William	2100	10	4	9	E506			
tower								
ard	95	11	1	6				
	72 3/4	11	1	6				
tower John								
s of	220	10	6	9				

Owners Names	Acres	Dist	Range	Sect.	Entry or Grant	Water Course	Town lots & No.	Remarks
(p-340con.)								
Joiner Littleton	133 1/3	10	4	9				
Jones Edmond	786	10	5,6	10	G406			part of
Knight James	57	10	5	8				
Moore, William H.	12	10	4	6				Emt.by Kavanaugh
McCutcheon John & others	288½	11	1	9				pt of S. Edmonson's 390
Murry John	640	10	4	8	G21524	formerly in I Terrills name 241.45		
Same	100	10	5	9				
Same	100	10	6	9	E1963			pt of Russells 200 A
Same	25	10	4	7				pt of W.Treadways 100
Same	53½	10	5	7				
Same	128	10	4	7.8	E987			pt of Catrons
Same	10	10	4	6	E1504			
Same	15	10	6	8	E1322			pt of Gholson 70 A.
Same	21	10	5	9	E1944			pt of E.Bryans 200
Same	45	10	5	8,9	E1330			pt of I.King 72½ A
Same	30	10	4	9				pt of Flowers 120 A
Murry James H.	200	10	5	9				entered by A. Stewart
Murry,John and John C.McLemore	50	10	4	6	E1576			
(p-341)								
Murry John & Jno. C.McLemore	20	10	6	8				
Same	25 22/100	10	6	8	1577			
Same	20	10	4	6	1503			
Same	4	10	4	7				
Same	1	10	4	6				
Owens Saml. & Henry	200	10	6	8	G287			pt of Rices 5000
Reese Solomon	365	10	4	8	E91			formerly W.B. Hills

rs Names	Acres	Dist	Range	Sect.	Entry or Grant	Water Course	Town lots & No.	Remarks
4lcon.)								
es Tyre	263	10	5	9	G18004			
ers Williams	100							
ggs James	250	10	5	9				
lferro								
	666 2/3	10	6	6	E145			pt of Benj. Talliferros 1000
s Samuel	342	10	4	11	E179			pt of Wells & Gibbons 640

(p-341con.) Whereupon it is considered by the court that Judgement
be and the same is hereby entered against the aforesaid several tracts
of land in the name of the State of Tennessee for the amount of taxes,
costs and charges severally Due thereon for the year 1828, and it is
further considered by the court that said several tracts of land and town
lots or so much thereof as shall be sufficient of each of said tracts
and town lots sold to satisfy the taxes, costs and charges due thereon
as the law directs.

(p-Editor's note: original paragraph illegible)

(p-342) State of Tennessee Haywood County Court of pleas and quarter
sessions March Term 1829, whereas I, Thomas Potter, constable and collector
of the public Taxes for the corporation of the Town of Brownsville and
State aforesaid report to court the following lots in said Town as having
been omitted to be returned for the corporation Taxes for the year 1828
that the same is liable for double taxes and that the double Taxes remain
due and unpaid and that the respective owners or claimants thereof have
no goods or chattels within the corporation on which I can destrain for
the said Taxes to wit,

Owners Names	Town Lots	No. of Lots
Andrew Hamilton	1	72
Andrew Hamilton	1	84
Robert Clanton	1	135
Robert Clanton	1	143
Robert Clanton	1	137
Robert Clanton	1	147
Duncan McIver	1	122
Bennet R.Butler	1	45
Bennet R.Butler	1	41
Henry L.Gray	1	48
Joshua Martin	1	91
William W.Douthit	1	56
William W.Douthit	part of 111	
William Crutcher	1	55
Same	1	57
Same	1	60
Issued	1	60

Wherefore it is considered by the court that Judgement be and the
same is hereby entered up against the aforesaid several Town lots in the
name of the Mayor and Alderman of of the corporation of the Town of
Brownsville for the amount of Double Taxes, costs and charges severally
due thereon for said year 1828 and it is ordered by the court that said
several town lots be sold (p-343) to satisfy said double taxes costs
& charges, as the law directs.

State of Tennessee)
Haywood County   ) March Term 1829

    I,Thomas Potter constable in & for the corporation of the Town of
Brownsville and collector of the Taxes thereof make report to the court of
the following lots in said Town listed for Taxation for the year

(p-343con.) 1828, the Taxes on which remain due and unpaid and that respective owners or claimants thereof have no goods or chattels in said Town on which I could destrain for the satisfaction of said Taxes for said year, to wit,

Persons Names	Town Lots	No. of Lots
Francis L.Dilliard	1	26
Francis L.Dilliard	1	35
Thomas Rankin	1	19
Samuel Elliott	1	4
Joseph Findly	1	98
Jesse Brown	1	138 (taxes costs & charges pd. (to Shff by Haralson 5 Oct. (1829
Sidney P.Smith	1	30
Sidney P.Smith	1	46

Whereupon it is considered by the court that Judgement be and the same is hereby entered up against the aforesaid several town lots in the name of the major and Alderman of the Corporation of the Town of Brownsville for the amount of single Taxes, costs & charges severally due thereon for said year 1828, and it is ordered by the court that said several town lots be sold to satisfy said single Taxes, costs & charges as the law directs.

Court adjourned until tomorrow morning o'clock.

Rich. Nixon,Char.
Sam. P.Ashe,J.P.
L.McGuire

Issued

(p-344) Wednesday morning March 11th 1829

Court met according to adjournment Present the worshipful Richard Nixon, Samuel P.Ashe, N.T.Perkins, Jonathan T.Jacocks and Lawrance McGuire esquires Justices.

An Instrument of writing purporting to be the last will and testament of William S.Lambert late of said county deceased, was this day exhibited in open court, and the Execution thereof was duly proved by the oaths of William B.Grave & John Perkins, witnesses thereto & ordered to be recorded.

It is ordered by the court that the Taxes for the present year be as follows to wit
That there be a county tax of 18 3/4 cents on each hundred acres of land, a jury Tax of thirty seven & one half cents on each hundred acres of land and a Tax of $12\frac{1}{2}$ cents on each hundred acres of land for the purpose of building bridges in addition to the State Tax- that there be a county Tax of 25 cents on each slave, twelve and one half cents on each white poll and a tax of $6\frac{1}{4}$ cents on each white & black poll for a poor tax, and a county Tax of $37\frac{1}{2}$ cents on each Town lot all in addition to the State Tax-

'p-344con.) The court proceeded, agreeable to public notice, appointment of three Justices of the peace as a quorum court for twelve months, when upon counting the votes it appeared that Richard Nixon, Samuel P.Ashe and Lawrence McGuire were duly elected as quorum Justices for twelve months .

(p-345) It is ordered by the court that Lawrence McGuire, Nelson Hargrove, John R.McGuire, Green L.Haralson, Herndon Haralson, George Watts, Oliver Woods, Elijah Arnold, and Benjamin G.Alexander, or any any five of them be and are hereby appointed a Jury of view to view and mark a road from Brownsville in a direction to Bolivar the nearest and best way as far as the county line and to cross big Hatchie at the most suitable place on a direct course & make report to next court.
Iss'd.

It is ordered by the court that Daniel Cherry, David Hay Lawrence McGuire, Samuel P.Ashe, Herdon Haralson, Jonathan T.Jacocks, Charles Wortham, Joel Estes, Thomas G.Nixon, Joshua Abstain, James W.Russell, Henry H.Turner, Wilson A.W.Mann, Samuel Owens, Simon Turner, Lewis Foscue, William Conner, John P.Majors, Albert M.Estes, James Henderson, James Sanders, Edwin Tias Richard Taylor, Nicholas T.Perkins, Charles White & John Roddy be summoned to attend at the next Circuit Court for this county to be holden in the first Monday in July next then & there to serve as grand or petit jurors, and that Jordan M.Hansborough, & Mansfield Ware be summoned to attend said court as constables & that a venire facias issue accordingly-

Deed of Trust from Herndon Haralson to Robert Hughes for certain property in said deed of Trust mentioned was this day produced in open court and duly acknowledged by the said Herndon Haralson and Robert Hughes to be their act & deed for the purposes in said deed of trust mentioned & ordered to be certified for Registration.

A Deed of Gift from Eliza H.Leigh to her son William R.Leigh for certain property in said Deed of gift mentioned was this day proved in open court by the oaths of Jonathan J.Nixon and George R.Jordan witnesses thereto & ordered to be certified for registration.

(p-346) Deed of Conveyance from Samuel Elliott to Levi Richards for two acres and Eighty five poles of land was this day acknowledged in open court by the said Samuel Elliott to be his act and deed & ordered to be certified for Registration.

The Grand Jury came into court & there appearing no further business for their consideration at the present term, were discharged, and the following Jurors of the venire facias proved their attendance, to wit

John Marberry	2 days	Eli Farris----	2 days
Samuel Elliott	2 "	Edward West	2 "
Littleton Joiner	2 "	William Weddle	2 "
Philip Bruce	2 "	Bird Link	2 "
John H.Freeman	2 "	Allen H.Howard	2 "
Robert Burnes	2 "	James W.Russell	2 "
Henry Welch	2 "	John Potter	2 "
James Thompson	2 "	Francis Lamoin	2 "

(p-346con.) William Terrill 2 days
            Richard Moore   2 "

And Jordan M.Hansborough, constable three days, Matthew Ray, constable Two days-

It is ordered by the court that Cornelius Buck be permitted to turn the road from the south to the north side of his field, the distance of about 2or 300 yards, provided he cuts out & puts the same in good repare at his own expense.
Iss'd.

It is ordered by the court that John G.Carithers sheriff and collector of this county be allowed in the settlement of his accounts with the Treasurer of the Western District the sum of four dollars & seventy five cents the State Tax on 2535 acres of land improperly listed for Taxation for the year 1828.

It is ordered by the court that John G.Carithers, Sheriff and collector be allowed a credit in his settlements with the county Trustee of this county for the sum of sixteen dollars sixty two & one half cents on 2535 acres of land improperly listed for Taxation for the year 1828.
Issued

(p-347) Hiram Bradford)
               vs   )
         Enos. Short   )

This day came the said Defendant by his attorney and saith he can not gainsay the said plaintiffs action against him for ninety six dollars, forty two & one half cents and confesses judgement for the same.
It is therefore considered by the court that the said plaintiff do recover against the said Defendant the said sum of ninety six dollars forty & one half cents, by the defendant assumed, and the costs in this behalf expended & the defendant in mercy etc.

James S.Steele   )
        vs   )
Herndon Haralson)

This day came the said plaintiff by Robert Hughes his agent and saith he intends no further to prosecute his action against the said defendant.
It is therefore considered by the court here that the said defendant go hence without day and recover against the said plaintiff his costs by him about his defence in this behalf expended etc.

William H.Haralson)
        vs   )
Herndon Haralson   )

This day came the said plaintiff by Robert Hughes his agent and saith that he intend no further to prosecute his action against the said Defendant
It is therefore considered by the said Defendant go hence without day and recover against the said plaintiff his costs by him

(p-347con.) about his defence in this behalf expended etc.

James W.Haralson)
    vs)
Herndon Haralson)

This day came the said plaintiff by Robert Hughes his agent and saith that he intends no further to prosecute his said action against the said defemdant. It is therefore considered by the court that the said Defendant go hence without day and recover against the said plaintiff his costs by him about his defence in this behalf expended-

(p-348) An Instrument of writing purporting to be the last will and testament of John R.Leigh deceased, late of this county, was this day exhibited in open court for probate, and was proven by this testimony of Peter J.Mattett one of the subscribing witnesses thereto, who swore that he knew said John R.Leigh at the date of said instrument, and that he saw him sign, seal, execute & deliver the same & declared the same to be his last will & testament in the presence of this defendant and the Revd. John Wetherspoon of Hillsborough, North Carolina, the other subscribing witness thereto & that this deponent and said John Weatherspoon did, in presence of the said Leigh and at his request & in the presence of each other, subscribe the same with their proper names as witnesses- And that at the time thereof the said John R. Leigh was of same despairing mind and memory.

Whereupon John W.Guion, the Executor named in said last will and testament, makes known to this court his relinquishment of the Executorship under the said last will & testament of said John R.Leigh deceased, and thereupon Thomas G.Nixon, was by the request of Eliza H. Leigh, widow of said John R.Leigh deceased, appointed administrator, with the will annexed, of said John R.Leigh Deceased, and entered into bond in the sum of Ten thousand dollars with Richard Nixon & N.T. Perkins_____his securities.

John Moore was this day appointed Guardian for Frank Hill minor heir of Edward Hill dec'd who entered into bond in the sum of two thousand dollars with James W.Russell & Philip Bruce as security.

(p-349) The State of Tennessee)
    vs) Sci Fa for non attendance as a
Joseph Curry) juror

Upon affidavit of the Defendant the fine heretofore assessed against the defendant for his non-attendance as a juror is remitted on the defendants paying the costs of the Sci Facias.

The State)
    vs)
John McWhite)

John McWhite acknowledges himself indebted to the State of Tennessee in the sum of $100 be levied of his goods and chattels lands and tenments, but to be void on condition that he makeshis personal appearance at the next Term of this court, then & there to answer the charge of the State against him & not depart without leave of court.

(p-349)   The State of Tennessee   )
                 vs   )
          John McWhite   )

James W. Russell acknowledges himsslf indebted to the State of Tennessee in the sum of Fifty Dollars but to be void on condition that John McWhite shall make his personal appearance at the next term of this court to answer a charge of the State against him and not depart without leave of court.

Upon the Petition of Eliza H.Leigh setting fourth his desire to emancipate and set free a certain negro man slave named Harry, the property of the said Eliza H.Leigh, for his faithful services heretofore rendered to her & to her late husband John R.Leigh, late of said county deceased, and for reasons appearing to this court it is considered by the court here there being a majority of the Justices of said county present that the petition be granted, and that the said negro man Harry be manumitted and fervor set free upon the said Eliza H.Leigh's giving bond and security as the state in that case requires. And thereupon the said Eliza H.Leigh entered into bond in the sum of one Thousand Dollars with Thomas G.Nixon, Jonathan J.Nixon and William H.Loving her securities to indemnify and save unless the county of Haywood from becoming charge-able with the support of said man Harry etc.

(p-350)   Caleb Warren assee   )
                 vs   )
          James H.Walker &   )
          James Sampson

This day came the said plaintiff by his attorney and saith he intends no further to prosecute his said action against the said De-fendants. And thereupon the said by defendant by his attorney assumes to pay all costs in this behalf expended- Wherefore it is considered by the court that the said plaintiff recover against the defendants, the costs in this behalf assumed and the said defendant in mercy etc-

Joseph G.Swift (use   )
of James Sampson)   )
         vs   )
Richard Nixon   )

This day came the said plaintiff by his attorney & saith he in-tends no further to prosecute his suit against the said Defendant by his atty. assumes to pay all costs considered by the court that the said plaintiff recoveragainst the said Defendant the costs by him in this behalf assumed.

Alexander B.Bradford   )
Edwin H.Childress   )
         vs   )
Blackman Coleman   )
Daniel Madding &   )
Champness Mading   )

This day came the said parties by their attornies & thereupon came also a jury of good & lawful men, to wit William Terrill, James W.

(p-350con.) Russell, Francis Lamoin, John Wynne, Monroe P.Estes, James Boothe Richard Moore, John Potter, Thomas Potter, Joseph Ables and Thomas Nixon who being elected, tried & sworn well and truly to inquire what Damages the said plaintiff hath sustained upon their oaths aforesaid do say they assess the plaintiffs Damages to five hundred and Eighty three dollars, besides costs. It is therefore considered by the court that the said plaintiff do recover against the said defendants the (p-351) Damages aforesaid by the jury in form aforesaid assessed & the costs in this behalf and the Defendants in mercy etc.

From which judgement the Defendants have prayed and obtained an appeal to the next Circuit Court of this county he having given bond & security therefor.

William H.Henderson   )
        vs   )
Michael Miller   )

On motion of the said plaintiff by his attorney and it appearing to the satisfaction of this court that William Lawrence did on the 24th day of December 1827 obtain a judgement in the Circuit Court of this county against Michael Miller & William H.Henderson his security for the sum of sixty two dollars & sixty eight cents besides costs of suit - And it also appearing satisfactorilly to this court that William H. Henderson the plaintiff, hath said on said Judgement as security for said defendant, the sum of sixty five dollars and sixty five cents on the 8th of October 1828. Therefore, on motion of the said plaintiff by his attorney it is considered by the court that the said plaintiff do recover against the said Defendant the said sum of sixty five dollars and sixty five cents with interest from the 8th of Oct. 1828 amounting to one Dollar & sixty three cents and the costs of this motion.

Richard Nixon & Herndon Haralson who were at the last term of this court appointed to make application to the county Court of Madison for the Taxes due this county make report that they have not accomplished the object for which they were appointed & pray to be continued. Whereupon it is ordered by the the court that they be continued & act accordingly.

(p-352) It is ordered by the court that William H.Henderson, Thomas G.Nixon, Nicholas T.Perkins, Jonathan T.Jacocks, Blackman Coleman and Mansfield Ware, or a majority of them be and are hereby appointed a jury of view to view and mark a road from the Town of Brownsville to the Tipton County line in a direction to Paynes Ferry, Covington etc. and said jury of view are hereby required also to view Estes road and report to the next court which of the two roads, the one now contemplated to be cut out or the Estes road is the nearest and best and report to the next term.
Iss'd.

Court adjourned until tomorrow nine o'clock.

                    Rich'd Nixon Char.
                    Dan'l Cherry
                    L.McGuire

(p-352con.)　Thursday morning March 12, 1829

Court met in pursuance to adjournment. Present Richard Nixon,
Daniel Cherry & Lawrence McGuire, esqrs. justices.

George W. Hockley　)
     vs　　　　)
Bird Link　　　　)

The Defendant being dissatisfied with the Judgement rendered
against him at this term hath prayed and obtained an appeal to the next
Circuit Court of this County, he having entered into bond and security
to prosecute the same.

George W. Hockly　)
     vs　　　　)
Bird Link　　　　)

The Defendant being dissatisfied with the judgement rendered
against him at this Term hath prayed and obtained an appeal to the next
Circuit Court of this county he having given bond and security to prosecute the same.

(p-353) Samuel P. Ashe, the Executor named in the last will and testament
of William S. Lambert, late of said county dec'd. this entered in the
bond with William B. Grave and David Hay his securities in the sum of
Eight thousand Dollars.

Joseph Ables &　)
Berry Dearin　　)
   vs　　　　)
Jesse Kimp　　　)

The defendant being dissatisfied with the judgement of this court
hath prayed an appeal to the next Circuit Court of this County. He
having given bond & security to prosecute the same.

Samuel P. Ashe, Daniel Cherry, Richard Nixon, Lawrence McGuire
and Herndon Haralson were this day appointed commissioners to make
contracts for erecting Bridges, causeways, cutting out roads across the
bottoms on the main rivers in said county and to receive from the
sherrif and pay out the monies arising from the taxes laid for that
purpose agreeable to an act of the General Assembly passed on the
second of November 1827.

It is ordered by the court that Simon Turner & Hiram Bradford
be appointed commissioners to settle with the clerks of the Circuit
and County Court, sherriff and county trustee for the present year.

A power of attorney from James S. Steele to John W. Steele was this
day acknowledged in open court by the said James S. Steele to be his act
and deed for the purposes therein mentioned, and ordered to be certified.

It is ordered by the court that John Wells, Joseph T. Haralson,
Jedidiah Cusick, Jonathan Nixon, Stephen Boothe, Joseph Curry, James C.
Hart, John Young, Benjamin Weaver, Begnal Crook, Francis M. Wood, Jesse
Embre, Azariah Thompson, John Sanderlin, Aron T. Brooks, Sidney P. Smith

(p-353con.) William Johnson sen, Milton McDearman, James Axley, Joseph Murphy, Griffith Edwards, Mark Spence & John Stone be summoned to attend at the next court of pleas & quarter sessions of said county then and there to serve as grand or petit jurors as the case may be & that Jordan M.Hansborough and Matthew Ray be summoned to attend said court as constables.

(p-354) The jury of view who were at the last term of this court appointed to view & mark a road from Wortham's Ferry to Madison County line in a direction to Trenton make report that they have done the same which is received by the court.

It is ordered by the court that David Hay, Lawrence McGuire Richard Nixon, Archibald McNeal, Philip Bruce, Henry McCoy, & Stokely D.Hays be appointed to view and mark a road from the Jackson road leading by Col. Nixons to Hatchie River and make report to next court. Iss'd.

Rec./of Britain H.Sanders Alexander B.Bradford attorney Genl. called upon the clerk of this court for his receipts for monies due to the Treasurer of the Western District, and Trustee of this county, when he produced the following:

Rec'd. of Britain H.Sanders, clerk of the County Court of Haywood County, three hundred and sixty three dollars and eighty cents the amount of State tax by him collected for the year ending the first day of October 1828 Feby. 21st 1829-

(Signed) I.Carithers
T.W.Dist.

Rec'd of Britain H.Sanders clerk of Haywood County Court two dollars it being the amount of taxes and forfeitures collected by him agreeable to his report up to the first day of October, 1828-March 9th-1829-

(Signed) Rich'd Nixon, Cty.Trustee

(p-355)   State of Tennessee)
           Haywood County   )

Court of pleas and quarter sessions March Term 1829. I,John G. Carithers sheriff and collector of the public Taxes for the County of Haywood report to court the following tracts of land and town lots as having been omitted to be returned for the public taxes for the year 1828 that the same is liable for double taxes and that the double taxes remain due and unpaid, and that the respective owners or claimants thereof have no goods or chattels within his county on which he can destrain for said Taxes   (to wit)

ers Names	No. of Acres	Dist.	Range	Sect.	No.of Entry or Grant	Town lots	Gen'l Remarks
355con.)							
n Brown	4000	10			Gt.117		F.D.
n Rice	5000	11	1	7&8	E2199		B.H.
n Rice	5000	11	1	7&8	E2200		B.H.
es Tisdale rs of	7606	11	2	11	Gt412		F.D.
es Tisdale rs of	5000	11	1	9	Gt414		T.D.
es Tisdale rs of	5592	10	6	10	Gt415		F.D.
es Tisdale rs of	3496	10	6	10	Gt410		
es Tisdales rs of	6934	10&11	1&6	10	Gt411		F.D.
dale & aton	12	10					F.D.
dale & Wheaton	640	11	1	9	E355		F.D.
ert Searcy rs of	731 3/4	10	6	8 &9	Gt.291		part of J.Rices 5000-not to be advertised
t.Searcy rs of	801	10	6	8 &9	Gt282		
ert Searcy irs of	482	10	5	7&8	Gt294		
t.Searcy rs of	240	10	5	7	Gt294		
ert Searcy rs of	284	11	1	8	Gt295		
y Wheaton	5796	11	1	10 &11	Gt413		F.D.
y Wheaton	2786	10&11	1&6	10	Gt411		F.D.
y Wheaton	2393	11	1	11	Gt407		F.D.
liams uel H.	800	10	5	9	E787		F.D.
bblefied, ment	228	10	5	6	E364		B.H.

Owners Names	No of Acres	Dist	Range	Sect.	No ofEntry Grant	Town Lots	Genl. Remarks
(p-355con.)							
Jesse Steed	1035	10	4	7&8	G308		B.H.
William B.Graves	1500	10	5	7&8	E2149		B.H.
Amelia Johnson	1000	10	5	8	E2522		B.H.
John Jinkins	230	10	4	9	970		
(p-356)							
John Jinkins	1000	10	4	8&9	1002		
Ezekiel Polk	500	10	6	6&7	562		B.H.The single tax pd. to shff. & my fees to me B.C.Coleman the single tax to shff & my fees to me B.Coleman
Alexander A.R.& J.H.Bills	371				E908		
A.R.Alexander	640	10	4	10	174		
A.R.Alexander	410				970		
John C.McLemore	640	10	6	8	E1163		in the name ofpresident & trustees of NC
John C.McLemore	640	10	5	11	E463		in the name of Jacob Walker
John C.McLemore	298	10	4	11	E197		pt. of Wells & Givins
William P.Rowan	660	10	4	7	Gt275		pt of W.Moore's 1320
John Rice	5000	10&11	6&1	7&8			above McGuires Ferry
William T.Lewis	1000	10			Gt60		
William T.Lewis	1000	10			Gt90		
Thos.Williamson &Heirs						no194	
Amos Warner						no 1.31	
Robt.Clanton						no1.135	
Robt.Clanton						no1.143	
Robt.Clanton						no1.137	
Robt.Clanton						no1.149	
John McCampbell Heirs of	475	10	6	8	pt of Gt.291		
John McCampbell Heirs of	502	11	1	8	Gt295		
John McCampbell Heirs of	546	10	6	8	pt of Gt.282		
John McCampbell Heirs of	675	10	5	7	pt of Gt.294		
John McCampbell Heirs of	240	10	5	7	pt of Gt.294		
Thos. Palmer					2.21&24		

(p-356con.) Whereupon it is considered by the court that Judgement be and the same is hereby entered up against the aforesaid several tracts of land & town lots in the name of the State of Tennessee for the amount of Double taxes, costs and charges severally due thereon, for said year 1828, and it is ordered by the court that said several tracts of land

and town lots or so much thereof of each as shall be sufficient to satisfy the taxes, charges & costs be sold as the law directs-

(p-357) State of Tennessee) March Term 1829
Haywood County)

Court of pleas and quarter sessions

Whereas it appears to the satisfaction of this court that the taxes remain due and unpaid upon the following tracts of land for the year 1827 and that the said land have heretofore reported and ordered to be sold, and advertised and offered for sale as the law directs, and that said land would not sell for the costs and taxes or any part thereof and that the taxes costs and charges remain due and unpaid and that the respective owners or claimants thereof have no good or chattels in Haywood County whereon the sheriff could distrain for said taxes costs & charges, all of which lands lie in in Haywood County (to wit)

Owners Names	Acres	Dist.	Ran.	Sect.	No.E or G	Wat. course	T.L	Re-marks
Anderson John	200	10				F.D.		
Arthur William	480	10	5	9	E1137			
Brown Peter	500	10			E307			
Bledsoe Anthony Hs. of	428	10	5:6	9	E587			
Barnet Robt.W.	50	10	6	6	E2980			
Baker Robert	50	10	6	6	E2181			
Brown James	420	10	6	8	E1801			
Brown James	2875	10	4:5	7:8	E1803			
Brown John	1000	10	5	7:8	G271			
Canady John	240	11	2					

Owners Names	Acres	Dist.	Range	Sect.	No.Entry or Grant	Water course	Town Lots	Remarks
(p-357con.)								
Caldwell James	200	10	5:6	11	part of Grant 155			
Crawford Wm.W.	320	10						
Chester,Robt J.	1000	11	1	6	E1740			
Cobbs Robt L.	50	10	5	9	E703	F.D.		
Denson Wm.	360	10	5	11	E776			
Dougherty Thos.	500	10	4	7	E77			
Dobson,Mathew	250	11	2	6				
Dixon William	500	10	4	6		B.H.		
Dixon William	50	10	3:4	10		F.D.		
Freeman Green	700	10	4	9	2249			
Goodlow Marthy E	117	10	5	11				
Givins & Wells	512	10	4	10	E179			
Grave William B.	1500	10	5	7:8	E2149			
Greer Joseph	1500	10	5	8				
Green James S. & Wm.B.Sims	125	11	6	9				
Henderson Robt.	150	10	4	8	E2270			
Harris Western	200	10	6	11	E2368	F.D.		
Hart Anthony	261	10	5	10		F.D.		
Hart Anthony	434	11	2	7	E230	B.H.		
Johnston Cane	640	11	1.2	9:10	E685			
Jones Henry	45	10	5	8	E1331			
(p-358)								
McClure,William	150	10	5	6	E2220			
McCampbell,John	475	10	6	8	part of Gt.291			
McCampbell John Hs. of	502	11	1	8	part of Gt.295			
Same	546	10	6	8	part of Gt.282			
Same	675	10	5	7	part of Gt.294			
Same	240	10	5	7	part of Gt.294			
McLellon John	3	10	4	10	E1796			
Newton Edward	640	11	2	9&10	E572			
Polk Ezekial	500	10	6	6&7	E652			
Philpot John W.	500	10	4	8	E319			
Same	360	11	1	8				

ers Names	Acres	Dist.	Range	Sect.	No.Entry or Grant	Water c course	Town Lots	Remarks
358con.)								
c Thomas	1434	10	5	6	E406			
e	500	10	4	7				
e John	1046	10	6	8	part of Gt.287			
e	2296	11	1	8	E2205			
e	2728	11	1&2	8	E2210			
glet James	57	10	5	8				
llen James	100	10	4	9	2312			
e Walter B.	60	11	1	6				
ed,Jesse	1035	10	4	7.8	G308	B.H.		
ale James								
rs of	7606	11	2	11	G412			
e	5000	11	1	9	Gt.414			
e	5592	10	6	10	G415			
e	3496	10	6	10	Gt410			
e	6934	10,11	1&6	10	Gt411			
ker Green H.	89	10	4	6	2386	B.H.		
liams John H.	1000	10	6	8	E219			
ker Alfred M.	20	10	4	6	E2405			
ton Robert							4no135,143,137,149	
liamson Thos.Heirs of							no 1,94	
ner Amos							no 1,31	

(p-358con.) Whereupon it is considered by the court that judgement be and the same is hereby entered up against the aforesaid several trusts of land and town lots in the name of the State of Tennessee for the amount of Taxes, costs and charges severaly due thereon for said year 1827 as also the costs and charges occasioned by the report and it is ordered by the court that said several tracts of land and Town lots (p-359) for so much thereof of each as shall be sufficient to satisfy the taxes costs and charges aforesaid be sold as the law directs.

On motion it is ordered by the court that all persons whose land or town lots are reported at this term for Double taxes, have leave to pay the single tax provided the do the same within thirty days immediately after the adjournment of this court, and paying all costs & charges for reporting the same & the clerks fees thereon, and all persons who shall pay the single Tax and the costs thereon within the time before specified are hereby released from the Double Tax-

Matthew Ray   )
    vs   )
Rowlett Patran)

On motion of the plaintiff and it appearing to the satisfaction of this court that the said plaintiff did on the 11th day of October 1828 obtain as judgement against the said Defendant before Richard Nixon esquire a justice of the peace for this county for the sum of $23 6¼/100 & fifty cents costs of suit. That an execution paid on said Judgement which came into the hands of Jordan M.Hansborough a constable of this county who by virtue of said execution hath made the following return to wit, Levied on 100 acres of land in the 10th District 6 Range, 9 section part of Entry No. 1961, there being no personal property to be found. It is therefore considered by the court that said tract of land levied on as aforesaid, be sold to satisfy the Judgement & costs aforesaid & the costs of this motion-
(p-360)
William Balch   )
    vs   )
William Lawrence)

This day came the Defendant by his attorney and dismisses his certiorari & thereupon the said plaintiff by his atto William Balch by his atto assumes to pay all costs in this behalf expended.

Whereupon it is considered by the court that the said William Lawrence recover against the said William Balch the costs in this behalf expended-

It is ordered by the court that the following tracts of land be released from the Double tax, the same having been reported at this term, and that they be sold, unless the single tax is paid before the day of sale, for the single taxes only to wit-

John Rice 5000 acres 11 district-1 range-7 & 8 Section E2199.

Same-------5000 acres 11 district----1 range---7 & 8 Section E2200 Same----5000 acres -- 10 &11--- 1 & 6 range 7 & 8, E---- John C.McLemore 640 acres--10 district---6 range 8 section E.1163 Same 640 acres, 10 district--6 range, 11 section---E 463. Same----298 acres---

(p-360con.) 10 district 4 range 11 part of E197

William P.Rowan 660 acres 10 district 4 range 7 part Gt 275

John Rhea 640 acres 10 district, 4 range, 11, E.214 Gt.7430

It is ordered by the court that Thomas Potter & the sheriff of this county be authorised to procure suitable locks & have the same put on the jail of this county in such way as to them may seem best for which this court will make a suitable allowance.

Court adjourned till court in course.

Rich'd Nixon Char-
Sam P.Ashe J.P.
L.McGuire

(p-361) State of Tennessee)
Haywood County) Set

At a Court of pleas and quarter sessions began and holden for the county of Haywood at the Court House in the Town of Brownsville on the second Monday in June A.D.1829. Present the worshipful Richard Nixon, Lawrence McGuire and Nicholas T.Perkins, esqrs. Justices (it being the 8th of the month)

Asa Biggs produced in open court that the scalps of six wolves, under the age of four months, and proved the killing of the same in this county. It is therefore ordered by the court that he be allowed the sum of two dollars each to be paid by the Treasurer of the Western District
Iss'd.

James B.Powell this day produced in open court the scalp of a wolf over the age of four months and proved as the law directs, the killing of the same in this county. It is therefore ordered by the court that he be allowed the sum of Three Dollars to be paid by the treasurer of the Western District
Iss'd.

Edward S.Johnson this day produced in open court the scalp of a wolf, over the age of four months and proved the killing the same in this county. It is therefore ordered by the court that he be allowed the sum of three Dollars, to be paid by the Treasurer of the Western District.
Iss'd.

(p-362) Monday June 8th 1829

Deed, Matthew Ray to William Conner for two hundred and four acres of land was this day acknowledged in open court by the said Matthew Ray and ordered to be registered.

Deed, an Indenture of bargain and sale from Jesse Embry, and Elizabeth his wife of Haywood County Tennessee to Jonothan C. Doss of Smith County & State aforesaid for seventy acres of land was this day produced in open court and the Execution thereof was duly acknowledged by the said Jesse Embry to be his act and deed for the purposes (p-362con.) therein mentioned, and thereupon the court proceeded to take the private examination of the said Elizabeth separates and apart from her said husband the said Jesse who saith that she did of her own free will and accord & without the coertion of her said husband make and execute the said deed of conveyance for the purposes in said deed mentioned all of which is ordered to be certified for registration.

Deed of conveyance from Matthew Ray to James W.Strother for one hundred and thirty acres of land was this day acknowledged in open court by the said Matthew Ray to be his act and deed and ordered to be certified for Registration.

Deed of conveyance from Thomas Rutherford to Francis S.Coxe for two acres & sixteen poles of land was this day proved in open court by the oaths of James Smith and Thomas B.Coleman witnesses thereto and ordered to be certified for Registration.

Deed of conveyance from Samuel Dickens to Charles White for three hundred acres of land was this day proved in open court by David Jeffreys one of the witnesses thereto.

(p-363) Monday June 8th 1829

William Stoddart esqr. was this day appointed Guardian for Eliza Cockrill who entered into bond in the sum of Five Thousand Dollars with Alexander B.Bradford & James Caruthers his securities.

Deed of Conveyance from David Jeffreys to Samuel Townsend for two acres of land was this day acknowledged in open court by said Jeffreys & ordered to be certified for registration.

An Instrument of writing purporting to be the last will and testament of George Ables, late of said county dec'd was this day produced in open court and the due execution thereof was proved by the subscribing witnesses thereto and ordered to be recorded and thereupon James Maulden, one of the Executors named in the said last will and testament came into court and entered into bond as Executor of said last will and testament in the sum of one thousand Dollars.

Hiram Bradford)
      vs   )
Enos Short   )

The Defendant Enos Short this day surrendered himself in open court in discharge of his bail, and thereupon it is considered by the court that his bail be and are hereby discharged from all liability or responsibility and on motion of the plaintiff by his attorney the Defendant is prayed in Custody of the Sherriff of Haywood County

Court adjourned till tomorrow morning nine o'clock.

Rich'd Nixon Cha
Jesse L.Kirk
Sam. P.Ashe

(p-364) Tuesday June 9, 1829

(p-364con.) Court met according to adjournment. Present the worshipful Richard Nixon, Sam'l. P. Ashe and Jesse L.Kirk, esqrs Justices.

Robert S.Wilkins a constable, presented to the court his resignation as such which is accepted by the court.

John G.Carithers esquire Sheriff makes return of the venire facias returnable to this court which is as follows, to wit:

State of Tennessee

At a court of pleas and quarter sessions began and holden for the county of Haywood at the Courthouse in the town of Brownsville on the second Monday in March in the year of our Lord 1829, it being the ninth day of said month, present the worshipful Richard Nixon, Daniel Cherry and Lawrence McGuire & others their fellow Justices of the peace It is ordered by the court that John Wells, Joseph T.Haralson, Jedediah Cusick, Jonathan J.Nixon, Stephen Boothe, Joseph Curry, James C.Hart, John Young, Benjamin Weaver, Bignal Crook, Francis M.Wood, Jesse Embry, Azariah Thompson, John Sanderlin, Aron T.Brooks, Sidney P.Smith, William Johnson Senr. Milton McDearman, James Axley, Joseph Murphy, Griffith Edwards, Mark Spence and John Stone (p-365) TUESDAY JUNE 9th 1829 - be summoned to attend at our court of pleas and quarter sessions on Tuesday after the second Monday in June next then and there to serve as grand or petit jurors or the case may be and that Jordan M.Hansborough and Matthew Ray be summoned to attend said court as constables.

Test B.H.Sanders, Clk
by B.Coleman Dep.

STATE OF TENNESSEE
TO THE SHERIFF OF HAYWOOD COUNTY GREETING:

You are hereby commanded to summon the aforesaid persons to serve as jurors at the next court of Pleas and quarter sessions to be held at the court house in the Town of Brownsville on Tuesday after the second Monday in June next, and this they shall in no wise omit under the penalty prescribed by law, Herein fail not and have you then and there this writ, Witness Britain H.Sanders clerk of our said court at office the second Monday in March 1829.

B.H.Sanders, clk
by B.Coleman Dep.

Upon the back of which said writ the sheriff of Haywood County hath made the following return, to wit Come to hand 10th of April 1829 by virtue of this venire facias I have summoned all the persons named in this writ, except Francis M.Woods and such persons so summoned are free holders or householders of said county and of lawful age.

Jno. G.Carither,
Shff.

(p-366) Tuesday 9th June 1829

Jedediah Cusick & Jonathan J.Nixon jurors, are excused from attending as such at this term.

(p-366con.) The following persons good and lawful men were elected
drawn sworn and charged as a grand jury from the present Term Joseph
Murphy Foreman, John Wells, Benjamin Weaver, Joseph T.Haralson, John Young,
James Axley, Azariah Thompson, John Stone, Bignal Crook, Joseph Curry,
Mark Spence, Stephen Boothe and Sidney P.Smith, who having received
their charge retired to consider of the duties assigned them. Matthew Ray
constables sworn to attend the grand jury.
Grand Jury

It is ordered by the court Joseph Curry, James C.Hart, Jesse Embry,
John Sanderlin, Aron T.Brooks, Milton McDearman and Griffith Edwards each
be fined in the sum of five dollars for their non attendance as jurors at
this court, they having been summoned on the venire facias returnable to
this court & on motion it is ordered by the court that the fine on each of
the above Jurors be remitted.
Remitted

(p-367) The Grand Jury returned into court and returned an Indictment
The State of Tennessee vs John L.Conduit for an assault and battery on the
body of Albert G.Ellis, a true bill and retired to consider of other duties.

Dulaney D.L.Whitehurst records the Ear mark of his stock thus, a
smothe crop & under bit in the right ear, and a swallow fork in the left
Ear.

George Robison   )
         vs   )
Thomas G.Nixon   )

This day came the said parties by their attornies and thereupon
came also a jury of good and lawful men, James C.Hart, Herndon Haralson,
Nathan Bridgeman, William Little, Daniel Shaw, James Henderson, Hermes
Champ, Ezekiel Blackshire Wilson A.W.Mann John G.Flowers & John McWhite
who being elected tried and sworn the truth to speak upon the matters in
dispute upon their oathsaforesaid do say they find for the plaintiff and
assess his Damages to fifty dollars besides costs. It is therefore considered by the court that the said plaintiff do recover against the said
Defendant & on motion against Jonathan J.Nixon his security in appeal the
Damages aforesaid by the Jury assessed with 12½ pr. cent interest thereon
from the third day of January 1829 the date of the Judgement before the
Justice, up to this day & the costs aforesaid in this behalf expended etc.

The defendant prayed & obtained an appeal to the Circuit Court, he
having given bond and security for the same.

JOHN INGRAM JR. BY HIS   )
(NEXT FRIEND) JOHN INGRAM SENR.)
         VS   )
JOHN McFARLAND   )

This day came the said parties by their attornies and thereupon
came also a jury of good and lawful men, to-wit: James C.Hart, Herndon
Haralson, Griffith Edwards Nathan Bridgeman, William Little, Daniel
Shaw, James Henderson Hermes Champ, Ezekiel Blackshire, Wilson A.W.
Mann, John G.Flowers, and John McWhite, who being elected tried and sworn
well and truly to try the issue joined between the parties upon their oaths

(p-367con.) aforesaid do say that the said (p-368) TUESDAY 9th JUNE 1829- defendant hath not paid the debt of Sixty-five Dollars in the declaration mentioned as the said plaintiff in replying hath alledged and they assess the plaintiff's damages by reason of the detention of that Debt to one dollar, seventy seven and one half cents, besides that/ costs. It is therefore considered by the court that the said plaintiff do recover against the said defendant the debt aforesaid in the declaration mentioned and the damages aforesaid by the jury assessed and the costs in this behalf expended, and the defendant in mercy etc.

It is ordered by the court that Herndon Haralson, Allen J.Barbee & Wilson A.W.Mann be appointed commissions to settle with Sarah D.Dyer Guardian for the minor heirs of Joel Dyer Dec'd and make report to next court.

It is ordered by the court John Williams overseer of the road be allowed in addition to the hands heretofore allowed the following, to-wit: Joseph Meredith, William Meredith, Elisha Bryant, John Bryant, Isaac Woods Elisha Ring, Benja. Rucker and Son and Captain Milton McDearman. Iss'd.

It is ordered by the court that Bird Link, Parson Bayes Joseph Eddins, Hardy Sills_____ Mathews, Bowen Rynolds James Carlton Robert Sanders Thomas West, Benj. Dearing or any five of them be appointed a jury of view to view and mark a road from the corner of Benj. Dearins fence to the Tipton County line to intersect the Covington (p-369) TUESDAY 9th JUNE 1829- road at Everetts Ferry & make report to next court. Isd.

It is ordered by the court Henry Welch, William H.Loving, William R. Hess, Hiram Bradford, William H.Henderson, be appointed a jury of view, to view and mark a road beginning at the west end of Main Street & to continue west till they pass Samuel Elliotts lot of ground on which he now lives thence to the one mile tree on the McGuire road and make report to next court. Iss'd.

It is ordered by the court that an order made at the December Term of this court 1828, granting to David Hay leave to turn the McGuire Road on which he lives be recinded and it is further ordered by the court that George Watts, Nelson Hargrove, Herndon Haralson, William Haralson, John A.Key, & William Morrison be appointed a jury of view to view and report to the next court whether said road should be turned & if it, should in what manner. Iss'd.

The commissioners appointed to settle with Susah J.Dyer Guardian for the minor heirs of Joel Dyer Deceased, make report that they have done the same which is ordered to be recorded.

Allen Westbrook and Jesse L. Kirk acknowledge themselves indebted to the State of Tennessee that is to say the said Allen Westbrooks in the sum of two hundred and/ dollars & the said Jesse L.Kirk in the sum of two hundred dollars, to be levied of their goods & chattels, lands & Tenements, but to be void on condition that the said Allen Westbrooks shall (p-369con.) make his personal appearance at our next court of pleas & quarter sessions to be held on the second Monday in September next, then & there to answer the State of Tennessee for an assault & battery on the body of Vordeman Halsel & not depart without leave of this court.

(p-370) Tuesday the 9th of June 1829

The grand jury returned into court with the following indictments- The State of Tennessee against Isaac Dial, Horton Dial and Allen Westbrooke for an assault and battery, on the body of Vardeman Halsel, "a true bill "- The State of Tennessee against Horton Dial for an assault and battery on the body of Francis Booby " a true bill ". The State of Tennessee against Archibald Robison for an assault and battery on the body of Daniel Smith, "a true bill." The State of Tennessee against William Jones, Reese Porter, Anthony Clark and Thomas Clark for a riott, assault and an affray" a true bill " The State of Tennessee against Isaac Dial and Horton Dial for an assault and battery on the body of Francis Booby and a Bill of indictment against James Harris for an assault and battery on the body of Jesse L.Kirk,"a true bill" & retired for the consideration of other duties.

It is ordered by the court that Samuel P.Ashe, John Roddy and Lewis Foscue be appointed Judges of the ensuing election for menbers of Congress & Governor, and member to the State Legislature at the cross Roads near Sam'l. P.Ashe's - that Richard Nixon Herndon Haralson & Blackman Coleman and/ be appointed Judges of the Election at Brownsville- that Oliver Woods, Benjamin G.Alexander, & Benjamin Wilkes be appointed Judges of the election at Wood's and that Daniel Cherry, Charles Wortham and Adam Hawkins be appointed Judges of the election at Cherrys.

(p-371) Tuesday 9th June 1829

It is ordered by the court that the following persons be summoned to attend on the first Tuesday after the second Monday in September next to serve as grand or Petit Jurors as the case may be to wit James Armstrong, Nehemiah Hardy, Robert M.Spicer, Thomas G.Nixon, Herndon Haralson, Henry Welch, Joseph Eddings, Bird Link, Edward West, Robert Burnes, Thomas White Tobias C.Henderson, Henry McCoy William Hollings - worth, Harmon Frazier, Philip Bruce, Richard T.Moore, John McFarland, Adam Hawkins, Francis M.Woods, Thomas Thweatt, William Conner, Philip Koonce, Robert T.Smith, Robert Perry, John Albright and that James Kinny and Jordan M.Hansborough be summoned to attend said court as con- stables.
Iss'd.

An Indenture of bargain and sale from Thomas Brown to Delany D.S. Whitehurst for ninety two & one half acres of land was this day produced in open court and the execution thereof was duly proved by the oath of Griffith Edwards one of the witnesses thereto who also made oath that George Ables the other witness thereto became a subscribing witness with him and in the presence of the said Thomas Brown, and that the said George Ables has departed this life- all of which is ordered to be certified for registration-
Deed

(p-371con.) It is ordered by the court Lawrence McGuire, Nelson Hargrove, John R.McGuire, Green L.Haralson, George Watts, Oliver Woods Elijah Arnold and Benjamin G.Alexander or any five of them be and are hereby appointed a jury of view to view and mark a road from Brownsville in a direction to Bolivar the nearest and best way as for as the County line & to cross Big Hatchie at the most suitable place on a direct course and make report to next court .
Iss'd.

Bill of sale from Thomas N.White to Alexander Scott for a negro boy named Solomon was acknowledged in open court by said White & ordered to be certified for registration.

(p-372) Tuesday June 9th 1829

James Axley this day produced in open court the scalp of a wolf over the age of four months and proved as the law directs that he killed the said wolf in the County of Haywood. It is therefore ordered by the court (there being five Justices on the bench) that the said James Axley be allowed the sum of three dollars to be paid by the Treasurer of the Western District.
For Hansborough.

It is ordered by the court John O.Tanner, John Rogers, John Albright, Samuel Green, James Russel, & William Patton, be appointed a jury of view to view the Estes & Fulton roads and to ascertain whether it would not conduce to the interest of the public to have the two consolidated & if in their opinion it should be done, report to the next court at what point they should be united-
Iss'd.

It is ordered by the court William H.Henderson Robert Sanders, Britain H.Sanders, Herndon Haralson, Thomas West, James Carlton and Allen Howard be appointed a jury of view and mark a road the nearest and best way from the town of Brownsville to Hatchie River at or near the mouth of Sugar Creek and make report to next court.
Iss'd.

(p-373) Tuesday 9th June 1829

It is ordered by the court that the clerk, the sheriff and the attorney General each be allowed their respective fees in the following state cases (there being a majority of the Justices Present & each voting in the affirmative to wit: S.P.Ash, Oliver Woods, N.T.Perkins, Lawrence McGuire, J.T.Jacocks, Jesse L.Kirk, & Richard Nixon) to wit:

(p-373con.)

Name of the Case	Atty fees	Clks fees	Shffs fees
The State vs Amos Chambers 5"		7.62½	3.22½
The State vs Amos Chambers 5"		5.20	1.87½
The State vs Benj.McDonald 5"		5.20	2.22½
The State vs John Young		4.12½	1.62½
The State vs John M.Smith		4.62½	1.62½
The State vs Peter Lankford		7.17½	
The State vs Lee H. Burks		5.45	1.37½
The State vs Edward Harris		5.32½	1.87½
The State vs S.H.Copeland 5		5.20	1.85
The State vs Thos Stokely		5.32½	2.75
The State vs Stephen S.Childress		3.65	" 75
The State vs F.L.Dillard		3.65	" 25
The State vs James Haggard		4.65	1.37½
The State vs James Haggard		5.15	1.75
The State vs John A.Key 5		5.05	1.62½
The State vs Thos J.McGuire5		5.55	1.87½
The State vs John R.McGuire5		5.45	2.87½
The State vs Watt F. Tweedy	5	4.93	2.37½
The State vs Reese Porter		3.10	1.00

Issued for the clerks part-Issued to the Shff.
Iss'd to Bradford

(p-374) Tuesday 9th June 1829

Samuel H.Shannon)
      vs   )   In Debt
Stephen S.Childress)

    This day came the said parties by their attornies and thereupon
came also a Jury of good and lawful men to wit : James C.Hart,
Griffith Edwards, Nathan Bridgeman, William Little, Daniel Shaw James
Henderson, Hermis Champ Ezekiel Blackshire, Wilson A.W.Mann, John G.
Flowers & John McWhite who being elected tried and sworn well and truly
to try the issue joined upon their oath aforesaid do say that the Defendant hath not paid the Debt of seventy eight dollars in the plaintiffs
declaration mentioned as the plaintiff in declaring hath alledged and
they assess the plaintiffs damages by reason thereof to five dollars &
eighty five cents besides.
    It is therefore considered by the court that the plaintiff do re-
cover against the defendant the debt aforesaid in the declaration mentioned
and the damages by the Jury assessed & the costs in this behalf expended
& the Defendant in mercy etc.

Joseph H.Felts assee)
      vs   )
Reubin Golden   )
    This day came the said plaintiff by his attorney and saith intends
no further to prosecute his action against the defendant and thereupon
the defendant by his attorney assumes to pay all costs in this behalf

(p-374con.) expended. It is therefore considered by the court that the plaintiff do recover against the defendant the costs in this behalf expended etc.

(p-375) Tuesday 9th June 1829

William H.Henderson)
       vs)   Assumpsit
Hardy Hightower)

This day came the plaintiff by his attorney and saith he intends no further to prosecute his suit against the said Defendant. It is therefore considered by the court that the defendant go hence without day and recover against the said plaintiff his costs by him about his defence in this behalf expended etc.

Matthew Barrow & others)
       vs)   In debt
Hiram Bradford adm. &)
Matthew Ray

This cause is continued on the affidavit of Matthew Ray, one of the Defendants, until the next term of this court.

John H.Porter)
       vs)   In debt
Simon Turner &)
Richard Nixon

This day came the said parties by their attornies and thereupon came also a jury of good and lawful men to wit, James C.Hart, Herndon Haralson, Griffeth Edwards, Nathan Bridgeman, William Little, Daniel Shaw James Henderson, Hermes Champ Ezekiel Blackshire, Wilson A.W. Mann, John G.Flowers and John McWhite who being elected, tried and sworn well and truly to try the issue joined between the parties upon their oath aforesaid do say that the said defendants have not paid the debt of six hundred and forty Dollars in the plaintiffs declaration mentioned as the plaintiff in replying hath alledged, and the jurors aforesaid upon their oath aforesaid do further say that there is no set off as the plaintiff in replying hath alledged, and they assess the said plaintiff damages by reason of the non payment of that debt to ninety three dollars and eighty cents besides (p-376) Tuesday 9th June 1829 costs. It is therefore considered by the court that the said plaintiff do recover against the said defendant the debt aforesaid in the declaration mentioned and the damages aforesaid by the jury in form aforesaid assessed and the costs in this behalf expended and the said defendants in mercy From which Judgement the Defendants have prayed and obtained on appeal to the Circuit Court of this county they having given bond with Nicholas T.Perkins and Thomas G.Nixons to prosecute the same.

Samuel D.Lowell)
       vs
Thomas Furguson)

(p-376con.) Continued on affidavit of the Defendant.

William Armon assee   )
        vs   )
Joseph Eddings   )   In debt

       This day came the said parties by their attornies and thereupon
came also a jury of good and lawful men, to wit   James C.Hart, Herndon
Haralson, Griffith Edwards, Nathan Bridgeman, William Little, Daniel
Shaw, James Henderson, Hermes Champ, Ezekiel Blackshire, Wilson A.W.
Mann John G.Flowers & John McWhite who being elected tried and sworn
well and truly to try the issue joined upon their oath do say that the
Defendant hath not paid the debt of three hundred & sixty two dollars
& fifty cents in the plaintiffs declaration mentioned as the plaintiff
in declaring hath alledged and they assess the plaintiffs damages by
reason of the detention of that debt to ten dollars and Eighty seven
cents, besides costs. It is therefore considered by the court that the
said plaintiff do recover against the said defendant the debt aforesaid
in the declaration mentioned and the damages aforesaid by the jury (p-
377) Tuesday 9th June 1829   in form aforesaid assessed and the costs
in this behalf expended and the defendant in mercy etc.

Robert Caruthers   )
      vs   )
Jediah Cusick   )

       The death of the plaintiff in this suit is suggested

Christopher E.McEwen   )
     vs   )
Thomas Potter and   )
Robert T.Smith   )

       This day came the said parties by their attornies and thereupon
came also a jury of good and lawful men to wit   James C.Hart, Herndon
Haralson, Griffith Edwards, Nathan Bridgeman William Little Daniel
Shaw, James Henderson, Hermes Champ, Ezekiel Blackshire, Wilson A.W.
Mann John G.Flowers & John McWhite who being elected tried and sworn
well and truly to try the issues joined, upon their oath aforesaid do
say that the defendants have not paid the debt of one hundred and forty
one dollars, thirty seven and one half cents, and the jurors aforesaid
upon their oath aforesaid do further say that there is no set off as the
said plaintiff in replying hath alledged and they assess the said plaintiffs damages by reason of the detention of that debt to three dollars
and fifty cents besides costs. It is therefore considered by the court
that the said plaintiff do recover against the said defendants the debt
aforesaid in the declaration mentioned and the damages aforesaid by the
jury assessed and the costs in this behalf expended, and the said defendants in mercy etc.

(p- 378) Tuesday 9th June 1829

Hiram Bradford admr. of   )
Robert A. Penn, dec'd.   )   In debt
        vs   )
Green L.Haralson and   )
Herndon Haralson

(p-378con.)

This day came the said parties by their attornies and thereupon came also a jury of good and lawful men James C.Hart, Vardemon Halsel, Griffeth Edwards, Nathan Bridgeman William Little, Daniel Shaw, James Henderson, Hermes Champ Ezekiel Blackshire, Wilson A.W.Mann, John G. Flowers and John McWhite who being elected, tried and sworn well and truly to try the issue joined upon their oath aforesaid do say that the Defendants have not paid the Debt of one hundred and nine dollars in the plaintiffs declaration mentioned as the plaintiff in replying hath alledged and they assess the said plaintiffs damages by reason of the detention of that Debt to two dollars and seventy two cents besides costs. It is therefore considered by the court that the said plaintiff do recover against the said Defendant the debt aforesaid in the Declaration mentioned and the damages aforesaid by the Jury assessed and the costs in this behalf expended and the said defendants in mercy etc.

Peter R.Booker   )
vs   )   In debt
Henry L.Gray   )

This day came the said parties by their attornies and thereupon came a jury of good and lawful men to wit, James C.Hart, Herndon Haralson, Griffith Edwards, Nathan Bridgeman, William Little, Daniel Shaw, James Henderson, Hermes Champ, Ezekiel Blackshire, Wilson A.W. Mann, John G.Flowers, & John McWhite, who being elected, tried and sworn well and truly to try the issue joined between the parties upon (p-379) Tuesday 9th June 1829- their oath do say that the defendant hath not paid the debt of two hundred and fifty dollars in the plaintiffs declaration mentioned and the jurors aforesaid upon their oath aforesaid do further say that there is no sett off as the said plaintiff in replying hath alledged and they assess the said plaintiffs damages by reason of the detention of that Debt to seventy nine dollars & seventy five cents- besides costs. It is therefore considered by the court here that the said plaintiff do recover against the Defendant the debt aforesaid in the declaration mentioned and the Damages aforesaid by the Jury assessed and the costs in this behalf expended etc.

Joseph Spence   )
)
    vs   )
James H.Walker   )

By consent of the parties it is ordered by the court that the parties in this suit without further notice have leave to take deposition of Amons Vincent & others in the town of Mooresville, Alabama at the house or Tavern house of Griffin Lamkin on the 14th August next & succeeding day between the hours of 9 o'clock of the forenoon or six o'clock of the afternoon those or others of those days to be read in evidence on the trial of the above called-

(p-379con.) William H. Hewlite)
       vs   )   In debt
    Samuel Henderson   )

    This day came the said parties by their attornies and thereupon
came a jury of good and lawful men to wit, James C.Hart, Herndon
Haralson, Griffith Edwards Nathan Bridgeman William Little Daniel Shaw,
James Henderson Hermes Champ, Ezekiel Blackshire Wilson A.W.Mann, John
G.Flowers, and John McWhite, who being elected tried and sworn well and
truly to try the issues joined upon their oath do say that the Defendant
hath not paid the Debt of one hundred and sixty dollars in the plaintiffs
declaration mentioned as the plaintiff in replying hath alledged, and the
jurors aforesaid do further say that there is no set off as the said
plaintiff in replying hath alledged, and they assess the said plaintiffs
damages by reason of the detention of that Debt to two Dollars & sixty
cents besides costs.

    It is therefore considered by the court here that the said plaintiff
do recover against the said (p-380) Tuesday 9th June 1829 defendant
the debt aforesaid in the declaration mentioned and the Damages aforesaid
by the jury assessed and the costs in this behalf expended etc.

Samuel Smith assee   )
)
     vs   )   In debt
Aaron T.Brooks   )

    This day came the said parties by their attornies and came also a
jury of good and lawful men to wit James C.Hart, Herndon Haralson,
Griffith Edwards, Nathan Bridgeman William Lyttle, Daniel Shaw, James
Henderson Hermis Champ, Ezekiel Blackshire, Wilson A.W.Mann, John G.
Flowers and John McWhite who being elected tried and sworn well and
truly to try the issues joined upon their oath aforesaid do say that
the defendant hath paid all the debt in the declaration mentioned except
the sum of one hundred and fifteen dollars and they assess the plaintiffs
damages by reason of the detention of the residue of the debt in the
declaration mentioned to two dollars thirty seven & one half cents besides
costs.
    It is therefore considered by the court that the plaintiff recover
against the Defendant the residue of the debt aforesaid, and the damages
aforesaid by the Jury assessed & the costs in this behalf expended and
the Defendant in mercy from which Judgement the Defendan (p-381)
Tuesday 9th June 1829 hath prayed and obtained an appeal to the Circuit
Court of this county- He having given bond with Jordan M.Hanborough and
John T.Turner to prosecute to the same.

Caleb Warren   )
    vs   )   In debt
Richard Nixon   )

    This day came the said parties by their attornies and came also a
jury of good and lawful men to wit James C. Hart, Herndon Haralson,
Griffith Edwards, Nathan Bridgeman, William Little, Daniel Shaw, James
Henderson, Hermes Champ, Ezekiel Blackshire, Wilson A.W.Mann, John G.
Flowers, and John McWhite who being elected tried and sworn well and

(p-381con.) truly to try the issue joined upon their oath do say
that the defendant hathnot paid the debt of two hundred and fifty one
dollars and three cents in the plaintiffs declaration mentioned as the
plaintiff in replying hath alledged and they assess the said plaintiff
damages by reason of the detention of that debt to three dollars and
seventy five cents besides costs. It is therefore considered by the
court there the plaintiff do recover against the said Defendant the Debt
aforesaid in the declaration mentioned and the Damages aforesaid by the
Jury assessed and the costs in this behalf expended and the Defendant
in mercy etc. From which Judgement the Defendant had hath prayed and
obtained an appeal to the Circuit Court of this county who gave bond with
Nicholas T.Perkins and Thomas G.Nixons securities to prosecute the same-

(p-382) Tuesday 9th June 1829

Matthew Ray & others)
    vss   ) Certioraro
Hiram Paget   )

  On motion of the said plaintiff to dismiss the Certiorari in this
cause and upon solemn argument being heard thereon and by the court here
fully understood it is considered by the court that the motion be sustained and that the plaintiff recover against the said Matthew Ray, Herndon
Haralson, Lawrence McGuire and on motion against Robert T. Smith their
security in the Certiorari the sum of ninety six dollars & Twenty five
cents with 12½ per cent interest thereon from the 24th day of May 1829,
the date of the Judgement before the Justices up to this day as also the
costs in this behalf expended.

Jesse L. Kirk)
  vs   )
Albert G.Ellis)   Certiorari

  This day came the said plaintiff by his attorney and moved the
court to dismiss the Certiorari in this cause, and upon solemn argument
being had thereon and by the court here fully understood it is considered
by the court that the motion be sustained and that the said plaintiff
recover against the said Jessee L.Kirk and on motion against Thomas M.
Smith his security in the certiorari fifty two dollars and thirty two
cents with 12½ per cent interest thereon from the 25th day of April
1829, the date of the Judgement before the Justice up to this day as
also the costs in (p-383) Tuesday 9th June 1829, this behalf expended
with the defendants in mercy etc.

Abia Weaver)
  vss   )
John Taylor)

  This day came the said Defendant Abia Weaver by his attorney, and
the said plaintiff being solemnly called to prosecute his suit against
the Defendant came not, not does he prosecute the same wherefore it is
considered by the court that the said Defendant go hence without day and
recover against the plaintiff his costs in this behalf expended etc.

(p-383con.) Jesse L.Kirk)
          vs   )   Certiorari
Albert G.Ellis)

On motion of the said plaintiff by his attorney to dismiss the
certiorari in this cause and upon solemn argument being had thereon and
by the court here fully understood it is considered by the court that
the motion be sustained and that the plaintiff recover against the defendant, and on motion against Thomas M.Smith his security in the
certiorari the sum of twenty four dollars and one cent with $12\frac{1}{2}$ per cent
interest thereon from the 25th of April 1829, the date of the Judgement
before the magistrate up to this day & the costs in this behalf expended
etc.

The Grand jury returned into court and there appearing no further
business for their ## consideration at this Term were discharged.

Court adjourned until tomorrow morning nine o'clock

                        Rich'd Nixon Char-
                        Sam. P.Ashe
                        L.McGuire

(p-384) The court met according to adjournment. Present the worshipful Richard Nixon, Samuel P.Ashe, and Lawrence McGuire esquire Justices.

Bowen Reynolds records the Ear Mark of his stock thus, to wit,
One underslip off of each ear from rear to the point- taken off the point

William Armoin assee)
          vs   )
Joseph Eddings   )

The defendant being dissatisfied with the Judgment obtained
against them prayed an appeal to the Circuit Court which is granted-
     He having given bond with Bowen Reynolds & Bird Link as securities.

William H.Hewlett)
          vs   )
Samuel Henderson)

The Defendant being dissatisfied with the Judgement of the court
hath prayed an appeal to the next Circuit Court . He having given bond
and security therefor.

Upon the petition of James Denin praying this court to appoint commissioners to lay off, divide and set apart to him the said James Denin
and to the other heirs of James Robison deceased their respective lots
and portions of a one thousand acre tract of land in the 10th surveyors
District range six and (p-385) Wednesday 10th June 1829- sections six
and seven, and it appearing to the satisfaction of this court that publication has been made as required by law. It is therefore considered by
the court that Benjamin G.Alexander, Oliver Woods, Jonathan Burlison,
David Jarrett and Jesse Walling be appointed commissioners to divide said
tract of land between the said heirs, to wit, Osborn Robison the heirs of
Thompson Robison, James Denin in right of his wife, Davey and Milas

(p-385con.) Robinson and make report to the next term of this court. Is'd.

Upon the petition of Samuel P.Ashe agent and attorney for John C.McLemore, paying this court to appoint commissioners to lay off and set apart to John C.McLemore his locative interest, to wit one fourth part of a twenty five hundred and sixty acre tract of land in range two Section six granted to James Hart and it appearing to this court that legal publication has been made. It is therefore ordered by the court that Griffith Edwards, Joseph Welker, John Roddy, Anderson Britt and Lawrence McGuire be appointed commissioners to divide and set apart to said John C. McLemore his proportion of said tract of land.
Petition Is'd.

It is ordered by the court that the sheriff refund to Lee Sullivan two Dollars fifty one & one fourth cents, it being the one half of the Double tax, costs & charges on three hundred acres of land for the year 1828, upon which the Single tax only should have been collected
P̶e̶t̶i̶t̶i̶o̶n̶/̶I̶s̶d̶/

Wednesday June 10th 1829-

(p-386)   The State of Tennessee)
                    vs   )
          John McWhite   )

This day came as well the State of Tennessee by the attorney General as the said Defendant in his proper person , and the said Defendant being solemnly charged saith he is not Guilty in manner & form as charged in the bill of Indictment, and for his trial puts himself upon the country and the attorney General doth the like, and thereupon came also a jury of good and lawful men to wit, Griffith Edwards, Archibald McNeal, William P.Young, Thomas N.White, Caleb Warren, James Russell, Benjamin Weaver, George Weddle, Thomas M.Smith, Nelson Hargrove, A̶b̶n̶e̶r̶ Abner Spence and Mason F.Johnson who being elected, tried and sworn well and truly to try the issue of traverse upon their oaths do say that the defendant is guilty in manner and form as charged in t̶h̶e̶/ the bill of Indictment. It is therefore considered by the court that the defendant make his fine with the State of Tennessee by the payment of five Dollars and all costs and that he be taken etc.

Thomas J.Dobyns was this appointed Guardian for Wareck W.McGary who gave bond as the law directs.

(p-387) Wednesday 10 June 1829

The State   )
     vs   )
Reese Porter   )

This day came as well the State of Tennessee by the attorney General as the defendant in his proper person, and the Defendant being solemnly charged saith that he is not guilty in manner and form as charged in the bill of Indictment and for his trial puts himself upon the country & the attorney General doth the like, and thereupon came also a jury of good and lawful men to wit Griffith Edwards, Archibald, McNeal, William P. Young, Thomas N.White, Caleb Warren, James Russell, Henry Welch, George Weddle, Thos. M.Smith, Nelson Hargrove, Abner Spence and Mason F.

(p-387con.) Johnson who being elected, tried and sworn well and truly
to try the issue of traverse upon their oaths do say that the defendant
is Guilty in manner and form as charged in the bill of Indictment. It
is therefore considered by the court that the Defendant be confined in
the common jail of this county for the space of ten days, unless he should
previous to that time pay as a fine the sum of five dollars and all costs
or secure the same by giving good security for the payment thereof to the
clerk of this court.

(p-388) Wednesday 10th June 1829

Thomas N.White who stands security for Alexander M. Kirksey to
appear at this court at the instance of James S.Steele to surrender a
schedule, pay the debt due, or take the benefit of the insolvent debtors
oath, this day surrendered in court, the body of said Alexander M.
Kirksey in complyance with the said bond.

Sidney P.Smith who was elected at this Term as constable for this
county gave bond and security & took the oaths prescribed by law.

An Indenture of bargain & sale from John G.Blount by James Caruthers
to Abner Spence for 100 acres of land was this day proved in open court
by the oaths of William H.Henderson and Nelson Hargrove, witnesses thereto
& ordered to be registered.
Deed.

Caleb Warren to Thomas Carnahan for two hundred & twenty five acres of
land was this day acknowledged in open court by the said Caleb Warren
to be his act & deed for the purposes in said deed mentioned and ordered
to be registered.
Deed.

Deed of Conveyance from Matthew Ray to Benjamin Weaver for fifty
acres of land was this day acknowledged in open court by the said
Matthew Ray to be his act and deed for the purposes in said deed mentioned & ordered to be registered.

(p-389) Wednesday June 10th 1829

George Weddle)
)
vs)
)
William Weddle and)
Levi Gardner)

On motion of the said plaintiff by his attorney and it appearing
to the satisfaction of the court that heretofore to wit on the sixth
day of January 1829. Isaac White obtained a judgement in the Circuit
Court of this county against Levi Gardner, William Weddle and against
the said George Weddle as their security said Judgement as security aforesaid the sum of thirty three dollars and seventy-two cents. Therefore
on motion of the said plaintiff by/his/attorney it is considered by the
court that the said plaintiff do recover against the said defendants the
said sum of thirty three dollars and seventy two cents as also his costs
by him about his motion on this behalf expended.
* and that he hath paid on

(p-389con.)   GEORGE WEDDLE   )
                    vs   )
            LEVI GARDNER & WILLIAM WEDDLE)

On motion of the plaintiff by his attorney and it appearing to the satisfaction of the court that heretofore, to wit: in the 6th day of January 1829, Isaac White obtained a judgment in the Circuit Court of this county against Levi Gardner--William Weddle, and against the said Plaintiff as their security and that he hath paid on said Judgment as security aforesaid the sum of twenty-six dollars and ninety cents. Thereupon on motion of the said plaintiff by his attorney it is considered by the Court that the said plaintiff do recover against the said defendants the said sum of twenty-six dollars and ninety cents & costs by him about his motion in this behalf expended.

(p-390)   Wednesday June 10th 1829

Thomas Carnahan   )
         vs   )
Thomas G.Nixon admr. of   )
John R.Leigh Dec'd.   )

This day came the said plaintiff by his attorney and saith he intends no further to prosecute his said action against the defendant and thereupon each party by their attornies assumes to pay one half the costs in this behalf expended.

The jurors to the present term claimed their attendance as follows to wit.

Joseph Murphy	1 day	John Wells	1 day
Benj. Weaver	1 do	Jas. T.Haralson	1 do
John Young	1 do	James Axley	1 do
Azariah Thompson	1 do	John Stone	1 do
Begnal Crook	1 do	Jas. Curry	1 do
Mark Spence	1 do	Stephen Boothe	1 do
Sidney P.Smith	1 do	Milton McDearman	1 do
John Sanderlin	1 do	Jesse Embry	1 do
James C.Hart	1 do	Griffith Edwards	2 do

Court adjourned until tomorrow morning nine o'clock.

                              Rich. Nixon char.
                              L.McGuire
                              B.Coleman

Thursday June 11,1829, the court met pursuant to adjournment Present the worshipful Richard Nixon, Lawrence McGuire & Blackman Coleman Justice.

Christopher E.McEwen   )
           vs   )
Thomas Potter and   )
Robert T.Smith   )

(p-390con.) The defendants being dissatisfied with the Judgements
rendered against them hath prayed and obtained an appeal to the next
Circuit Court of this county who gave bond with Henry Welsh and John
Mott to prosecute the same. And the court then adjourned until court in
course.

                                    Rich. Nixon char-
                                    L.McGuire
                                    B.Coleman J.P.

(p-391) Monday September Term 14th day 1829

State of Tennessee   )
Haywood County Court) Set.

        At a court of pleas and quarter sessions began and holden for
the County of Haywood at the courthouse in the town of Brownsville on
the second Monday in September A.D.1829 present the worshipful Richard
Nixon Saml. P.Ashe, Daniel Cherry and others their fellow Justices of
the peace this 14th September 1829

        The Jury of view who were at the last term of this court appointed
to view the Estes & Fulton roads and to ascertain whether it would
not conduce to the interest of the Public to have the two consolidate &
if in their opinion it should be done at what point they should be
united make report to this court as follows:

        We the   Jury the/jury of review have viewed and agreed that the
Estes road should be confined to the Fulton road from Brownsville four
miles and three quarters, then leaving the Fulton road at a certain
point marked, and then to intersect the Estes road again near Smith
Mounces at a certain point marked. Given under our hands this the
11th Sept. 1829.

                                    John O.Tanner
                                    John Rogers
                                    John Albright
                                    Saml. Green
                                    William Patton

        Which report is received by the court & (p-392) Monday September
14, 1829 is thereupon ordered by the court that the Estes road be discontinued from the town of Brownsville and that the same shall be consolidated & run with the Fulton road to the point marked by the Jury of
view, where it shall turn off and intersect the Estes road at or near
Smith Mounces. Eli Ozment produced in open court the scalp of a wolf
over four months old and proved the killing the same in the County of
Haywood according to law . It is therefore ordered by the court (there
being seven Justices of the peace on the bench) that the said Eli
Ozment be allowed the sum of three Dollars to be paid by the Treasurer
of the Western District.
Iss'd.

        Delany Whitehurst this day produced in open court the scalps of
two wolves over the age of four months & proved the killing of the
same in the County of Haywood (in Haywood County) agreeably to law. It
is therefore ordered by the court that the said Delany Whitehurst be

(p-392con.) allowed the sum of six dollars to be paid by the treasurer
of the Western District (there being seven Justices of the peace on the
bench)
Iss'd.

Hardy L.Blackwell produced in open court the scalp of a wolf over
the age of four months and proved the killing the same in Haywood County.
It is therefore ordered by the court (there being seven Justices of the
peace on the bench) that the said Hardy L.Blackwell be allowed the
(p-393) Monday September 14th 1829- sum of three dollars to be paid by
the treasurer of the Western District
Issued 14th Septr. 1829

On motion it is ordered by the Court, Adam R.Alexander & John H.
Bills, be released from the Double tax on 371½ acres of land reported
for the double taxes on the payment of the single tax & all costs &
charges- and that Ezekial Polk be released from the double tax on 500
acres of land also reported for the double tax on the payment of the
single tax costs & charges-

It is ordered by the court that Dorsey Biggs overseer of a road,
be allowed Martin Frazier & Harrison P.Womble in addition to his former
hands.
Iss'd

William Johnson produced in court that scalp of a wolf over four
months old and proved the killing of the same in Haywood County as the
law directs. It is therefore ordered by the court (there being seven
Justices of the peace on the bench) that he be allowed the sum of three
Dollars, to be paid by the Treasurer of the Western District.
Iss'd.

Jonathan R.Burleson produced in open court the scalps of three
wolves under the age of four months & proved by his own oath, he having
no other testimony whereby he could prove the same, that he killed the
wolves in Haywood County. It is therefore ordered by the court (there
being seven justices present) that he be allowed two Dollars & fifty
cents for each of said scalp to be paid by the Treasurer of the Western
District.
Iss'd. - - wolf scalp

(p-394) September Term 14th Septr. 1829.

Nimrod Axley this day produced in open court the scalp of a wolf
over the age of four months & proved by his own oath the killing of the
same he having no other evidence whereby he could prove the same.
It/is/therefore/ordered/by/the/court here/

It is therefore ordered by the court here that the there being
seven justices present, be allowed three dollars to be paid by the
treasurer of the Western District.
Issued to V. Lanier by order of Haresborough

Eli Faris this day produced in open court the scalp of a wolf over
the age of four months and proved the killing of the same by his own oath

(p-394con.) (he having no other evidence whereby he could prove the same).
Iss'd.

It is therefore ordered by the court that the said Eli Farris be
allowed the sum of three dollars to be paid by the Treasurer of the
Western District.

James Malden Executor of George Ables, makes return of an Inventory
of said Estate which is ordered to be recorded-

Deed of Conveyance from Samuel P.Ashe to John J.Wells for one
hundred and twenty three acres and third of an acre of land was produced
in open court and acknowledged by the said Sam'l. P.Ashe & ordered to be
certified.

Bill of sale from Jesse L. Kirk to Robert S.Wilkins for a certain
negro man slave named Casey was produced in open court & acknowledged by
the said Kirk and ordered to be certified for Registration.

(p-395) Monday Sept. 14 1829

Deed of Conveyance from Isham W.Olive to Thomas S.Yancy for his
interest in two & a half acres of land was proved in open court by the
oaths of James W.Strother & John Sevier witnesses thereto & ordered to
be certified for Registration.

James L.Wortham esquire a Justice of the peace in & for the County
of Haywood this day tendered to court his resignation as a justice of
the peace which is received by the court.

Isaac Hardman produced in open court the scalp of a wolf over four
months of age & proved the killing of the same as the law directs in
Haywood County. It is therefore ordered by the court (there being
seven Justices on the bench) that the said Isaac Harman be allowed three
dollars to be paid by the Treasurer of the Western District
Iss'd.

James Story & John T.Clark were this day appointed constables of
this county, who entered into bond & security & took the oaths prescribed
by law.

Bill of sale from Jesse Green to William L.Lambert for a negro
woman named Dolly aged about thirty eight and her three children Ezekiel,
Mary and Betsy was this day proved in open court by the oath of G.Edwards
a subscribing witness thereto

Bill of sale from William L.Lambert to Jesse Green for a negro
woman named Dolly aged about thirty eight and three children Ezekial,
Mary and Betsy was this day proved in open court by the oath of G.Edwards
a witness thereto.

(p-396) Monday September 14th 1829

Lawrence McGuire, John Roddy, & Joseph Walker three of the commissioners appointed at the last Term of this court to lay off , divide and

(p-396con.) set apart to John C.McLemore his locative interest, to wit. one fourth part of a twenty five hundred & sixty acre tract of land in range two section six granted to James Hart this day made their report in writing under their hands have they had divided and apportioned the same. It is therefore ordered by the court after due inspection of said report of said commissioners, that said report be received and entered of record and certified for Registration. It is therefore considered by the court that said petitioner pay the costs in and about his petition in this behalf expended and that venir facias issue accordingly and it is further ordered that Lawrence McGuire as commissioner & surveyor be allowed the sum of ten dollars, John Roddy a commissioner four dollars & and Joseph Walker a commissioner four dollars.

A Power of attorney from Lee Sullivan to Griffith Edwards Edwards/ & Isaac Edwards was produced in open court and the execution thereof proved by the oath of Mary Edwards, a witness thereto.

(p-397) Monday 14th September 1829

Oliver Woods, Jesse Walling, J.R.Burlison and Benjamin G.Alexander four of the commissioners appointed at the last term of this court to lay off, divide and set apart to James Dunn, the petitioner, and to the other heirs of James Robertson dec'd their respective lots and portions of a one thousand acre tract of land in the tenth surveyors District, range six & sections six and seven this day made their report in writing under their hands how they have divided and apportioned the same. It is therefore ordered by the court, after due inspection of said report of said commissioners, that the said report be received and entered of record and certified for registration. It is therefore considered by the court that said Petitioner pay all costs in and about his petition in this behalf expended and that Venir Facias issue according and it is further ordered that Samuel Erwin the surveyor be allowed the sum of thirteen dollars, Oliver Woods a commissioner four dollars. Jessee Walling a commissioner four dollars, J.R.Burlison a commissioner four dollars and B.G.Alexander a commissioner four dollars .

Upon the application of John G.Flowers it is ordered by the court that said John G.Flowers be authorised to keep a Ferry at his landing on Hatchie River on his entering into bond & security as the law directs.

(p-398) Monday 14 Sept. 1829

It is ordered by the court that all the hands of Daniel Cherry work on the Trenton road.

It is ordered by the court that John Roddy, Lewis Foscue, Joseph Walker, Samuel P.Ashe, James Story and Robt. Haywood be and are hereby appointed a Jury of view to view and mark a road from or near the cross roads on the lands of Samuel P.Ashe the best and nearest way in a direction to Somerville and also one towards Raleigh or Memphis & make report to next court.
Iss'd.

It is ordered by the court that Thomas Furgerson, James Dorris, James M.Henderson, & Isaac Woods be appointed a jury of view to view (p-398con.) & mark a road leading from Brownsville the best & nearest way in a direction to Dyersburg so far as Haywood County line. Iss'd.

Court adjourned until tomorrow morning nine o'clock.

Rich'd Nixon char.
L.McGuire
Sam.P.Ashe

(p-399) Tuesday Sept. 15, 1829

Tuesday morning 15th September 1829 the Court met according to adjournment Present the worshipful Richard Nixon, Samuel P.Ashe, Lawrence McGuire and others their Justices .

John G.Carithers Sheriff of Haywood County makes return of the venire Facias returnable to this court which is as follows to wit:

State of Tennessee
At a court of Pleas and quarter sessions began and held for the County of Haywood at the court-house in the town of Brownsville on the second Monday in June in the year of our Lord 1829 it being the 8th day of said month. Present the worshipful Richard Nixon, Samuel P.Ashe and Jesse L. Kirk, Esqrs and others their fellow justices of the peace. It is ordered by the court that James Armstrong Nehemiah Hardy, Robert M.Spencer, Thomas G.Nixon, Herndon Haralson Henry Welsh, Joseph Eddins Bird Link, Edward West, Robert Burns., Thomas White, Tobias C. Henderson, Henry McCoy, William Hollingsworth, Harman Frazier, Philip Bruce, Richard T.Moore , John McFarland, Adam Hawkins, Francis M.Wood, Thomas Thweatt, William Conner Philip Koonce, Robert T.Smith, Robert Perry, & John Albright be summoned to attend at the next court of pleas & quarter sessions on Tuesday after the second Monday in September next then and there to serve as grand or petit Jurors as the case may be and that James Kinny and Jordan M.Hansbrough be summoned (p-400) Tuesday 15th Sept. 1829, to attend said court as constables.

Test B.H.Sanders clk by
B.Coleman Dep.

State of Tennessee
To the sherriff of Haywood County, Greeting:
You are hereby commanded to summon the aforesaid persons to serve as jurors at the next court of Pleas and quarter sessions to be held at the courthouse in the Town of Brownsville on Tuesday after the second Monday in September next, and this they shall in no wise omit under the penalty prescribed by law. Herein fail not and have you then and there this writ. Witness Britain H.Sanders clerk of our said court at office the second Monday in June 1829

B.H.Sanders, clk

Upon the back of which said writ aforesaid the sherriff of Haywood county made the following return viz-
by virtue of the within venire Facias I have proceeded to summon all

(p-400con.) the within named persons to serve as grand and petit jurors, and such persons so summoned are freeholders or householders of said county.

Jno. G.Carithers shff-

The following persons were elected, drawn & sworn and as a grand jury for the present Term to wit Herndon Haralson Foreman, Philip Koonce, Thomas G.Nixon, Robt. M. Spicer, Adam Hawkins, Bird Link, Edward West, Francis M.Woods, John Albright, Robert Burns, Henry McCoy, William Conner & Tobias C.Henderson who having receive their charge retired to consider of the duties assigned them.
G.Jury.

(p-401) Tuesday 15 Sept. 1829

James C.Kinney constable sworn to attend the Grand Jury.

Robert Caruthers)
    vs   )
Jedediah Cusick)

On motion & it appearing to the satisfaction of this court that the plaintiff in this cause is dead & that his death was suggested at the last term of this court, that this suit be revived in the name of Elizabeth B. Caruthers, Samuel Caruthers and Parry W.Porter administrators of the said deceased.

Deed of Conveyance from Thomas H.Taylor by his attorney in fact Matthew Ray to Samuel Elliott for five acres of land was this day acknowledged in open court by the said Matthew Ray attorney as aforesaid & ordered to be certified for Registration.
D.

Deed of Conveyance from Matthew Ray to Jordan & Nixon for a lot of ground in the Town of Brownsville known & designated in the plan of said Town by no. 20 was this day acknowledged in open court by said Matthew Ray and ordered to be certified for registration.

Deed of Conveyance from Richard Nixon to Caleb Warren for one hundred acres of land was this day acknowledged in open court by the said Richard Nixon to be his act and deed & ordered to be certified for registration.

Albert G.Ellis)
    vs   )
Burwell Wilkes)

This day came the said plaintiff in his proper person and saith he intends no further to prosecute his said appeal in this cause. It therefore considered by the court here that the Defendant go hence without day and recover against the said plaintiff his costs in this behalf about his Defence in this behalf expended.

Abia Weaver produced in open court the scalp of a wolf over the age of four months & proved the killing of the same in Haywood County. It is therefore considered by the court (there being five Justices of (p-401con.) the peace on the bench) that he be allowed the sum of three Dollars to be paid by the Treasurer of the Western District. Issued to Jno. H.Freeman

Pages 402-Blank
        403-Blank

(p-404)   TUESDAY 15th SEPT. 1829

Elizabeth B.Caruthers)
Samuel Caruthers &)
Parry W.Porter admns.)
of Robert Caruthers)
                vs)   No. 3
Jedediah Cusick)

        This day came the said parties by their attornies & thereupon came also a jury of good lawful men to wit, Robert Perry, William Hollingsworth, Joseph Eddins, John McFarland, Nehemiah Hardy, Thomas N. White, William Powell, William Proudfit, Samuel Elliott, Thomas Potter, William H.Burton and Benjamin Wilkes who being elected, tried and sworn well and truly to try the issue joined upon their oaths aforesaid do say that the defendant hath not paid the Debt of seven hundred and six dollars & fifty cents in the declaration mentioned as the plaintiff in declaring hath alledged, and they assess the plaintiffs damages by reason of the detention of that debt to fifty four dollars and seventy five cents, besides costs- It is therefore considered by the court that the said plaintiffs do recover against the said defendant the Debt aforesaid in the declaration mentioned and the damages aforesaid by the Jury in form aforesaid assessed & their costs by them in this behalf expended, and the said defendant in mercy-

William Alred (to the use)
of James Axley)
                vs)
Azariah Thompson)

        This day came the said Defendant in his proper person and withdrawing his plea by him heretofore pleaded saith he cannot gainsay the said plaintiffs action for one hundred and eighty eighty dollars.
        It is therefore considered by the court that the said plaintiff do (p-405) Tuesday 15th Sept. 1829, recover against the said Defendant the said sum of one hundred and eighty eight dollars, and his costs by him in this behalf expended. From which Judgement of the court the defendant prayed and obtained an appeal to the next Circuit Court. He having given bond and security to prosecute the same

Henry S.Meeks)
        vs
Jedediah Cusick)

        This day came the said parties by their attornies & thereupon came also a jury of good & lawful men to wit, Robert Perry, William Hollingsworth, Joseph Eddins, John McFarland, Nehemiah Hardy, Thomas N.

(p-405con.)

White, William Powell, William Proudfit, Samuel Elliott, Thomas Potter, William H. Burton and Benjamin Weaver, who being elected tried and sworn well and truly to try the issue joined upon the oath do say that the defendant hath not paid the debt of seventy dollars in the plaintiffs declaration as the plaintiffs in replying hath alledged and they assess the plaintiffs damages by reason of the detention of that debt to one dollar and ninety cents besides costs. It is therefore considered by the court that the plaintiff do recover against the defendant the debt aforesaid in the declaration mentioned and the damages aforesaid by the Jury assessed & the costs in this behalf expended & the defendant in mercy etc.

(p-406) Tuesday 15 Sept. 1829

Joseph Spence   )
      vs   )
James H. Walker)

    The Death of the plaintiff is suggested by his attorney.

ROSE MILLER   )
    VS   )
WILLIAM H. HENDERSON)
& REUBIN ALPHIN   )
)

    This day came the said parties by their attornies and thereupon came also a jury of good and lawful men to wit: Robert Perry, William Hollingsworth, Joseph Eddins, John McFarland, Nehemiah Hardy, Thomas N. White, William Powell, William Proudfit, Samuel Elliott, Thomas Potter, William H. Burton & Benjamin Wilkes who being elected tried & sworn well and truly to try the issue joined upon their oath do say that they find the issue in favour of the plaintiff and assess his damages to one hundred and sixteen dollars. It is therefore considered by the court that the said plaintiff do recover against the said Defendants the damages aforesaid by the jury assessed and the costs in this behalf expended & the defendants in mercy, etc.

William Word &)
William Moss   )
    vs   )
Thomas N. White)

    This day came the said parties by their attornies and thereupon came also a jury of good and lawful men to wit: Robert Perry, William Hollingsworth, Joseph Eddins, John McFarland, Nehemiah Hardy, Thos. N. White, William Powell, William Proudfit, Samuel Elliott. Thomas Potter, William H.Burton and Benjamin Wilkes who being elected (p-407) Tuesday 15th Sept. 1829, - tried and sworn well and truly to try the issue joined upon their oath do say that the defendant hath not paid the Debt of three hundred and fifty dollars in the plaintiffs declaration mentioned as the Plaintiffs in replying have alledged & they assess the plaintiffs damages by reason of the detention thereof to eleven dollars besides costs.
    It is therefore therefore considered by the court that the plaintiffs recover against the defendant the debt aforesaid in the declaration mentioned & the damages aforesaid by the jury assessed & the costs in this behalf expended etc.

(p-407con.) Thomas Elms   )
                vs   )
          Francis S.Coxe)

This day came the said parties by their attornies and thereupon
came also a jury of good & lawful men, to wit, Robert Perry, William
Hollingsworth, Joseph Eddins, John McFarland, Nehemiah Hardy, Thomas N.
White, William Powell, William Proudfit, Samuel Elliott, Thomas Potter,
William H.Burton, and Benjamin Wilkes who being elected, tried and sworn
well and truly to try the issues joined upon their oaths do say that the
defendant hath not paid the debt of one hundred of four dollars & fifty
cents in the plaintiffs declaration mentioned as the plaintiff in replying
hath alledged- and the jurors aforesaid upon their oath aforesaid do further
say that there is no set off as the plaintiff in replying hath alledged
and they assess the plaintiffs damages by reason of the detention of that
debt to ten dollars & eighty five cents besides costs. It is therefore
considered by the court that the plaintiff do recover against the Defendant the debt of aforesaid in the declaration mentioned & the Damages
aforesaid by the Jury assessed and the costs in this behalf expended etc.

(p-408) Tuesday 15 Sept. 1829

Thomas Forest   )
        vs   )
Albert G.Ellis)

This day came the said parties by their attornies and thereupon came
a jury of good and lawful men, to wit, Robert Perry, William Hollingsworth
Joseph Eddins, John McFarland, Nehemiah Hardy, Thomas N.White, William
Powell, William Proudfit, Samuel Elliott, Thomas Potter, William H.
Burton and Benjamin Wilkes who being elected tried and sworn well and
truly, to try the issues joined upon their oath do say that the defendant
hath not paid the debt of four hundred and fifty dollars as the plaintiff
in replying hath alledged, and the jurors aforesaid upon their oath aforesaid do further say that there is no set off as the plaintiff in replying
hath alledged and they assess the plaintiffs damages by reason thereof to
fourteen dollars and sixty two cents besides costs.
        It is therefore considered by the court that the said Plaintiff do
recover against the said defendant the debt aforesaid in the declaration
mentioned and the damages aforesaid by the Jury assessed & the costs in
this behalf expended & the defendants in mercy.

(p-409) Tuesday 15th Sept. 1829

Albert G.Ellis   )
        vs   )
Burwell Wilkes   )

This day came the said plaintiff in his proper person and sath he
intends no further to prosecute his said appeal in this cause.

Wherefore it is considered by the court that the Defendant go hence
and recover against the said plaintiff his costs in this behalf expended.

The court adjourned until tomorrow morning nine o'clock.

(p-409con.)   Rich'd. Nixon char.
                                Sam. P.Ashe J.P.
                                L.McGuire

(p-410) Wednesday 16 Septr. 1829

Wednesday 16 September 1829. Court met pursuant to adjournment. Present the worshipful Richard Nixon, Samuel P.Ashe & Lawrence McGuire, esqrs. Justices-

On motion of the attorney General it is ordered by the court that that Alexander B.Bradford ,esquire attorney Genl. file a bill of Indictment Ex officio against John Louis conduitt for an assault and battery on Reubin Golden.

The State of Tennessee   )
         vs   )
Anthony Clark   )

This day came as well the State of Tennessee by the attorney General as the defendant in his proper person, and the Defendant being solemnly charged says he is guilty in manner and form as charged in the bill of Indictment and puts himself upon the grace and mercy of the court. It is therefore considered by the court that the defendant make his fine with the State by the payment of five dollars & all costs and that he be taken and thereupon James Clark acknowledges himself security for the payment of fines & costs aforesaid and agrees that execution may issue jointly against him & the Defendant for the fine & costs aforesaid.

The State of Tennessee   )
         vs   )
William Jones   )

This day came as well the State of Tennessee by Alexander B.Bradford esquire attorney General as the Defendant in his proper person and the Defendant being solemnly charged saith_____he is guilty in manner and form as charged in the Bill of Indictment & puts himself upon the grace and mercy of the court. It is therefore considered by the court that the Defendant make his fine with the state by the (p-411) Wednesday 16 Sept 1829 payment of five dollars and all costs and that he be taken.

And thereupon Samuel P.Ashe came into court and acknowledges himself bound as security for the payment of the fine & costs aforesaid and that execution may issued jointly against him & the said Defendant for the same.

The State of Tennessee)   For an assault & battery on
         vs   )   Francis Booby
Isaac Dial   )

This day came as well the State of Tennessee by Alexander B. Bradford esqr. attorney General as the defendant in his proper person and the defendant being solemnly charged saith that he is not guilty in manner and form as charged in the bill of Indictments and for his trial puts himself upon the country, and the attorney General doth the like, and thereupon came a Jury of good and lawful men, to wit Robert Perry, (p-411con.) William Hollingsworth, Joseph Eddins , John McFarland, Nehemiah Hardy, Philip Bruce, Thomas N.White, William Powell, Abia Weaver, Robert Sanders, James Carlton and Archibald Robison who being elected tried and sworn well and truly to try the issue of Traverse . And thereupon by the knowledge and direction of the court a Nole Prosequi is entered.

The State of Tennessee)
   vs   )
Hastings Dial   )

  This day came as well the State by Tennessee by Alexander B. Bradford esqr. attorney General as the Defendant in his proper person and the defendant being charged saith he is not Guilty in manner and form as charged in the bill of Indictment & for his trial puts himself upon the country and the attorney General doth the like. And thereupon came a jury of good and lawful men to wit Robert Perry (p-412) Wednesday 16th Septr. 1829, William Hollingsworth, Joseph Eddins, John McFarland, Nehemiah Hardy, Philip Bruce, William Powell, Abia Weaver, Robert Sanders James Carlton and Archibald Robison, Thomas N.White, who being elected tried & sworn well & truly to try the issue of traverse upon their oath do say that the defendant is Guilty in manner and form as charged in the bill of Indictment. It is therefore considered by the court here that the Defendant make his fine with the state of Tennessee by the Payment of fifteen- dollars and all costs, and there he be taken etc. And thereupon Benjamin Wilkes acknowledges himself bound as security for the fine & costs and agrees that execution may issue jointly against him and the Defendant for the fine & costs aforesaid.

The State of Tennessee)
   vs   )
Archibald Robison)

  This day came as well the state of Tennessee by A.B.Bradford esqr. attorney Gen 'l. as the Defendant in his proper person & the defendant being solemnly charged saith he is guilty in manner and form as charged in the bill of Indictment and puts himself upon the grace and mercy of the costs. It is therefore considered by the court that the Defendant make his fine by the payment of five dollars and all costs & that he be taken and thereupon James Sanders acknowledges himself bound as security for the fine and costs aforesaid and agrees that execution may issue jointly against him & the Defendant therefor.

(p-413) Wednesday 16th Septr. 1829

    The State of Tennessee) No. 1 assault & battery in
        vs   ) A.G.Ellis
    John L.Conduitt)

  This day came as well the State of Tennessee by Alexander B. Bradford esqr. attorney General as the defendant in his proper person and the Defendant being charged saith he is guilty in manner and form as charged in the Bill of Indictment & for his trial puts himself upon the grace and mercy of the court. It is therefore considered by the court here that the defendant make his fine with the state by the pay-

(p-413con.) ment of thirty dollars & all costs & that he be taken etc. And thereupon William Fitzerald comes into open court and acknowledges himself bound with the Defendant for the fines and costs aforesaid and agrees that Execution may issue jointly against them for the same.

The State of Tennessee) No. 2 For an assault & battery on
            vs   ) A.G.Ellis
John L.Conduitt   )

        This day came as well the State of Tennessee by Alexander B. Bradford esquire attorney General, as the Defendant in his proper person, and the Defendant being solemnly charged saith that he is not guilty in manner and form as charged in the bill of Indictment & for his trial puts himself upon the country, and the attorney General doth the like, and thereupon came also a Jury of good and lawful men to wit, Henry Welsh, Benjamin Wilkes James Sanders, William Weddle, William H.Mann, John Stone, Thomas M.Smith, Benjamin F.Neely, James W.Russell, Thomas N. White, Robert Perry, and Simon Turner who being elected tried and sworn well and truly to try the issue of traverse upon their oaths aforesaid do say that the defendant is_____ Guilty in manner and form as charged in the bill of Indictment . It is therefore considered by the court that the Defendant make his fine with the state by the payment of Twenty dollars & all costs & that he be taken.
And thereupon William Fitzgerald acknowledges himself bound as security for the fine & costs aforesaid and agrees that execution issue jointly against the Defendant & himself for the same.

(p-414) Wednesday 16, Septr. 1829.

        It is ordered by the court that David Hay, Lawrence McGuire, Richard Nixon, Archibald McNeal, Philip Koonce, Henry McCoy Stokely D. Hays, Joshua Abstain and John G.Flowers be appointed a jury of view to view a road from the Jackson road leading by Col. Nixon's to Hatchie river & make report to this court.

The State of Tennessee) No. 5 For an assault & battery on V.
            vs   ) Halsel
Hastings Dial   )

        This day came as well the State of Tennessee by Alexander B. Bradford esqr. attorney Gen'l. as the defendant in his proper person and the Defendant being solemnly charged charged saith that he is guilty in manner and form as charged in the bill of Indictment puts himself upon the grace and mercy of the court. It is therefore considered by the court that the defendant make his fine with the State by the payment of five dollars & all costs & that he be taken. And thereupon Benjamin Wilkes comes here into open court and acknowledges himself bound as security for the fine & costs aforesaid and agrees that Execution may issue jointly against the Defendant and himself thereto.

The State   )
    vs   )
Abia Weaver)

(p-414con.) This day came as well the State of Tennessee by A.B. Bradford esqr. attorney Genl. as the Defendant in his proper person and the Defendant being charged says he is guilty in manner and form as charged in the Bill of Indictment & puts himself upon the grace and mercy of the court.

It is therefore considered (p-415) Wednesday 16 Sept 1829, by the court that the Defendant make his fine with the State by the payment of fifty cents and all costs and that he be taken etc. and thereupon Albert G.Ellis comes into court and acknowledges himself bound with the Defendant for the fine and costs aforesaid and agrees that execution issue jointly against them for the same.

The State   )
        vs   ) No. 3 a & B on R.Golden
John L.Conduitt)

This day came as well the State of Tennessee by A.B.Bradford esqr. atty. Genl. as the defendant in his proper person and the defendant being solemnly charged saith he is Guilty in manner and form as charged in the bill of Indictment & puts himself upon the grace and mercy of the court. It is therefore considered by the court that the Defendant make his fine with the State by the payment of one cent and all costs and that he be taken- and thereupon William Fitzgerald comes into court and acknowledges himself bound with the defendant for the fine and costs aforesaid, and agrees that execution may issue jointly against them for the same.

The State of Tennessee)
        vs   ) Assault & battery on A.Echols No. 4
John L.Conduitt   )

This day came as well the State of Tennessee by Alexander B. Bradford esquire attorney General as the Defendant in his proper person and the said Defendant being solemnly charged saith he is Guilty in manner and form as charged in the Bill of Indictment and puts himself upon the grace and mercy of the court. It is therefore considered by the court that the defendant make his fine with the State of Tennessee by the payment of fifty dollars and all costs and that he be taken. And thereupon William Fitzgerald comes here into court and acknowledges himself bound as security for the fine and costs aforesaid and agrees that execution may issue jointly against the defendant and himself for the same.

(p-416) Wednesday 16th Sept. 1829

The State of Tennessee)
        vs   ) No. 7
Hastin Dial   )

Hastings Dyal and Benjamin Wilkes acknowledge themselves indebted to the State of Tennessee, to wit, the said Hastings Dial in the sum of one hundred Dollars and the said Benjamin Wilkes in the sum of fifty Dollars to be levied of their & each of their proper goods & chattels, lands and tenements, but to be void on condition that the said Hastings Dial shall make his personal appearance at our next court of pleas &

(p-416con.) quarter sessions of this county then and there to answer a charge of the state of Tennessee against him for an assault and battery on the body of Frances Booby & not depart without leave of said court.

The State of Tennessee) No 8 for an assault & battery of
vs) V Halsel.
Isaac Dial)

This day came as well the state of Tennessee by A.B.Bradford esquire attorney Gen'l. as theDefendant in his proper person, and the Defendant being solemnly charged saith that he is Guilty in manner and form as charged in the bill of indictment, and puts himself upon the grace and mercy of the court. It is therefore considered by the court that the Defendant make his with the State of Tennessee by the payment of five dollars and all costs and that he be taken- And thereupon Benjamin Wilks comes here into court and acknowledges himself bound as security for security for the Defendant for the Payment of the fine and costs aforesaid and agrees that execution may issue jointly against them for the same.

(p-417) Wednesday 16 Sept 1829

Deed of Conveyance from Thomas Brown by his attorney in fact Alexander B.Bradford to Francis S.Coxe for one hundred acres of land was this day acknowledged in open court by the said Alexander B. Bradford, attorney as aforesaid, to be his act and deed & ordered to be certified for registration.

Deed of conveyance from Thomas H.Taylor by Matthew Ray attorney in fact to Samuel Elliott for five acres of land was this day acknowledged in open court by said Matthew Ray & ordered to be certified for registration.

It is ordered by the court William Hollingsworth, William H. Henderson, Valentine Sevier, Matthew Ray, Henry Welsh, Jordan Hansbrough and Allen R.Howard be and are hereby appointed a jury of view to view the McGuire Road from the Town of Brownsville to McGuires Ferry to ascertain what alterations if any, should be made in said road, and make report of their proceedings to the next term of this court.
Issd.

Court adjourned until tomorrow morning nine o'clock.

Rich'd Nixon char.
L.McGuire
Sam. P.Ashe

(p-418) Thursday 17th Sept. 1829

The court met pursuant to adjournment Present Richard Nixon, Sam'l. P.Ashe, & Lawrence McGuire, esqrs. Justices (p-418con.) James B.Furgerson this day obtained a licence to keep an ordinary in the Town of Brownsville, who entered into bond with Hiram Bradford as security.

William Worrd &)
William Moss)
  vs   )
Thomas N.White)

   The defendant being dissatisfied with the Judgment rendered against him hath prayed and obtained an appeal to the next Circuit Court he having given bond with Hiram Bradford as his security to prosecute the same.

The State of Tennessee)
   vs   )
Allen Westbrook)

   This day came as well the State of Tennessee by Alexander B. Bradford esquire attorney General as the Defendants in his proper person, and the said defendant being solemnly charged saith he is not guilty in manner and form as charged in the bill of Indictment and for his trial puts himself upon the country, and the attorney General doth the like - and thereupon came a jury of good and lawful men to wit Robert Perry, William Hollingsworth, Joseph Eddins, John McFarland, Philip Bruce , Thomas N.White, Henry Welsh, John Potter, John Hardwick, Paul P.Kelly, Thomas J.Dobbins and Robert Sanders who being elected tried and sworn well and truly to try the issue of traverse upon their oaths do say that the defendant is guilty (p-419) Thursday 17 Sept. 1829 in manner and form as charged in the bill of Indictment.

state of Tennessee by Alexander B. Bradford esquire attorney General as the Defendants in his proper person, and the said defendant being solemnly charged saith he is not guilty in manner and form as charged in the bill of Indictment and for his trial puts himself upon the country, and the attorney General doth the like - and thereupon came a jury of good and lawful men to wit, Robert Perry, William Hollingsworth, Joseph Eddins, John McFarland, Philip Bruce, Thomas N.White, Henry Welsh, John Potter, John Hardwick, Paul P.Kelly, Thomas J.Dobbins and Robert Sanders who being elected tried and sworn well and truly to try the issue of traverse upon their oaths do say that the defendant is guilty (p-419) Thursday 17 Sept. 1829, in manner and form as charged in the bill of Indictment.

   It is therefore considered by the court that the Defendant make his fine with the State by the payment of five dollars and all costs and that he be taken- and thereupon James Kinny comes into court and acknowledges himself bound for the fine and as to aforesaid, and agree that execution may issue jointly against the Defendant and himself for the same.

   Bill of sale from Jesse Green to William L.Lambert for four negroes, to wit, Dolly a negro woman about thirty eight years of age and her three children to wit, Ezekial, Mary and Betsey was this day proved in open court by the oaths of J.H.Simms, a witness, thereto and ordered to be certified for registration

(p-419con.)   S.D.Lowell   )
                    vs   )
             Thomas Furgerson   )

By consent of the parties by their attornies, it is agreed that
the deposition of Thomas Miller be taken at the office of the clerk of
the court on Thursday the 24th of this month between the hours of ten
o'clock A.M.& Six o'clock P. M. to be read as evidence in behalf of the
Defendant in this cause, and it is further agreed that this order shall
be taken and considered a lawful notice.

The Grand jury returned into court and there appearing no further
business for their consideration were discharged.

The following Jurors proved their attendance to wit:

Thomas N. White	3 days	Thos. G.Nixon	2 days
Joseph Eddins	3 days	Robt. M.Spicer	3 "
William Hollingsworth		Adam Hawkins	3 "
	3 days	Bird Link	3 "
Henry Welsh	3 days	Edward West	3 "
Philip Bruce	2 days	Frs. M.Wood	3 "
Robert Perry	3 days	John Allbright	3 "
John McFarland	3 days	Robt. Burns	3 "
Nehemiah Hardy	2 days	Henry McCoy	3 "
Herndon Haralson	3 "	William Conner	3 "
Philip Koonce	3 "	Tobias C.Henderson	3 " & James

Kinny constable to the grand Jury 3 -

(p-420) Thursday 17th Sept 1829

It is ordered by the court that Tobias C.Henderson overseer of a
road be allowed the following hands in addition to those heretofore
allowed him to wit, William Bolling and hands, and that they be released from working on any other road-
Iss'd.

William Powell)
          vs   )
Berry Dearen   )

On motion of the plaintiff by his attorney and it appearing to the
satisfaction of the courthere that the said plaintiff as security for the
defendant hath paid on a Judgement rendered in this court at the September
Term thereof 1828 in favour of William A.Johnson against Berry Dearin,
John Hardwick, & this plaintiff, the sum of sixteen dollars & fifty
seven cents. It is therefore considered by the court here that the said
plaintiff do recover against the said defendant the said sum of sixteen
dollars & fifty seven cents and the costs in this this behalf expended etc.

Simon Turner   )
       vs   )
Richard Nixon &   )
Thomas G.Nixon   )

(p-420con.) This day came the said parties in their proper persons and thereupon the said Defendants say they cannot gainsay the said plaintiffs action for three thousand and sixty dollars & costs.

It is therefore considered by the court here that the said plaintiff do recover against the said Defendants the said sum of three thousand and sixty dollars and the costs in this behalf expended. And it is agreed by and between the said parties that the above Judgement of three thousand and sixty dollars may be discharged by the payment of the debt, interest and all costs and damages and charges that have accrued or that may accrue in the following named suits viz

The first at the instance of John H.Poston assignee of Frederick W. Huling vs Simon Turner and Richard Nixon instituted in the County Court of Haywood where a Judgement was obtained against the defendants and an appeal was taken up to the Circuit Court original debt $640. The other at the instance of William L. Brown assignee of Frederick W.Huling (p-421) Thursday 17th Sept. 1829, against Simon Turner also instituted in this court and returned to the present Term, original debt $640, which said suits were brought on the bond given by Simon Turner and Richard Nixon to Frederick W.Huling and was contracted to have been taken in and delivered over to said Turner by said Nixon by the bond given by him the said Richard Nixon and Thomas G.Nixon on which this suit is founded and which is filed.

Nathan Bridgeman)
  vs)
Sam'l. P.Ashe Exr. adm.)

This day came the said plaintiff by his attorney and saith he intends no further to prosecute his said action against the said defendant. It is therefore considered by the court here that the Defendant go hence without day and recover against the said Plaintiff his costs by him about his Defence in this behalf expended.

Netherland Fait)
  vs)
Stokely D.Hays & Christopher)
E.McEwen & William M.Ewen Exrs.)
of Felix Staggs dec'd.)

This day came the said defendants by their attorney and the said plaintiffs being solemnly called to come into court and prosecute their suit came not but made default. It is therefore considered by the court that the Defendants go hence without day and recover against the said Plaintiffs their costs by them about their Defence in this behalf expended etc.

The State of Tennessee)
  vs)
Peters & Demeranville)

This day came the state of Tennessee by Alexander B.Bradford esqr. attorney General, and who saith he intends no further to prosecute his suit against the defends. And thereupon the defendants assume the payment of all costs etc.

(p-422) Thursday 17 Septr. 1829

(p-422con.) Robert A.Steele)
              vs   )   Debt
     Jessee L.Kirk)

    This day came the said parties by their attornies and the defendants
Demurr being solemnly agreed and by the court here fully understood, it is
considered by the court here that the said Demurr be overruled, and that the
said Plaintiff do recover against the said Defendant two hundred and eleven
dollars and twenty five cents, the debt in the declaration mentioned and
twenty three dollars and twenty five cents Damages for the detention
thereof & the costs in this behalf expended.

Jesse L.Kirk)
     vs   )
Albert G.Ellis)

JAMES S. STEELE   )
ALEXANDER M.KIRKSEY &)   Motion
THOMAS N.WHITE   )

    On motion of the said plaintiff by his attorney for a Judgement
against defendants bond executed by the said Defendant Alexander M.Kirksey
and Thomas N.White his security to John G.Carithers Sheriff of said Haywood
County for the sum of Eighty Dollars conditioned the said Alexander M.
Kirksey should well and truly keep the Prison rules of said Haywood County
till regularly discharged by Lane in a case wherein said Kirksey had
been arrested by virtue of a ca sa in favour of James S.Steele- the
Plaintiff for the sum of thirty Dollars or thereabouts. And upon solemn
argument being had and fully understood by the court it is considered by
the court that the said motion be overruled and that the said Defendants
go hence without day and recover against the Plaintiff their costs in
this behalf expended from which Judgement the Plaintiff has prayed and
obtained an appeal to the Circuit Court he having given bond and security
as the law directs.

(p-423) Thursday 17th Septr. 1829

A.G.Ellis   )
    vs   )   Appeal
Jessee L.Kirk)

    This day came the plaintiff in his own proper person and says he
intends no longer to prosecute his suit against the said Defendant. It is
therefore considered by the court that the Defendant go hence with day and
that he recover his costs in this behalf expended.

Joshua Abston who was at this term elected coroner of this county came
into court and entered into bond with Archabald McNeal, Henry McCoy and
James Henderson as his securities and took the oath of office.

    The Jury of view who was at this term appointed to view and mark a
road from the Jackson road leading by Col. Richard Nixon to Hatchie River
make report that they have done the same which is viewed by the court.

    Power of attorney from Daniel Cherry to John Harbert was this day (p-423con.) produced in open court and duly acknowledged by the said Daniel Cherry to be his act and Deed and ordered to be certified.

It is ordered by the court that Joshua Abston, Lawrence McGuire, Archibald McNeal, John G.Flowers and David Hay be appointed a Jury of view to view the road from Brownsville to the bluff on Hatchie River and to ascertain and report to next court whether in there opinion said road shall be changed or altered, and if so in what manner. Iss'd.

It is ordered by the court that the order made at the June court 1829 - appointing Levi Sullivan overseer of a road be recinded and that the hands heretofore allowed to him work under A.A.Tucker overseer of a Road from Estanaula to the Bolivar Road below Mauldins. Iss'd.

Court adjourned until tomorrow morning nine o'clock.

Rich'd. Nixon char.
L.McGuire
Sam. P. Ashe

Iss'd.

(p-424) Friday 18th Septr. 1829

The court met persuant to adjournment Present the worshipful Richard Nixon, Sam'l. P.Ashe and Lawrence McGuire, esqrs. Justices.

A power of attorney from John Blackwell to Sterling Smith was acknowledged in open court by said John Blackwell and ordered to be certified.

Albert G.Ellis   )
    vs   )
Samuel N.Woods &   )
Matthew Ray

On motion of said plaintiff by his attorney to dismiss the certiorari in this cause and upon solemn argument being had thereon and by the court fully understood, it is considered by the court here that said motion be sustained, and that the said Plaintiff do recover against the said Defendant, and on motion against Matthew Ray his security in the certiorari the sum of forty dollars, with $12\frac{1}{2}$ per cent interest thereon from the 10th of April 1829, the date of the Judgement before the Justice, up to this day and all costs in this behalf expended.etc.

John G.Flowers, who at this term at/this Term prayed & obtained leave to keep a Ferry on Hatchie river, came into court & gave bond as the law directs.

THE STATE OF TENNESSEE   )
    vs   )
JAMES HARRIS   )
UTLEY HOULTON   )
SIMION SULLIVAN   )

(p-424con.) This day came the State of Tenn. by Alexander B.Bradford esqr. attorney Gen'l. and the said Defendants, who were bound in a recognizance in the sum of five hundred Dollars, being solemnly called to come into court as they were bound to do to answer a charge of the State against the said Deft. Harris for an assault & battery on Jessee L.Kirk came not but made default. It is therefore considered by the court that the State of Tennessee recover against the said Defendants the said sum of five hundred dollars, and that Sciri facias issue severally against them, etc. Sci fa to issue.

(p-425) Friday 18th Sept 1829

It is ordered by the court that Lawrence McGuire, Nelson Hargrove, John R.McGuire, George Watts, Oliver Woods Elijah Arnold, Benjamin G. Alexander, Benjamin Huckaby and Joel Pace or any five of them be and are hereby appointed a jury of view to view and mark a road from Brownsville in a direction to Bolivar, the nearest and best way as for as the County line, and to cross Big Hatchie at the most suitable place in a direct course and make report to next court.
Iss'd.

It is ordered by the court (there being a majority of the acting Justices of the county present on the bench) that William H. Henderson, Henry Welsh Valentine Sevier, Matthew Ray and Stokely D.Hays be appointed a jury of view to view and mark a road from the end of Main Street to intersect the Fulton road as such point as they may think proper & correct & make a report to this court.

WILLIAM CAMPBELL)
  vs   )
JAS. T. HARALSON)
TOBIAS C. HENDERSON)
JAMES HENDERSON)

This day the said Plaintiff by his attorney & saith he intends no further to prosecute his action against the Defendants. And thereupon the Defendants by their attorney assumes to pay all costs in this behalf expended. It is therefore considered by the court that the Plaintiff recover against the said Defendants in this behalf expended.

James S.Steele)
  vs   ) Original Attachment
Isham Olive)

This day came the Plaintiff by his attorney and the said Defendant being solemnly called came not but made default. It is therefore considered by the court that the Plaintiff do recover against the said Defendant but because the court is not advised what damages the Plaintiff has sustained therefore it is ordered by the court that a Jury came at the next court to enquire of the Damages aforesaid.

Herndon Haralson-Commissioner)
  vs   )
Isham Olive   )

(p-425con.) This day came the said Plaintiff by his attorney and the said Defendant being solemnly came not but made default. It is therefore considered by the court that the said Plaintiff recover of the said Defendant - One hundred Dollars the Debt in the said Detention mentioned and (p-426) two Dollars damages for the detention thereof and his costs in this behalf expended.

McCrab & Jarrettvs)
Walker Wilson &   )
Reuben Golden   )

On motion of the Plaintiff for a judgement against the Defendants upon a paper purporting to be a bond executed by the said Defendants for their personal appearance here to make a surender etc. and upon argument being heard thereon it is considered by the court here that said motion be overruled and that the Defendants go hence without day and that they recover there costs in this behalf expended.

Robertson & Davenport)
        vs   )
Allen Westbrooks   )

On motion of the Plaintiff for a Judgement against the Defendants upon a paper purporting to be a bond executed by said Defendants. It is considered by the court here after solemn argument that said motion be over ruled and that said Defendants go hence without day and that they recover their costs in this behalf exepended.

C.P.Wilman   )
        vs   )
Sidney P.Smith   )

On motion of the Plaintiff for a Judgement against the Defendants upon a paper perporting to be a bond etc. It is therefore considered by the court here after solemn agreement that said motion be overruled and that said Defendants go hence without day and that they recover their costs in this behalf expended.

It is ordered by the court that Richard Nixon, Lawrence McGuire Samuel P.Ashe, Daniel Cherry, Daniel Shaw Jonathan T.Jacocks, Joel Estes Simon Turner, Nicholas T.Perkins, Wilson A.W.Man, James Carlton, Richard Taylor, John Williams, Edward West, Herndon Haralson, David Hay, Hiram Bradford, John Roddy, John Marbarry, James Henderson Senr. Joshua Abston, Archabald McNeal, John Rodgers, Nelson Hartgrove, Joseph Murphy (p-427) James Mauldin be summoned to attend at the next Circuit Court of this county then and there to serve as grand or petit Jurors as the case may and that Mansfield Ware be summoned as constable to attend said court.

It is ordered by the court that McFarland, William Johnson Senr., Charles White, William Proudfit, Edward Daney, Thomas G.Nixon, Mason F. Johnson, Harvey Womble, Elisha Roberts, Samuel Owens, Caleb Warren, William A.Terry, William A.Burton, Henry Welsh, James W.Russell, Benjamin Weaver, Paul P.Kelly, Thomas Potter, William C.Bruce & Mark Spence, John Stone Robert Burns, Eli Jones, William Weddle, Thomas M.Smith and William H. Mann, is summoned to attend at the next County Court of this county to

(p-427con.) serve as Grand or Petit Jurors and that Mathew Ray be summoned
to attend said court as constable.

William H.Henderson, Mathew Ray, Stokely D.Hays, Henry Welsh, and
Valentine Severe who was appointed at this term a Jury of view to view
a road from the west end of Main Street and connect it with the Fulton
Road make the following report to wit "We the undersigned being appointed a jury of view to view the Fulton Road leading westwardly make the
following report that the road be continued due west with Main Street
and with the avenue now open untill it reaches the Hatchie connection
thence the best way to intersect the present road and is ordered by
the court that John Rogers overseer of the Fulton Road be authorised
and required to cut out the same.
Iss'd.

(p-428) Friday 18th Septr. 1829

It is ordered by the court (there being a majority of the Justices
present) & the ayes & noes being taken that Matthew Ray, James Smith &
Hiram Bradford, will be allowed the sum of seven dollars for settling with
the Sheriff and county Trustee of this county for the years 1826 & 1827,
to be paid by the county Trustee out of any unappropiated monies in his
hands.
James Smith's certificate issued to him- Issued to Ray Bradford's issued
and delivered to J.G.Carithers.

Deed of Conveyance from Thomas H.Taylor by Matthew Ray his attorney
in fact to James Coe for two & one tenth acres of land was acknowledged
in open court & ordered to be registered.

Mansfield Ware   )
        vs   )
Francis L.Dillard)

On motion of the Plaintiff and it appearing to the satisfaction of
this court that the Plaintiff, hath paid as appearance bail for the Defendant the sum of thirty five Dollars and judgement rendered in this court
at March Term 1829*favour of Rhodah Horton as the Plaintiff upon a sciri
facias. It is therefore considered by the court that the Plaintiff do recover against the Defendant the said sum of thirty five dollars & his
costs by him about his motion in this behalf expended etc.

Court adjourned until court in course

                              Rich'd. Nixon char.
                              Sam'l P.Ashe
                              L.McGuire

(p-429) December Term 1829

At a court of Pleas and quarter sessions began & holden for the
County of Haywood at the courthouse in the Town of Brownsville on the
second Monday, it being the 14th day of December A.D.1829. Present,the
worshipful Richard Nixon Nicholas T.Perkins, Lawrence McGuire, Joel
Estes, Jonathan T.Jacocks, Oliver Woods, esquires Justices.
*in

(p-429con.) William Anderson produced in open court the scalp of a wolf over the age of four months and proved, as the law directs, that he killed said wolf in this county. It is therefore, ordered by the court (there being five Justices on the bench) that he be allowed the sum of three dollars, to be paid by the Treasurer of the Western District.
For V.Sevier

Joshua Abstain this day produced in open court the scalp of a wolf over the age of four months, and proved as the law directs, that he killed said wolf in the county of Haywood. It is therefore ordered by the court (there being five Justices on the bench) that he be allowed the sum of three dollars, to be paid by the Treasurer of the Western District.

John H.Henderson this day produced in open court the scalp of a wolf over the age of four months and proved the killing of said wolf in Haywood County as the law directs. It is therefore ordered by the court (there being five Justices of the Peace on the Bench) that said John H. Henderson be allowed the sum of three dollars to be paid by the Treasurer of the Western District.
Fee paid, Iss'd.

Articles of agreement between Lucy Koonce, Isaac Koonce & David Munn were this day produced in open court & the Execution thereof duly proved by the oaths of B.W.Hargett & Council Miller, witnesses thereto & ordered to be certified for Registration.

(p-430) Monday December 14, 1829

A Deed of Conveyance from Sidney P.Smith and Mary his wife, to James W.Strother for two lots of ground in the Town of Brownsville, nos. thirty & forty six was exhibited in open court and the Execution thereof duly acknowledged by said Sidney P.Smith to be his act and deed, and thereupon the court proceeded to take the private examination of said Mary Smith, seperate and apart from her husband, who saith that she did of her own free will and accord, sign said deed for the purposes therein expressed & that she did not execute to the same through the fears, pursuation or coertion of her said husband- all of which is ordered to be certified for registration.
Deed

A Deed of conveyance from John G.Carithers sheriff and collector of Haywood County to Asa Biggs for one thousand acres of land was this day acknowledged by said John G.Carithers & ordered to be certified for registration.
Deed

A Deed of conveyance from Washington Cusick to Joshua Abstain for Twenty one & one fourth acres of land was this day acknowledged in open court & ordered to be certified for Registration.
Deed

A Deed of conveyance from Francis M.Woods to Jessee Embry for Fifty acres of land was this day acknowledged in open court by said Francis M.Woods & ordered to be certified for Registration.
Deed

(p-430con.) A Deed of conveyance from Matthew Ray to Samuel Green for one hundred acres of land was proved in open court by the oaths of William Conner & C.E.Parrish witnesses thereto & ordered to be certified for Registration.

(p-431) Monday 14th December 1829

Deed of Conveyance from Joshua Kelly to Humphrey Donalson for two hundred acres of land lying in the County of Wilson was produced in open court and proved by the oaths of Paul P.Kelly and Jas. R.Kelly, witnesses thereto and ordered to be certified for Registration.
Deed.

A power of attorney from Albert M.Estes of this county to Joshua Bonner of Stokes County & State of North Carolina was exhibited in open court & the execution proved by the oaths of Lawrence McGuire and Blackman Coleman and ordered to be certified for registration.

William Barcroft was this day appointed Administrator of William Barcroft late of said county dec'd who gave bond in the sum of four hundred dollars with Jonathan T.Jacocks & Elisha Bryans security.

Edward West was this day appointed a constable in this county who entered into bond & took the oaths required by law.

Thomas W.Pugh this day prayed & obtained leave to keep an ordinary at his now dwelling to use, who gave bond and security.

The non Cupative will of Richard T.Moore late of said county dec'd was produced in open court and proved by the oaths of Allen J.Barbee and John Y.Taylor and thereupon Mary Moore, the Executrix, came into court and entered into bond and security & took the oath directed by law.

Upon the Petition of Joel Estes of Haywood County, it is ordered by the court that said Joel Estes have leave to erect a Mill on Lagoon Creek on the lands heretofore purchased by him from George W.Hockly, which Mill, when completed, is hereby established, as a Public Mill according to law.

(p-432) Monday 14 December 1829

It is ordered by the court, the following Justices being on the bench (who are a majority of the Justices of the County), to wit Richard Nixon, Lawrence McGuire Nicholas T.Perkins, Jonathan T.Jacocks, Oliver Woods and Joel Estes, and the ayes & noes being taken and each of said Justices voting in the affirmative, that Alexander B.Bradford esqr. attorney General, be allowed the sum of Forty dollars for his Ex- officio services for the year ending at this Term, to be paid by the County Trustee out of any unappropriated money in his hands.
Iss'd to the order of A.B.Bradly, J.Carithers in favour of the Shff.
Jno. C.C.

It is ordered by the court, a majority of the Justices being on the bench, to wit, Richard Nixon, Lawrence McGuire, Nicholas T.Perkins , Jonathan T.Jacocks, Oliver Woods & Joel Estes and the ayes & noes being (p-432con.) taken & each of said Justices voting in the affirmative, that John G.Carithers Sherriff, be allowed the sum of Forty dollars for his Ex officio services for the year ending at this term, to be paid by the County Trustee out of any unappropriated monies in his hands. Issd.

(p-433) Monday 14th December 1829

It is ordered by the court, a majority of the Justices being present, to wit, Richard Nixon Lawrence McGuire, Nicholas T.Perkins, Jonathan T. Jacocks, Oliver Woods, & Joel Estes, and the ayes and noes being taken and each of said Justices voting in the affirmative, that the clerk of this court be allowed the sum of Thirty dollars for his Ex officio services for the year ending at this Term as also the further sum of Twenty five dollars for making out & recording the Tax lists for the present year to be paid by the county Trustee out of any unappropriated monies in his hands Issued Febry 16th 1830

It is by the court that Lawrence McGuire, David Hay, Herndon Haralson, Alexr. D.Gordon, John Marberry, William Morrison and Francis Lamoin or any five of them be and are hereby appointed a Jury of view to view the road called the McGuire road (leading from Jackson to McGuires Ferry on Big Hatchie river) and to ascertain and report to the next term of this court what alterations and changes are necessary to be made in said road.

Robert Perry (for the	)
use of Jordan M. Hansbrough	)
vs	)
Jedediah Cusick & Newton Cusick	)

The Defendant Jedediah Cusick who had been taken by virtue of Ca Sa issued in this cause by Blackman Coleman, a Justice of the Peace for said county and who entered into bond for his appearance at this Term, this day appearance in open court and filed a Schedule of his property which (p-434) Monday 14 December 1829, Schedule is as follows, to wit.
A Schedule of Jedediah Cusick in case of a Ca Sa against him in favour of Jordan M.Hansbrough, & for his use, to wit 400 acres of land, 4 Range Section and a note of hand against Joshua Kelly for about $250, which is now in suit in the County Court of Haywood County, Tennessee with the exception of five pr. cent or the whole amount which Edmond Richmond is entitled to as a fee for bring suit on the same by agreement with me this 14th day of December 1829, Sworn to in open court.

B.H.Sanders, Clk.)
by B.Coleman Def.)   Jedediah Cusick

Mansfield Ware	)
vs	)
Francis Lamoin	)
Joseph Ewing & J.D.Stamps	)

The defendant Francis Lamoin who had been arrested at the instance of the Plaintiff by virtue of a Ca sa issued from the Circuit Court of this county & who had given bond & security for his appearance at this (p-434con.) court this day appeared in open court - and thereupon appeared also the said plaintiff in his proper person & release & discharges the defendant from all responsibility on said Ca Sa Bond.

(p-435) Monday 14th December 1829

It is ordered by the court that Joshua Abstain, Lawrence McGuire Archibald McNeal, John G. Flowers, David Hay, William Morris and Philip Bruce, Valentine Sevier, Thomas J.Dobyns & Young E.Allison be appointed a Jury of view to view the road the road from Brownsville to the Bluff on Hatchie River & to ascertain and report to this court whether in their opinion said road should be changed or altered, & if so in what manner.

It is ordered by the court there being a majority of the acting Justices on the Bench, and the ayes and noes being taken as the law directs, and each of said Justices voting in the affirmative to wit Richard Nixon, Lawrence McGuire, Nicholas T.Perkins, Jonathan T.Jacocks Oliver Woods, & Joel Estes, that the clerk of this court be allowed the sum of Twenty Eight dollars on Twenty tracts of land reported for the taxes of 1828 and not sold for the want of Bidders. Also the sum of fourteen dollars on two tracts of land reported for the double tax for 1828 & not sold for the want of bidders and also the sum of fifty one dollars & Eighty cents on thirty seven tracts of land reported for the Taxes for 1827 & not sold for the want of bidders to be paid by the County Trustee out of any unappropriated monies in his hands.
Issued to B.Coleman

(p-436) Monday 14 December 1829

Benjamin G.Alexander, Jesse Walling, William Pace, William C.Bruce, Littleton Joiner, William H.Burton, Thomas Thweatt, William H.Henderson Isaac M.Johnson, and John Fitts, who were appointed Justices of the Peace for Haywood County this day produced their commission in court & severally took the oath prescribed by law.

It is ordered by the court that Malcom Johnson, Archibald Brazeal, Oliver Woods, Henning Pace , Jesse L.Kirk and Levi Arnold be appointed a Jury of view to view the road leading from Estanaula in a direction to Covington & to turn the same if in their opinion, the public convenience will not be prejudiced so that the same will not injure the lands of William Pace & John Adams & make report to next court.
Iss'd.

It is ordered by the court that Jonathan R.Burlison, Jesse Walling, Thomas Richardson, Matthew George James King & John Walling be appointed a jury of view to view & lay off a road from Palestine to Estanaula & make report to next court.
Issd.

Court adjourned until tomorrow morning nine o'clock.

Rich. Nixon char.
L.McGuire
Sam. P.Ashe
Joel Estes

(p-437)   Tuesday 15th December 1829

The court met according to adjournment. Present the worshipful
Richard Nixon, Samuel P.Ashe & Lawrence McGuire, esqrs. & others their
fellow Justices.

The Sheriff of Haywood County makes return of the venire facias returnable to this court, which is as follows, to wit,

State of Tennessee
        At a court of Pleas and quarter sessions began and held for
the County of Haywood at the Courthouse in the Town of Brownsville on the
second Monday in September 1829, being the 14th day of said month, present
the worshipful, Richard Nixon, Samuel P.Ashe, Daniel Cherry and others
their fellow Justices of the peace. It is ordered by the court that John
McFarland, William Johnson, Senr. Charles White, William Proudfit, Edward
Davie, Thomas G.Nixon, Mason F.Johnson, Henry Womble , Elisha Roberts
Samuel Owens, Caleb Warren, William A.Terry, William H.Burton, Henry Welsh
James W.Russell, Benjamin Weaver, Paul P.Kelly, Thomas Potter, William
C.Bruce, Mark Spence, John Stone, Robert Burnes, Eli Jones, William
Weddle, Thomas M.Smith, William H.Mann, be summoned at the next County
Court of this County to serve as grand or petit Jurors as the case may be
and that Matthew Ray, be summoned to attend said court as constable.

        STATE OF TENNESSEE
            TO THE SHERIFF OF HAYWOOD COUNTY, GREETING:
        You are hereby commanded to summon the aforesaid persons to serve
as jurors at   the next Court of Pleas and Quarter sessions to be held
for said county at the courthouse in the Town of Brownsville on the second Monday in December next, and this they shall in no wise omit under
the penalty prescribed by law. Herein fail not and have you then and there
this writ, witness Britain H.Sanders clerk aforesaid court at office the
second Monday in September 1829

                                B.H.Sanders clk.
                                by B.Coleman Dep.

        Upon the Back of which said writ (p-438) Tuesday 15th December
1829. the sheriff makes the following return to wit By virtue of the
within venire Facias to me directed, I have proceeded to summon all the
within named persons to serve as Jurors, and such persons so summoned are
inhabitants of said county and free holders of said County

                                Jno. G.Carithers, Shff

        The following persons were elected drawn and sworn as a grand
Jury for the Present Term to wit, Mason F.Johnson, Foreman, Caleb Warren,
Eli Jones Mark Spence, William H.Mann, William A.Terryl, Thomas M.
Smith, Robert Burnes, John McFarland, Henry Welsh, William Proudfit,
Edward Davie & James W.Russell, who having received their charge, retired
to consider of the duties assigned them. Wyatt F. Tweedy, a constable,
sworn to attend the Grand Jury etc.
Grand Jury.

(p-438con.)   Samuel D.Lowell   )
                    vs   )
              Thomas Furgerson)

  This day came the said parties by their attornies and thereupon
came also a jury of good and lawful men, to wit, Thomas G.Nixon, Charles
White Harvey A.Womble, John Stone, William Johnson Senr. Benjamin Weaver
Paul P.Kelly, Frederick Tyus, Nelson Hargrove, Isaac Dial, Giles Bulock,
and James M.Henderson who being elected, tried and sworn well & truly the
issue joined between the parties upon their oath aforesaid do say they
find the issue in favour of the Defendant. It is therefore considered by
the court that the said Defendant go hence without day and recover of the
said Plaintiff his costs by him about his defence in this behalf expended.

(p-439) Tuesday 15th December 1829

John Wills asee   )
      vs   )
John T.Bryan &   )
Stephen S.Bryan   )

  This day came the said parties by their attornies, and thereupon
came also a jury of good and lawful men to wit Thomas G.Nixon, Charles
White, Harvey A.Womble, John Stone, Wm. Johnson senr. Benjamin Weaver,
Paul P.Kelly, Frederick Tyus, Nelson Hargrove, Isaac Dial, Giles Bullock
and James H. Henderson who being elected tried and sworn well and truly
to try the issues joined between the parties, upon their oath do say that
they find the issues in favour of the Plaintiff and assess his damages to
sixty six dollars, one cent and a half besides costs.
  It is therefore considered by the court that the said plaintiff do
recover against the said Defendants the damages aforesaid by the Jury in
form aforesaid assessed and the costs in this behalf expended & the defendants in mercy etc.

Jedediah Cusick   )
      vs   )
)
Joshua Kelly   )

  This day came the said Plaintiff by his attorney, and saith he intends no further to prosecute his suit against the Defendant. And thereupon the Defendant assumes to pay all costs . It is therefore considered
by the court that the said plaintiff do recover against the Deft. the
costs in this behalf expended.

Mansfield Ware   )
      vs   )
Francis L. Dillard   )

  Joseph Taylor who was regularly summoned as a Guarnishe to appear
at this court to declare upon oath what he was indebted to the defendant
Francis L. Dillard, this day personally appeared in open court and being
duly sworn upon the Holy Evangelist of Almighty God, saith that he does,
not nor did he at the time of the service of said Guarnishment owe the
said Francis L.Dillard anything that he has no effects of said Dillard

(p-439con.) in his hands nor does he know of any person who is indebted to the said Dillard or who has any of his effects in their hand.

(p-440) Tuesday 15th December 1829

Mathew Barrow, John C.McLemore & James P.Clark)
)
vs)
Hiram Bradford admr. & Mathew Ray)

This day came the parties by their attornies whereupon the matters of law arising upon the Demurrer of the Plaintiffs to the second plea pleaded by the Defendants having been seen & inspected and argument thereon had in the presence of counsel on both sides, and by the court fully understood, it is ordered and directed by the court that the demurrer of the Plaintiffs aforesaid be sustained and thereupon by permission of the Plaintiff & by leave of the court the Defendants were permitted to plead to the merits which was accordingly done whereupon came a jury of good & lawful men to wit Thomas G.Nixon, Charles White, Harvey Womble, John Stone, William Johnson Senr. Benjamin Weaver, Paul P.Kelly Frederick Tyas, Nelson Hargrove, Isaac Dyall, Giles Bullock & James M.Henderson, who being elected tried & sworn the truth to speak upon the issue joined upon their oaths do say that they find the issues in favour of the Plaintiffs, and that the Defendants do owe & detain the said sum of four hundred & nine dollars as the Plaintiffs thereof against them hath complained, & they assess their damages by occasion of the detention thereof to sixty nine dollars five cents. It is therefore considered by the court that the Plaintiffs recover of the Defendants the debt & damages aforesaid found & assessed as aforesaid amounting to four hundred & seventy eight dollars & five cents besides their costs by them about their suit in this behalf expended to be levied (as regards Defendant Bradford as administrator etc) of the goods & chattels, rights & credits which were of Robert Penn late deceased in the hands of said administrator unadministered to be found etc & the Dfts. in mercy etc.

And now the Defendants by attorney come & move in arrest of Judgment & file their reason accordingly.

It is ordered by the court that William Weddle a Juror summoned as a juror on the venire Facias returnable to this court, was this day called to come into court to serve as a juror came not, but made Default. It is therefore ordered that he be fined Five Dollars & that Sciri facias issue
Sci Fa.

(p-441) Tuesday 15th December 1829

It is ordered by the court (there being a majority of the Justices present) that John G.Carithers sheriff and collector of Haywood County be allowed a credit with the Treasurer of the Western District for the sum of Fifty five Dollars Eighty & one half cents for the lands reported for the single Tax for 1828, and not sold for the want of bidders. Also the further sum of Sixty two dollars and forty cents on lands reported for the double tax for 1828 and not sold for the want of bidders, as also the sum of one hundred and forty dollars & forty one cents on lands reported for the single Tax for 1827 & not sold for the want of bidders. Iss'd.

(p-441con.) It is ordered by the court (there being a majority of the Justices Present) that John G.Carithers Sheriff and collector of Haywood County be allowed a credit with the county Trustee of Haywood County for the sum of one hundred and six dollars eighty Seven & one half cents on lands reported for the single tax for 1828 & not sold for the want of bidders, also the sum of one hundred and nineteen dollars and forty three cents on lands reported for the double tax for 1828 & not sold for the want of bidders, and the sum of two hundred and sixty eight dollars and seven cents on lands reported for 1827 and not sold for the want of bidders Issued

It is ordered by the court that the county Trustee of Haywood refund to John L.Wheaton the sum of sixteen dollars & thirty eight cents the county part of the Taxes on 2393 acres of land Grant No. 407 it appearing that the said 2393 acres lies in the County of Dyer.
Issued. 7 May 1831

(p-442) Tuesday 15 December 1829

It is ordered by the court that the clerk of this court receive lists of Taxable property and polls from such persons as have not listed their property for 1829 during the setting of this court. That he at the same time receive the Taxes on the same and receipt therefor & attach the same to his return for 1830.

William H.Loving esquire was by the court appointed attorney General pro Term from the present term of this court.

Court adjourned until tomorrow morning nine o'clock.

Rich'd. Nixon Char
L.McGuire
Sam. P.Ashe

(p443) WEDNESDAY 16th DECEMBER 1829

Wednesday 16th December, 1829-
This court met pursuant to adjournment. Present the worshipful Richard Nixon, Sam'l. P. Ashe and Lawrence McGuire esquires

James Armstrong was this day appointed administrator of John Armstrong late of said County dec'd who entered into bond in the sum of two thousand dollars with Samuel P.Ashe & Jessee Kemp as his securities and took the oath prescribed by law.

James Armstrong was this day appointed administrator of James Morrison deceased who entered into bond in the sum of one thousand dollars with Samuel PAshe and Jesse Kemp as his securities and took the oath.

A Deed of Conveyance from John L.Wheaton to Ebenezer G.Young for 200 acres of land was this day acknowledged in open court by William H. Henderson attorney in fact for said Wheaton and ordered to be registered. Deed

A Deed of Conveyance from John L.Wheaton to Richard N.Eubanks for

(p-443con.) seven hundred and fifty acres of land was this day proved in open court by the oaths of J.M.Hansbrough & William H.Henderson witnesses thereto and ordered to be registered .
Deed

A Deed of Conveyance from Ramsey Henderson and Thomas B.Coleman to William M.Allen and Thomas J.Dobyns for six hundred and thirty nine acres of land was acknowledged in open court by the said Henderson and Coleman and ordered to be registered.
Deed

(p-444) Wednesday 16th December 1829

A deed of conveyance from William C.Russell to George Stalcup for a lot of ground in the Town of Brownsville No. 18 was this day proved in open court by the oaths of William H.Loving and George R.Watts, witnesses thereto & ordered to the registered.
Deed

A Deed of conveyance from John G.Carithers sheriff and collector of Haywood County to Henderson and Coleman for six hundred and thirty nine acres of land was this day acknowledged in open court by said John G.Carithers, Sherriff etc. and ordered to be certified for registration.
Deed

The Grand Jury returned into court and there appearing no further business for their consideration at this term, were discharged.

A Deed of Conveyance from John C.McLemore to John G.Carithers & Hiram Bradford in trust for Sephrona Longly and children was this day produced in open court and proved by the oath of Joel S.Dyer one of the witnesses thereto.
Deed

John P.Perkins was this day appointed Guardian for William R.Leigh minor heir of John R.Leigh deceased, who entered into bond in the sum of six thousand Dollars with Nicholas T.Perkins, John H.Nixon and Thomas G.Nixon & took the oath prescribed by law.

(p-445) Wednesday 16th December 1829

It is ordered by the court that James Tisdale's heirs be released from the double Tax on 7606 acres of land, grant 412,5000 acres grant 414- 5592 acres grant 415; 3496 acres Grant 410; 6934 acres grant 411; reported for the Double Tax for the year 1828.

It is ordered by the court that Mary Wheaton be released from the double tax on 5786 acres of land grant 413; 2786 acres grant 410; 2393 acres grant 407, reported for the Double Tax for 1828.

It is ordered by the court that Samuel H. Williams be released from the Double Tax on 800 acres of land , Entry 787 reported, for the double Tax for 1828.
Iss'd.

(p-445con.) It is ordered by the court that Clement Subblefield be released from the double tax on 228 acres of land. Entry 364 reported for
the double tax for 1828.

It is ordered by the court that John G.Carithers Sherriff and
collector of Haywood County be allowed a credit with the State Treasurer
of the Western District for the sum of Eighty six dollars, twelve, and
three fourth cents on five tracts of land reported for the double tax
for 1828 in the name of the heirs of James Tisdale amounting to twenty
eight thousand, s ix hundred & 28 and the double tax on which has been
released by this court.
Issd- acres

It is ordered by the court that John G.Carithers sheriff be allowed a credit with the County Trustee for $104.43 cents on twenty eight
thousand six hundred & twenty eight acres reported for the Double tax in
the name of the heirs of James Tisdale for 1828, the double tax on which
has been released from by the this court.

(p-446) Wednesday 16 December 1829

Joseph Spence   )
        vs   )
James H.Walker   ) .

The death of the Plaintiff having been suggested at last term of
this court, now on motion of John Read, attorney & for reason appearing
to the court it is ordered by the court that the suit in this case be
revived in the name of Marmon Spence administrator of all & singular
the good & chattels rights & credits of said Joseph Spence deceased.

It is further ordered that the parties have leave to take depositions of witnesses by giving ten days notice if taken in the State &
twenty out.

It is ordered by the court that John G.Carithers sheriff and
collector of Haywood County be allowed a credit with the Treasurer of
the Western District for the sum of thirty two dollars and sixty four
cents on 10,965 acres of land reported for the double tax for 1828 , in
the name of Mary Wheaton, the Double tax on which has been released by
this court.
Iss'd in Jany. 27th 1830

It is ordered by the court that John G.Carithers sheriff be allowed
a credit with the county trustee of Haywood County for the sum of sixty
two dollars & thirty five cents on 10, 965 acres of land reported for the
double tax for 1828 in the name of Mary Wheaton, the Double tax on which
has been ommitted by this court.
Iss'd.

(p-447) Wednesday 16 December 1829

It is ordered by the court that John G.Carithers and collector of
this county be allowed a credit with the Treasurer of the Western District

(p-447con.) for the sum of sixty nine cents on 228 acres of land reported for the Double tax for 1828 in the name of Clement Subblefield, the double tax on which has been released by this court.
Iss'd. Jany 27,

It is ordered by the court that John G.Carithers sheriff be allowed a credit with the Treasurer of Haywood County for the sum of one dollar and twenty cents on 228 acres of land reported for the Double Tax for 1828 in the name of Clement Subblefield, the double tax on which has been released by this court.
Iss'd.

It is ordered by the court that John G.Carithers sheriff and collector of this county be allowed a credit with the Treasurer of the Western District for the sum of two dollars forty three and one one half cents on 800 acres of land reported for the Double Tax for the year 1828 in the name of Samuel H.Williams, the Double tax on which has been released by this court.
Iss'd.

It is ordered by the court that John G.Carithers sheriff be allowed a credit with the county Trustee for the sum of four dollars, fifty six & one half cents on 800 acres of land reported for the double Tax for 1828 in the name of Samuel H.Williams, the double tax for 1828 in the name of Samuel H.Williams the double tax on which has been released by the court.
Iss'd.

Court adjourned until tomorrow morning nine o'clock.

Rich 'd. Nixon char.
Sam. P. Ashe
L.McGuire

(p-448)   THURSDAY 17th DECEMBER 1829

Thursday 17th December 1829

The court met according to adjournment Present, the worshipful Richard Nixon, Samuel P. Ashe and Lawrence McGuire esqrs.Justices.

A deed of conveyance from Thomas Windsor to David Gill for one hundred and fifty five acres of land was proved in open court by the oaths of M.H.Bradford & Hiram Bradford, witnesses thereto and ordered to be registered.
Deed.

A Deed of Conveyance from John G.Carithers sheriff of Haywood to Joel Estes for 800 acres of land was this day acknowledged in open court by said John G.Carithers sheriff and ordered to be certified for registration.
Deed

It is ordered by the court that Vincent Haralson, Joseph T.Haralson, Stephen Terry, John Shaw, Doctor James H.Walker, Samuel Brown, Doctor

(p-448con.) Joseph Jones and Charles White be appointed a Jury to view and mark a road from Jeffers Bluff on Hatchie River to the Madison County line in a direction to Jackson at such place as said Jury may think proper and make report to next Term.
Deed

A Deed of Conveyance from Kinchen Lewter to Valentine Sevier & James W.Strother for lot No. 17 in Brownsville was acknowledged in open court & ordered to be registered.
Deed

Deed of Conveyance from James W.Strother to Valentine Sevier for lot No. 17 in the Town of Brownsville, was acknowledged in open court & ordered to be registered.
Deed

It is ordered by the court that Thomas Furgerson, James Dorris, James Axley, James M. Henderson and Isaac Woods be appointed a Jury of view to view & mark a road leading from Brownsville the best way in direction to Dyerburg as far as the county line & make report to the next court.
Iss'd.

(p-449) Thursday 17th December 1829

The State of Tennessee   )
           vs   )
John L.Conduitt   )

This day came as well the State of Tennessee by William H.Loving esqr. attorney General Pro Term as the Defendant being charged saith is guilty in manner and form as charged in the Bill of Indictment, and puts himself upon the grace and mercy of the court. It is therefore considered by the court that the Defendant make his fine with the State of Tennessee by the Payment of Twenty five Dollars and all costs. And thereupon William Fitzgerald and Mansfield Ware came into open court and acknowledge themselves bound as security for the payment of the fine and costs aforesaid and agree that Execution may issue against them with the Defendant for the fine and costs aforesaid- And it is agreed by said parties & by the defendant by his counsel & the attorney General that no appeal, or any exceptions whatever shall be here after taken to any irregularity or imformality to any of the proceedings had in this court.

The State of Tennessee   )
           vs   )
James H.Clark & George   )
M.Penn   )

The defendants were bound in a recognizance in the same of Five hundred dollars to appear at this term to answer a charge of the State of Tennessee against the Defendant James H.Clark for Treating in contrary to the act of Assembly in such case made and provided , it being this day solemnly called to come into court as they were bound to do, came not but made default. It is therefore considered by the court that the State of Tennessee recover against the said James H.Clark and George M. Penn the

(p-449con.) said sum of five hundred dollars and that a writ of Sciri
facias issue requiring the said Defendants to appear at the next term of
this court to show cause if any they have why said Jedgement should not
be made final against them
Sci fa to issue

(p-450) Thursday 17th December 1829

The State of Tennessee)
      vs   )
Hastings Dyall   )

By the knowledge and direction of the court a nole Prosequi is
entered and it is ordered by the court that the Trustee Pay to the Sheriff
attorney Gen'l. Pro Term and clerk their respective fees.

The State of Tennessee)
      vs   )
William Anderson   )

The Defendant who was bound in a Recognizance to appear at this
Term to answer a charge of the State appeared in open court and there
appearing no charge was discharged. And thereupon the Defendant and
Caleb Warren came into court & assumed all costs in this behalf expended.

It is ordered by the court that James S.Steele, Herndon Haralson be
appointed commissioners to take the private examination of Margaret
McGuire wife of Lawrence McGuire, at his house respecting her dower right
in and to a certain lot or parcel of land No ____ in the Town of Harrodsburg
in the State of Kentucky conveyed by said Lawrence & Ware to Ann McAbee.
It appearing to the satisfaction of this court that the said Margaret
McGuire is too infirm to attend the court to be priviley examined.

Francis S.Coxe, Thomas J. Dobyns and Charles Guiger who were at this
Term appointed to settle with Hiram Bradford Administrator of Robert A
Penn, Dec'd makes report that they have done the same which reports is
returned into court & ordered to be Recorded.

(p-451) Thursday 17 December 1829

The Jury of view appointed to view and mark a road for a Public
road leading from the new landing at the Lime Kelse Bluff on Hatchie
River to the Town of Brownsville make report that they have done the same
and that said road shall begin at the landing and run up the ridge on
the rights hand of a large Gulley or Ravine above the Bluff to the summit
of the River Ridge then North right of McGuires and left of Hays clearing
across three branches of Hurricane Creek, then along a ridge to the nearest
point of the Sugar Creek ridge, then with said ridge round the leads of
the Spring Hollows and several others on the left to the Bridge on Sugar
Creek at the enterance of the Town which report was received and accepted
by the court. And thereupon,

It is ordered by the court that David Hay be appointed overseer to
cut out and put in repair said road and that he be allowed all the hands
east of Sugar Creek to the 4 Range line and the hands north of Hatchie
river to Hills Road as also all hands in the town of Brownsville to

(p-451con.)   assist in cutting out said road.
Iss'd.

Deed of conveyance from Nicholas T.Perkins and David Jeffers to
William Hart, Joseph Cowan & Susan his wife Obediah Smith and Elizabeth
N.Smith his wife, Wynn Dixon and Rebecca Dixon his wife of the County of
Henderson and State of Kentucky for seven hundred and fifty acres of
land was produced in open court and proved by the oath ofY.E.Allison
one of the witnesses thereto.
Deed.

(p-452)   Thursday 17 December 1829

A Deed of conveyance from William Hart, Joseph Cowan, Susan Cowan
Obediah Smith, Elizabeth N.Smith, Wynn Dixon, Rebecca Dixon, by their
attorney in fact Archibald Dixon to Nicholas T.Perkins, and David Jeffers
for seven hundred and fifty acres of land was this day proved in open court
by the oath of Y.E.Allison, one of the witnesses thereto.
Deed

Bill Sale from John G.Carithers sheriff to Hiram Bradford for a
negro Girl named Elinor was this day acknowledge in open court and ordered to be registered.

A Bill of Sale from John G. Carithers Sheriff to Hiram Bradford
for a negro woman Jude & her child Melia was acknowledged in open court
and ordered to be Registered.

Jno. H.Freeman this day prayed & obtained a license to keep an
ordinary at his now dwelling house in this county who gave bond etc.

Deed of Conveyance from Matthew Ray, attorney in fact for Thomas
H.Taylor to Thomas Rutherford for one acre and seventy five poles o f
land was this day proved in open court by the oaths of William H.
Loving & Young E Allison witnesses thereto & ordered to be registered.

Deed of Conveyance from Samuel Elliott to Robert M. Logan and
Thomas Rutherford, for three & a fourth acres of land was this day proved
in open court by the oath of William H.Henderson & William H.Loving,
witnesses thereto & ordered to be Registered.

Court adjourned until tomorrow nine o'clock.

                              Rich'd. Nixon, Char.
                              Sam. P. Ashe
                              L. McGuire

(p-453)   FRIDAY 18th DECEMBER 1829

Friday Morning 18th of December 1829 The court met pursuant to
adjournment. Present the worshipful Richard Nixon Samuel P.Ashe and
Lawrence McGuire esqrs. Justices.

Deed of Conveyance from Britain H.Sanders to Henry Sweney for lot

(p-453) fifty one in the town of Brownsville, was proved in open court
by the oath of Nicholas T.Perkins one of the witnesses thereto and ordered
to be registered.

Deed of Conveyance from Matthew Ray to Samuel Steel for lot no.
43 in Brownsville was this day proved in oepn court by the oaths of N.W.
Dill & T.L.Steele, witnesses thereto and ordered to be registered.

An Instrument purporting to be the last will & Testament of Henry
H. Turner was produced in open court and the Execution thereof was duly
proved by the oaths of N.T.Perkins and J.W.Fort witnesses thereto and
ordered to be recorded- And thereupon Mary S.Turner having relinguished
her right of administration on said estate Nicholas P.Perkins was appointed
administrator, with the will annexed who gave bond with
(Not finished)

It is ordered by the court that Richard Nixon, Lawrence McGuire
and William C.Bruce be appointed to take lists of Taxable property and
poles in Captain Elliotts conpany for 1830 Joel Estes in Capt. Estes
Company ___ Littleton Joiner Esqr. in Burtons Company, Jesse L. Kirk, &
William Pace, in Sullivan's Company, Sam'l. P. Ashe in Johnsons Company
Benja. G. Alexander for Wilsons Company- Obion Woods for Kinneys Company
Isaac M.Johnson for Tweedys Company- Daniel Cherry for Worthams Company
and Blackman Coleman for McDearmons Company .

Iss'd.

(p-454) Friday 18th December 1829

Joseph Spence   )
        vs   )
James H.Walker   )

On motion it is ordered by the court that this suit be revived in
the name of Morman Spence administrator of Joseph Spence deceased and
by consent of the parties by their attornies leave is granted to take
depositions Generally by Jury ten days notice within and Twenty days
notice if without the state.

Thomas Perciful)
       vs   )
Jesse Walling   )

This day came the said parties by their attornies & thereupon
came also a jury of good and lawful men, to wit: Charles White,
Benjamin Weaver, Thomas G.Nixon, Henry A.Womble, John Stone, William
Johnson, Paul P.Kelly, James M.Henderson, William Powell, Thomas
Fergerson & Young E.Allison who being elected, tried & sworn well and
truly to try the matters in dispute between the parties upon their oaths
do say they find for the Defendant.

It is therefore considered by the court that the defendant go hence
and recover against the said plaintiff his costs by him about his defence
in this behalf expended.

(p-454con.) James S.Steele)
       vs)
     Isham W.Olive)

  This day came the said parties by their attornies & thereupon
came also a jury of good and lawful men, to wit, Charles White, Benjamin
Weaver, Thomas G.Nixon, Henry A.Womble, John Stone, William Johnson,Paul
P.Kelly, James M.Henderson, William Powell, Thomas Furgerson, and Young E.
Ellison who being elected tried and sworn well and truly to inquire what
damages the Plaintiff hath sustained upon their oath do say they assess
the Plaintiffs damages to one hundred & forty five dollars besides costs.
It is therefore considered by the court that the said (p-455) Friday
18th December 1829 plaintiff do recover against the said defendant the
damages aforesaid by the jury assessed and the costs in this behalf expended and the Defendant in mercy etc.

  It is ordered by the court that John G.Carithers Sheriff and collect-
or of Haywood County be allowed a credit with the commissioners of the
Bridge fund for six months from the first day of January next for lands
to be reported for 1829 to the amount of two hundred and eighty one dollars and forty cents. It appearing to the court that amount was uncollected & had to be reported, and that the clerk certify the same.
Iss'd. Feb. 10th 1830

  It is ordered by the court that John G.Carithers Sheriff and collect-
or of Haywood County be allowed a credit for six months from the first day
of January next with the Treasurer of the Western District for the sum of
four hundred and twenty two dollars & ten cents for lands to be reported
for 1829, it appearing to the court that that amount is uncollected & had
to be reported, and that the clerk certify the same.
Iss'd. 27 Jany. 1830

  It is ordered by the court that John G.Carithers sheriff and collect-
or of Haywood County be allowed a credit with the County Trustee of this
county for six months from the first day of January next for the sum of
twelve hundred and sixty six dollars and thirty cents for lands to be reported for 1829, it appearing to the court that that amount is uncollected
and had to be reported and that the clerk certify the same.
Issued

(p-456) Friday 18th December 1829

Benjamin Perry assee)
     vs)
Blackman Coleman &)
Daniel Mading)

  This day came the said parties by their attornies & thereupon came
also a jury of good and lawful men to wit, to wit, Charles White, Benjamin
Weaver, Thos, G.Nixon, Henry A.Womble, John Stone, William Johnson
Paul P. Kelly, James M.Henderson, William Powell, Thomas Furgerson,
Young E.Ellison & John McWhite who being elected, tried and sworn well
and truly to try the issue joined upon their oaths do say that the Defendants have not paid the Debt of one hundred dollars in the declaration
mentioned as the plaintiff in declaring hath alledged, and they assess the

(p-456con.) Plaintiffs damages by reason of the detention of that Debt to two dollars & fifty cents- It is therefore considered by the court that the said plaintiff do recover against the Defendants the debt aforesaid in the declaration mentioned and the Damages aforesaid by the Jury assessed & the costs in this behalf expended & the Defendants in mercy-from which Judgement the Defendants prayed an appeal to the Circuit Court they having given bond & security.

Andrew Montgomery)
      vs)
Sarah J.Dyer)

    This day came the said parties by their attornies and thereupon came a jury of good and lawful men to wit; Charles White, Benjamin Weaver, Thomas G.Nixon Harvey A.Womble, John Stone, William Johnson,Paul P.Kelly, James M.Henderson, William Powell, Thomas Fergerson, Young E. Allison, John McWhite who being elected tried (p- 457) <u>Friday 18th December 1829</u>, and sworn well and truly to try the issue joined upon their oath do say that the defendant hath not paid the Debt of one hundred dollars & 70/100 in the plaintiff declaration mentioned as the plaintiff in declaring hath alledged, and they assess the plaintiffs damages by reason thereof to six dollars and fifty cents besides costs.
    It is therefore considered by the court that the said plaintiff do recover against the said Defendant the debt aforesaid in the declaration mentioned and the damages aforesaid by the Jury assessed & the cost in this behalf expended.

John C.McLemore)
      vs)
Robert Sanders)

    This day came the said parties by their attornies & came also a jury of good and lawful men, to wit: Charles White, Benjamin Weaver, Thomas G. Nixon, Henry A.Womble, John Stone, William Johnson, Paul P.Kelly James M.Henderson, Thomas Fergerson, Young E. Allison & John McWhite who being elected tried and sworn well and truly to try the issue joined upon their oath do say that the Defendant hath not paid the debt of five hundred and fifty dollars in the plaintiffs declaration mentioned as the Plaintiff in declaring hath alledged and they assess the Plaintiffs damages by reason of the detention of that debt to sixty four dollars and fifty cents besides costs. It is therefore considered by the court that the said Plaintiff do recover against the said defendant the debt aforesaid in the declaration mentioned and the damages aforesaid by Jury assessed and the costs in this behalf expended etc.

(p-458) Friday 18th December 1829

William L.Brown)
      vs)
Simon Turner)

    This day came the said Parties by their attornies & thereupon came also a jury of good and lawful men to wit: Charles White , Benjamin Weaver, Thomas G.Nixon, Harvy A.Womble, John Stone, William Johnson, Paul P. Kelly, James M.Henderson, William Powell, Thomas Fergerson, Young E. Allison & John McWhite, who being elected, tried and sworn the truth to

(p-458con.) speak upon the issue joined upon their oath aforesaid do say
that the defendant hath not paid the debt of six hundred and forty dollars
in the plaintiffs declaration mentioned as the Plaintiff in the declaring
hath alledged and they assess the Plaintiff damages by reason of the detention of that debt to one hundred and thirteen dollars and fifty cents,
besides costs.   It is therefore considered by the court that the said
Plaintiff do recover against the said defendant the debt aforesaid in the
declaration mentioned and the Damages aforesaid by the Jury assessed and
the costs in this behalf expended & the defendant in mercy from which
Judgement the Defendant prayed an appeal to the Circuit Court of Haywood
County which is granted. He having given bond with Richard Nixon &
John P.Jordan as securities.

(p-459) Friday 18th December 1829

Henry Lake   )
   vs   )
Richard Nixon   )

     This day came the said parties by their attornies and thereupon
came also a jury of good and lawful men to wit Charles White, Benjamin
Weaver, Thomas G.Nixon, Harvy A.Womble, John Stone, William Johnson, Paul
P.Kelly, James M.Henderson, William Powell Thomas Furgerson, Young E.
Allison and John McWhite, who being elected, tried and sworn well and truly
to try the issue joined upon their oaths aforesaid do say that the Defendant hath not paid the debt of one hundred and seventeen dollars & thirty
eight cents in the Plaintiffs declaration mentioned as the plaintiff in
declaring hath alledged and they assess the Plaintiffs Damages by reason
of the detention of that debt to twelve dollars and fifty cents besides
costs. It is therefore considered by the court that the said plaintiff
do recover against the said defendant the debt aforesaid in the declaration
mentioned and the damages aforesaid by the Jury assessed & the costs in
this behalf expended & the defendant in mercy etc.

Samuel Dickins   )
   vs   )
William H.Henderson &   )
Henry A.Powell   )

     This day came the said parties by their attornies and thereupon
came also a jury of good and lawful men, to Charles White, Benjamin
Weaver, Thomas G.Nixon, Harvy A.Womble, John Stone, William Johnson,Paul
P. Kelly, James M.Henderson, William Powell, Thomas Furgerson, Young E.
Allison and John McWhite who being elected tried & sworn the truth to
speak upon the issue joined upon their oath do say that the said Defendants
have not paid the debt of four hundred and forty eight dollars and thirty
eight cents in the plaintiffs declaration mentioned as the Plaintiff in
declaring hath alledged and they assess the Plaintiffs Damages by reason
thereof to sixteen dollars besides costs. It is therefore considered by
the court that the said Plaintiffs do recover against the defendant the
Debt aforesaid in the declaration

(p-460) Friday 18th December 1829

(p-460con.) mentioned and the damages aforesaid by the Jury assessed and the costs in this behalf expended & the defendants in mercy etc.

James Woods & Co.)
   vs   )
Francis S.Coxe)

  This day came the said parties by their attornies and came also a jury of good and lawful men, to wit, Charles White, Benjamin Weaver, Thomas G.Nixon, Harvey A.Womble, John Stone, William Johnson, Paul P.Kelly James M.Henderson, William Powell, Thomas Furgerson, Young E.Allison, & John McWhite who being elected, tried and sworn well and truly to try the issue joined between the parties upon their oath do say that the defendant hath paid all the debt in the Plaintiffs declaration mentioned except one hundred and eighty dollars and fifty seven cents which sum remains due and unpaid and they assess the Plaintiffs damages by reason of the detention of the residue of that Debt to nine dollars and fifty cents besides costs. It is therefore considered by the court that the said Plaintiffs do recover against the Defendant the residue of the debt aforesaid & the damages aforesaid by the jury assessed and the costs in this behalf expended etc.

Mason F.Johnson)
  vs   )
William R.Hess &)
F.W.Punkard   )

  This day came the said parties by their attornies and came also a jury of good and lawful men to wit, Charles White, Benjamin Weaver, Thomas G.Nixon, Harvy A.Womble, John Stone, (p-461) Friday 18th December 1829 William Johnson, Paul P.Kelly, James M. Henderson William Powell, Thomas Furgerson, Young E.Allison, and John McWhite who being elected tried and sworn well and truly to try the issue joined upon their oath do say they find the issue in favour of the Plaintiff and assess his damages by reason thereof to fifty four dollars thirteen & one half cents, besides costs-
  It is therefore considered by the court that the plaintiff do recover against the said defendants the damages aforesaid by the jury assessed and the costs in this behalf expended & the said Defendants in mercy etc.

John Brooks (use of)
George Barcroft &)
Samuel Pope)   )
  vs   )
Stephen Terry   )

  This day came the said parties by their attornies and thereupon came also a jury of good and lawful men to wit, Charles White, Benjamin Weaver, Thomas G.Nixon, Henry A.Womble, John Stone, William Johnson, Paul P.Kelly, James M.Henderson, William Powell, Thomas Furgerson, Young E.Allison and John McWhite who being elected tried and sworn the truth to speak upon the issue joined upon their oaths do say that the defendants hath not paid the debt of one hundred and six dollars & eighty one cents in the declaration mentioned, as the Plaintiff in declaring hath alledged & they assess the Plaintiffs damages by reason of the detention of that debt to fourteen dollars & twenty five cents, besides costs. It is there-

(p-461con.) fore considered by the court that the Plaintiff do recover against the said the debt aforesaid in the declaration mentioned and the damages aforesaid by the Jury assessed & the costs in this behalf expended etc.

(p-462) Friday 18th December 1829

Samuel Dickins   )
        vs   )
J.Terry & J.Bilbro)

        This day came the parties by their attornies & thereupon came a jury of good and lawful men to wit, Charles White, Benjamin Weaver, Thomas G.Nixon, Harvy A.Womble, John Stone, William Johnson, Paul P. Kelly, James M.Henderson, William Powell , Thomas Furgerson, Young E.Allison and John McWhite, who being elected tried and sworn well and truly to try the issue joined upon their oaths do say that the defendants have not paid the debt of six hundred dollars in the Plaintiffs declaration mentioned as the Plaintiff in declaring hath alledged and they assess the plaintiffs damages by reason thereof to seventy dollars & fifty cents besides costs. It is therefore considered by the court that the said plaintiff do recover against the said defendants the debt aforesaid in the declaration mentioned and the damages aforesaid by the jury assessed and the costs in this behalf expended and the said defendants in mercy etc.

George W.Hockley)
        vs   )
Bird Link   )

        This day came the said parties by their attornies and thereupon came also a jury of good and lawful men to wit, Charles White, Benjamin Weaver, Thomas G.Nixon, Harvey A.Womble, John Stone, William Johnson, Paul P.Kelly, James M.Henderson, William Powell, Thomas Furgerson,Young E.Allison and John McWhite who being elected tried & sworn well & truly to try the issue joined upon their oath do say that the defendant hath not paid the (p-463) Friday 18th December 1829 debt of one hundred & thirty three dollars, thirty three and one third cents in the plaintiffs declaration mentioned as the Plaintiff in declaring hath alledged and they assess the Plaintiffs damages by reason of the detention of that debt to two dollars & fifty cents besides costs. It is therefore considered by the court that the said Plaintiff do recover against the said defendant the debt aforesaid in the declaration mentioned & the damages aforesaid by the Jury assessed & the costs in this behalf expended. From which Judgement the Defendant prayed and obtained an appeal to the Circuit Court of this county. He having given bond and security therefor.

James Woods & Co.   )
        vs   )
Jedediah Cusick   )
Washington Cusick &)
William Cusick   )

        On motion of the Plaintiff by William H. Loving Esqr. attorney and it appearing to the satisfaction of the court that the Defendant Jedediah Cusick was arrested by virtue of a Ca Sa issued by Blackman Coleman a (p-463con.) Justice of the peace for this county at the instance of the plaintiff against the said Jedediah Cusick to satisfy the said plaintiff in the sum of Twelve dollars & costs which the plaintiff recovered against him before said Justice on the 18th of April 1829, and that the said defendant entered into bond with the said Washington Cusick and William Cusick as his securities to appear at this court to satisfy the debt or surrender a schedule etc. and the said Defendants having failed to appear as they were bound to do, therefore, on motion of the said Plaintiff by his said attorney it is considered by court that the Plaintiff do recover against the said Defendants the Debt aforesaid in said writ _____ (p-464) Friday 18 December 1829, and fifty cents interest thereon from the date of the Judgement before the Justices as also the costs in this behalf expended.

_____ Harper)
      vs)
Thomas Furgerson)

On motion of the Plaintiff by his attorney to dismiss the Petition in this cause for a certiorari and upon argument had thereon & by the court here fully understood it is considered by the court that the motion be sustained & on motion it is ordered by the court that a Procedents issue to Daniel Cherry esquire , directing him to issue execution against the defendant Thomas Furgerson on the Judgement before him. And it is further considered that the said plaintiff do recover against the said Thomas Furgerson and John Hardwick & Jordan M.Hansbrough his security the costs of this motion.

It is ordered by the court that Joseph N.Meredith Samuel Owens, William Conner, Stephen Booth, Henry McCoy, Ephrain Stanfield, Henry Welsh Joseph Curry, Thomas N.White, Joseph T.Haralson, James M.Henderson Benjamin Boothe, John Albright, Joseph Terry, James Bilbro, William Fitzgerald William Barcroft, Thomas G.Nixon, Edward Matthews, Nathl. D. Lilly, Benjamin Wilkes, John G.Flowers, Allen J. Barbee, William C.Russell, Calvin E.Parish, and James C.Jones be summoned to attend at the next County Court as Jurors and that Edward West be summoned as constables. Jury

(p-465) Friday 18th December 1829

Nicholas T.Perkins was this day appointed administrator with the will annexed, of Henry H.Turner late of said county deceased who gave bond in the penalty of twelve thousand dollars with Richard Nixon, John T.Turner Charles White, John P.Perkins, and Thos G.Nixon as his securities and qualified as the law directs.

Deed of conveyance from Sion Hunt to Henry H.Turner for five hundred and fifty one and one half acres of land was this day proved in open court by the oath of Charles White one of the witnesses thereto.

Deed of Conveyance from Matthew Ray attorney in fact for Thomas H.Taylor to Samuel Steele for a certain piece of ground in said deed mentioned was proved in open court by the oaths of N.W. Dill & Ferdinand L.Steele witnesses thereto and ordered to be registered.

Deed of Conveyance from Charles White to Francis S.Coxe for two

311

(p-465con.) lots of ground in Brownsville No. 29 & 37 was acknowledged
in open court and ordered to be registered.

Deed of Conveyance from Britain H.Sanders to Henry Sweeny for a
lot in Brownsville No. 51 was acknowledged in open court and ordered to
be registered.
(See entry before)

There being no further business for the Jury at this term they
were discharged & proved their attendance as follows to wit:

Charles White 4 day____John Stone 4 days Benja. Weaver 4___ Thos. G.
Nixon 4____ Henry A.Womble 4 ____ William Johnson 4_____ Paul P.Kelly
4 days.

Ordered by the court that Herndon Haralson and Simon Turner be
appointed commissions to settle with Thomas G.Nixon administrater of
John R.Leigh deceased and make report to the next term of this court.
Issd.

(p-466) Friday December 18th 1829

Upon the petition of William B.Grove. It is ordered by the court
that Lawrence McGuire, David Hay, Henry Sheppard, Samuel P.Ashe, and
Henry Johnson be appointed commissioners to divide a tract of land of
1500 acres between the heirs of Wm. B. Grave dec'd and set off and allott
to the several parties entered in said land and make return of their
proceedings to the next term of this court as the law directs.
Iss'd.

Ordered by the court that William Hollingsworth Wm. H. Henderson
Vallentine Sevier, Henry Welsh, Jordan M.Hansbrough, Allen H.Howard,
Thos. West, and Nicholas T.Perkins be appointed a jury of view to view
the McGuire road from Brownsville to the McGuire ferry in Big Hatchie
River to assertain what alterationn or changes should be made on said
road and make report of their proceedings to the next term of this court.
 Iss'd.

The Jury of view appointed at last Term to view from or near the
cross roads on the lands of Samuel P.Ashe in a direction to Somerville
and also one towards Raleigh make report that they have done the same
which is received by the court.

Court adjourned until tomorrow morning nine o'clock.

Rich'd. Nixon Char.
L. M. Guire
Sam. P. Ashe

(p-467) Saturday 19th December 1829

The court met in pursuance to adjournment-
Present the worshipful Rich'd. Nixon, Samuel P.Ashe, & Lawrence McGuire
esqrs. Justices.

(p-467con.) John C. McLemore)
vs)
Robert Sanders)

The defendant being dissatisfied with the Judgement of the court prayed and appeal to the Circuit Court of this County which is granted-He having given bond & security.

Andrew Montgomery)
vs)
Sarah J. Dyer)

The defendant being dissatisfied with the Judgement rendered against her hath prayed and appeal to the Circuit Court who gave bond and security to prosecute the same.

Court adjourned until court in course.

> Rich'd. Nixon Char.
> L. McGuire
> Sam. P. Ashe

(p-468) March 8th 1830

State of Tennessee)
Haywood County)

At a Court of pleas and quarter sessions began & holden for the County of Haywood at the Courthouse in the Town of Brownsville on the second Monday in March, 1830. It being the eight day of said month-Present the worshipful Samuel P. Ashe, Joel Estes, Nicholas T. Perkins, Lawrence McGuire, Jonathan T. Jacocks, Oliver Woods, William H. Henderson Isaac M. Johnson, Thomas Thweatt, Littleton Joyner, & Blackman Coleman.

John T. Clark a constable in Captain Wilsons Company this day tendered to the court his resignation as a constable which is accepted by the court.

John Alexander and Crowder Holloway were this day elected constables the first for Wilson's Company & the latter for in Capt. Estes Company who severally took the oaths prescribed by law, and entered into bond & security.

James H. Sims who this day produced in open court a commission from his Excelly, the Governor of this state, appointing him a Justice of the Peace in & for this County and thereupon took the several oaths prescribed by law.

John T. Turner Guardian for Simon T. Turner this day returned into court on account current for the year 1829 which is received and ordered to be recorded.

William H. Loving esquire was this day (the attorney Gen'l. being absent) appointed by the court attorney Gen'l. Pro-TTem for the Present term.

(p-469) Monday March 8th 1830

A Bill of Sale from Joseph W. Hawkins to Elisha Roberts for a negro Girl, Lucy was this day produced in open court and duly proved by the oath of Charles Wortham and John W.Wortham, subscribing witnesses thereto and ordered to be certified for registration.

Joseph N.Meredith & William Fitzgerald, jurors summoned in the venire Facias to this term are, for reasons shown, excused from attending as such at this court.

The clerk of this court being called upon by the attorney Genl. Pro-Tem for his receipts etc. for 1829 produced them of which the following are true copies viz:

Jackon, Jany. 29th 1830 . Received of Britain H.Sanders Clerk of Haywood County Court by his deputy B.Coleman six hundred and sixty two dollars and ninety six and 3/4 cents the amount of the State revinue by him collected for the year 1829 according to the commissioners return.

Jas. Caruthers
T.of Western
District,Term

Received of Britain H.Sanders, clerk of Haywood County Court by the hands of Blackman Coleman his deputy, the sum of Twenty dollars, the amount of fines & forfeitures due by said Sanders to the county trustee, agreeably, to his report from the first of October 1828 up to the first of October 1829 March 1st 1830.

Richard Nixon County Trustee

A Deed of Conveyance from Thomas Brown to David Allen for one hundred and fifty acres of land was this day proved in open court by the oaths of William C.Bruce and Harmon Frazier witnesses thereto & ordered to be registered.
Deed

A deed of conveyance from George Currie and Judieth his wife to Thomas W.Chandler for fifty three & two sevenths acres of land lying in the County of Caswell and State of North Carolina was this day produced in open court and the execution thereof was duly acknowledged in open court by the said George Currie to be his act and deed and thereupon the court proceeded to take the private examination of Judith Currie, separate apart from her husband who saith that she did of her own free will and accord execute the said deed of conveyance for the purposes in said deed mentioned-all of which is ordered to be certified.
Deed- No state tax paid.

(p-470) Monday March 8th 1830

John Moore, Guardian for Frances Hill makes a return of his account current which is ordered to be recorded.

A Bill of sale from Robert T.Smith to Polly Smith for a negro man (p-470con.) named Dick was this day acknowledged in in open court by said Robert T.Smith and ordered to be certified for registration.

A paper purporting to be the last will and testament of David Allen late of said County, deceased, was exhibited in open court & the execution thereof was duly proved by the oaths of William C.Bruce and Hial S.Allen witnesses thereto and ordered to be recorded.

Mary Allen was this day appointed administrator with the will annexed of David Allen, late of said County deceased, who took the oath prescribed by law & entered into bond with Harman Frazier, Philip A.Bruce & Hial S. Allen securities in the sum of two thousand dollars.

John Potter to Henry Welsh for one half of lot No. 68 in the Town of Brownsville was this day proved in open court by the oaths of Jacob Vick & Y.E.Allison witnesses thereto and ordered to be certified for registration. Deed

On the Petition of Joseph Jones It is ordered by the court that Charles White, Stephen Terry, Mexico B.Shearman, James Bilbro, Eli Jones, George Curry, Thomas White, or any five of them be appointed a jury to view and ascertain whether it would be any inconvenience or injury to the Public to turn the road leading by Charles Whites gin in a direction to Harrisburg so that the same will not injure the farm & plantation of Joseph Jones but which, if in the opinion of the jury should be turned, is to remain the eastern boundary of Doctor Jones land.
Iss'd.

The Jury of view appointed at last term to lay off a road from Palestine to Estanaula make report that they have done the same.

(p-471) Monday 8th March 1830

It is ordered by the court that William Johnson, senr. David Nunn, Charles R.Johnson, James Wyse, John Sanderlin, John Felts, Charles Howard & Christopher Felts, Charles Wortham, be and are hereby appointed a jury of view to view and mark a road from Harrisburg to the County line in a direction to Dyerburg and make report to the next court.
Iss'd.

William P.Young was this day fined five dollars for a contempt shown to the court & was ordered in custody of the sheriff until he secures the fine- And thereupon Joel Estes acknowledges , himself as security and agrees that execution issue jointly against them.
Iss'd.

Berry Rucker was fined five dollars for a contempt shown to this court and was ordered in custody, till the fine & costs were paid- And thereupon Joshua Abstain acknowledges himself bound as security and agrees that execution may issue jointly against them.
Iss'd.

Court adjourned until tomorrow nine o'clock.

Sam. P.Ashe J.P.

(p-471con.)   Wm. H. Henderson J.P.
                                     N.T. Perkins J.P.

(p-472)   Tuesday March 9th 1830

     The court met according to adjournment. Present the worshipful
Samuel P.Ashe, William H.Henderson, Nicholas T.Perkins, and others their
fellow justices.

     An inventory of the Estate of William Barcroft Dec'd was returned
into court & ordered to be registered.

     Deed of Conveyance from Vincent Haralson to Doctor Joseph Jones for
725 acres of land was acknowledged in open court by said Haralson & ordered to be registered.
Deed

     An Inventory of the Estate of Richard T.Moore Dec'd was this day re-
turned into court and ordered to be recorded and filed.

     The court proceeded to the election of a quorum Court for the first
year and upon balloting Samuel P.Ashe, Lawrence McGuire and John Felts
Esquires were duly elected.

     A Deed of bargain and sale from John McWhite to Henry Welsh for thirty
nine and one half acres of land was this day produced in open court and
duly acknowledged.

     A Deed of bargain & sale from Ezekiel Blackshire, to Henry Welsh for
two hundred acres of land was acknowledged in open court & ordered to be
registered.

     It is ordered by the court the following Justices being on the bench
& the ayes and noes being taken as the law directs and each of said justices voting in the affirmative, to wit: Lawrence McGuire, Samuel P. Ashe
Jesse L.Kirk, Isaac M.Johnson, William Burton, Littleton Joyner, Jono T.
Jacocks, Oliver Woods, B.Coleman, that James B.Furgerson be allowed the
sum of seven Dollars for a book purchased from him by the County Trustee
of this county for this office, to be paid by the County Trustee out of
any monies in his hands not otherwise appropriated.

(p-473)   Tuesday March 9th 1830

     It is ordered by the court (the following Justices of the peace
being on the bench & the ayes & noes being taken as the law directs, and
each of said Justices voting in the affirmative) to wit: Sam. P. Ashe,
William H.Henderson, Lawrence McGuire Jesse L.Kirk, Jonathan T.Jacocks,
L.Joyner, Isaac M.Johnson, William Burton,John Felts & Oliver Woods-
That Simon Turner and Hiram Bradford, each be allowed the sum of two dol-
lars & fifty cents pr. day for Eight days, in settling with the county
Trustee and with the sheriff of Haywood County to be paid by the County
Trustee out of any unappropriated monies in the hands of the county Trus-
tee.
Iss'd. to Turner- Iss'd. to H.Bradford Sept. 1832.

(p-473con.) It is ordered by the court that Herndon Haralson be allowed
the sum of Twenty five Dollars and Richard Nixon the sum of seventeen dollars
& fifty cents for their attention to & for settling with the county of
Madison for monies due by that county to them, the following Justices of the
peace being on the bench, to wit: Sam'l. P.Ashe, W.H.Henderson, Lawrence
McGuire Jesse L.Kirk, J.T.Jacocks, L.Joyner, Isaac M.Johnson, William
Burton, John Felts & Oliver Woods and each voting in the affirmative which
sum is to be paid by the county Trustee so soon as he received the monies
due by the County of Madison to this county.
Issued to Haralson- Issued to Nixon.

A Deed of Conveyance from Thomas H.Taylor to Robert Perry for three
acres & one hundred and twenty poles of land was this day proved in open
court by the oaths of James Carlton and Miles H.Bradford, witnesses thereto
& ordered be registered.
Deed.

(p-474) Tuesday March 9th 1830

John G.Carithers sheriff and collector of Haywood County produced in
open court his receipts from the State Treasurer and from the County Trustee
for the amount severally due them.

The court proceeded to the election of a sheriff and collector of
the public taxes for the ensuing two years, when upon counting the votes
it appeared that John G.Carithers received sixteen votes Johua Abstain
two votes and John P.Jordan one vote whereupon it was declared by the court
that John G.Carithers was duly and constitutionally elected sheriff and collector of & for the County of Haywood for the ensuing two years, who thereupon entered into bond & security and took the several oaths prescribed by
law.

The court proceeded to the election of a County Trustee in & for the
County ofHaywood when upon counting the votes it appeared that Richard
Nixon had fourteen votes and Henry Welsh had six votes- whereupon it was
declared by the court that Richard Nixon was duly & constitutionally elected County Trustee for said county, who thereupon entered into bond and
security and took the oath prescribed by law.

John G.Carithers Esqr. sheriff of Haywood County makes return of the
Venire Facias in the words and figures following (to wit)

State of Tennessee)
Haywood County   )

At a court of pleas and quarter sessions began and held for the
County of Haywood at the courthouse in the town of Brownsville on the
second Monday (p-475) Tuesday March 9th 1830 in December in the year of
our Lord 1829 It being the 14th day of said month, Present the worhsipful
Richard Nixon, Samuel P.Ashe, and Lawrence McGuire, and others their fel-
low Justices. of the peace.
It is ordered by the court that Joseph N.Meredith, Sam'l. Owen,
William Conner, Stephen Boothe, Henry McCoy, Ephraim Stanfield, Henry
Welsh, Joseph Curry, Thomas N.White, Joseph T.Haralson, James M. Henderson
Benjamin Boothe, John Albright, Joseph Terry, James Bilbro, William

(p-475con.) Fitzgerald, William Barcroft, Thomas G.Nixon, Edward Mathews, Nathaniel D.Lilly, Benjamin Wilks, John G.Flowers, Allen J. Barbee,William C.Russell, Calvin E.Parish, and James C.Jones be summoned to attend at the next court of pleas and quarter sessions on Tuesday after the second Monday in March next then and there to serve as grand or petit jurors as the case may be & that Edward West be summonedto attend said court as constable.

                              Test   B.Sanders,clerk
                                     B.Coleman Depty.

State of Tennessee

        To the sheriff of Haywood County, Greeting

        You are hereby commanded to summon the aforesaid persons to serve as Jurors at the next court of pleas and quarter sessions to be held at the Courthouse in the town of Brownsville on Tuesday after the second Monday in March next, and this they shall in no wise under the penalty prescribed by law. Herein fail not and have you then and there this writ, witness Britain H.Sanders clerk of our said court at office the second Monday in December 1829.

                              B.H.Sanders, clk
                              By B.Coleman Depty.

        Upon the back of which said return the sheriff of Haywood County hath made the following return, to wit: (p-476) Tuesday March 9th 1830, By virtue of the within Venire Facias to me directed. I have proceeded to summon all the within mentioned persons except Samuel Owens, Joseph Curry, Thomas N.White Joseph Terry, and James C.Jones, and such persons so summoned are freeholders or householders in said county.

                              J.G.Carithers, Shff.

        The following persons good and lawful men were elected drawn, sworn and charged as a grand jury for the present term (to wit) James M. Henderson, John Albright, Edward Mathews, Thomas G.Nixon, James Bilbro, John Y. Flowers, William Barcroft, Henry McCoy foreman Benjamin Wilks, Joseph T.Haralson, William C.Russell, Benjamin Booth and Ephraim Stanfield and retired under the care of Edward West a constable sworn to attend them. Grand Jury

        It is ordered by the court that Thursday next be set apart for the transaction of county business.

        Hiram Bradford and Simon Turner the commissions heretofore appointed by this court to settle with the sheriff and collector of this county and with county trustee of this county this day made report upon oath that they have done the same. which report is received and accepted by the court and ordered to be recorded.

        James Clark overseer of the road from Fayette County line to big Muddy, handed in his resignation as such which was accordingly received.

(p-477) Tuesday March 9th 1830

(p-477con.) William H.Henderson this day handed into the court a paper of which the following is a true copy, viz:

Be it remembered that on Tuesday the ninth day of March 1829 at the courthouse in the Town of Brownsville, being the second day of March term of the court of Pleas and Quarter sessions for County of Haywood in the State of Tennessee and the day pointed out by law to elect a sheriff for said county- and whereas John G.Carithers former sheriff and collector for said county John P. Jordan, Joshua Abstain, and William H.Henderson were candidates, and the said Henderson and others did then and there contend that the former shff. etc. was not eligible for the following reasons to wit first- that a legal settlement has never been made and received by the said court, altho-several several has been had except the last which had not been read to & recorded by the court & secondly that he was a defaulter to a considerable amount & that he has received considerable sums of money which he has obtained credits for by said court, and should have paid over on or before this court, neither had he made the report required of him by law to make at this term and that the court elected him without knowing whether he was not a defaulter and thereby not eligible to the said office, all of which was contrary to law and the practice of the County Courts of this State, and particularly the law regulating the sheriffs election in this State- All of which said Henderson alledges appears from the records and papers filed in said court and other testimony and the laws of the land, and that all the papers and proceedings of said court be carried up to the Circuit Court for further proceedings to be had thereon. Wm. H. Henderson.

And also the following to wit,
State of Tennessee)
Haywood County   )

Court of Pleas and Quarter sessions for Haywood County March Term 1830

(p-477A) This day a report of the commissioners of the revinue for Haywood County who had examined and re-examined the accounts between the sheriff and Trustee of said county for the last six years was produced in open court when after argument had thereon Joel Estes one of the members of said court moved the court first to recommit, said accounts to said commissions for their amendment and reversion of the same with instructions forever the want to require of the sheriff either or through the trustee to account with them for any and all monies-received by him as taxes each and every one of the six years from the property on which the court within said time had allowed him contigent credits, that they should strike a balance to shew what was, and what had not been collected thereof at the end of each year, and the amount, which was certified to remain uncollected, and at the end of the year, to be carried forward as a charge to the next years account, to keep up said balance or balances thus uncollected at the end of each year as a charge against said sheriff and Trustee till this time especially to ___ why there is so much difference between the amount of taxes in the year of 1824 & 1825, and between 1827 and 1828 and note the cause thereof, especially to call on the sheriff through the Trustee for the amount of taxes he has received, since a certain contingent credit of 1266 dollars-was allowed him at the last December Term of this court which allowance or credit he the said member of the court intended was premature and illegal and therefore don't excuse said sheriff from paying over agreeable to law such part thereof as have been since collected which motion was overruled

(p-477A) the court refusing recommitted said account to said commissioners
Secondly we the said members of the court move the court to strike the name
of John G.Carithers from the test of candidates for the office of said
sheriff of said county, for the next two years, as he had been sheriff and
collector for said county for the last six years, during which time his
accounts had not been settled in that strict and special manner pointed by
law and had not produced his list insolvents for the last year, nor sub-
scribed the oath required by law, although he was requested or required by
several of the court, not a majority, to do that as received by him since
last December him has not been accounted and not denied that a (p-478)
Tuesday March 9th 1830, a propotion of said acres has not been accounted
for, he has not produced the receipts the law requires to inable him to
be elligible to that office, that during the space of six years, in which
he has been collector of said county the taxes due the county amount to
near $12000- as shown by said report of commissioners and by the same show-
ing he has only paid over to the trustee, during the same space of time
$5645 or there abouts that within the said time he has been allowed by the
court contingent credits to the amounts of about 5240 dollars that the receipts he has obtained from the Trustee amounting to upwards of eleven
thousand dollars include their contingent credits in such phraseslogy
and form as to induce a belief that the whole was actually paid in and that
only a small portion of the credit by unreadable to 5240 dollars appear by
said report in its first part to be on lands which could not be sold for
want of bidders the residue appear to have been only temporary credits, to
allow him time collect, and therefore chargeable to him as money actually
in hand until legally accounted for, the said sheriff and collector re-
fused and wholly failed to account for these items of taxes and therefore
was inelligiable to said office, which motion was also overruled, the said
John G.Carithers was admitted as a candidate for said office, and elected
by the court for said county for the next two years to which proceeding
the said Joel Estes member of said bourt as aforesaid enters his protest,
he believeing it improper, illegal and tending much to the injury and cost
of revineu for said county as also to the Injury and oppression of the
good citizens thereof and to the end that Justice may be done in relation
to all the matters and things at first prays that the whole matter with the
accounts of settlement of said commissioners the sheriff and collectors re-
ceipts- and vouchers on which the court have acted, with all other papers
and ceficates and vouchers- which may have relation to said matters may be
carried up and laid before the Honorable the Judge of the Circuit Court of
law at the next term of said court, to be holden for said county for his
decision or said accounts (p-479) Wednesday March 10th 1830 and said
motion and the said William H. Henderson- adopts the foregoing, as additional part and reasons- and prays it may be incorporated as a part of his exceptions on the records.

Wm. H. Henderson

The court then adjourned until tomorrow nine o'clock.

Sam. P. Ashe J.P.
L.McGuire J.P.
John F.Felts J.P.

Wednesday March 10th 1830, The court met in pursuance to adjournment
Present the worshipful Samuel P.Ashe, Lawrence McGuire and John F.Felts
esquires Justices.

(p-479con.) Jesse L.Kirk   )
                     vs   )
              Albert G.Ellis   )

This day came the said parties by their attornies and thereupon
came also a jury of good and lawful men, viz, Calvin E.Parrish, William
Conner, Henry Welsh, Allen J.Barbee, Nathaniel D.Lylly, Stephen Terry,
Isaac Woods, Julius Sanders, Thomas M.Smith, David Hay, John Young and
Herdnon Haralson, who being elected, tried & sworn well & truly to try the
issue joined upon their oath do say they find the issue in favour of the
Plaintiff and assess his Damages to ten dollars and costs.

It is therefore considered by the court here that the plaintiff do
recover against the said Defendant the Damages aforesaid by the jury in
form aforesaid assessed and the costs in this behalf expended & the Defendant in mercy etc.

(p-480) Wednesday March 10th 1830

Michael M Cody   )
              vs   )   No. 4
Francis S.Coxe   )

This day came the said parties by their attornies and thereupon
came also a jury of good and lawful men, to wit, John Gamble, Bird Link,
Nelson Hartgrove, Thomas W. Pugh, Mason F.Johnson John J. James, Amos
Moore, Abia Weaver, Alexander Kirksey, Thomas N. White, James Dorris and
Wm. P. Young who being elected, tried and sworn well and truly to try the
issue joined upon their oaths aforesaid do say that they find the issue
joined in favour of the Plaintiff and assess his damages to three hundred
& fifty two dollars and fifty seven cents besides costs.
It is therefore considered by the court here that the said plaintiff
do recover against the said Defendant that Damages aforesaid by the jury
in form aforesaid assessed and the costs in this behalf expended & the
Defendant in mercy etc.

Michael M.Cody   )
              vs   )   No 5
Francis S.Coxe   )

This day came the said parties by their attornies and thereupon
came also a jury of good and lawful men to wit, John Gamble, Bird Link,
Nelson Hartgrove, Thomas W. Pugh, Mason F.Johnson, John J.James Amos Moore
Abia Weaver, Alexander Kirksey, Thomas N·White , James Dorris and William
P.Young, who being elected, tried and sworn well and truly to try the issue
joined between the parties, upon their oaths do say they find the issue
joined in favour of the Plaintiff and assess his damages to two hundred &
eleven dollars, besides costs.

It is therefore considered by the court here that the said plaintiff
do recover against the said Defendant the Damages aforesaid by the jury in
form aforesaid assessed and the costs in this behalf expended & the said
Defendant in mercy etc.

(Wednesday March 10-1830

(p-481) Alexander M.Kirksey)
     vs   ) No. 6
   Ezekial Blackshire &)
   James S.Steele   )

   This day came the said parties by their attornies and thereupon came also a jury of good & lawful men, to wit, John Gamble, Bird Link,Nelson Hargrove, Thomas W.Pugh, Mason F.Johnson, John J. James, Amos Moore, Abia Weaver, James Dorris, William P. Young, Calvin E.Parish and William Conner who being elected, tried and sworn well and truly to try the issue joined upon their oath do say they find the issue in favour of the defendants.

   It is therefore considered by the court that the Defendants go hence without day and recover against the said plaintiff their costs by them about their defence in this behalf expended etc.

John McFarland (use of J.)
 Embry   )
     vs   )
James M.Henderson   )-

   This day came the said Plaintiff by his attorney and saith that he intends no further to prosecute his said action against the said Defendant, and thereupon the said defendant by his attorney comes into court & assumes all costs in this behalf expended etc.

  Alexander M.Kirksey)
     vs   )
  Ezekial Blackshire &)
  James S.Steele   )

   Thomas Boon who was duly summoned to give evidence in behalf of the plaintiff in this cause, was this day solemnly called to come into court and give evidence as he was bound to do, came not but made default. It is therefore, on motion of said plaintiff by his attorney, considered by the court that said plaintiff do recover against the said Thomas Boon the sum of one hundred and twenty five dollars and that a sciri facias issue, etc.
Sci Fa

(p-482) Wednesday March 10, 1830

   A power of attorney from Samuel Burton to William H.Henderson was this day proved in open court by the oaths of Edmond Richmond and James B Furgerson witnesses thereto and ordered to be certified for Registration.

   A Deed of conveyance from Robt. Sanders to James C.Jones for lot No. 4, in Brownsville was proved in open court by the oaths of Edmond Richmond Simon Turner witnesses thereto & ordered to be registered.
Deed

   A deed of Trust from John Wynn & Thomas Hugh to Thomas Yandle for purposes in said deed mentioned was this day acknowledged in open court and ordered to be certified for registration (no state tax- it being personal property-

(p-482con.) James Axly this day produced in open court the wolf scalp over four months old and proved as the law directs that he killed the wolf in Haywood County. It is therefore ordered by the court (there being five Justices on the bench) that the said James Axly be allowed the sum of three dollars to be paid by the Treasurer of the Western District. Iss'd.

Daniel Johnson produced in open court the scalp of a wolf over the age of four months, and proved the killing of the wolf in Haywood County as the law directs. It is therefore ordered by the court (there being five Justices on the bench) that the said Daniel Johnson be allowed the sum of three dollars to be paid by the Treasurer of the Western District. D. Cherry- Issd.

William Bays produced in court the scalp of a wolf over four months old, and proved as the law requires that he killed said wolf in Haywood County. It is therefore ordered by the court (there being five Justices on the bench), that the said William Bayso be allowed the sum of three dollars to be paid by the Treasurer of the Western District. Issued.

(p-483) Wednesday 10th March 1830

A Deed of Conveyance from Samuel Elliott to Andrew Hamil for one acre & one hundred and twenty poles of land was proved in open court by the oaths of Hiram Bradford one of the witnesses thereto.

John P.Perkins Guardian for William R.Leigh returns into court his account current of said estate which is ordered to be recorded.

Court adjourned until tomorrow morning nine o'clock.

John F.Felts J.P.
Sam. P.Ashe J.P.
L.McGuire J.P.

Thursday morning March 11th 1830. The court met according to adjournment . Present the worshipful, John F.Felts, Samuel P.Ashe and Lawrence McGuire esqr. Justices of the Quorum.

```
Thomas N.White      )
       vs           )   No. 8
Jordan M.Hansbrough )
```

This day came the said parties by their attornies and thereupon came also a jury of good and lawful men to wit; William Powell, William Downs, Berry Rucker, Caleb Warren, Francis S.Coxe, John Mott, William P. Young, Ichabod Herring, Thomas M.Smith, Calvin E.Parish, Allen J.Barbee & Nathaniel D.Lilly who were elected tried & sworn well & truly to try the issue joined- And thereupon the said Plaintiff by his attorney comes into court and enters a non suit. It is therefore considered by the court that the Defendant go hence and recover against the Plaintiff his cost by him about his defence in this behalf expended. etc.

(p-484) Thursday 11th March 1830

(p-484con.) A Deed of bargain and sale from John G.Carithers Esqr. sheriff and for the County of Haywood to Kendal Davie was this day produced in open court and duly acknowledged for one certain part or parsel of ground being situated in the town of Brownsville known as part No. 6 as designated in the plan of said town which is duly acknowledged by John G.Carither shff. etc. and ordered to be certified for registration.

Joseph Spence's Adm.)
       vs   )
James H.Walker   )

    This cause is on the affidavit of John D.Martin esqr. continued until the next term of this court.

Jesse Kemp   )
    vs   )
Reese Porter)

    This cause is continued until the next term of this court as on the affidavit of Defendant.

    It is ordered by the court that Thomas Furgerson James Axly, Isaac Woods, James Wise, Charles Wortham, John McFarland, & John Williams or any five of them be appointed a jury of view to mark out a road from Brownsville to the county line in a direction to Dyersburg in Dyer County the nearest and best way to the county line & make report to next term.

    It being represented & made to appear to the satisfaction of this court that Benjamin Huckaby is two poor to support his infant daughter, Caroline Huckaby and that some provision should be made by this court. It is therefore ordered by the court that William H.Henderson & Blackman Coleman be appointed by this court to procure some suitable person to take charge & care of said child for one year & that said Henderson & Coleman be & are hereby authorised to draw from the County Trustee the sum of (p-485) Thursday 11 March 1830 forty dollars to be by them appropriated for the use of said child which sum the county Trustee is hereby authorized to pay (there being nine Justices on the bench & each voting in the affirmative.)
Issued to Wm.Hollingsworth for $2
    It is ordered by the court (there being nine Justices present & each voting in the affirmative) that Mrs. Nelson be allowed the sum of twelve dollars for taking care of Caroline Huckaby daughter of Benj. Huckaby to be paid by the County Trustee.
Iss'd.

    It is ordered by the court that A.B.Bradford esqr. attorney Gen'l. be allowed his tax fee of five Dollars in the following state Cases entered in this court upon which the parties were convicted of Gambling & from whom the tax fee could not be collected, to wit:
The State of Tennessee vs John Young...................... $5.00
The State vs John M.Smith.................................$5.00
The State vs Peter Lankford...............................$5.00
The State vs Stephen Childress............................$5.00
The State vs Edward Harris................................$5.00
The State vs Fra.L.Dillard................................$5.00
The State vs James Haggard................................$5.00
The State vs James Haggard................................ $5.00

(p-485con.) there being nine Justices present to wit: Saml.P.Ashe,Lawrence McGuire Dan'l.Cherry,Littleton Joiner,Oliver Woods,W.H.Henderson,Joel Estes,John M.Felts,& B.Coleman (p-486) and each of said Justices voted in the affirmative which are to be paid by the county Trustee amt. of any unappropriated money in his hands.

It is ordered by the court that Simon Turner and David Hay be and are hereby appointed commissioners of the revenue to settle with the clerk of this Circuit Court, the clerk of the County Court, the trustee of this county and with the sheriff and collector of said county for the present year.   Oral- Iss'd.

A deed of conveyance from Reubin Alphin and Polly his wife to Henry Welsh for thirty nine and one-half acres of land was proved in open court by the oaths of James W.Strother and John Mott and ordered to be register- ed.   Deed

Samuel P.Ashe Esqr.was this day unanimously chosen chairman pro tem of this court for the term.

Reece Poter was this day appointed administrator of Samuel Porter deceased who gave bond and took the oaths prescribed by law.

It is ordered by the court that Herndon Haralson, David Hay,Lawrence McGuire, Nelson Hargrove, and Alex'd. D.Gordon be appointed a jury of view to view and assertain what alterations if any should be made in the McGuire road leading from Jackson to McGuires Ferry to commence about one and a half mile above the residence of said Gordon thence down the road to McGuires Ferry and make report to the next term of this court.
Deed-Iss'd.

It is ordered by the court that Thomas Henderson be released from the double tax on 640 acres of land in the 6th Range & 9th section not listed for taxation for the year 1829.
Double tax released

It is ordered by the court that David Battle be released from the double tax on 414 acres of land in 10th District 6 range & 6 section, which has not been listed for taxation for the year 1829.

It is ordered by the court that Alfred Norman be appointed overseer of the road leading from Solomon Keltner by Thos.Nights Lewis Camels & John Smiths in a direction to the Key corner to the Dyer County line.

(p-487) David Jeffers Ind.   )
             vs   )
        James Bilbro & Stephe Terry)

This day came the said parties by their attorney and thereupon came also a jury of good and lawful men,Viz: William Powell,William Downs,Berry Rucker,Caleb Warren, Francis S.Coxe, John Mott,William P. Young,Ichabod Herring,Thomas N.White, Calvin E.Parrish,Allen J.Barbee,& Nathaniel D.Lilly who being elected tried and sworn well and truly to try the issue joined between the parties uppon their oaths do say that they find the issue in favour of the Plaintiff mentioned as the Plaintiff in declaring hath alleged and they assess the Plaintiffs damages by reason (p-487con.) thereof to Eleven dollars besides costs.

It is therefore considered by the court that the said Plaintiff do recover against the said defendants their debt in the declaration aforesaid mentioned and the damages aforesaid by the Jury assessed and his costs in that behalf expended and by agreement of the attornies for the said parties this case is to lie over untill next term when the said Deft may take an appeal to the Circuit Court.

Britain H.Sanders)
     vs)
Albert G.Ellis)

This day came the said defendant in his own proper person and says that he intends no further to prosecute his writ of certiorari and dismisses the same. It is therefore considered by the court that the said Britain H.Sanders recover against the said defendant his cost in this behalf expended.

John Lea)
   vs)
S.D.Hays)

This day came the said defendant in his proper person and saith he cannot gainsay the said plaintiff action against him for seventy eight dollars sixty one cents besides costs. It is therefore considered by the court that the said plaintiff do recover against the said Defendant the said sum of seventy eight dollars and sixty one cents and his cost in this behalf expended.

Samuel Dickens)
     vs)
James Bilbro &)
Mexico B.Sherman)

On motion of the said plaintiff by his attorney and it appearing to the satisfaction of this court that the said Plaintiff did at the December Term of this court 1829 recover against the said Defendant Bilbro and one Stephen Terry the sum of $670.50 and that an execution (p-487A) issued thereon which came into the hands of Jordan M.Hansbrough a Deputy Sheriff of this county who has made return thereon that he did on the 6th of February 1830 receive from Stephen Terry the sum of three hundred and forty nine dollars and fifty five cents and that he had on the 10th day of February levied the said execution on a negro boy named Wyatt as the property of James Bilbro to satisfy the balance of said execution and took a delivery bond for the said boy at the courthouse in the town of Brownsville on the 22nd day of February with Mexico B.Sherman security to said bond which bond was forfeited by the failure of said Bilbro and Sherman to deliver him as bound to do by their bond. Wherefore on motion of the said plaintiff by his attorney it is considered by the court that the said Plaintiff do recover against the said defendants James Bilbro and Mexico B.Sherman the sum of three hundred and forty five dollars and forty two cents it being the residue of the amount due on the Judgement aforesaid as also the costs in this behalf expended.

(p-487A) The State of Tennessee)
               vs   )
          Berry Rucker   )

This day came as well the State of Tennessee by Aled. B.Bradford attorney General as the Defendant in his proper person and the Defendant being charged says that he is guilty in manner and form as charged in the bill of Indictment and puts himself upon the mercy of the court.

It is therefore considered by the court that the defendant make his fine with the State by the payment of five dollars and all costs and that he be taken. And thereupon Jno. P. Jordan acknowledged himself bound as security with the said defendant for the payment of the cost and fine aforesaid and agrees that execution issue against them jointly for the same

Court adjourned until tomorrow nine o'clock.

                          Sam. P. Ashe Ch. Pro tem
                          John F.Felts J.P.
                          L.McGuire

Omit 488)
(p-489) Friday March 12, 1830

The court met according to adjournment Present the worshipful Saml. P.Ashe, John F. Felts and Lawrence McGuire Esqrs. Justices of the quorum.

Thornton W.Pinkard)
          vs   )
Mason F.Johnson   )

This day came the said parties by their attornies & thereupon came also a jury of good and lawful men to wit, Henry Welsh Nathaniel D.Lilly, Calvin E.Parish , Thomas M.Smith, John J.James, William Powell, William P. Young, John H.Freeman, John Young, John Gamble, Allen J.Barbee and Frederick Tyus who being elected, tried and sworn well and truly to try the issue joined & thereupon by consent of the Parties by their attornies & with the assent of the court Henry Welsh, one of the jurors of the jury aforesaid is withdrawn & the rest of the Jurors from rendering their verdict are wholly discharged.

A Deed of conveyance from Henry Welsh to Robert Bough and David Gill for one half of lot No. 68 in the Town of Brownsville was acknowledged in open court by said Welsh & ordered to be registered.
Deed

A Deed of Conveyance from Nicholas T.Perkins and David Jeffers to William Hart, Joseph Cowan and Susan his wife, Obediah Smith andElizabeth N.Smith, his wife, Wynn Dixon and Rebecca Dixon his wife of the County of Henderson and State of Kentucky for seven hundred and fifty acres of land, the execution of which was heretofore proved in open court by the oath of Young E.Allison was again produced in open court and proved by the oath of James L.Winfield, a witness thereto & ordered to be registered.
The state tax is only to be charged once-

(p-490) Friday March 12, 1830

Mason F.Johnson   )
      vs   )
Thomas G.Nixon adm.)
of John R.Leigh   )

     This day came the said plaintiff by his attorney and saith that he
intends no further to prosecute his said action against the said Defendant
and dismisses the same. It is therefore considered by the court here that
the Defendant go hence without day and recover against the said Plaintiff
his costs in this behalf expended & the Plaintiff in mercy etc.

     It is ordered by the court that Samuel P.Ashe, Lawrence McGuire,
Daniel Cherry, Benjamin G.Alexander, Jonathan T.Jacocks, David Hay,
Wilson A.W.Mann, Simon Turner, Hiram Bradford, John Roddy, Littleton
Joyner, John Williams, Richard Taylor, Isaac M.Johnston, John F.Felts,
James Carlton, James Malden, Joseph Jones, Nicholas T.Perkins, Joseph
Murphy, Charles White, Samuel Green, Robert Pickins, William H. Burton,
Joel Estes, Jessee Walling be summoned to attend at the next Circuit
Court to be holden for this county, then and there to serve as Grand or
Petit jurors as the case may be, and that Mansfield Ware be summoned to
attend said court as constables.
Jury

     It is ordered by the court that John Young, Francis S.Coxe,
Benjamin Weaver, Matthew Picket, Henry Welsh, Samuel Owen, James Sanders,
James Henderson Philip Bruce, Thomas W.Pugh, David Nunn, Thomas G.Nixon,
James Armstrong, Griffeth Edwards, Robert M.Spicer, James Burton, Isaac
Koonce, Adam Hawkins, Herndon Haralson, Daniel Shaw, Alfred Simpson,
Lancaster Given, Azariah Thompson, Bird Link, Nelson Hargrove, and Milton
McDearman be summoned to attend at our next County Court then & there to
serve as Grand Petit jurors- and that Edward West be summoned to attend
said court as constables .

     A Deed of conveyance from William Hart, Joseph Cowan Susan Cowan,
Obediah Smith, Elizabeth Smith, Wynn Dickson, Rebecca Dixon, by their attorney
in fact Archibald Dickson to David Jeffers & Nicholas T.Perkins for seven
hundred & fifty acres of land the Execution of which was heretofore proved
in this court by the oath of Y.E.Allison was again presented to the court
& proved by the oath of James L.Winfield a witness to the same & ordered
to be Registered.
Deed, the State Tax is only to be charged once
(p-491) Friday 12 March 1830

     A deed of conveyance from Samuel P.Ashe to Fountain G.McGee for
one hundred & sixteen & one fourth acres of land was acknowledged in open
court by said Ashe and ordered to be registered.
Deed.

     A Deed of conveyance from Samuel P.Ashe to Ephraim Walls for three
quarters   acres or thereabouts of land was acknowledged in open court
by said Ase and ordered to be Registered.
Deed

(p-491con.) A Deed of conveyance from Sam. P.Ashe to Fountain McGee for three quarter acres or thereabouts of land was acknowledged in open court by said Samuel P.Ashe & ordered to be Registered.
Deed

A deed of conveyance from Samuel P.Ashe to Lawrence McGinnis for about three quarter acres of land was acknowledged in open court by said Ashe and ordered to be registered.
Deed

Simon Turner & Herndon Haralson commissioners appointed to settle with Thomas G.Nixon administrator of the estate of the estate of John R. Leigh dec'd make report to this term that they have done the same which is received by the court & ordered to be recorded.

```
Robert Jaffray &      )
David Brown Crane     )   No. 13
        vs            )
James H.Clark         )
```

This day came the said parties by their attornies & came also a jury of good & lawful men, to wit, Henry Welsh, Nathaniel D.Lilly, Calvin E.Parish, Thos. M. Smith, John J.James, William Powell, William P.Young, John H.Freeman, John Young, John Gamble, Allen J.Barbee and Frederick Tyus who being elected tried and sworn well & truly to try the issue joined upon their (p-492) Friday March 12, 1830 oath do say that they find the issue in favour of the said plaintiff and assess their damages to six hundred and twenty six dollars and sixty two cents besides costs. It is therefore considered by the court that the said Plaintiffs do recover against the said Defendant the damages aforesaid by the Jury in form aforesaid assessed and the costs in this behalf expended etc. and the Defendant in mercy etc.

```
Robert Jaffray & Co.  )
        vs            )
James H.Clark         )
```

This day came the said parties by their attornies & came also a Jury of good and lawful men viz, Henry Welsh, Nathaniel D.Lilly, Calvin E.Parish, Thomas M. Smith, John J.James, William Powell, William P.Young, John H. Freeman, John Young, John Gamble, Allen J.Barbee and Frederick Tyus, who being elected, tried & sworn well and truly to try the issue joined upon their oath do say that they find the issue in favour of the plaintiffs and assess, their damages to seven hundred and fifty seven dollars and fifty nine cents & costs.

It is therefore considered by the court that the plaintiffs do recover against the Defendant the damages aforesaid by the jury assessed and the costs in this behalf expended etc. & the defendant in mercy etc.

```
John R.Acre           )
        vs            )
Thomas G.Nixon        )
```

This day came the parties by their attornies and came also a Jury of good & lawful men to wit, Henry Welsh, Nathaniel D.Lilly, Calvin E.

(p-492con.) Parish, Thomas M.Smith, John J.James, William Powell,William P.Young,John H.Freeman,John Young,John Gamble,Allen J.Barbee and Frederick Tyus who being elected, tried and sworn well and truly to try the issue joined upon their oaths do say that the Defendant hath not paid the Debt of one hundred dollars in the Plaintiffs declaration mentioned as the Plaintiff in declaring hath alledged, and they assess the Plaintiffs damages by reason thereof to four dollars and seventy five cents besides costs. It is therefore (p-493) considered by the court that the said Plaintiff do recover against the said defendant the Debt aforesaid in the declaration mentioned and the damages aforesaid by the jury in form aforesaid assessed and costs in this behalf expended & the Defendant in mercy etc.

Nancy Bigley   )
            vs)
William Powell)

      This cause, is by consent of the parties by their attornies set for trial at the next term of this court.

      Samuel Dickins assigned of H.R.W.Hill Executor, of Joseph Branch Dec'd.
      vs
Blackman Coleman

      This day came the defendant in his proper person & saith that he cannot gainsay the said plaintiffs action against him for the sum of five hundred and seventy dollars besides costs & confesses Judgement for the same. It is therefore considered by the court that the Plaintiff do recover against the Defendant the said sum of five hundred & seventy dollars & the costs in this behalf expended & the Defendant in mercy etc.

The State of Tennessee)
            vs   )
William P.Young   )

      This day came as well the state by Alexander B.Bradford esqr. atto. Genl. as the Defendant in his proper person, and the Defendant being charged saith is guilty in manner & form as charged in the bill of Indictment & puts himself upon the grace & mercy of the court. It is therefore considered by the court that the Defendant make his fine with the state by the Payment of five dollars & all costs & that he be taken & thereupon John Young. acknowledges himself bond as security for the fine & costs aforesaid and agrees that Execution may issue against them therefor.

(p-494) Friday March 12,1830

      It is ordered by the court that the order made at the last term of this court upon the petition of William B.Grove,appointing Lawrence McGuire, David Hay, Henry Sheppard, Samuel P.Ashe & Henry Johnson, commissioners to divide a tract of land of 1500 acres between the heirs of William B.Grove dec'd and to set off to said parties interested in said land their respective portions, be revived & issued accordingly. Iss'd.

And the court adjourned until tomorrow morning nine o'clock.

(p-494con.)   W.H.Henderson J.P.
                               John F.Felts J.P.
                               Dan'l.Cherry J.P.

        Saturday morning March 13,1830 The court met according to adjourn-
ment Present the worshipful William H.Henderson, John F.Felts and Daniel
Cherry esqrs. Justices

William J.Herbert assee)
            vs   )
 John Wilson   )

    This day came the said plaintiff by his attorney and the said De-
fendant being solemnly called and came not but made default It is therefore considered by the court here that the said plaintiff do recover
against the said Defendant the residue of the Debt in the declaration
mentioned of one hundred dollars and six dollars damages for the detention
thereof, besides the costs in this behalf expend.

Michael M.Cody   )
        vs   )
Francis M.Coxe   )

    The defendant being dissatisfied with the Judgement rendered against
him hath prayed and obtained an appeal to the next Circuit Court of this
County- He having given bond and security to prosecute the same.

Michael M.Cody   )
        vs   )
Francis S.Coxe   )

    The defendant being dissatisfied with the judgement rendered
against him hath prayed an appeal to the next Circuit Court of this county
He having given bond and security to prosecute the same.

    (p-495) Saturday March 13, 1830

John B.Acre   )
        vs   )
Thomas G.Nixon   )

    The defendant being dissatisfied with the Judgement Judgement
rendered against them prays and appeals to the next Circuit Court of this
county, who gave bond and security therefor.

        Nicholas T.Perkins administrator with the will annexed of Henry H.
Turner deceased makes report to this court of an inventory & amount of
sales of the Estate of said H.H. Turner which is ordered to be recorded.

State of Tennessee) March Term 1830
Haywood County   )

    I, John G.Carithers sheriff and collector of the public taxes for
the County of Haywood make report to court of the following tracts of
land and town lots listed for Taxation in said county for the year 1829
the Taxes on which remains due and unpaid and that the respective owners

or claimants thereof have no goods or chattels in said county on which I could
strain for the satisfaction of said taxes for said years to wit:

ers Names	No.Acres	Dist	Range	Sect.	No.Entry or Grant	Water course	Town Lots	Number
e,S.P.&								
drick	1500	10	5	8	E2147	B.H.		
xander &								
.Bills	371	10			E908			
d Robert	480	10	6	8	996			
ant Stephen	4	10						
ant Stephen							3	
ckfan,Jesse	860	11	1	9	407			
low E.							1	102
d Andrew	338 3/4	10	6	9	part of B.Smiths 5000	acre tract		
ton Samuel	200	10	4	7&8	part of grant 308			
ton Thos.H.	200	"	"	"	part of Do			
ar Elisha	278	10	5	10	part of W.T.Lewis 15000 acre tract			
okBignal	500	11	2	8				
rk,James P.	640	11	1	6	part of Campbells tract			
b,Robert L.	345	10	6	8&9				
ment Simon	185	10	4	11	256			
pbell Arthur	640	11	1	6		B.M.		
496)								
ldress John's								
resentative	935	11	1	6	453	B.M.		
ick Jedediah	833	10	4	8&9				
sm James	2100	10	4	9	20,202			
wford W.H.	320	10	5	11	128	part of J.C.McLemore's 500 acres		
ldress, Stepeh S.								
rdian for his								
Joel	465	10	5	11				
kins Samuel	200	10	4	8	E219			
son William	223¼	10	5	11	776			
iel Robert	75	10	4	10	entered in the name of E.Howard			
ke Robert Heirs								
	1000	10	5&6	10,11	part of D.Sheltons 3000 acre			
l George W-	47	10	6	10	90 part of W.T.Lewis 1000 acres			

Owners Names	No.Acres	Dist	Range	Sect.	No.Entry or Grant	Water course	Town Lots	Number
Same	230	10	5	10		part of Lewis 1500 acres		
Earl Jno.B .	290	10	6	10	90 part of Lewis 1500 acres			
Earl Jno.B.	45	10	5	10	part of Lewis 1500 acres			
Ditto	237	10	5	10	90 part of 1000 acres to Lewis			
Foster Robert	3000				part of grant 403			
Fort Jacob							1	
Green Thos.J.	200	10	4	8				
Gibbs,George W.	500	10	6	6	413 in the name of the Repr. of Armstrong			
Groves Wm.B.								
Heirs	1500	10	5	7.8	B.H.			
Hughs Robert	124				2140			
Houston Robt.	100	10	5	11	638			
Henderson Thos.	480	10	4.5	9	part of 640			
Ditto-do-							5	
Same	200	11	1	6.7	entered in the name of A.H.Howard			
Same	100				entered in the name of G.W.Jones			
Same	100	10	4	10	entered in the name of W.H.Henderson			
Same	50				entered in the name of Redding Hare			
Andrew Hamilton							2	
Hockly,Geo:(W:) for P.Wescott)	1368	11	2	9	295 part of Rices 5000 acres			
Same	2848	11	1	8.9	291 " " " " "			
Same	1596	11	1	8.9	282 " " Do Do			
Same	1017	10	6	8	287 " " Rices 5000 acres			
Same	1981	10.11	6.1	7.8	294 part of Rices 5000 acres			
Hockly, G.W.	833	10	5.6	11	60 part of 1000 acres Grant to W.Lewis			
Hart James	984	11	2	6	part of 2560 in the name of James Hart (p-497)			
Hannon William	39	10	6	10	part of 1000 acres Granted to W.T.Lewis			
Same	241	10	5	10	part of 1500 Grant to do			
Harman Edward	282	--	5		part of do			
Hollady Samuel	108	10	4	10.11	in the name of J.W.Pike			
Harrelston Henry P.50								
Jones Calvin	560	10	5	9	E514			
Jackson Andrew	640	10	5	11	772	Entered in the name of McLemore		
Same	180	10	5	11	128	part of 500 acres in the name McLemore		

ers Names	No.Acres	Dist	Rang	Sect.	No.Entry or Grant	Water course	Town Lots	Number
nes Silas	357	10	5.6	11	60	part of Grant in the name of W.T.Lewis		
anaugh,								
liam	12	10	4	6				
is John	82	10	6	10		part of Lewis 1000 acres tract		
ne	222	10	5	10		part of Lewis 1500 acres		
ver, John	1000	11	2	10.11	E795			
ne	640	10	5	6	556			
ne	674	10	5	10	406	part of Grant		
ne	1851	10	5.6	10				
ver Duncan							3 Town lots	
phrey A.D.	600	10	6	7.8		B.H.		
emore Robt.								
rs	480	10	6	6	E1116			
emore & Wilson	5000	10.11	6.1	7.8	₵200/	the name of Rice		
ne	5000	11	1.2	7.8	2199			
rton Thos,								
rs	1000	10	5	7	G272			
k & Deveraux	500	10	5	11				
k Ezekial	500	10	6	6.7				
lips Abraham	1000	10	6	8	E2175			
nce William	225	10	6	10		part of Lewis 1000 acre tract		
ne	59	10	5	10		part of Lewis 1500 acre tract		
l Labon P.	40	10	6	10		part of Lewis 1000 acre tract		
ne	239	10	5	10		part of Lewis 1500 tract		
y Mathew	360	10	6	9				
ne	1250	10	4	11	E632			
d John &								
ers	200	10	5	11	126			
J C M)								
wen William P.	660	10	4	7	589	party of the Moore tract		
J C M)								
ddy Ephraim	275	10	5	10		part of Lewis Tract		
th William H.	67½	10	6	11				
th Furdenan	1085	10	6	11		part of Grant 403		
dder Philip J.	1000	10	5	9	E328			
ns Wattes B.	640	11	1	6				

Owners Names	No.Acres	Dist	Rang	Sect.	No.Entry or Grant	Water course	Town Lots
Shelton James	2000	10	5.6	10.11	part of D Shelton 3000		
(p-498)							
Talbot & Bryant							1
Tisdell James							
Heirs	4000	10,11	6	8.9	G414 part		
Tishell James							
Heirs	5592	10	6	8-9	G415	1	
Same	5883	11	1	11	412	11	
Same	3296	10	6	9	410	"	
Same	5344	10	6	11	411	"	
Taylor Thos H.	525	10					1
Webb,James	980	11	2	9	690		
Williamson Benj.	1280						
Windsor,John							
Heirs	850	10	5	7.8	279 part of 1000 acre tract		
William Robt. W.	170	10	5	11			
Wheaton Jno. L.		10	6	11	403 part of grant		
Same	2218	11	1	10	400 part of		
Wheaton Mary	2786	10	6	10	410 part of		
Whitton Silas R.	51	10	5	10	part of Lewis 1500 acre tract		
Same	225	10	6	10	90 part of		
Murry John	100	10	5	9	entered in the name of Barcroft		
Same	100	10	6	9	part of Russells Entry		
Same (53½)	53 3/4	10	5	7			
Same	10	10	4	5	1504		
Same	21	10	5	9	1944 by E.Bryans		
Same	50	10	4	9	1809 part of		
Same							2 nos 41-45
Same	72	10	5	8.9	1330		
Same	228	10	4	7.8	part of E.Robertson Entry		
Murry James	200	10	5	9	entered in the name of Stewart		
James David	640	10	5	9			
Bond Eaton	100	10	4	7	2283		
Bond Thomas	100	10	4	7			
Joiner Matthew	185						
Overton John	1000	10	5	11	155		

(p-498con.) Whereupon it is considered by the court (there being a majority of the Justices of said county present) that judgment be and is hereby entered against the said several tracts of land and town lots in the name of the State of Tennessee for the amount of Taxes,costs and charges severally due thereon for the year 1829, and it is further order-ed by the court that said several tracts of land and town lots or so much (p-499) respectively as shall be sufficient of each of each of said tracts and Town lots be sold to satisfy the taxes costs and charges severally due thereon.

Jordan M.Hansbrough who was at this term elected a constable for Haywood County in Captain Elliotts Company this day appeared in open court and took the several oaths prescribed by law and gave bond with Edward West & William H.Loving as security.

It is ordered by the court that Samuel Conyers be released from the double tax on eight acres of land & 1 white poll for 1829 and pay the sheriff the single tax, and that Thomas Needham be released from the Double Tax on 1000 acres for 1829 not being given in & pay the single Tax on the same.
Double Tax released.

It is ordered by the court that William H.Henderson and Blackman Coleman be appointed to superintend the repairing the jail of this county that they be authorised to employ some person to repair the jail, and that they be allowed the sum of twenty five dollars to be by them applied for that purpose which sum is to be paid by the county trustee out of any unappropriated monies in his hands not otherwise appropriated (there being nine (p-500) justices on the bench & each of said justices voting in the affirmative.

The Grand jury returned into court and there appearing no further business for their consideration at this term were discharged and _____ their attendance,viz: Henry McCoy 5 days James M.Henderson five days
 John A Wright 5___   Edward Matthews 5 days
Thomas G.Nixon 5, James Bilbro 5 John G.Flowers 5_ William Barcroft 5

Benjamin Wilkes 5   Joseph T.Harralson 5   William C.Russell 5
Benjamin Boothe 5   Ephraim Stanfield 5   Edward West constable five-
and Sidney P.Smith constable five days.

Bowen Reynolds was this day appointed of Gideon Pace who gave bond and security and took the oath prescribed by law.

It is ordered by the court that the following persons be and are hereby appointed commissioners under the act of the General assembly of the State of Tennessee of 1829 for the purposes in said acts mention-ed in the following Captains Companies in this county, to wit:
in Capt. Tweedys company John F.Felts Esqr. in Captain Worthams Company, Daniel Cherry esqr. in Captain Parkers company, James Sanders,in Captain Estes Company- Joel Estes Esqr. In Captain Elliots company- Bowen Reynolds
In Captain McDearman's Company- Blackman Coleman.
In Captain Burtons Company W.H.Burtons
In Captain Sullivans Company- James H.Walker
In Captain Kennys Company, William Pace

(p-500con.) In Captain Johnson's Company- Samuel P.Ashe
In Captain Wilson's Company Alfred Simpson and that the clerk of this
court issue an order notifying each of said commissioners of their appointment & that the sheriff proceed forth-with to serve such notifica-
tions.
Iss'd.

It is ordered by the court (there being a majority of the justices
present) that the Taxes for the present year be as follows: in addition
to the State Tax, to wit, that there be a county tax of 18 3/4 cents on
each 100 acres of land, on each slave 18 3/4 , on each white poll $12\frac{1}{2}$
cts, on each pleasure carriage one half the amount of the state Tax, on
each merchant five dollars, on each stud horse or Jack half the price
of the State Tax, on each Town lot $37\frac{1}{2}$ cents, and that there be a poor
tax of $6\frac{1}{4}$ cents on each 100 acres of land & on each slave, also a jury
tax of 25 cents on each 100 acres of land & a Bridge Tax of $12\frac{1}{2}$ do on
each 100 acres of land (tax 1830-)

(p-501) The State of Tennessee   )
                    vs   )
              James S.Steele   )

This day came as well the state of Tennessee by Alexander B.
Bradford esqr. attor. Genl. and the Defendant in his proper person and
the Defendant being solemnly charged saith he is guilty in manner and
form as charged in the bill of Indictment & puts himself upon the grace
and mercy of the court. It is therefore considered by the court that
the said Defendant make his fine with the state of Tennessee upon the
payment of one dollar & all costs and that he be taken.

The State of Tennessee)
                vs   )
John H.Freeman   )

This day came as well the State of Tennessee by A.B.Bradford esqr.
atto. Gen'l. as the Defendant in his proper person and the defendant being charged says he is guilty in manner and form as charged in the bill
of Indictment and puts himself upon the grace and mercy of the court,
It is therefore considered by the court that the Defendant make his fine
with the State of Tennessee by the payment of one dollar & all costs.

It is ordered by the court that John G.Carithers sheriff & collect-
or of this county be allowed a credit with the Treasurer of the western
District for the sum of nine dollars, thirty seven and one half cents on
five thousand acres of land improperly listed for Taxes for 1829 in the
name of McLemore & Wilson- and- also that he be allowed a credit - with
the commissioners of the Bridges Fund of $ 6.25 on said tract of land
and also a credit of nine Dollars thirty seven & $\frac{1}{2}$ cents with the county
Trustee on said tract of land and (p-502) also a credit with the
county Trustee on account of jury tax of Eighteen Dollars & seventy five
cents on account of the jury Tax, etc.

(p-502con.) Matthew Barrow)
John C.McLemore &)
John P.Clark) Motion in arrest of
vs) Judgment
Hiram Bradford adm. of)
Robert A.Penn & Matthew Ray)

This day came the parties by their attornies & the matters of law
arising upon the defendant being heard by the court and fully understood
by the court, it is considered by the court that the said motion in arrest
of judgment be overruled and for nothing held, and that the said plaintiffs
have execution on the judgement heretofore at the last term of this court
rendered in this cause

It is ordered by the court that the commissioners of the county
Revenue, appointed for the year 1830 be directed to call on the clerk of
Haywood County Court for the report of the late commissioners, together
with all the papers or documents he may have in relation thereto, or
will afford any information in ascertaining the items which constitute
the balances due the County of Haywood in each and every year, according
to the said report, as well as the balances due in (to tax) the persons
from whom due and to whom chargeable to carry those balances forward and
charge them as they should be - To compare the Tax lists of the several
years past and the present, and determine, if possible, the cause of the
difference in the amount of the several years past and the present,and
correct all errors & irregularities in the proceedings, if any by which
the county has or may sustain any injury in the single or double taxes or
any other way and apply the remedy , if practicable, and suggest such
plans, ways or means as they may approve of for the benefit of the (p-503)
county revenue to the next term of this court and that the clerk of this
court issue a copy of this order to each of the commissioners of the
revenue appointed for the present year.

The court adjourned until court in course.

Sam.P.Ashe chr. Pro.Tem
Joel Estes J.P.
John F.Felts J.P.
Dan'l. Cherry J.P.
William H.Henderson J.P.

(p-504) blank

(p-505) Record of the returns of the constables of Haywood County on
elections for Common School Commissioners held on the 1st Saturday in June
1838

Joab Harrell constable for District No. 1 reports that he advertised
and met agreeable to law at the election presinct of said District for
the purpose of electing five common school commissioners, and could not
hold an election for want of voters, June 2nd 1838.
District no. 1

Signed,
Joab Harrell, constable

(p-505 con.) Constable for District No. 2 reports that Dist. No. 2
held an election agreeable to law at election presinct of District No.
2 and that the following named persons were duly and constitutionally
elected common school commissioners for said District, to wit: Silas
M.Caldwell, Solomon Payne, Benjamin G.Alexander, Isaac Dancey & John
Coppage, June 2nd 1838. Dt. No. 2

Mitchell Tate constable for District No. 3 reports that he opened
and held an election agreeable to the election presinct of said District
No. 3 for the purpose of electing common school commissioners, and that
the following named persons were duly & constitionally elected, to wit:
David L.Ray N.Hardy, James Coxe, Joseph B.Stanton, & John Ianery, June
2nd 1838.
Dist No. 3

Signed,
M.Tate C.H.C

Abel Jones constable of District No. 4 makes report that he
opened and held an election at the eledtion presinct of said District
agreeable to law, for the purpose of electing common school commissioners
for said District No. 4 and that Wright Nicholson, Samuel Brown, William
Barbee, Washington Currie and John Brantley were duly and constitutionally
elected June 2nd 1838.
Dist. No. 4

Signed
Abel Jones,Const.H.C.

John H.Cobb constable in District No.5, makes report that he opened
and held an election at the election prect. in said in said District
agreeable to law, for the purpose of electing common school commissioners
and that Richard Taylor, McNairy Newell, Edward Jones, Jesse D.Joyner
and Joel L.Abston were duly and constitutionally elected June 2nd 1838
No. 5

Signed,
Jno. H.(editors note; torn off)

(p-506) Whitehead constable of District No. 6, makes report that he
opened and held an election at the election presinct in sd. District
agreeable to law for the purpose of electing common school commissions
and that Hamilton W.Cotter, John P.Perkins, Jacob Smith, John Chilton &
James C.Jones were duly and constionally, June 2nd 1838
No.6

Whitehead const.

Edward Ware constable of District No.7 certifies that he opened and
held an election in the town of Brownsville, agreeable to law for the pur-
pose of electing common school commissioners for said district,and that
Herndon Haralson, Robert McLogan, Howell Taylor, Thomas Owen & John
Sangster Sen. were duly elected.
No. 7

No election in District No. 8 for the reason no voters attended.
No 8,

(p-506con.) There being no constable for District No.9 Wm.G.Turner D.S.
Certified that he opened and held an election agreeable to law for com-
mon school commissioners for said District,and that Green H.Bradford,
Thornton Easley, Richard O.Britton, George W.Young & Anthony Carlton were
duly & constitutionally elected 2nd June 1838.
No. 9

                                        Signed
                                        W.G.Turner D.S.

        Constable of the 10th Civil District reports that he opened and
held an election agreeable to law at the election pressinct of said
District, and that Alexander Boyd, Matthew D.Anderson, Allen J.Barbee,
 Jas.L.Green and John Coltart were duly & constitutionally elected common
school commissioners for said District June 2nd 1838
No.10

        James F.Smothers the constable of District No.11 certifies that he
opened and held an election at the election precinct of District No.11,
agreeable to law, and that John McFarland,M.S.Moss,J.F.Wortham,R.Burns,
and A.Lewis, were duly & conditionally elected common School Commissioners
for said District June 2nd,1838.
No.11

                                        Signed
                                        J.F.Smothers,Cons. of the 11
                                        District

        The constable of District No. 12 certified that he opened and held
an election at the election presint of said District,agreeable to law, and
that George Henry,Giles Hawkins,Henry Winburn, G.R.Johnson, H.L.Blackwell
were duly and constitutionally elected common school commissioners for said
District No. 12_____   June 2nd 1838
No. 12
                        Jas.P.Cavanaugh C.H.C

(p-507) RECORD OF THE REPORT OF THE CONSTABLES OF HAYWOOD COUNTY ON THE
ELECTIONS BY THEM HELD FOR COMMON SCHOOL COMMISSIONER FOR THE YEAR 1840

District No. 1 Election 7th March at improper time

District No.2 Election held at improper time-

District No.3 election held at improper time

District No.4 Samuel Brown,Wright Nicholson, and Joseph Stokely,elected
as pr report.

District No.5 John Williams Dempsey Nowell & Jessee Currie elected as pr.
report (J.H.Cobb const.)

District No. 6 James C.Jones Jacob C.Smith & John Chilton elected, said
Chilton having since died the board has appointed Thomas J.Mulhollan to
fill the vacancy.

District No.7 William A.W.Mann, John Sangster and John Tugwell, elected
as pr. report of A.F.McCann Const.

(p-507con.) District No. 8 no election at the proper time.

District No.9 no election at the proper time.

District No. 10, Jno. Coltart, M.D.Anderson & Jno.H.Halliburton elected
as pr.report.

District No.11, Thomas Green, Ralph Williams & Wm.Edwards elected,
Thomas Green, refusing to act, the vacancy is filled by appointing Isaac
M.Johnson.

District No.12, David Whitaker John F.Felts & David Nunn, elected as
pr. report-

THE END

-A-

AANDERSON [SIC]
DANIEL, 153
ABBOT
CHARLES R., 95
ABLE
GEORGE, 120
MORRIS, 23
ABLES
GEORGE, 112, 113,
114, 115, 125,
126, 252, 256,
270
JOE, 200
JOSEPH, 171, 184,
187, 217, 226,
242, 243
ABSTAIN
JOEL, 175, 181,
193(2), 205
JOEL L., 163
JOHUA [SIC], 316
JOSHUA, 11, 31, 35,
36, 39, 53, 88,
101, 120, 151,
180, 187, 193,
203, 227, 228,
233, 238, 279,
290, 293, 314,
318
JOSIAH, 227, 228
ABSTEN
JOSHUA, 26, 31, 55
ABSTON
JOEL L., 338
JOSHUA, 67, 285,
286, 288
ACRE
JOHN B., 330
JOHN R., 328
ADAMS
JOHN, 293
AKIN
WILLIAM A., 144
ALBERTSON
JOHN, 203
RUTH, 203
ALBRIGHT
JOHN, 142(2), 256,
257, 268, 272,
273, 310, 316,
317
ALEXANDER
A.R., 246
ADAM R., 269
B.G., 271
BENJA. G., 304
BENJAMIN G., 238,
256, 257, 264,
271, 287, 293,
327, 338
HENDRICK, 331
JOHN, 312

ALFIN
REUBEN, 36
REUBIN, 10, 11(2),
14, 16, 22, 28,
31, 52, 71
RUBIN, 16(2)
ALLBRIGHT
JOHN, 137, 283
ALLEN
DAVID, 92, 111, 112,
120, 313, 314(2)
EDWARD, 92
HIAL S., 314
HIED., 92
MARY, 314
WILLIAM M., 298
ALLISON
Y.E., 303, 314, 327
YOUNG E., 293, 303,
304, 306, 307,
308, 309, 326
ALLPHIN
REUBEN, 106, 110,
125, 137
REUBIN, 162, 164
ALLREAD
WILLIAM, 153
ALPHIN
JAMES R., 94
POLLY, 324
REUBEN, 44, 85, 94,
44a
REUBIN, 50, 110,
116, 121, 140,
142, 148, 151,
175, 176, 203,
275, 324
ALPIN
REUBEN, 47
ALREAD
WILLIAM, 35
WM., 51
ALRED
WILLIAM, 22, 230,
274
ALSTON
ALFRED, 75
ANDERSON
GEORGE, 153
JOHN, 153, 247
M.D., 340
MATTHEW D., 339
WALKER, 153
WILLIAM, 290, 302
ANDREWS
CULLIN, 182
HARRIET, 182
JAMES, 182
JANE, 182
JOHN, 151, 164, 165,
167, 182, 193,
204
LEMUEL, 182
MARY, 182
SARAH, 182

APLIN
JAMES R., 95
APLING
JAMES R., 152
ARMOIN
WILLIAM, 264
ARMON
WILLIAM, 260
ARMOUR
WM., 216
ARMSTRONG
JAMES, 256, 272,
297, 327
JAS. S., 230
JOHN, 297
MARTIN, 7, 75
MARTIN R., 17
ARNOLD
ELIJAH, 238, 257,
287
ELISHA, 174
LEVI, 293
MATTHEW, 165
WILLIAM, 103, 128,
166
WM., 115
ARTHUR
WILLIAM, 7, 17, 75,
153, 247
ASH
MARY B., 87
S.P., 257
SAMUEL P., 50, 68,
87, 92
ASHBROOK
MOSES, 153
ASHE
& STRUDWICK, 233
BENSON, 69
J.P., 161
S.P., 159, 331
SAM P., 134, 177,
251
SAM'L P., 150, 176,
177, 253, 281,
284, 286, 289,
297, 304, 316
SAM. P., 91, 147,
170, 178, 181,
204, 216, 252,
293, 312, 314,
328, 337
SAML. D., 88
SAML. P., 175, 203,
268, 324, 326
SAMUEL D., 87
SAMUEL P., 31, 33,
34, 39, 67, 69,
88, 102, 104,
118, 120, 134,
136, 137, 141,
151, 152, 164,
170, 171, 178,
181, 193, 202,
203, 204, 207,

208, 209, 211,
212, 219, 220,
221, 222, 223,
237, 238, 243,
256, 264, 265,
270, 271, 272,
277, 288, 294,
300, 303, 311,
312, 315, 316,
319, 322, 324,
327, 328, 329,
336
ATCHISON
[BLANK], 181
AXELY
JAMES, 301
AXLEY
JAMES, 39, 52, 53,
94, 95(2), 101,
244, 253, 254,
257, 267, 274
NIMROD, 100, 101(2),
125, 138, 187,
269
ROBERT, 10(2), 11,
25, 101
ROBT., 107
AXLY
JAMES, 322, 323

-B-

BAGLER
NATHAN, 7
BAKER
ROBERT, 153, 247
BALCH
WILLIAM, 122, 166,
174, 197, 201,
250
WM., 108, 109, 122
BALDRIDGE
ALFORD, 153
ALFRED, 230
FRANCES, 17
FRANCIS, 7, 230
BANE
& WALKER, 189
BAPTIST
JOHN G., 195
RICHARD H., 195
WILLIAM, 195
BARBE
ALLEN J., 190
BARBEE
ALLEN J., 129, 193,
204, 213, 214,
255, 291, 310,
317, 320, 322,
324, 326, 328,
329, 339
WILLIAM, 338
BARCROFT
GEORGE, 308
WILLIAM, 171, 175,

181, 226, 228,
291, 310, 315,
317(2), 335
BARICROFT
WM., 107
BARNET
ROBT. W., 247
BARRET
ROBERT W., 153
BARRINGTON
JAMES, 11, 27, 31,
39, 53, 54
WASHINGTON, 26
BARRINTINE
WASHINGTON, 35
BARROW
& VAULX, 7, 17
MATHEW, 296
MATTHEW, 259, 337
BARRY
W., 65
BARRYCROFT
WILLIAM, 183
BATTLE
DAVID, 324
BAXTER
JAMES, 32
JOSEPH, 206, 213
BAYES
PARSON, 255
BAYLER
NATHAN, 17
BAYS
WILLIAM, 322
BENJAMIN
ANDREW [?], 233
GEO., 233
BENTON
SAMUEL, 331
THOS. H., 331
BERRYCROFT
[BLANK], 66
BEVILL
JOHN, 169, 172
BEVINS
WILLIAM, 111
BIGGES
PARSON, 23
BIGGS
ASA, 82, 148, 251,
290
DORSEY, 269
PARSON, 67
BIGHAM
ALVIN, 175
JAMES, 142
[BLANK], 142
BIGLEY
NANCY, 329
BIGLOW
E., 331
BILBRO
& FERRY, 179
J., 309
JAMES, 310, 314,

316, 317, 324,
325, 335
BILES
ROBT., 143
BILLS
J.H., 246, 331
JOHN H., 269
BINGHAM
ALVAN, 92, 183
ALVIN, 130, 181
BLACK
HUGH, 32
JOHN, 32
BLACKBURN
SAMUEL, 184
BLACKFAN
JESSE, 331
JESSEE, 17
JESSIE, 7
BLACKMAN
SAMUEL, 163
BLACKSHEAR
E., 186
EZEKIEL, 184
BLACKSHER
EZEKIEL, 105
BLACKSHIRE
EZEKIAL, 113, 114,
115, 206, 321(2)
EZEKIEL, 110(2),
112, 159, 169,
205, 254, 258,
259, 260, 261,
262, 315
BLACKWELL
CAPT., 34
H.L., 339
HARDY L., 10, 28,
67(2), 68, 108,
138, 184, 269
JOHN, 286
BLACWELL
CAPT., 61
BLAN
THOMAS, 75
BLEDSOE
ANTHONY, 75, 153,
247
BLOUNT
JOHN G., 266
BLOWERS
JOHN G., 335
BLYTHE
CHAMPION, 203
F.J., 165
JOHN, 104
JOSEPH, 2, 22
T., 166
T.J., 166
THOMAS, 109, 122
THOMAS J., 139, 141,
151, 164, 174,
180, 184
THOS., 66
THOS. J., 163

BODDIE
NATHAN, 75
BOLES
ROBERT, JR., 207
WILLIAM, 207
BOLLING
WILLIAM, 283
BOMAR
ELISHA, 331
BOND
DAWSON, 10, 29
EATON, 153, 233, 334
THOMAS, 233, 334
BONNER
JOSHUA, 291
BOOBY
FRANCIS, 256, 277
BOOKER
PETER R., 261
BOON
THOMAS, 321
BOOTH
BENJAMIN, 65, 317
STEPHEN, 26, 67,
101, 310
STEPHEN, SR., 151
BOOTHE
BENJA., 107
BENJAM, 148
BENJAMIN, 122, 203,
310, 316, 335
HENRY, 50
JAMES, 226, 228, 242
STEPHEN, 243, 253,
254, 267, 316
BOSWEAL
CRAVER, 146
BOSWELL
CRAVEN, 97
BOUGH
ROBERT, 326
BOURLAND
& FOX, 200
BOWEN,
REYNOLDS AND SMITH,
32
BOWERS
GEORGE, 75, 153
BOWLING
LEWIS, 162
WILLIAM, 162
BOYAN
ELISHA, 181
BOYCE
PARSON, 178
BOYD
ALEXANDER, 339
ANDREW, 331
MARAIS, 232
MARCUS, 123
ROBERT, 331
BOYLER
NATHAN, 75, 153
BOZE
WILLIAM, 93

BRADBERY
ELIJAH, 116
BRADFORD
A.B., 24, 42, 91,
98, 127, 128,
143, 147, 152,
173, 209, 213,
278, 280, 281,
323, 336
ALED. B., 326
ALEXANDER B., 13,
24, 28, 29, 42,
43, 48, 57, 58,
59, 60, 71, 72,
73, 80, 81, 82,
97, 98, 117, 122,
127, 135, 148,
151, 152, 202,
241, 244, 252,
277, 278, 279,
280, 281, 282,
284, 287, 291,
329, 336
ALX. B., 28
GREEN H., 339
H., 157
HIRAM, 2, 4, 6,
10, 11, 12,
22, 23, 32, 33,
38, 42, 53, 55,
100, 106, 122,
128, 130, 157,
158, 171, 175,
176, 182, 214,
219, 222, 239,
243, 252, 255,
259, 260, 282,
288, 289, 296,
298, 300, 302,
303, 315, 317,
322, 327, 337
HYRAIM, 151
HYRAM, 11, 39, 88,
139, 147, 149,
150, 159, 161,
162, 167, 178
HYRUM, 120
M.H., 109, 175, 203,
300
MILES H., 316
RAY, 289
BRADLY
A.B., 291
BRAHAM
JOHN, 7, 17
BRANCH
JOSEPH, 75, 153,
191, 329
BRANDFORD
A.B., 80
BRANTLEY
JOHN, 338
BRAZEAL
ARCH'D, 62
ARCHIBALD, 184, 293

BRAZZEAL
  [BLANK], 32
BRETT
  ANDERSON, 181
BRIANT
  J.H., 17
BRIDGEMAN
  NATHAN, 10, 11(2),
    69, 115, 206,
    208, 209, 213,
    254, 258, 259,
    260, 261, 262,
    284
BRIDGEMEN
  NATHANIEL, 188
BRIDGEMENT
  NATHANIEL, 27
BRIDGEMOND
  NATHAN, 74
BRIDGMAN
  NATHAN, 10, 24, 33,
    50, 67, 112, 116
BRIDGMEN
  NATHAN, 113, 114,
    131
BRIGHAM
  JAMES H., 65
BRIT
  ANDERSON, 175, 183
BRITT
  ANDERSON, 265
BRITTON
  RICHARD O., 339
BROOKS
  A.T., 184
  AARON T., 179(2),
    262
  ARON T., 224, 243,
    253, 254
  ARRON T., 224
  CAPT., 208
  JOHN, 308
  ROBERT, 7, 17, 75
BROUGHTON
  THOS., 233
BROWN
  ALEXANDER, 145
  JAMES, 65, 153, 247
  JESSE, 63, 85, 237
  JOHN, 7, 17, 85,
    101, 153(2), 160,
    245, 247
  JOHN H., 109
  PETER, 7, 17, 153,
    247
  REUBIN S., 171
  SAMUEL, 51, 65, 88,
    93, 94, 104,
    110, 130, 137,
    142, 151, 163,
    164, 182, 185,
    300, 338, 339
  THOMAS, 7, 17, 75,
    91, 153, 256,
    281, 313

WILLIAM L., 284, 306
BRUCE
  PHILIP, 70, 71, 72,
    82, 83, 87, 184,
    195, 225, 226,
    238, 240, 244,
    256, 272, 278,
    282, 283, 293,
    327
  PHILIP A., 62, 65,
    68, 314
  PHILLIP, 33, 70,
    188, 221
  PHILLIP A., 121,
    125, 126
  W.C., 142
  WILLIAM C., 62, 68,
    69, 94, 95, 98,
    129, 131, 134,
    142, 188, 195,
    288, 293, 294,
    304, 313, 314
  WM. C., 49, 137
BRUNSON
  JOSHUA, 111
BRYAN
  E., 234, 334
  ELICK, 107
  ELISHA, 175, 291
  J.H., 7
  JOHN T., 175, 295
  JOSEPH, 52
  STEPHEN, 75, 175,
    230(2), 233
  STEPHEN S., 295
BRYANT
  & TALBOT, 334
  & TALBOTT, 160
  & TOLBOT, 85
  ELISHA, 185, 186,
    207, 255
  J.H., 76
  J.T., 230
  JNO. T., 85
  JOHN, 255
  JOHN T., 160
  STEPHEN, 85, 160,
    331
BRYEANS
  ELISHA, 171
BUCK
  CORNELIUS, 106, 184,
    239
BUCKHANNON
  JOHN, 7, 17
BULLOCK
  GILES, 184, 227,
    228, 295, 296
  MR., 138
BULOCK
  GILES, 295
BURKS
  LEE H., 40(2), 42,
    46, 58, 61, 62,
    68, 72, 97, 117,

131, 132, 133,
    258
  WILLIS H., 46
BURLESON
  JONATHAN R., 269
BURLISON
  J.R., 271
  JAMES A., 172(3)
  JOHNATHAN R., 172
  JONATHAN, 174, 264
  JONATHAN R., 172(2),
    197, 198, 201,
    293
BURNES
  ROBERT, 192, 238,
    256, 294(2)
BURNS
  R., 339
  ROBERT, 26, 35, 39,
    53, 67, 88, 93,
    94, 101, 107,
    121, 221, 225,
    226, 272, 273
  ROBT., 53, 283
BURTON
  JAMES, 143, 198, 327
  SAMUEL, 321
  WILLIAM, 315, 316
  WILLIAM A., 288
  WILLIAM H., 274,
    275, 276, 293,
    294, 327
BURTONS
  CAPT., 335
  W.H., 335
BUTLER
  BENNET R., 11, 131,
    236
  BENNETT R., 20
  WILLIAM, 131, 212,
    219
BUTTER
  BENNET R., 116

-C-

CALDWELL
  JAMES, 248
  JOHN, 210, 222
  NATHANIEL, 230
  SILAS M., 338
CALWELL
  JAMES, 154
CAMELS
  LEWIS, 324
CAMPBELL
  ARTHUR, 7, 17, 75,
    331
  WILLIAM, 75, 287
  WM., 230
CANADY
  ALFRED, 5
  JOHN, 153, 247
CARITHER
  JNO. G., 253

JOHN G., 225
CARITHERS
  I., 244
  J., 291
  J.G., 205, 289, 317
  JNO. G., 69, 89, 94,
    124, 142, 273,
    294
  JOHN F., 330
  JOHN G., 1, 3, 4, 7,
    10, 13, 14, 16,
    17, 20, 22, 25,
    27, 31, 32, 36,
    47, 48, 49, 51,
    52, 55, 59, 66,
    68, 74, 81, 84,
    91, 93, 106, 110,
    121, 122, 125,
    126, 128, 129,
    132, 134, 136,
    137, 138, 139,
    140, 141, 149,
    151, 152, 153,
    159, 160, 161,
    163, 164, 166,
    175, 176, 181,
    182, 183, 192,
    198, 201, 202,
    204, 205, 207,
    210, 211, 220,
    222, 226, 229,
    239, 244, 253,
    285, 290, 292,
    296, 297, 298,
    299, 300, 303,
    305, 316, 318,
    319, 323, 336
  MARY, 207
  MATTHEW C., 207
  ROBERT, 178
CARLTON
  ANTHONY, 339
  JAMES, 177, 181,
    183, 185, 193,
    196, 255, 257,
    278, 288, 316,
    327
  JOHN, 175
CARNAHAN
  THOMAS, 13, 266, 267
  THOS., 133
CARPENTER
  BENJ., 75, 154
  BENJAMIN, 7, 17
CARROLL
  WILLIAM, 1
CARRUTHERS
  JOHN G., 5(2)
CARSON
  CHARLES, 38
CARTER
  MARGARET, 35(2)
CARTNEY
  ALEXANDER W., 142
CARUTHERS

ELIZABETH B., 273, 274
JAMES, 175, 203, 252, 266
JAS., 313
JNO. G., 142
JOHN G., 6, 12, 23, 25
ROBERT, 260, 273, 274
SAMUEL, 273, 274
CASBY
JAMES, 24(2), 47
JANE, 48
CATRAN
JNO., 204
CAVANAUGH
JAS. P., 339
CHAMBERS
AMOS, 30(2), 59, 105, 258
JAMES, 30, 59, 105
CHAMP
H., 86
HARMIS, 147
HERMES, 192, 227, 228, 254, 259, 260, 261, 262
HERMIS, 131, 132, 133, 134, 147, 226, 258, 262
CHANDLER
THOMAS W., 313
CHANEY
THOMAS, 40
CHELTON
JOHN M., 171
CHERRY
D., 208, 322
DAN'L, 5, 67, 88, 97, 116, 124, 147, 150, 161, 170, 175, 185, 189, 202, 203, 204, 206, 216, 242, 324, 330, 337
DANIEL, 1, 2, 5, 11, 23, 25, 28, 30, 33, 34, 38, 65, 67, 69, 92, 95, 97, 101, 106, 109, 116, 120, 124, 125, 126, 137, 141, 150, 151, 152, 161, 164, 185, 189, 192, 193, 202, 203, 204, 207, 208, 209, 211, 212, 217, 220, 221, 222, 223, 224, 238, 243, 253, 256, 268, 271, 285, 286,

288, 294, 304, 310, 327, 330, 335
DANL., 31, 69, 101, 109, 126
DARLING, 75
DAVID, 39
CHESTER
R., 8, 17
ROBERT I., 12
ROBERT J., 75, 154, 201
ROBT. J., 248
CHILDRES
JOHN, 75
STEPHEN, 117, 126
CHILDRESS
E.H., 173(2)
EDWIN H., 144, 147, 149, 218, 219, 241
JOEL, 331
JOHN, 7, 17, 154, 331
S.S., 205
STEPEH S., 331
STEPHEN, 193, 204, 323
STEPHEN S., 73, 190, 205, 258(2)
STEPHENS S., 152
CHILTON
JOHN, 338, 339
CHINAG
FRANCIS, 62
CHISM
JAMES, 331
CLANTON
ROBERT, 85, 160, 236, 249
ROBT., 246
CLARK
ANTHONY, 256, 277
JAMES, 69, 92, 104(2), 108, 110(2), 122, 184, 277, 317
JAMES H., 301, 328(2)
JAMES P., 296, 331
JOHN C., 337
JOHN P., 337
JOHN T., 270, 312
THOMAS, 184, 256
CLARKE
JAMES, 110
CLAUSE
JOSEPH B., 195
CLEMENT
SIMON, 331
CLIFTON
JOHN H., 217
COBB
J.H., 339
JOHN H., 338

ROBERT L., 331
COBBS
ROBT. L., 154, 230, 248
COCKRAM
& PECK, 165
COCKRELL
MARK R., 153
COCKRILL
ELIZA, 252
MARK R., 59
CODY
MICHAEL M., 320(2), 330
COE
JAMES, 289
COLART
JOHN, 232
COLEMAN
B., 41, 56, 59, 63, 67, 80, 119, 121, 124, 173, 177, 201, 202, 246, 253, 268, 272, 292, 293, 294, 313, 315, 317, 324
B.C., 246
BLACKMAN, 3, 4, 5, 6, 10, 11, 12, 21, 23, 25, 26, 27, 28, 29, 31, 32, 35, 38, 39, 41, 45, 47, 63, 67, 68, 69, 80, 83, 91, 95, 113, 121, 124, 141, 146, 152, 171, 173, 176, 180, 182, 185, 191, 194, 201, 202, 206, 215, 218, 219, 220, 222, 224, 241, 242, 256, 267, 291, 292, 304, 305, 309, 312, 313, 323, 329, 335
DANIEL, 213
JOS. H., 230
THOMAS B., 252, 298
ZACHARIAH, 213
COLQUEHAUN
ANGUS, 122
COLQUEHOUS
ANGUS, 108
COLTART
JNO., 340
JOHN, 339
CONDUIT
JOHN L., 254
CONDUITT
JOHN L., 278, 279, 280(2), 301
CONNER

SAMUEL, 10(2), 11, 39, 52, 54, 110
WILLIAM, 238, 251, 256, 272, 273, 283, 291, 310, 316, 320, 321
CONYERS
SAMUEL, 1, 5, 25, 30, 67, 68, 104, 110, 335
COOK
JOHN W., 91
WILDS, 175
COOKE
JOHN W., 109
COONCE
PHILLIP, 31
COONTS
PHILIP, 55
COPELAND
S.H., 258
SAM'L, 62
SAMUEL, 73, 124
SAMUEL S., 21
COPPAGE
JOHN, 338
COSBY
JAMES, 13(3), 62, 63, 65, 96, 124, 128, 129
COTTER
HAMILTON W., 338
COUTCHER
WILLIAM, 85
COWAN
JOSEPH, 303(2), 326, 327
SUSAN, 303(2), 326, 327
COX
ENOCH, 93
ENOS, 111
FRANCIS L., 98, 99
COXE
ENOS, 108, 111, 112
F.S., 181
FRANCIS M., 330
FRANCIS S., 63, 131, 132, 133, 158, 167, 171, 182, 186, 193, 195, 206, 217, 252, 276, 281, 302, 308, 310, 320, 322, 324, 327
JAMES, 338
TENCH, 186
WHITEHURST, 108
COY
HENRY M., 182
CRAIG
JOHN, 7, 17, 75
CRANE
DAVID BROWN, 328
CRAWFORD

W.H., 331
WM. W., 154, 248
CROCKET
JOSEPH, 75
CROOK
BEGNAL, 201, 243,
267
BIGNAL, 11, 29, 50,
93, 102, 108,
123, 151, 193,
201, 204, 205,
253, 254, 331
BIGNELL, 88
JAMES, 50, 193
CRUTCHER
THO., 24
THOMAS, 51, 107,
120, 151, 179
THOS., 65, 88, 94,
143
WILLIAM, 51, 160,
236
CURRAY
CAPT., 61
JOSEPH, 107
CURRIE
GEORGE, 313
JESSEE, 339
JUDIETH, 313
JUDITH, 313
WASHINGTON, 338
CURRIN
J., 113, 119
CURRY
CAPT., 22, 26, 208
GEORGE, 314
JAS., 267
JOSEPH, 151, 164,
191, 193, 205,
240, 243, 253,
254, 310, 316,
317
CUSICK
JEDEDIAH, 10, 11,
26, 28, 31, 39,
51, 53, 107,
178, 179, 226,
253, 273, 274,
292, 295, 309,
310, 331
JEDIAH, 226, 260
JEDIDIAH, 243
JEREDIAH, 11
NEWTON, 292
NEWTON M., 178
WASHINGTON, 290,
309, 310
WASHINGTON M., 226
WILLIAM, 309, 310
CUTCHER
THOMAS, 93

-D-

DABYNS

THOMAS J., 228
DANCEY
ISAAC, 338
DANEY
EDWARD, 288
DANIEL
ROBERT, 331
DANNET
ROBERT, 17
DARRIS
JAMES, 100, 101(2),
107, 125, 179
DAUGHERTY
GEORGE, 7, 17
THOMAS, 17
DAVENPORT
& ROBERSON, 288
DAVIE
DOCTOR EDWARD, 151
EDWARD, 294(2)
KENDAL, 323
KINDLE, 233
DEAREN
BERRY, 283
DEARIN
BERRY, 178, 215,
216, 226, 243,
283
DEARING
B., 118, 200
BENJ., 255
BERRY, 104, 118,
122, 124, 125,
126, 130, 187,
188, 193, 194,
200, 204, 212,
216, 217, 218
DEARINS
BENJ., 255
DEERING
BERRY, 120, 123, 176
DEMERANVILLE
& PETERS, 284
DENIN
JAMES, 264
DENNET
ROBERT, 7, 109
DENNIT
ROBERT, 109
DENSON
WILLIAM, 154, 331
WM., 248
DERIN
B., 171, 217
BERRY, 143, 144,
145, 147, 148,
149, 178, 186,
189, 191, 192,
193, 209
DEVENEUX
& POLK, 75
DEVERAUX
& POLK, 333
DIAL
HASTIN, 280

HASTINGS, 278, 279,
280
HORTON, 256
ISAAC, 256, 277,
281, 295
DICKENS
SAMUEL, 21, 24, 252,
325
DICKINS
SAMUEL, 179, 307,
309, 329, 331
DICKSON
ARCHIBALD, 327
REBECCA, 327
WILLIAM, 75
WYNN, 327
DILL
N.W., 304, 310
NOAH W., 204
DILLARD
F.L., 68, 174, 228,
258
F.S., 31
FRA. L., 323
FRANCES L., 104,
116, 193
FRANCIS, 37
FRANCIS F.L., 69
FRANCIS L., 11, 42,
57, 58, 61, 62,
81, 96, 98, 99,
115, 131, 134,
137, 142, 143,
144, 145, 147,
148, 149, 150,
152, 157, 176,
187, 190, 191,
210, 230, 289,
295
THOMAS F., 29
DILLIARD
FRANCIS L., 38, 43,
46, 56, 57, 110,
237
DILLIRD
FRANCIS L., 88
DILLON
DANIEL, 203
ISAAC, 203
MARY, 203
NATHAN, 203
SALLY, 203
WILLIAM, 203
DIXON
ARCHIBALD, 303
REBECCA, 303(2), 326
WILLIAM, 154(2), 248
WYNN, 303(2), 326
DOBBINS
THOMAS J., 282
DOBSON
MATHEW, 154, 248
DOBYNS
THOMAS J., 227, 265,
293, 298, 302

DODD
W., 39
WILIE, 34, 35, 120,
137
WILLIE, 10, 28, 31,
35(2), 39, 40
DONALSON
HUMPHREY, 291
DONELL
WILLIAM, 230
DONELSON
& KING, 231
DORRIS
JAMES, 2, 11, 16,
28, 31, 39, 40,
50, 53, 57, 214,
271, 301, 320,
321, 44a
DOSS
JONOTHAN C., 251
DOUGHART
WM. W., 15
DOUGHERT
WILLIAM W., 14
DOUGHERTY
THOMAS, 7, 75, 221
THOS., 154, 248
DOUTHEATT
WILLIAM W., 11
DOUTHET
WILLIAM W., 42
DOUTHETT
WILLIAM W., 15
WM. W., 15
DOUTHIT
W.W., 47
WILLIAM W., 29(2),
31, 53, 55, 70,
71, 104, 236
WM. W., 154
DOWNS
WILLIAM, 199, 322,
324
DRAKE
DAVID, 163
ROBERT, 331
ROBT., 232
DUNCAN
WILLIAM L., 168
DUNN
JAMES, 271
DuPONCEAU
PETER S., 186
DYAL
HASTINGS, 280
DYALL
HASTINGS, 302
ISAAC, 296
DYER
CHARLES C., 175
CORNELIA J., 175
JAMES M., 175
JOEL, 35, 162, 175,
255(2)
JOEL H., 152

JOEL S., 175, 298
ROBERT H., 152
SARAH, 69
SARAH ANN, 175
SARAH D., 255
SARAH J., 35, 306,
  312
SARAH L., 175
SUSAH [SIC] J., 255
W.B., 85
WILLIAM H., 27
WILLIE B., 23
DYNE
  JOEL, 7
DYRE
  CHARLES, 4(2)
  CHARLES C., 21
  CORNELIA, 4(2), 21
  DRUCELLA, 21
  DRUCILLA, 4(2)
  JAMES, 4(2)
  JAMES W., 21
  JOEL, 3, 4(5),
    11(2), 17, 21,
    27(2), 76
  JOEL H., 27
  JOEL S., 21
  MAJOR, 6
  MARIAH T., 21
  SARAH ANN, 4(2), 21
  SARAH J., 21
  WILL H., 3(2)
  WILLIAM B., 26
DYSON
  EQILLA, 154

-E-

EARL
  GEORGE W., 331
  JNO. B., 332
EARLE
  JOHN, 122
EASLEY
  THORNTON, 339
ECHOLS
  A., 280
EDDINGS
  JOSEPH, 256, 260,
    264
EDDINS
  JOSEPH, 255, 272,
    274, 275, 276,
    278, 282, 283
EDMONDSON
  SAMUEL, 76
EDMONSON
  SAMUEL, 154
EDMUNSON
  JOHN, 233
  WILLIAM, 233
EDNEY
  & PHIPPS, 198
  SAMUEL, 106, 196,
    198

EDWARD
  CAPT., 50
  ISAAC, 111
  ISAAC D., 70
EDWARDS
  BENJA W., 117
  CAPT., 61, 111, 208
  G., 270(2)
  GRIFFETH, 33, 34,
    50, 181, 259,
    261, 327
  GRIFFITH, 69, 88,
    92, 120, 175,
    244, 253, 254,
    256, 258, 260,
    261, 262, 265,
    267, 271
  GRIFITH, 67
  ISAAC, 33, 50, 69,
    104, 110(2), 271
  ISAAC D., 70
  ISAC, 67
  MARY, 271
  WM., 340
EDWARS
  GRIFFETH, 93
  WM. M., 117
ELIOT
  SAMUEL, 57
ELLIOT
  AND PERKINS, 4
  CAPT., 208, 335
  JAMES, 53
  SAMUEL, 55, 56, 57,
    58, 68, 69, 128,
    129, 131
ELLIOTT
  CAPT., 162
  JOHN, 66, 165, 174
  JOHN B., 174
  SAM'L, 31
  SAML., 25
  SAMUEL, 11, 29, 31,
    32, 46, 62, 88,
    93, 100, 106,
    127, 137, 142,
    143, 144, 145,
    147, 148, 149,
    150, 151, 162,
    167, 168, 169,
    186, 187, 188,
    189, 191, 192,
    193, 194, 199,
    202, 206, 209,
    212, 213, 215,
    216, 221, 225,
    226, 230, 237,
    238, 255, 273,
    274, 275, 276,
    281, 303, 322
ELLIS
  A.G., 278, 279, 285
  ALBERT G., 254, 263,
    264, 273, 276,
    280, 285, 286,

320, 325
ELLISON
  L.H., 42
  LEWIS H., 43
  YOUNG E., 305
ELMS
  THOMAS, 276
EMBRE
  JESSE, 243
EMBRY
  ELIZABETH, 251
  J., 321
  JESSE, 251, 253,
    254, 267
  JESSEE, 290
ERWIN
  ALEXANDER, 8, 17
  SAMUEL, 271
ESTES
  A.M., 71
  ALBERT M., 71, 238,
    291
  CAPT., 41, 93, 335
  JOEL, 1, 11, 25,
    26, 28, 39, 50,
    59, 71, 88, 92,
    104, 108, 118,
    133, 136, 143,
    161, 174, 176,
    185, 193, 198,
    202, 203, 204,
    206, 207, 219,
    225, 238, 288,
    289, 291, 292,
    293, 300, 304,
    312, 314, 318,
    324, 327, 335,
    337
  M.P., 71
  MARCEAU P., 187
  MONROE P., 82, 83,
    124, 127, 128,
    129, 131, 132,
    133, 206, 227,
    228, 242
  MORE P., 87
ESTICES
  CAPT., 217
ESTIS
  JOEL, 61, 116, 181
EUBANKS
  RICHARD N., 297
EWEN
  WILLIAM M., 284
EWING
  ALEXANDER, 76(2),
    154, 233
  ALEXANDER C., 154,
    233
  JOSEPH, 292

-F-

FAIT
  NETHERLAND, 284

FARIS
  ELI, 43, 51, 125,
    126, 162, 221,
    225, 226, 269
  ELI, 65
FARRIS
  ELI, 31, 33, 37,
    38(2), 40, 42,
    62, 65, 68, 238,
    270
  JAMES, 13
FARZIER
  HARMON, 126
FASCUE
  LEWIS, 88, 92, 151
FELTS
  CAREY, 69
  CHRISTOPHER, 314
  JOHN, 314, 315(2),
    316
  JOHN F., 319, 322,
    326, 327, 330,
    335, 337, 340
  JOHN M., 324
  JOSEPH H., 258
FERGERSON
  THOMAS, 127, 184,
    304, 306
FERGUSON
  THOMAS, 2, 5, 11,
    23, 26, 173
FERRY
  & BILBRO, 179
FIELD
  JOHN, 85
FIELDS
  JAMES, 33, 50, 67
FIGURES
  MATHEW, 48, 56, 60,
    68, 71, 98, 99,
    133, 154
  MATTHEW, 60, 62, 69,
    72
FINDLEY
  JOSEPH B., 162
FINDLY
  JOSEPH, 136, 237
  JOSEPH B., 163
FITSGERALD
  [BLANK], 141
FITTS
  JOHN, 293
FITZERALD [SIC]
  WILLIAM, 279
FITZGERALD
  OBEDIAH, 117
  WILL, 109
  WILLIAM, 66(2), 83,
    104, 122, 279,
    280(2), 301, 310,
    313, 317
  WM., 117
FLOWERS
  BENJ., 76, 154
  DAVID, 76, 154, 233

JOHN G., 227, 228, 254, 258, 259, 260, 261, 262, 271, 279, 286, 293, 310, 317
JOHN Y., 317
FOREST
THOMAS, 151, 276
FORREST
THOMAS, 164
FORT
ELIAS, 76
J.W., 304
JACOB, 332
JACOB H., 24, 85
JANE N., 122
JOSEPH W., 85
FOSCUE
LEWIS, 92, 120, 238, 256, 271
FOSTER
ROBERT, 332
FOWLER
SILAVANUS, 154
FOX
& BOURLAND, 200
FRAZIER
HARMAN, 121, 272, 314
HARMON, 83, 126, 256
MARTIN, 269
MARTIN G., 174
FREEMAN
CATER, 26, 51, 142
CATO, 22, 40, 53, 105, 110, 126, 137, 167, 168, 169, 193, 204, 205, 209, 212, 213, 214, 215, 216, 219
CHRISTOPHER, 208
GREEN, 154, 248
I., 76
J., 7, 17, 52
JAMES, 140, 192
JNO. H., 274, 303
JOHN H., 203, 206, 208, 213, 214, 221, 225, 226, 238, 326, 328, 329, 336
FRIEND
E.T., 60
EDWARD T., 42, 43, 56, 57, 58, 61
FUDGE
CAPT., 6, 34, 61, 64, 68
JOHN, 31
JOHN B., 36, 70, 96, 98, 99, 100
FULLER
EZEKIEL, 172(3)
FURGERSON

JAMES B., 282, 315, 321
JOEL, 180, 181
THOMAS, 34, 125, 213, 271, 283, 295, 301, 305, 307, 308, 309, 310, 323
FURGESON
THOMAS, 220
FURGUSON
THOMAS, 34, 180, 181, 259

-G-

GAINES
WILLIAM W., 143
GAINS
WM. P., 116
GAMBLE
JOHN, 227, 228, 320, 321, 326, 328, 329
GARDINER
LEVI, 88
GARDNER
& McCRORY, 147
LEVI, 28, 31, 39, 71, 121, 125, 126, 143, 144, 145, 147, 151, 157, 167, 168, 169, 173, 199, 266, 267
GARNER
LEVI, 11
GARRETT
DANIEL, 230
GEORGE
BENJAMIN, 153, 187, 213, 214
MATTHEW, 293
GERARD
CHARLES, 8, 17
GERRARD
CHARLES, 76
GHOLSON
A.S., 124
ALONDUS, 43
ALONDUS S., 71, 72, 206
B., 18, 77
BENJAMIN, 17
GHOLSTON
ALONDUS, 96
J.B., 155
GIBBONS
& WELLS, 235
GIBBS
GEORGE W., 332
GILL
DAVID, 300, 326
GIVEN
LANCASTER, 327

GIVENS
& WILLS, 79
DICKSON, 201
GIVINS
& WELLS, 154, 246, 248
GLASS
DAVID, 207
GLENN
FRANKLIN, 197
GOFF
ANDREW, 154
GOLDEN
JESSE, 220
R., 280
REUBEN, 224, 288
REUBIN, 184, 258, 277
GOLSON
B., 8
BENJAMIN, 8
GOOCH
NATHAN, 176
GOOD
EDWARD, 5, 67, 69
GOODE
EDWARD, 1, 6, 11
GOODLOW
MARTHY E., 154, 248
GOODMAN
CALEB, 118
LEVI, 53
GOODMEN
CALEB, 119
GORDAN
ALEXANDER D., 93, 94
GORDEN
ALEX. D., 88
ALEXANDER D., 35
GORDON
A.D., 11, 97, 98, 99, 146
ALEX'D D., 324
ALEXANDER, 146, 187
ALEXANDER D., 39, 53(2), 94, 95, 96, 108, 120, 124, 137, 142, 146, 148(2), 163
ALEXR. D., 292
CAPT., 67
GRADDY
QUINNY, 107
GRAINS
WM. P., 133
GRAVE
WILLIAM B., 237, 243, 246, 248
WM. B., 311
GRAVES
WILLIAM B., 154
WM. B., 76
GRAY
H.L., 85, 124
HENRY L., 3, 13, 36,

47(2), 74, 83, 89(3), 90(2), 99, 103, 124(2), 128, 129, 162, 236, 261
MARY H., 13
GREEN
A. HAYS, 154
HAYS, 76
J.S., 76, 137, 154
JAMES, 43
JAMES S., 248
JAMES W., 140
JAS. L., 339
JESSE, 224, 270(2), 282
JOSEPH, 17
ROBERT G., 40, 55
ROBT. G., 42
SAML., 268
SAMUEL, 140, 223, 257, 291, 327
SAMUEL B., 213, 214
THOMAS, 223, 340(2)
THOS. J., 332
WILLIAM H., 154
GREER
J., 9, 19, 79
J.S., 8, 17
JOSEPH, 8, 76, 154, 248
THOMAS, 8, 17
THOS., 230
GREY
HENRY L., 27
M.H., 128
GRISHAM
G. JARRAD, 159
GARRET P., 65
GRISUM
[BLANK], 33
GROVE
SALLY, 87
WILLIAM B., 311, 329(2)
WM. B., 332
GUARDNER
LEVI, 54, 55, 93, 94, 107, 164
GUIGER
CHARLES, 302
GUION
JOHN W., 240

-H-

HAGGARD
JAMES, 102, 117, 128, 148, 151, 258, 323
HALE
JOHN M., 141
HALL
BIAS, 212
TOBIAS, 206

HALLIBURTON
JNO. H., 340
HALLOWELL
JOHNATHAN, 109
HALSEL
V., 279, 281
VARDEMAN, 163, 256
VARDEMON, 261
VORDEMAN, 256
HALSELL
VARDY, 22
HALSEY
VARDY, 2, 32
HAMEL
ROBERT, 205, 206
HAMIL
ANDREW, 322
ROBERT, 31, 184,
186, 225, 226
HAMILL
ROBERT, 88, 93
HAMILTON
ANDREW, 76, 236, 332
HAMMEL
ANDREW, 65
ROBERT, 37, 112, 126
HAMMELL
ANDREW, 177
JAMES, 177
ROBERT, 2, 11, 29,
33, 37, 38, 94,
101, 113, 114,
115, 120, 125,
169, 221
HAMMELS
ANDREW, 121
HAMMET
ROBERT, 68
HAMMIL
ANDREW, 149
ROBERT, 107, 110
HAMMILL
ANDREW, 98
JAMES, 96, 97
ROBERT, 62, 113, 114
HAMONDS
ROBT., 23
HANBOROUGH
JORDAN M., 262
HANNER
RODDY, 122
WM., 107
HANNON
WILLIAM, 65, 139,
332
HANNOR
WILLIAM, 92
HANSBOROUGH
JORDAN, 222
JORDAN M., 151, 159,
163, 168, 170,
175(2), 181, 217,
238, 239, 244,
250, 253, 256
JORDON M., 193

JOURDAN, 117
JOURDAN M., 133,
141, 193, 205
JOURDON M., 127
HANSBROUGH
J.M., 298
JORDAN, 281
JORDAN M., 272, 292,
310, 311, 322,
325, 335
JOURDAN, 80
JOURDEN, 80
JOURDON, 73
HARALSEN
VINSENT, 26
HARALSON
CAPT., 6
GREEN L., 108, 122,
238, 257, 260
HERNDON, 1, 22, 25,
42, 88, 91, 106,
108, 122, 124,
128, 131, 134,
137, 139, 143,
144, 145, 146,
147, 150, 151,
164, 165, 170,
175, 177, 182,
185, 193, 202,
204, 205, 217,
219, 238, 239,
240, 242, 243,
254, 255, 256,
257, 259, 260,
262, 263, 272,
273, 283, 287,
288, 292, 302,
311, 316, 320,
324, 327, 328,
338
JAMES W., 240
JAS. T., 267, 287
JOSEPH, 139
JOSEPH T., 121, 243,
253, 254, 300,
310, 316, 317
VINCENT, 88, 107,
151, 163, 180,
185, 186, 187,
193, 300, 315
WILLIAM, 255
WILLIAM H., 175, 239
HARBERT
JOHN, 285
HARDWICH
JOHN, 44, 45, 56
HARDWICK
JOEL W., 30, 36, 61
JOHN, 39, 44, 46,
53, 55, 57(2),
60(2), 82, 100,
103, 123, 191,
200, 209, 213,
218, 221, 282,
283, 310

JONATHAN J., 36
JONATHAN P., 30, 61
LINDSAY, 218, 221
HARDY
N., 338
NEHEMIAH, 256, 272,
274, 275, 276,
278, 283
HARELSON
HERNDON, 29, 149
SILAS, 154
HARESBOROUGH
JORDAN M., 140
HARGETT
B.W., 290
HARGROVE
CAPT., 107
NELSON, 88, 93, 94,
101, 108, 120,
123, 124, 125,
126, 164, 182,
193, 204, 224,
238, 255, 257,
265, 266, 287,
295, 296, 320,
321, 324, 327
HARLASON
HERNDON, 108
HARMAN
EDWARD, 332
ISAAC, 270
HARNELSON
THOS. B., 154
HARPER
[BLANK], 310
HARRALSON
GREEN L., 98
H., 66
HERNDON, 33, 97,
121, 127, 142,
161
JOSEPH, 37, 67
JOSEPH T., 65, 335
VINCENT, 65, 93, 94,
120, 176, 180
HARRELL
JOAB, 337
HARRELSON
GREEN L., 1, 2,
3(2), 23, 49
H., 12, 49
HENNDON, 120
HERNDON, 2, 3(2),
11, 32, 39, 57,
58, 148
JOSEPH T., 38, 214
VINCENT, 10(2),
11(2), 21, 35, 39
HARRELSTON
HENRY, 332
HARRILSON
GREEN L., 16, 42
HERNDON, 23, 41
JOSEPH T., 37
HARRIS

EDWARD, 73, 82, 258,
323
JAMES, 256, 286
JOHN, 173
WESTERN, 154, 248
WILLIAM, 21, 35
HARRISON
GREEN L., 42
HART
ANTHONY, 8, 17, 76,
154, 248
JAMES, 76, 89, 151,
154, 221, 225,
226, 230, 265,
271, 332(2)
JAMES C., 177, 185,
243, 253, 254,
258, 259, 260,
261, 262, 267
WILLIAM, 303(2),
326, 327
HARTGROVE
NELSON, 148, 149,
151, 152, 288,
320
NILSON, 205
HARVY
WINSTON, 83, 124
HAWKINS
ADAM, 256(2), 272,
273, 283, 327
GILES, 339
JOSEPH W., 313
HAY
D., 36, 208
DAVID, 50, 87, 151,
193, 208, 222,
238, 243, 244,
255, 279, 286,
288, 292, 293,
302, 311, 320,
324, 327, 329
SUSAN, 87(3)
SUSAN J., 87, 88
HAYS
A.C., 232
O.B., 8, 17, 76, 154
OLIVER B., 125
S.D., 325
STOKELY D., 244,
279, 284, 287,
289
HAYWOOD
ROBT., 271
HEAD
WILLIAM, 17
HEARTGROVE
NELSON, 71
HENDERSON
J.L., 26
JAMES, 64, 65, 67,
88, 93, 94,
101, 107, 120,
151, 164, 193,
238, 254, 258,

259, 260, 261,
262, 285, 287,
327
JAMES H., 309
JAMES M., 271, 295,
296, 301, 304,
305, 306, 307,
308, 310, 316,
317, 321, 335
JAMES, SR., 288
JOHN H., 290
MICHAEL, 213
R., 64
RALINGS, 56
RAMSEY, 298
RAWLING, 179
RAWLINGS, 178
ROBT., 154, 248
ROLLINGS, 64(2)
SAMUEL, 223, 262,
264
THOMAS, 8, 17, 324
THOS., 154, 232, 332
THS., 85
TOBIAS, 26, 65, 88,
107
TOBIAS C., 10(2),
11, 31, 36, 62,
68, 69, 175, 181,
183, 256, 272,
273, 283(2), 287
W.H., 316, 324, 330,
332
WILLIAM, 8, 17, 23,
32, 47, 217
WILLIAM H., 21, 24,
32, 71, 123,
124, 162, 176,
191, 201, 206,
226, 242, 255,
257, 259, 266,
275, 281, 287,
289, 293, 297,
298, 303, 307,
312, 315, 318,
319, 321, 323,
330, 335, 337
WM. H., 19, 20, 25,
97, 103, 106,
107, 108, 109,
162(2), 311, 315
HENDRICK
JOHN, 173
HENRY
GEORGE, 339
JOHN, 20
HERBERT
WILLIAM J., 330
HERMIS
CHAMP, 160
HERNDON
JAMES, 209
HERRIN
ICABOD, 140
HERRING

ICHABOD, 226, 322,
324
JOEL M.B., 2
HERRINS
ICHABOD, 107
HESS
W.R., 105
WILLIAM R., 21, 73,
83, 101, 105,
117, 124, 135,
147, 157, 173,
185, 202, 214,
222, 255, 308
WM. R., 102, 105,
111, 220
HEWLETT
WILLIAM H., 264
HEWLITE
WILLIAM H., 262
HICKS
& SLATER, 100
HIGHTOWER
HARDY, 259
JOHN, 233
RICHARD, 76, 232,
233
HIGHTOWERS
RICHARD, 123
HILL
EDWARD, 228, 240
FRANCES, 313
FRANK, 228, 240
H.R.W., 329
HENRY R.W., 191
JOHN, 32
W.B., 234
WILLIAM B., 8, 17
WM., 222
HOARD
WILLIAM, 233
WM., 76
HOCKLEY
GEORGE W., 228, 243,
309
HOCKLY
G.W., 332
GEO. W., 332
GEORGE W., 106, 123,
162, 175, 196,
228, 243, 291
HODGES
PRESTON G., 71, 91,
144, 154, 201
HOLLADY
SAMUEL, 332
HOLLAND
WILLIS, 37, 38, 62,
81, 105, 110(2)
WILLIS C., 123, 203
HOLLINGSWORTH
JAMES, 38, 40, 42,
43
WILLIAM, 31, 39, 53,
54, 104, 256,
272, 274, 275,

276, 278, 281,
282, 283, 311
WM., 110, 323
HOLLOWAY
CROWDER, 312
HOLLOWELL
JOHN, 167
JOHNATHAN, 94
JONATHAN, 88, 93(2),
121, 125, 126,
137, 142, 164,
167, 168, 169,
173
JORDAN, 151
HOLLWELL
JONATHAN, 142
HOLMON
[BLANK], 223
HORD
WILLIAM, 160
HORTON
RHODA, 228
RHODAH, 289
RODAH, 176, 188,
193, 210
RODOH, 171
HOULTON
UTLEY, 286
HOUSTON
ROBT., 154, 332
SAMUEL, 137
HOWARD
A.H., 332
ALLEN, 30, 31, 82,
83, 85, 257
ALLEN H., 10, 11,
16, 38, 39, 40,
43, 53, 70, 87,
123, 125, 137,
142, 147, 214,
219, 220, 221,
225, 226, 238,
281, 311
ALLIN H., 57
CHARLES, 5, 11, 64,
314
E., 331
MEEKERS, 230
SEPHEN, 179
STEPHEN, 5, 227
HUCKABEE
BENJ., 53
BENJA., 10
BENJAMIN, 31, 36, 53
HUCKABY
BENJAMIN, 10, 11(2),
29, 39, 206, 214,
287, 323
CAROLINE, 323
GRAY, 175, 176, 230
HUGH
THOMAS, 321
HUGHES
ROBERT, 230, 238,
239(2), 240

THOMAS, 151
HUGHS
ROBERT, 3(2), 8, 17,
61, 76, 106, 121,
332
ROBT., 27, 41, 49
THOMAS, 164, 192
THOS., 164
HULING
F.W., 22
FREDERIC W., 17
FREDERICK W., 8, 284
HUMMELL
ROBERT, 6
HUNT
LION, 208
SION, 310
HUNTER
BURRELL, 15, 16, 26,
70
HENRY, 16
HUNTSMAN
A., 17
ADAM, 8
HUTCHESON
WILSON, 160
HUTCHINSON
WILSON, 86

-I-

IANERY
JOHN, 338
INGRAM
JOHN, JR., 254
JOHN, SR., 254

-J-

JACKSON
ANDREW, 332
ELIZABETH, 92, 93,
120
JAMES, 24, 33, 92,
96, 97, 108, 120,
123, 125, 127,
128, 129, 131,
134, 179
JESSE, 92(2), 93,
108, 120
JESSEE, 120, 125,
126, 178
JOHN, 179
MALECHE, 93
MALICHE, 32
MALICHI, 108
WILLIAM, 2, 22(2),
32, 66, 67, 121,
125, 126, 138,
179(2)
WM., 77
JACOCBS [SIC]
JONATHAN T., 88
JACOCKS
J.T., 161, 257, 316

JON. T., 19, 56
JONA. T., 5, 10,
12(2), 20, 25, 50
JONATHAN, 193
JONATHAN F., 120
JONATHAN T., 1, 10,
11, 12, 19, 25,
26, 31, 39, 47,
52, 63, 93, 106,
107, 139, 178,
202, 203, 204,
206, 207, 208,
211, 212, 220,
221, 222, 223,
237, 238, 242,
288, 289, 291,
292, 293, 315,
327
JONO. T., 315
JONTHAN T., 312
T., 151
JACOKS
JONA. T., 126
JONATHAN T., 126
JAFFRAY
ROBERT, 328(2)
JAMERSON
GREEN B., 43, 72,
81, 95
JAMES
DAVID, 334
JOHN, 208
JOHN J., 320, 321,
326, 328, 329
MARY, 77
JAMESON
GREEN B., 43, 70
JAMISON
GREEN B., 43(2), 62,
210
JARRETT
& McCRAB, 288
DAVID, 91, 264
JEFFERIES
D., 141
JEFFERS
DAVID, 4, 12, 39,
141, 303, 324,
326, 327
JEFFREYS
DAVID, 1, 6, 11, 22,
24, 109, 134,
176, 179, 185,
252
JENKINS
JOHN, 77
JENNINGS
HIRAM, 231
JENSON
GREEN B., 87
JETTON
ISAAC, 166, 183, 198
JOHN, 183, 198
JOHN L., 166
JINKINS

JOHN, 246
JOCOCKS
JONA. T., 130
JONATHAN T., 130,
137
JOHNSON
AMELIA, 246
C.R., 339
CAPT., 336
CHARLES R., 314
DANIEL, 322
EDWARD S., 251
ELI, 184
HENRY, 311, 329
ISAAC M., 293, 304,
312, 315, 316,
340
M., 186
MACOM, 214, 215, 216
MALCOLM, 1, 2, 22
MALCOM, 209, 213,
293
MALCOMB, 31, 212
MASON F., 11, 38,
53, 55, 62,
68(2), 72, 88,
142, 152, 176,
178, 220, 265,
288, 294(2), 308,
320, 321, 326,
327
THOMAS, 231
THS., 85
WILLIAM, 11, 224,
244, 269, 304,
305, 306, 307,
308, 309, 311,
314
WILLIAM A., 89, 283
WILLIAM, JR., 198
WILLIAM, SR.,
151(2), 253, 288,
294, 295, 296
JOHNSTON
CANE, 248
G., 220
G.M., 220
GEO., 155
GEO. M., 155
ISAAC M., 327
JOHN, 25, 56, 213,
214
KANE, 154
MALCOM, 174
MALCOMB, 32, 33, 92,
109, 122, 169,
184, 216
MALCOMT, 104
MASON F., 32, 42,
69, 87, 104, 109,
110, 137
THOMAS, 8, 18
THOS., 77
WILLIAM, 53, 104
WILLIAM A., 103, 200

WILLIAM, JR., 34,
164
WILLIAM, SR., 164
WM., 5, 56
WM., SR, 110
WM., SR., 110
JOINER
DAVID, 8, 18, 137
LITTLELON, 221
LITTLETON, 225, 226,
234, 238, 293,
304, 324
MATHEW, 77
MATTHEW, 154, 334
JONES
ABEL, 338(2)
CALVIN, 155, 332
DOCTOR JOSEPH, 301,
315
EDMOND, 234
EDMUND, 155
EDWARD, 338
ELI, 11, 22, 26, 36,
37, 38, 39,
53, 104, 107,
110, 175, 181,
184, 186, 187,
188, 189, 190,
191, 192, 193,
194, 198, 294,
314
FREDERICK, 40
GEORGE W., 31, 36
HENRY, 8, 18, 77,
155, 248
JAMES C., 310,
317(2), 321, 338,
339
JOHN G., 148, 149,
178
JONATHAN, 32, 50
JONATHAN, SR., 108
JOSEPH, 314, 327
WILLIAM, 256, 277
JORDAN
& NIXON, 273
GEORGE R., 238
JNO. P., 326
JOHN P., 307, 316,
318
JOYNER
JESSE D., 338
L., 316
LITTLETON, 312, 315,
327

-K-

KAVANAUGH
WILLIAM, 32, 130,
333
WILLIAM W., 3(2),
26, 27, 34, 151,
192
KEATHLY

JOHN, 187
KEE
JOHN, 148, 149
KELLY
FIFER, 107
JAS. R., 291
JOSHUA, 65, 107,
178, 179, 291,
292, 295
PANE P., 178
PAUL P., 282, 288,
291, 294, 295,
296, 304, 305,
306, 307, 308,
309, 311
KELTNER
SOLOMON, 324
KEMP
JESSE, 171, 200,
213, 214, 217,
226, 297, 323
JESSEE, 297
KENADA
ALFRED, 28
KENADY
A., 31
KENEDY
ALFRED, 1, 5, 6, 10,
54
KENNABY
ALFRED, 184
KENNADY
ALFRED, 10, 11(2),
39, 125, 138
ROBERT, 203
W.E., 204
KENNEDY
ALFRED, 30, 53, 106
KENNY
CAPT., 335
KERKSEY
ALEXANDER, 127
KEY
JOHN A., 121, 122,
126, 128, 129,
131, 134(2), 135,
136, 214, 255,
258
KIMP
JESSE, 243
KINDAL
TRAVIS, 130
KINDLE
TRAVIS, 122
KING
& DONELSON, 231
BENJ., 53
BENJAMIN, 6, 11, 28,
31, 39, 53, 106,
112, 113, 114,
115, 120, 125,
126
I., 234
J.A., 123
JAMES, 174, 293

JOHN A., 82, 83, 87,
94(2), 95(2), 99,
100, 107, 123(2),
128, 129, 131,
134, 139, 150,
217
JOSEPH, 38
STITH M., 199
THOMAS, 8, 18, 155
KINNEY
JAMES, 203
JAMES C., 273
KINNY
JAMES, 256, 282, 283
KINSEY
JOHN, 160
KIRK
J.L., 161
JESSE L., 67, 137,
140, 141, 144,
147, 151, 163,
165, 166, 170,
174, 175, 176,
181, 185, 189,
193, 204, 206,
207, 208, 209,
211, 212, 216,
217, 220, 221,
223, 227, 252,
253, 255, 256,
257, 263, 264,
270, 272, 285,
293, 304, 315,
316, 320
JESSEE L., 163, 263,
285, 287
KIRKEY
ALEXANDER, 132
KIRKSEY
ABRAHAM, 131, 148
ALEXANDER, 128, 129,
131, 133, 134,
136, 320, 321
ALEXANDER M., 224,
266, 285, 321
BRANT H., 4
BRYANT H., 1, 64,
163
LUCINDA, 1
KIRKSY
BRYANT H., 161
KNIGHT
JAMES, 231, 234
KOONCE
ISAAC, 24, 36, 63,
120, 202, 224,
290, 327
JOHN, 66, 202, 224
LUCY, 290
PHILIP, 53, 71, 98,
115, 120, 143,
144, 145, 148,
149, 150, 151,
152, 184, 256,
272, 273, 279,

283
PHILLIP, 36, 93, 94,
95, 99, 100, 112,
113, 114, 125,
134, 137, 142,
144, 145, 147,
164, 208, 209,
215, 216
KOONTZ
PHILLIP, 88
KOUNTS
PHILIP, 212

-L-

LACKEY
ROBERT, 40
LAKE
HENRY, 307
LAMAIN
FRANCIS, 70
LAMB
WILLIAM, 102, 114(2)
LAMBERT
WILLIAM L., 270(2),
282
WILLIAM S., 224,
237, 243
LAMKIN
GRIFFIN, 261
LAMOIN
F., 65
FRANCES, 33, 70, 93,
212
FRANCIS, 31, 36, 39,
70, 71, 114, 142,
150, 178, 210,
215, 216, 225,
226, 227, 228,
231, 238, 242,
292
THOMAS, 22
LAMOYN
FRANCES, 133
FRANCIS, 94, 112
LANDFORD
PETER, 99
LANE
DAVID, 130
LANG
LUNSFORD, 231
LANGFORD
PETER, 120
LANIER
REV., 178
V., 269
LANKFORD
PETER, 38, 39,
40(2), 44, 53(2),
57, 258, 323
WILLIAM, 42, 43
[BLANK], 223
LARANCE
WILLIAM, 149
LAVING

WM. H., 83
LAWRENCE
& WARE, 302
W., 166
WILLIAM, 121, 150,
152, 163, 165,
166, 167, 168,
169, 184, 210,
222, 242, 250
WM., 109, 122
LEA
JOHN, 325
LEE
J.R., 65
LEIGH
ELIZA, 164
ELIZA H., 121, 147,
238, 240, 241
JOHN P., 149
JOHN R., 33, 38,
114, 121, 130,
133, 147, 163,
164, 176, 192,
240, 241, 267,
298, 311, 327,
328
WILLIAM R., 238,
298, 322
LEMOIN
FRANCIS, 88, 216,
221
LEMOYN
FRANCIS, 111, 113,
114, 115, 137
LENARD
JACOB, 52
LEONARD
JACOB, 8, 18, 52, 77
LEWIS
A., 339
JOHN, 333
W., 332
W.T., 331, 332, 333
WILLIAM T., 8, 18,
160, 246
WM. T., 85
LEWTER
KINCHEN, 301
LILLY
NATHANIEL D., 23,
121, 126(2), 151,
164, 167, 168,
169, 173, 317,
322, 324, 326,
328
NATHL. D., 310
LINK
BIRD, 181, 183, 221,
225, 226, 228,
238, 243, 255,
256, 264, 272,
273, 283, 309,
320, 321, 327
JOHN, 175, 178
LITTLE

WILLIAM, 231, 254,
258, 259, 260,
261, 262
LOCKE
SILAS, 56
LOGAN
ROBERT M., 303
LOGWOOD
CHARLES M., 167
LONG
NICHOLAS, 8, 18, 231
RICHARD H., 77
LONGLY
NATHAN A., 207
ROBERTSON Y., 207
SEPHRONA, 298
LORANCE
WILLIAM, 148
LOUIS
JOHN, 277
LOVING
WILLIAM, 47
WILLIAM H., 21, 49,
122, 224, 241,
255, 297, 298,
301, 303, 309,
312, 335
WM. H., 107
LOWELL
S.D., 283
SAMUEL D., 259, 295
LOWERY
TOBIAS, 101
LOWRY
JOSEPH, 32, 50
LUCKY
ROBERT, 44, 60, 72,
124
LYLLY
NATHANIEL D., 320
LYNN
BENJAMIN, 167
WILLIAM B., 137
LYTTLE
WILLIAM, 262

-M-

McABEE
ANN, 302
McALLISTER
JOHN, 8, 18, 52(2)
McALOVAN
& PARISH, 145, 146
& PARRISH, 74, 96,
112(2), 113, 116,
119
PARRISH, 99
McALVRAN
& PARRISH, 132
McCAIN
ARTHUR F., 128, 129,
131, 134, 150,
186, 188, 189,
190, 191, 192,

352

193, 194
ARTHUR T., 187
McCAMBELL
  JOHN, 248
McCAMPBELL
  JOHN, 246
  [HEIRS], 155
McCANN
  A.F., 339
McCHUNG
  ELI, 174
McCLUM
  ELI J., 158
McCLUNG
  ELI, 187, 190
McCLURE
  WILLIAM, 248
  WM., 155
McCOY
  HENRY, 51, 65, 88,
    104, 108, 110,
    120, 124, 193,
    204, 205, 244,
    256, 272, 273,
    279, 283, 285,
    310, 316, 317,
    335
McCRAB
  & JARRETT, 288
McCRAY
  GEORGE, 157
McCREE
  J., 155
McCRORY
  & GARDNER, 147
  GEORGE, 170
  JOHN, 147(2)
McCUTCHEON
  JOHN, 234
McDEARMAN
  CAPT., 224, 335
  MILTON, 244, 253,
    254, 255, 267,
    327
McDONALD
  BENJ., 258
  BENJAMIN, 30, 60,
    105
  JOHN, 8, 18, 159
McEWEN
  CHRISTOPHER E., 260,
    267, 284
McFARLAND
  JOHN, 175, 181, 183,
    254, 256, 272,
    274, 275, 276,
    278, 282, 283,
    294, 321, 323,
    339
  [BLANK], 288
McGAVOCK
  JACOB, 77
McGEE
  FOUNTAIN, 328
  FOUNTAIN G., 327

McGIMPSEY
  [BLANK], 165
McGIMSEY
  [BLANK], 166
McGINNIS
  LAWRENCE, 328
McGRAIN
  SICILLY W., 209
McGRAW
  SICILLY W., 209
McGUIRE
  CAPT., 14, 61
  J.R., 231
  JAMES M., 208
  JOHN R., 24, 33,
    49, 96, 97,
    102, 103, 112,
    113, 114, 115,
    118, 124, 128,
    210, 222, 238,
    257, 258, 287
  JOHN T., 166
  L., 5, 10, 12, 19,
    20, 31, 41, 45,
    47, 50, 62, 63,
    80, 93, 97, 101,
    105, 106, 109,
    116, 121, 126,
    130, 134, 136,
    137, 150, 159,
    161, 163, 174,
    177, 178, 198,
    202, 223, 242,
    251, 268, 293,
    312
  LAURANCE, 41, 50(2)
  LAURENCE, 1(2), 2,
    10, 11, 12(2),
    20, 23, 24, 26,
    32(2), 33(2)
  LAWRANCE, 237
  LAWRENCE, 6, 14, 19,
    20, 39, 47, 61,
    63, 66, 67, 68,
    80, 88, 91, 92,
    93, 97, 101, 106,
    108, 109, 116,
    121, 122, 125,
    126, 130, 134,
    136, 137, 139,
    141, 142, 146,
    150, 151, 152,
    159, 161, 163,
    164, 173, 174,
    175, 176, 177,
    178, 180, 181,
    182, 183, 193,
    198, 202, 203,
    204, 207, 208,
    209, 211, 212,
    220, 221, 222,
    225, 238, 243,
    244, 251, 253,
    257, 263, 264,
    265, 267, 270,

271, 272, 277,
  279, 281, 286,
  287, 289, 291,
  292, 293, 294,
  297, 300, 302,
  303, 304, 311,
  312, 315, 316,
  319, 322, 324,
  326, 327, 329
MARGARET, 302
RICHARD, 288
SAMUEL, 146
T.J., 63, 118, 231
THOMAS J., 49(2),
  73, 82, 96, 99,
  100, 102, 103,
  118, 119, 149,
  150, 166, 175,
  208
THOS. J., 103, 115,
  128, 231, 258
McHABE
  JOHN, 174
McIVER
  D.M., 143
  DUNCAN, 85, 236, 333
  EVANDER, 8, 18, 52
  IVANDER, 5
  JNO., 27
  JOHN, 8, 11, 18, 21,
    77, 155, 333
McKEN
  GRIFFITH, 155
McLAUGHTIN
  JAMES, 124
McLELLAND
  JOHN, 77
McLELLON
  JOHN, 155, 248
McLEMORE
  & WILSON, 333, 336
  H., 230
  J., 9, 18
  J.C., 8, 18, 331
  JNO. C., 89
  JOHN C., 124, 162,
    175, 202, 203,
    230, 231, 234,
    246, 250, 265,
    271, 296, 298,
    306, 312, 337
  ROBT., 77, 155, 333
  SUGARS, 77, 155
McLEOD
  DONALD, 111
McLEON
  D.M., 71
McLOGAN
  ROBERT, 338
McNAIRY
  JOHN, 155
  [BLANK], 155
McNARY
  BUTLER, 155
McNEAL

ALEXANDER, 148
ARCHABALD, 285, 288
ARCHIBALD, 88, 93,
  94, 131, 133,
  143, 144, 145,
  147, 148, 150,
  151, 152, 164,
  187, 190, 193,
  194, 201, 205,
  227, 228, 244,
  265, 279, 286,
  293
McNEALE
  ARCHIBALD, 132, 134,
    164, 204
McWHITE
  JNO., 86, 222
  JOHN, 11, 44, 50,
    58, 82, 83, 87,
    90, 98, 99, 101,
    105, 107, 110,
    124, 125, 137,
    142, 143, 144,
    145, 147, 148,
    149, 150, 151,
    152, 164, 167,
    168, 169, 173,
    199, 210, 221,
    222, 225, 240,
    241, 254, 258,
    259, 260, 261,
    262, 265, 305,
    306, 307, 308,
    309, 315
  JOHN C., 210
MADDEN
  DANIEL, 34
MADDING
  C., 173
  D., 173
  DANIEL, 218, 241
MADEN
  MARIAH T., 21
MADIN
  DANIEL, 8, 18
MADING
  CHAMPNESS, 218, 241
  D., 173
  DANIEL, 21, 69, 219,
    305
  MARIAH, 21
MAJORS
  J.P., 151
  JOHN, 227
  JOHN P., 67, 101,
    121, 148(2), 149,
    164(2), 226, 228,
    238
  JOHN T., 62, 68, 69
MALCOMB
  CAPT., 65
MALDEN
  JAMES, 4, 22, 36,
    67, 104, 120,
    161, 163(3),

183(2), 270, 327
MALDIN
  JAMES, 50, 55, 56,
    57, 58, 110(2),
    130, 181, 221
MALDING
  JAMES, 39
MALLET
  GILES, 213
MAN
  WILLIAM W., 137
  WILSON A.W., 288
MANN
  WILLIAM A.W., 339
  WILLIAM H., 279,
    288, 294(2)
  WILLIAM W., 142(2)
  WILSON A., 225
  WILSON A.W., 193,
    221, 238, 254,
    255, 258, 259,
    260, 261, 262,
    327
MANNING
  CHARLES G., 26
MARBARRY
  JOHN, 288
MARBERRY
  JOHN, 31, 35, 53,
    68, 69, 120, 151,
    225, 226, 238,
    292
  [BLANK], 11, 23
MARBERY
  JOHN, 88, 102, 108,
    114(2), 124, 193,
    205, 221
MARBRA
  JOHN, 28
MARBRY
  JOHN, 164
MARBURY
  JOHN, 55, 62, 164,
    182, 204
MARTIN
  JOHN D., 47, 95,
    197, 323
  JOSHUA, 86, 236
MATETT
  GILES, 183
MATETTE
  GILES, 181, 193
MATHEWS
  EDWARD, 317(2)
  [BLANK], 255
MATNEY
  B., 196
  BROADWATER, 103,
    196, 197, 198
  BROADWATERS, 23
MATTET
  GILES, 214
MATTETT
  GILES, 175
  PETER, 176

PETER J., 240
MATTHEWS
  EDWARD, 206, 310,
    335
  [BLANK], 178
MAULDEN
  JAMES, 53(2), 56,
    175, 252
MAULDIN
  JAMES, 4, 10, 58,
    64, 149, 185,
    193, 288
  LITTLEBERRY, 63
  WILLIAM, 32
MAYS
  ROBT. V., 143
MEEKS
  HENRY S., 274
MERDITH
  WILLIAM R., 195
MEREDITH
  JOSEPH, 255
  JOSEPH H., 310
  JOSEPH N., 313, 316
  MAY, 195
  WILLIAM, 255
MILLER
  CALEB, 143, 207
  COUNCIL, 290
  FELIX G., 91
  JOHN M., 65, 71
  MICHAEL, 242
  ROSE, 275
  THOMAS, 283
  WILLIAM B., 74, 201
MINTER
  GAB'L, 96
  GABRIEL, 47, 48,
    128, 129
  JOSEPH, 47, 48
MITCHELL
  JOHN, 96, 97, 98,
    99, 100
  WILLIAM, JR., 166
MONDAY
  MONTIN, 42
MONTGOMERY
  ANDREW, 306, 312
MOODY
  ISAAC L., 144, 200,
    201, 204, 221
MOORE
  AMOS, 187, 320
  AMOSE, 321
  E.A., 231
  E.H., 231
  J.H., 167
  JAMES A., 115(2)
  JOHN, 228, 240, 313
  MARY, 291
  RICHARD, 151,
    164(2), 193,
    205(2), 221, 225,
    226, 228, 239,
    242

RICHARD T., 121,
    192, 256, 272,
    291, 315
  ROBT. C., 155
  W., 246
  WILLIAM, 8, 155, 234
  WILLIAM H., 139,
    180, 224
MORE
  WILLIAM, 18
MORGAN
  JOHN, 107
MORISON
  WILLIAM A., 92
MORRIS
  HUDSON, 30, 32, 61
  WILLIAM, 62, 68, 69,
    293
MORRISON
  JAMES, 297
  WILLIAM, 47, 92,
    120, 255, 292
  WILLIAM A., 138, 180
MORROW
  WM., 231
MOSS
  M.S., 339
  WILLIAM, 47, 275,
    282
MOTT
  JOHN, 213, 214(2),
    268, 322, 324(2)
MOUNCE
  SMITH, 268
MULHOLLAN
  THOMAS J., 339
MUNN
  DAVID, 290
MURPHREY
  A.D., 333
MURPHY
  A.D., 3(2), 27(2),
    41, 61, 231
  ARCHIBALD D., 121,
    170, 176
  JOSEPH, 33, 62, 65,
    68, 111, 112,
    120, 151, 164,
    167, 168, 169,
    173, 188, 193,
    195, 204, 205,
    244, 253, 254,
    267, 288, 327
  THOMAS, 69
MURRAY
  J., 8, 18
  JOHN, 8(2), 14,
    18(2), 65, 104,
    107
MURRY
  J., 77
  JAMES H., 234
  JOHN, 77, 171, 177,
    180, 207, 234,
    334

-N-

NEAL
  HENRY, 77, 155, 202
  ROBERT, 28(2),
    39(2), 40, 41,
    45, 46, 72, 83
NEALE
  ROBERT, 37(2), 43,
    94(2)
NEEDHAM
  THOS., 231
NEELY
  BENJAMIN F., 279
NELSON
  HUGH D., 77
  JOHN, 223
  MRS., 323
  PLEASANT, 5
NESBIT
  WILSON, 170
NESBITT
  WILSON, 158(2)
NEWELL
  McNAIRY, 338
NEWMAN
  JOSHUA, 5, 52(2)
NEWSOM
  WILLIAM, 38
NEWTON
  E., 231
  EDWARD, 8, 18, 77,
    155, 248
NICHOLSON
  WRIGHT, 338, 339
NIGHTS
  THOS., 324
NIMROD
  JAMES, 107
NISBIT
  WILSON, 189
NISON
  THOMAS G., 187
NIXON
  & JORDAN, 273
  COL., 51, 244
  J.H., 91
  JOHN H., 130, 298
  JOHNATHAN J., 221
  JONATHAN, 13, 57,
    137, 140, 243
  JONATHAN J., 22, 23,
    53, 55, 58, 70,
    72, 91, 96, 97,
    130, 131, 132,
    133, 134, 148,
    200, 204, 213,
    238, 241, 253,
    254
  JONATHAN T., 42
  R.W., 2, 159
  RICH'D, 41, 91, 93,
    97, 105, 134,
    136, 137, 143,

159, 161, 170,
177, 178, 181,
202, 216, 242,
244, 251, 252,
311, 312
RICH'D W., 89
RICH., 47, 50, 59,
63, 67, 71, 80,
88, 101, 147,
189, 198, 268,
293
RICHARD, 6, 11, 12,
20, 23, 26, 31,
35, 39, 41, 47,
48, 56, 67, 68,
71, 80, 83, 88,
91, 92, 93, 97,
101, 103, 106,
107, 120, 121,
128, 130, 134,
136, 137, 138,
140, 141, 142,
146, 148, 151,
152, 161, 163,
164, 170, 176,
177, 181, 189,
193, 198, 199,
202, 203, 208,
209, 211, 212,
215, 217, 219,
221, 222, 223,
225, 226, 237,
238, 240, 241,
242, 243, 244,
250, 251, 253,
256, 257, 259,
262, 264, 267,
268, 272, 273,
277, 279, 281,
283, 284, 285,
286, 288, 289,
291, 292, 293,
294, 297, 300,
303, 304, 307,
310, 313, 316
RICHARD W., 1, 11,
12, 19, 38, 57,
89, 96, 124, 144,
204, 216
RICHD., 5, 12, 22,
25, 31, 35, 39,
45, 163, 175
T.G., 52, 141
THO. D., 88
THOMAS, 242
THOMAS G., 11, 13,
15, 19, 20, 21,
22, 29, 35, 39,
52, 62, 68, 70,
72, 82, 83, 87,
108, 109, 112,
120, 121, 125,
126, 130, 140,
141, 142, 143,
144, 145, 147,

149, 150, 151,
161, 163, 164,
177, 184, 185,
192, 193, 204,
206, 220, 227,
228, 238, 240,
241, 242, 254,
256, 259, 263,
267, 272, 273,
283, 284, 288,
294, 295, 296,
298, 304, 305,
307, 308, 309,
310, 311, 317,
327, 328, 330,
335
THOMAS S., 306
THOS. G., 25, 31,
32, 36, 49,
104, 109, 110,
130, 133, 137,
205, 283, 310,
311
NOAKE
BENJAMIN, 118
NOAKES
BENJ., 67
BENJAMIN, 24,
118(2), 119, 210
BINJ., 68
NOAKS
BENJAMIN, 33, 40,
45, 50(2), 52,
58, 103, 104,
111, 119, 210
NOAX
BENJAMIN, 11, 39,
40, 62
NORMAN
ALFRED, 324
NOVELL
ENOS, 138
NOWELL
DEMPSEY, 339
NUNN
DAVID, 314, 327, 340
DAVID S., 36, 63
FRANCIS, 213
JOHN, 179, 213

-O-

OLIVE
ISHAM, 2, 287
ISHAM W., 270, 305
ONEAL
JOHN, 151, 192
OSBERN
JOHN, 147
OSBORN
EDWIN J., 47
OSBORNE
EDWIN J., 40
EDWIN JOY, 22
OSBURN

JOHN, 143, 144, 145,
148
OSMENT
JOHN, 72(2)
OVERTON
JOHN, 8, 18, 77,
155, 231, 334
THOMAS, 155
THOS., 333
OWEN
SAM'L, 316
SAMUEL, 327
THOMAS, 338
OWENS
HENRY, 234
SAML., 234
SAMUEL, 238, 288,
294, 310, 317
OZMENT
ELI, 268

-P-

PACE
DEMPSEY, 109
DEMSEY, 122, 174
GIDEON, 36, 65, 88,
104, 106, 108,
109, 116(2), 122,
125, 335
GUIDIAN, 66
HENNING, 33, 293
HENRY, 66
JOEL, 1, 2, 22, 32,
65, 92(2), 141,
175, 181, 183,
184, 213, 287
WILLIAM, 1, 187,
210, 212, 213,
214, 215, 216,
293(2), 304, 335
PADDY
EPHRAIM, 24
PAGET
HIRAM, 263
PALMER
THOS., 246
PARISH
& McALOVAN, 145, 146
AUSTIN A. DAVID, 11
CALVIN E., 310, 317,
321, 322, 326,
328
PARKER
CAPT., 335
DANIEL, 159
FOSTER, 143, 207
JOEL, 69, 100
JOHN, 11, 28, 31,
35, 78
JOHN, SR., 69
MATTHEW, 231
NEWMAN, 143
PARRISH
& McALOVAN, 74, 96,

112(2), 113, 116,
119
& McALVRAN, 132
C.E., 291
CALVIN E., 320, 324
D.W., 47
DAVID W., 73, 82
PATRAM
RAWLIN, 148
PATRAN
ROWLETT, 250
PATRICK
JOHN, 9, 18, 77,
137, 155
PATTON
JOHN, 53
TRESTON, 184
TRUS, 32
WILLIAM, 137,
142(2), 257, 268
WILLIAM H., 186,
187, 188, 189,
191, 192, 193,
194, 219
WM., 106
PAYNE
SOLOMON, 338
PECK
& COCKRAM, 165
PEN
ROBERT A., 55
PENN
CAROLINA, 157
GEORGE M., 301
LUCY C., 165
ROBERT, 11, 23, 29,
32, 96, 122
ROBERT A., 30, 56,
62, 68, 70, 72,
81, 82, 83, 87,
96, 97, 98, 99,
100, 101, 115,
116, 130, 150,
157, 162, 167,
168, 171, 214,
260, 302, 337
ROBT. A., 53, 165
PENNE
ROBERT A., 56
PERCIFUL
THOMAS, 304
PERKINS
AND ELLIOT, 4
DANIEL P., 123(2)
JOHN, 237
JOHN P., 298, 310,
322, 338
N.T., 1, 19, 20, 22,
39, 124, 135,
136, 137, 141,
146, 150, 159,
176, 198, 209,
223, 237, 240,
257, 304, 315
NICHOLAS T., 1, 4,

11, 12, 19, 20,
22, 39, 61, 80,
88, 120, 121,
124, 125, 130,
134, 136, 141,
142, 146, 149,
150, 151, 152,
157, 176, 186,
187, 193, 198,
203, 206, 207,
208, 209, 211,
212, 220, 221,
222, 242, 251,
259, 263, 288,
289, 292, 293,
298, 303, 304,
310, 311, 312,
315, 326, 327,
330
NICHOLS T., 238, 291
PERRY
BENJAMIN, 305
BENJAMIN W., 207
ROBERT, 120, 122,
137, 142(2), 151,
175, 176, 178,
181, 182, 183,
193, 204, 205,
220, 256, 272,
274, 275, 276,
277, 278, 279,
282, 283, 292,
316
SANFORD, 187, 206,
213, 219(2), 226,
227, 228
PERSON
JOHN, 9, 18, 231
PERSONS
JOHN, 78
PETERS
& DEMERANVILLE, 284
PHARIS
ELI, 69, 71, 72, 121
PHILIP
ABNER, 18
PHILIPS
ABRAHAM, 333
PHILLIP
ABNER, 9
PHILLIPS
A., 231
ABNER, 77
ABRAHAM, 109, 232
PHILPOT
JNO. W., 77
JOHN W., 8, 155, 248
PHILPOTT
JOHN W., 18
PHIPPS
& EDNEY, 198
C.M., 196, 197, 198
PICKET
MATTHEW, 327
PICKINS

ROBERT, 327
PIKE
J.W., 332
PINKARD
THORNTON W., 326
POLK
& DEVENEUX, 75
& DEVERAUX, 333
EZEKIAL, 248, 269,
333
EZEKIEL, 155, 246
THOMAS, 9, 18, 77,
141, 155, 249
WILLIAM, 21
POOL
LABON P., 333
POPE
SAMUEL, 308
PORTER
JOHN H., 259
PARRY W., 273, 274
REESE, 208, 209,
256, 258, 265,
323
SAMUEL, 324
POSTON
J.H., 77
JOHN H., 284
POTER
REECE, 324
POTTER
JNO., 96
JOHN, 28, 37, 38,
39, 41, 45, 56,
57, 70, 71, 72,
88, 93, 94, 120,
125, 126, 132,
149, 151, 152,
164, 174, 181,
202, 221, 225,
226, 228, 238,
242, 282, 314
THOMAS, 23, 32, 36,
39, 46, 62, 69,
80, 83, 94, 96,
104, 142, 146,
150, 181, 186,
187, 188, 189,
191, 192, 193,
194, 195, 202,
207, 226, 227,
228, 236, 242,
251, 260, 267,
274, 275, 276,
288, 294
THOS., 31, 68,
110(2), 137, 169
POWELL
HENRY A., 11, 27,
36, 108, 192, 307
JAMES B., 179, 223,
251
WILLIAM, 200, 214,
274, 275, 276,
278, 283, 304,

305, 306, 307,
308, 309, 322,
324, 326, 328,
329(2)
POWERS
JESSE, 188, 195
LEWIS, 10(2), 11(2),
22, 32, 70, 130,
137, 142(2), 163,
185
PRIM
CHARLES H., 125
JOHN, 125
LOGAN D., 125
PRINCE
WILLIAM, 333
PROUDFIT
WILLIAM, 274, 275,
276, 288, 294(2)
PUGH
THOMAS W., 291, 320,
321, 327
PUNKERD
F.W., 308

-R-

RAINEY
BENJAMIN A., 170
RANKIN
THOMAS, 237
THOS., 231
RAY
DAVID L., 338
J.R., 177
JOHN, 223
JOSEPH R., 174
M., 121, 183
MATHEW, 14, 15, 27,
47, 52, 71, 87,
106, 120, 123,
124, 128, 136,
169, 199, 200,
289, 333
MATTHEW, 2, 4, 11,
20, 23, 29, 32,
39, 42, 53, 65,
70, 71, 90, 93,
105, 106, 130,
136, 150, 151,
152, 159, 160,
161, 163, 173,
174, 182, 187,
195, 205, 207,
209, 217, 226,
239, 244, 250,
251, 252, 253,
254, 259, 263,
266, 273, 281,
286, 287, 289,
291, 294, 303,
304, 310, 337
READ
JOHN, 155, 177, 299,
333

REAVES
ROBERT, 145
REED
JOHN, 19, 83
REESE
SOLOMON, 20, 78, 234
REYNOLDS
B., 1
BOWEN, 1, 22, 65,
107, 120, 130,
144, 163, 182,
185, 264, 335
REYNOLDS,
BOWEN AND SMITH, 32
RHODES
TYRE, 78, 235
RICE
J., 231
JOHN, 9, 18, 78,
155, 245, 246,
249, 250
RICHARDS
LEVI, 40(2), 41, 42,
46, 219, 238
RICHARDSON
SAMUEL, 208
THOMAS, 293
RICHMON
EDMUND, 91
RICHMOND
EDMOND, 21, 45(2),
60, 109, 292,
321(2)
EDMUND, 71
RING
ELISHA, 255
RINGLET
JAMES, 78, 156, 249
RINNEY
ROBERT, 184
ROBERTS
ELISHA, 288, 294,
313
ROBERTSON
& DAVENPORT, 288
E., 334
ELIJAH, 9, 18
JAMES, 9, 18, 78,
271
ROBERT, 182
ROBINSON
DAVEY, 264
MILAS, 264
ROBISON
ARCHIBALD, 256,
278(2)
GEORGE, 254
HUGH B., 140
JAMES, 156, 264
OSBORN, 264
ROBERT, 175, 181
THOMPSON, 264
RODDIE
NATHAN, 134
RODDY

ALEXANDER, 24, 33, 50, 67
E., 65, 92, 107, 139
ELIAS, 93, 182
EPHRAIM, 33, 158, 170(2), 189(2), 333
EPHRAIN, 158
JOHN, 11, 33, 50, 67, 69, 104, 110(2), 111, 120, 122, 158, 170, 189, 238, 256, 265, 270, 271(2), 288, 327
JOHN N., 88
JOHN R., 151, 193
NATHAN, 159
ROBERT, 88, 93, 101, 102, 175, 181, 184, 185, 186, 187, 188, 189, 190, 191, 192, 193, 194, 198
RODGERS
JNO., 87(2)
JOHN, 39, 41, 43, 62, 68, 69, 88, 93, 94, 95, 98, 99, 100, 111, 137, 142, 162, 288
MARGARET, 87
THOS. J., 199
ROGERS
JOHN, 23, 31, 32, 37, 38, 40, 41, 42, 87, 112, 142, 257, 268, 289
MARGARETE, 87
ROLAND
BENJAMIN, 31
ROSS
GREEN, 231
MARY, 203
SAMUEL, 203
[BLANK], 51
ROULAND
BENJAMIN, 71
ROWAN
WILLIAM P., 246, 251
ROWEN
WILLIAM P., 333
ROWLAND
BENJ., 94, 157
BENJAMIN, 56, 57, 58, 71, 96, 99, 100, 111, 112, 127, 129, 131, 132, 133, 134, 136, 153, 157
BINJAMIN, 128
THOMAS, 42, 56, 57, 58
ROY

MATTHEW, 88(2)
RUCKER
BENJ., 39
BENJA., 255
BERRY, 52, 53, 207, 314, 322, 324, 326
RUPELL
JAMES W., 42, 43
RUSSEL
JAMES, 68, 209, 257
RUSSELL
DAVID, 41
JAMES, 49, 62, 70, 71, 72, 82, 83, 87, 112, 113, 114, 115, 121, 125, 126, 212, 213, 214, 215, 216, 219, 265
JAMES C., 31
JAMES W., 27, 37, 38, 39, 40, 41, 62, 68, 69, 70, 93, 94, 137, 142, 187, 193, 221, 225, 226, 227, 228, 238, 240, 241, 242, 279, 288, 294
JAS. W., 88, 90
ROBERT, 170
WARE, 223
WILLIAM C., 170, 171, 184, 190(2), 298, 310, 317(2), 335
WM. C., 162, 170
RUTHERFORD
JOHN, 16, 28(2), 105
THOMAS, 39, 42, 70, 80, 87, 93, 94, 111, 112(2), 127, 128, 129, 131, 137, 142, 143, 144, 145, 147, 148, 149, 150, 152, 210, 214, 221, 225, 252, 303
THOS., 53(2), 88, 116
RUTLEDGE
H.M., 53
HENRY M., 113, 191, 201
RUTLETGE
HENRY M., 119
RYNOLDS [SIC]
BOWEN, 255

-S-

SAMPSON
JAMES, 93, 94, 137,

142(2), 176, 180, 241(2)
JAS., 176, 182
SAMUEL, 88
SANDERLAIN
JOHN, 11, 175
SANDERLIN
JOHN, 5, 28, 104, 110, 111, 112, 181, 196(2), 197, 198, 243, 253, 254, 267, 314
SANDERS
B., 317
B.H., 4, 22, 62, 68(2), 93, 94, 110, 126, 142, 164, 177, 178, 182, 205, 225, 253, 272, 292, 294, 317
BRITAIN, 210
BRITAIN H., 1, 10, 11, 20, 24, 26, 29, 31, 47, 48, 63, 68, 91, 93, 97, 106, 108, 110, 112, 116, 121, 123, 124, 125, 126, 130, 131, 132, 137, 142, 143, 161, 164, 176, 182, 185, 203, 205, 211, 223, 225, 244, 253, 257, 272, 294, 303, 311, 313, 317, 325
BRITTAIN H., 24
DAVID, 24, 85
JAMES, 177, 238, 278, 279, 327, 335
JULIAS, 205
JULIUS, 1, 2, 16, 23, 28, 33, 38, 39, 42, 50, 51, 91, 108, 109, 111, 115, 120, 122, 123, 125, 127, 128, 129, 131, 132, 134, 136, 167, 169, 181, 186, 193, 204, 205, 213, 218, 226, 320
JULLUS [SIC], 150
JULUS, 53
PERKINS, 13
ROBERT, 108, 115(2), 122, 127, 128, 129(2), 136, 167, 169, 172, 206, 255, 257, 278,

282, 306, 312
ROBT., 321
THEOPHILUS, 26
SANFORD
WILLIAM, 131
SANGSTER
JOHN, 339
JOHN, SR., 338
SAUNDERS
BRITTAIN H., 6
JULIUS, 212, 219
SAWYERS
WILLIAM, 61, 117
WILLIAMS, 235
SCOTT
ALEXANDER, 257
JAMES, 92, 121, 126
JO, 92
JOHN, 87
SCRUGGS
JAMES, 235
JOHN, 78
SCUDDER
P.J., 78
PHILIP J., 232, 333
PHILLIP J., 156
SCURLOCK
BEVERLY, 10, 160
SEARCY
GRANVILLE D., 204
ROBERT, 156, 245
SEAT
JAS. W., 65
SEAWEL
GERMAN, 57
SEAWELL
GERMAN, 56, 57, 58
SEIVER
JOHN, 270
SEVERE
JOHN, 212
VALENTINE, 289
SEVIER
J., 223
JOHN, 209, 215, 216
V., 290
VALENTINE, 206, 213, 214, 281, 287, 293, 301
VALLENTINE, 311
SEWELL
GERMAN, 88
SHANNON
SAMUEL H., 258
SHARRIN
WM., 107
SHAW
DANIEL, 139, 151, 176, 180, 182, 193, 204, 209, 212, 213, 214, 215, 216, 219, 254, 258, 259, 260, 261, 262, 288, 327

JOHN, 300
JOSEPH, 1, 32, 104
SHEARIAN
  HENRY, 66
  HUGH, 66
  JOSEPH, 66
  T., 66
  WILLIAM, 66
SHEARIN
  HENRY, 162, 223
  HUGH, 162, 223
  JARRET, 162
  JARRETT, 225
  JARROTT, 66, 223
  JOSEPH, 162, 223
  MARY, 190
  THOMAS, 190
  TURNER, 190
  WILLIAM, 162, 175,
    181, 184, 187,
    190(2), 196(2),
    197, 198(2), 223,
    225
  WM., 187
SHEARMAN
  MEXICO B., 314
SHEARRIN
  TURNER, 107
  WILLIAM, 104, 110(2)
SHELBON
  DAVID, 9
SHELTON
  D., 331
  DAVID, 18, 78
  JAMES, 232, 334
SHEPPARD
  HENRY, 311, 329
  MARGARETE, 87
  SALLY, 87
SHEPPERD
  EGBERT H., 87
  JAS. H., 87
  JAS. HENRY, 87
  MARGARETE, 87
  MARY B., 87
  SUSAN J., 87
  WILLIAM, 87
SHERIAN
  WILLIAM, 66
SHERMAN
  MEXICO B., 325
SHERRIN
  WILLIAM, 87
SHERRON
  WILLIAM, 82
  WM., 83
SHORT
  ENOS, 252
  ENOS., 239
SHROPHIRE
  DAVID, 156
SHURDWICK
  EDWARD, 87
SILAS
  JAMES, 333

SILLS
  HARDY, 255
SIMMS
  J.H., 282
  J.S., 224
  WALTER B., 78, 156,
    232
SIMPSON
  ALFRED, 327, 336
SIMS
  JAMES H., 312
  W., 9, 17, 18
  W.B., 8, 76, 154
  WALTER B., 9, 18,
    78, 249
  WATTES B., 333
  WM. B., 248
SKILLAN
  JAMES, 156
SKILLEN
  JAMES, 249
SKURLOCK
  BEVERLY, 86
SLATER
  & HICKS, 100
SMITH
  & TROUSDALE, 129
  & TRUISDALE, 115,
    136
  ALSEY H., 21
  B., 76(2), 331
  BENJAMIN, 9, 18, 21,
    78, 156
  DANIEL, 179(2), 256
  ELIZABETH, 327
  ELIZABETH N.,
    303(2), 326
  G., 9, 18
  JACOB, 338
  JACOB C., 339
  JAMES, 4, 69, 70,
    87, 88, 109,
    128, 134, 161,
    168, 176, 177,
    178, 198, 214,
    215, 216, 219,
    252, 289
  JNO. A., 52
  JOHN, 324
  JOHN M., 16, 30, 62,
    81, 105, 124,
    258, 323
  MARY, 290
  OBEDIAH, 303(2),
    326, 327
  ODLE, 51
  POLLY, 313
  RICHARD, 9, 18, 78,
    156
  ROBERT F., 10, 40,
    42(2), 43, 186
  ROBERT L., 103
  ROBERT T., 10,
    11, 21, 28,
    39, 40, 47, 53,

    55, 82, 87, 96,
    99, 100, 104,
    110, 111, 112,
    148, 149, 187,
    188, 189, 190,
    191, 192, 193,
    194, 195, 205,
    256, 260, 263,
    267, 272, 313,
    314
  ROBT., 31
  ROBT. F., 120
  ROBT. T., 53, 83
  ROSS, 23
  SAMUEL, 262
  SIDNEY P., 156, 169,
    186, 213(2), 214,
    218, 226, 232,
    237, 243, 253,
    254, 266, 267,
    288, 290, 335
  STERLING, 286
  THOMAS J., 40, 103,
    127, 147, 156,
    223
  THOMAS M., 263, 264,
    265, 279, 294(2),
    320, 322, 326,
    329
  THOS. J., 83, 89(2),
    117, 124
  THOS. M., 328
  THS. J., 85
  TURNER, 92
  WILLIAM H., 333
SMITH,
  BOWEN & REYNOLDS, 32
SMOTHERS
  J.F., 339
  JAMES F., 339
SPENCE
  ABNER, 265, 266
  JOSEPH, 158, 167,
    169, 194, 216,
    261, 275, 299,
    304, 323
  M., 138
  MARK, 11, 31, 37,
    38, 244, 253,
    254, 267, 288,
    294(2)
  MARMON, 299
  MORMAN, 304
SPENCER
  ROBERT M., 272
SPICER
  ROBERT M., 256, 327
  ROBT. M., 273
SPIDER
  ROBT. M., 283
STAGGS
  FELIX, 284
STALCUP
  GEORGE, 170, 171,
    190(2), 298

JAMES, 31, 36, 100,
  227
STALCUPS
  GEORGE, 170
STAMPS
  J.D., 292
  JOHN D., 187
STANFIELD
  EPHRAIM, 151,
    164(2), 316, 317,
    335
  EPHRAIN, 310
STANFORD
  WILLIAM, 133, 137,
    142(2)
  WM., 132
STANLEY
  DAVID, 182
STANLY
  DAVID, 175, 181
STANTON
  JOSEPH B., 338
STEED
  JESSE, 9, 156, 246,
    249
  JESSEE, 18, 78
STEEL
  SAMUEL, 304
STEELE
  FERDINAND L., 310
  JAMES S., 223, 239,
    243, 266, 285,
    287, 302, 305,
    321(2), 336
  JOHN W., 243
  ROBERT A., 285
  SAMUEL, 310
  T.L., 304
STEPHENS
  JAMES, 186, 214
STEVENS
  JAMES, 169
STEWART
  ALEXANDER, 40, 46,
    57, 58, 66, 71,
    97
  DAVID, 9, 18, 78
  THOMAS, 204
STITH
  FURDENAN, 333
STOCKELY
  THOMAS, 128
STODDARD
  WILLIAM, 21, 252
STODDART
  WILLIAM, 119
STODDERT
  WILLIAM, 83, 162
  WM., 113
STOKELY
  JOSEPH, 339
  THOMAS, 61, 63, 73,
    82, 94, 95, 98,
    100, 101, 102,
    125, 127, 186,

187, 188, 189,
191, 192, 193,
194, 210, 222
THOS., 89, 107, 124,
258
STONE
J., 138
JOHN, 244, 253, 254,
267, 279, 294,
295, 296, 304,
305, 306, 307,
308, 309, 311
R.P.T., 174, 177
STORMS
JOHN, 112, 113, 114,
115
STORY
JAMES, 93, 120, 270,
271
STRICKLAND
DOCTOR C., 29
STRICKLIN
DOCTOR C., 15(2)
DR. C., 28
STROTHER
JAMES W., 252, 270,
290, 301, 324
STRUDWICK
& ASHE, 233
STUART
A., 46
STUBBLEFIED
CLEMENT, 245
STUBBLEFIELD
CLEMENT, 9, 18
STUBLEFIELD
CLEMENT, 78
STWART [SIC]
DAVID, 175
SUBBLEFIELD
CLEMENT, 299, 300
CLIMART, 156
SULIVAN
LEE, 12, 18, 78
SULLIVAN
(AND SON), 32
CAPT., 335
HENRY, 142
LEE, 9, 75, 156,
231, 265, 271
LEVI, 286
SIMION, 286
SUTHERLAND
G., 56
J., 56
SWEENY
HENRY, 311
SWENEY
HENRY, 303
SWIFT
JOSEPH, 120
JOSEPH G., 241
SWINDLE
CALEB, 194

-T-

TAILAR
THOMAS H., 80
TAILOR
RICHARD, 68
TALBOT
& BRYANT, 334
TALBOTT
& BRYANT, 160
JOSEPH, 224
TALIAFERRO
BENJAMIN, 19
TALIFERO
BENJAMIN, 9
TALLIFERRO
BENJ., 235
JOHN, 235
TANNER
JOHN O., 257, 268
TAPSCOT
JOHN, 146
TAPSCOTT
JOHN, 97
TATE
M., 338
MARK, 19
MARK A., 9, 78, 156
MITCHELL, 338
TAYLOR
HOWELL, 107, 338
ISAAC, 32
JAMES, 174
JOHN, 88, 93, 263
JOHN T., 195
JOHN Y., 107, 195,
291
JOSEPH, 295
RICHARD, 30, 31, 39,
67, 88, 93, 94,
95, 98, 99, 100,
101(2), 107, 120,
139, 151, 193,
195, 238, 288,
327, 338
T.H., 69
THOMAS H., 23, 87,
150, 151(2), 173,
195, 273, 281,
289, 303, 310,
316
THOS. H., 78, 231,
334
WILLIAM, 22
WILLIAM B., 2
TERREL
WM., 107
TERRELL
JOHN, 9, 78
WILLIAM, 220, 221
TERRELLS
WILLIAM A., 123
TERRILL
JOHN, 18, 156
WILLIAM, 225, 226,

239, 241
TERRY
J., 309
JOSEPH, 310, 316,
317
STEPHE [SIC], 324
STEPHEN, 208, 300,
308, 314, 320,
325
WILLIAM A., 288, 294
TERRYL
WILLIAM A., 294
THOMISON
DAVID, 177, 221
GEORGE, 194
THOMPSON
AZARIAH, 33, 34(2),
65, 108, 139,
224, 243, 253,
254, 267, 274,
327
AZH., 67
DAVID, 225
JAMES, 220, 226, 238
ZACHARIAH, 5
THWEAT
THOMAS, 5
THOS., 67, 69
THWEATT
THOMAS, 37, 40, 42,
88, 164, 175,
181, 184, 186,
187, 188, 189,
190, 191, 192,
193, 194, 198,
256, 272, 293,
312
THOS., 40
THWEATTS
THOMAS, 207
THWEEAT
THOMAS, 37, 38
THWEET
THOMAS, 92
TIAS
EDWIN, 238
TISDALE
& WHEATON, 19, 79,
156, 245
AND WHEATON, 9
JAMES, 18, 19, 156,
245, 249, 298,
299
JAMES H., 9
JAS., 79
TISDELL
JAMES, 334
TISHELL
JAMES, 334
TISON
AA., 109
TODD
GEORGE, 9, 19, 78
TOLBOT
& BRYANT, 85

TOPCOT
JOHN, 231
TOTTEN
BENJ., 156
BENJAMIN, 78
TOWNSEND
SAMUEL, 138, 252
TRACEY
JOHN, 203
RACHEL, 203
TRAYTOR
JAS., 66
TREADWAY
W., 234
TROUSDALE
& SMITH, 129
TRUISDALE
& SMITH, 115, 136
TUCKER
A.A., 286
ABBOTT A., 221
TUGWELL
JOHN, 339
TURNER
H.H., 330
HENRY, 163, 182
HENRY H., 9, 18,
130, 137, 142(2),
149, 175, 181,
182, 185, 193,
204, 205, 238,
304, 310(2), 330
HENRY W., 39
J.P., 80
JANE N., 122
JOHN F., 10
JOHN T., 10, 50, 62,
68, 70, 72, 82,
83, 87, 88, 93,
96, 98, 99, 100,
115, 116, 122,
127, 130, 149,
152, 163, 175,
181, 183, 185,
193, 194, 224,
262, 310(2), 312
MARY S., 304
NANCY M., 80
NANCY M.J.P., 4, 146
NANCY T., 146
ROBT., 204
SIMON, 4(2), 22(2),
33, 65, 88, 131,
132, 133, 151,
177, 193, 204,
205, 238, 243,
259, 279, 283,
284, 288, 306,
311, 315, 317,
321, 324, 327,
328
SIMON T., 78, 80,
146(2), 149, 224,
312
THOMAS, 161

W.G., 339
WM. G., 339
TURPIN
ANDERSON, 10, 184
TWEEDY
CAPT., 208, 335
W.F., 66
WATT F., 258
WIATT F., 34(2), 37,
64, 69
WYATT, 31
WYATT F., 11, 25,
28, 39, 62, 139,
183, 198, 212,
217, 218, 294
WYATTE F., 68
TYAS
FREDERICK, 296
TYRRILL
WILLIAM, 227, 228
TYUS
FREDERICK, 295, 326,
328, 329

-V-

VALCH
ADRIAN, 9, 19, 78
VANIER
A.W., 217
VAULX
& BARROW, 7, 17
J., 202
JAMES, 203
VICK
JACOB, 314
VINCENT
AMONS, 261
VINDLE
TRAVIS, 176

-W-

WADDELL
WILLIAM, 11
WADDLE
WILLIAM, 28, 35, 37,
38, 39
WALKER
& BANE, 189
ALFORD M., 157
ALFRED M., 249
CLEMEN T., 68
CLEMENT F., 22, 142
CLEMENT T., 31, 62,
69, 138, 142
CLEMMENT T., 36,
111, 137, 177
GREEN H., 156, 249
J.W., 79
JACOB, 156, 246
JAMES, 9, 19, 139,
194, 233
JAMES H., 158, 167,
169, 176(2), 180,

189, 216, 241,
261, 275, 299,
300, 304, 323,
335
JAMES S., 233
JAMES W., 9, 19, 21
JAS. H., 182
JOSEPH, 270, 271(2)
[BLANK], 223
WALLACE
OSBORN, 62, 73
ROBT., 124
WALLICE
OSBURN, 105
WALLING
JESSE, 264, 271,
293(2), 304
JESSEE, 271, 327
JOHN, 194, 293
WALLS
EPHRAIM, 327
WANE
MANSFIELD, 114, 120,
152, 164
WARE
& LAWRENCE, 302
EDWARD, 338
M., 192
MANFIELD, 157
MANSFIELD, 56, 57,
58, 94, 95, 104,
110, 134, 151,
167, 168, 169,
173, 175, 181,
184, 186, 187,
188, 189, 191,
192, 193, 194,
198, 203, 206,
209, 212, 213,
215, 216, 221,
223, 224, 225,
228, 238, 242,
288, 289, 292,
295, 301
MANSIFLED, 173
WARNER
AMOS, 85, 246, 249
CALEB, 63, 226
MARRS, 156
WARREN
CALEB, 11, 15, 31,
35, 36, 39, 48,
53, 130, 131,
132, 133, 138,
143, 144, 145,
147, 148, 208,
215, 221, 225,
227, 228, 241,
262, 265, 266,
273, 288, 294,
302, 322, 324
ROBERT, 112, 113,
114, 115(2)
WARRNER
AMOS, 160

WATSON
JACOB, 22, 32
JOHN, 37
MATTHEW, 216
WATTS
CHARLES, 145(2)
GEORGE, 71, 101,
107, 108, 124,
238, 255, 257,
287
GEORGE R., 111, 298
WEAKLEY
ROBERT, 19
WEAKLY
ROBERT, 9
ROBT., 79
WEATHERSPOON
JOHN, 240
WEAVER
ABIA, 263, 273, 278,
279, 320, 321
BENJ., 267
BENJA., 204, 205,
311
BENJAMIN, 151, 164,
167, 168, 169,
173, 193, 205,
243, 253, 254,
265, 266, 275,
288, 294, 295,
296, 304, 305,
306, 307, 308,
309, 327
JONATHAN, 127
WILLIAM, 158
WEBB
JAMES, 334
WEDDLE
GEORGE, 125, 265,
266, 267
WILLIAM, 31, 70, 72,
88, 93, 94, 121,
125, 126, 151,
164, 167, 168,
177, 193, 198,
199, 205, 221,
225, 226, 238,
266, 267, 279,
294, 296
WM., 107
WELCH
HENRY, 23, 25, 29,
32(2), 36, 38,
39, 53, 176, 202,
203, 224, 225,
226, 238, 255,
256, 265
WELKER
JOSEPH, 265
WELLS
& GIBBONS, 235
& GIVINS, 154, 246,
248
JOHN, 212, 213, 214,
215, 220, 227,

228, 243, 253,
254, 267
JOHN J., 270
WELSH
HENRY, 31, 55, 56,
57, 58, 88, 104,
106, 109, 110,
124, 221, 268,
272, 279, 281,
282, 283, 287,
288, 289, 294,
310, 311, 314,
315, 316, 320,
324, 326, 327,
328
WESCOT
J., 162
PATIENCE, 156, 233
WESCOTT
P., 332
PATIENCE, 123
WEST
EDWARD, 177, 190,
221, 225, 226,
238, 256, 272,
273, 283, 288,
291, 310, 317,
327, 335(2)
HENRY, 121
THOMAS, 104, 108,
110, 122, 148,
159, 193, 204,
255, 257
THOS., 110, 205, 311
WESTBROOK
ALLEN, 255, 282
WESTBROOKE
ALLEN, 256
WESTBROOKS
ALLEN, 255, 288
WETHERSPOON
JOHN, 240
WHARTON
JOHN, 85
WHEATON
& TISDALE, 19, 79,
156, 245
AND TISDALE, 9
DANIEL, 9, 19
JNO. L., 232, 334
JOHN L., 79, 106,
123, 156, 297(2)
JOHN S., 123
MARY, 79, 156, 245,
298, 299, 334
WHITAKER
DAVID, 340
WHITE
C., 1, 65
CHARLES, 1, 4, 11,
21, 22, 27, 33,
35, 39, 51,
65, 107, 120,
130, 139, 141,
151, 163, 176,

180, 182, 185,
193, 204, 208,
224, 238, 252,
288, 294, 295,
296, 301, 304,
305, 306, 307,
308, 309, 310,
311, 314, 327
CHAS., 141
DELANY, 112, 114
HOLLAND, 214
ISAAC, 266, 267
JAMES, 29
JAMES F., 58
JAMES T., 37, 38(2),
40, 42, 43, 57,
72
JOHN M., 14, 15(3),
28, 29, 31, 36,
39, 53(2), 82,
199
JOHN M.C., 83
LITTLEBERRY, 85
RICHARD, 131, 162,
212, 219
SAMUEL, 40
THOMAS, 47, 62, 68,
69, 224, 256,
272, 314
THOMAS N., 257, 265,
266, 274, 275(2),
276, 278, 279,
282(2), 283, 285,
310, 316, 317,
320, 322, 324
THOS., 26
THOS. N., 193
WILSON, 214
WHITEHEAD
SAMUEL, 186
WHITEHERST
DULANEY, 93
WHITEHURST
DELANY, 123, 268
DELANY D.S., 256
DULANEY D.L., 254
WHITES
DELANY, 112, 113,
115
WHITLEY
SETH, 170
WHITSETT
JAMES, 161
WHITTON
SILAS R., 334
WIATT
JOHN, 160
WIDDLE
WILLIAM, 70, 204
WILKES
BENJ., 156
BENJAMIN, 141, 156,
175, 176, 180,
186, 189, 190,
191, 192, 193,

198, 256, 274,
275, 276, 279,
280, 310, 335
BURWELL, 273, 276
WILKINS
ROBERT S., 139, 142,
184, 253, 270
WILKINSON
WM., 233
WILKS
BENJAMIN, 32, 109,
122, 174, 181,
187, 188, 194,
281, 317(2)
JOSEPH, 32
WILLIAM
J.H., 156
ROBT. W., 334
WILLIAMS
DANIEL H., 227
EDWARD, 5
EDWARD, JR., 34
J., 101
JOHN, 1, 5, 11, 30,
39, 62, 67,
68(2), 69, 94,
101, 107(2),
110(2), 138, 151,
193, 204, 205,
255, 288, 323,
327, 339
JOHN H., 249
JOHN R., 125, 184
JOHN, SR., 110, 121,
125
N.W., 204
NATHAN, 40, 167
R.W., 79, 156
RALPH, 340
ROBERT, 74, 116, 131
ROBERT S., 67
SAM'L, 9
SAM'L H., 79(2)
SAML., 19
SAMUEL H., 156, 245,
298, 300
STITH, 86
THOS., 249
WILLIAMSON
BENJ., 334
BENJAMIN, 79
JOHN, SR., 104
NATHAN, 38, 40, 42,
94, 98, 99, 100,
111, 112, 168,
169
NATHANIEL, 95
THOMAS, 160
THOS., 246
THS., 85
WILLS
& GIVENS, 79
GEORGE, 190
JOHN, 209, 214, 215,
216, 295

WILMAN
C.P., 288
WILSON
& McLEMORE, 333, 336
BENJA., 174
BENJAMIN, 133
CAPT., 336
GEORGE, 9, 19, 79
J., 111
JOHN, 330
WALKER, 175, 181,
183, 184, 288
WIMBERLY
GUILFORD, 201
JOSEPH P., 55, 124
WINBURN
HENRY, 339
WINDSOR
JOHN, 9, 79, 97,
146, 156, 231,
334
JOSEPH, 97, 146
NEWMAN, 97, 146
THOMAS, 97, 146, 300
WINFIELD
JAMES L., 326, 327
WINSOR
JOHN, 19
WISE
JAMES, 323
[BLANK], 223
WOLF
ANDREW, 127, 128,
129, 131
WOMBLE
BIGGS, 23
HARRISON P., 269
HARRY, 69, 111
HARVEY, 288, 296
HARVEY A., 295, 306,
308
HARVY, 112, 121,
125, 126, 306
HARVY A., 307, 308,
309
HENRY, 62, 68, 111,
294
HENRY A., 304, 305,
306, 311
L.D., 65, 121, 125,
126, 131, 132,
133, 151
LARENZO D., 225
LARINZO D., 164
LORENZA D., 167,
168, 169, 173
LORENZO D., 221
LOWRENCE, 33
WOOD
F.M., 31
FRANCES M., 3, 26,
28, 68
FRANCIS, 23
FRANCIS M., 3, 6,
11, 25, 27, 34,

38, 67, 104,
110(2), 151, 193,
243, 253, 272
FRS. M., 283
ISAAC, 67, 143
OLIVER, 201, 222,
223, 289
OLIVER B., 65, 69
SAMUEL D., 65
WOODARD
BENJAMIN, 23
ELI, 33
PATON, 13
WILLIE, 53
WOODFOLK
WILLIAM W., 9, 19
WOODFORK
W.W., 79
WOODS
CAPT., 203, 208
FRANCIS M., 253,
256, 273, 290
ISAAC, 255, 271,
301, 320, 323
JAMES, 308, 309
O., 161
OBION, 304
OLIVER, 1, 65, 66,
140, 151, 165,
193, 208, 209,
238, 256, 257,
264, 271, 287,
291, 292, 293,
312, 315, 316,
324
OLIVER B., 92, 104,
136, 140, 141,
174
OLLIVER B., 88
SAMUEL, 201, 235
SAMUEL D., 92
SAMUEL N., 286
WOODWARD
WILY, 55
WOOTEN
HENRY, 29, 31,
33(2), 36, 37,
38, 39, 42, 50,
62, 68, 70, 72,
82, 83, 87, 95,
96, 104, 124
WORD
WILLIAM, 275
WORRD [SIC]
WILLIAM, 282
WORTHAM
CAPT., 208, 335
CHARLES, 1, 3, 4,
6, 11, 21, 25,
26, 27, 28, 29,
31, 33, 38, 39,
61, 64, 65, 66,
67, 88, 92,
108, 151, 162,
175, 181, 183,

190, 202, 224,
238, 256, 313,
314, 323
CHARLES A., 139
CHAS., 25, 28
J.F., 339
J.L., 35, 39, 140,
161, 221
JAMES, 65, 139, 180
JAMES F., 4, 25, 34,
104, 110, 162,
190, 224
JAMES F., JR., 30
JAMES H., 121, 125
JAMES L., 1, 31,
35(3), 51(2), 61,
68, 139, 140,
143, 159, 175,
202, 203, 207(2),
208, 209, 211,
212, 220, 221(2),
222, 223, 224,
225, 270
JAMES, JR., 23, 202
JOHN W., 162, 313
WILLIAM R., 4, 6,
31, 34
WRIGHT
JOHN A., 335
WYNN
JOHN, 321
WYNNE
JOHN, 226, 227, 228,
242
WYSE
JAMES, 314

-Y-

YANCY
THOMAS S., 270
YANDLE
THOMAS, 321
YARBORAUGH
DAVID, 232
YARBY
JOHN, 157
YOUNG
BENJAMIN H., 171
EBENEZER G., 297
GEORGE W., 339
JOHN, 61, 73, 119,
123, 124, 243,
253, 254, 258,
267, 320, 323,
326, 327, 328,
329(2)
PETER, 32, 62
WILLIAM P., 227,
228, 265, 314,
320, 321, 322,
324, 326, 328,
329(2)
WM. P., 320